THE BEATLES IN PERSPECTIVE

Studies in Popular Music

Series Editors: Alyn Shipton, Royal Academy of Music, London; and Christopher Partridge, Lancaster University

From jazz to reggae, bhangra to heavy metal, electronica to qawwali, and from production to consumption, Studies in Popular Music is a multi-disciplinary series which aims to contribute to a comprehensive understanding of popular music. It will provide analyses of theoretical perspectives, a broad range of case studies, and discussion of key issues.

Published:

Do You Want to Know a Secret?: The Autobiography of Billly J. Kramer
Billy J. Kramer with Alyn Shipton

Dub in Babylon: Understanding the Evolution and Significance of Dub Reggae in Jamaica and Britain from King Tubby to Post-Punk
Christopher Partridge

Falco and Beyond: Neo Nothing Post of All
Ewa Mazierska

Global Tribe: Technology, Spirituality and Psytrance
Graham St John

Heavy Metal: Controversies and Countercultures
Edited by Titus Hjelm, Keith Kahn-Harris and Mark LeVine

Nick Cave: A Study of Love, Death and Apocalypse
Roland Boer

Open up the Doors: Music in the Modern Church
Mark Evans

Send in the Clones: A Cultural Study of Tribute Bands
Georgina Gregory

Technomad: Global Raving Countercultures
Graham St John

The Lost Women of Rock Music: Female Musicians of the Punk Era (second edition)
Helen Reddington

The Northern Soul Scene
Edited by Sarah Raine, Tim Wall and Nicola Watchman Smith

The Rosary and the Microphone: Religious Impulse in U2's Mediated Brand
Nicholas P. Greco

THE BEATLES IN PERSPECTIVE

A CARNIVAL OF LIGHT

EDITED BY
JAMES MCGRATH AND PETER MILLS

SHEFFIELD UK   BRISTOL CT

Published by Equinox Publishing Ltd.

UK: Office 415, The Workstation, 15 Paternoster Row, Sheffield, South Yorkshire, S1 2BX
USA: ISD, 70 Enterprise Drive, Bristol, CT 06010

www.equinoxpub.com

First published 2023

© James McGrath, Peter Mills and contributors 2023

All rights reserved. No part of this publication may be reproduced or transmitted in any form or by any means, electronic or mechanical, including photocopying, recording or any information storage or retrieval system, without prior permission in writing from the publishers.

British Library Cataloguing-in-Publication Data
A catalogue record for this book is available from the British Library.

ISBN-13 978 1 78179 195 0 (hardback)
　　　　　978 1 78179 242 0 (paperback)
　　　　　978 1 78179 196 7 (ePDF)
　　　　　978 1 80050 399 1 (ePub)

Library of Congress Cataloging-in-Publication Data
Names: McGrath, James, 1978- editor. | Mills, Peter, 1963- editor.
Title: The Beatles in perspective : a carnival of light / edited by James McGrath and Peter Mills.
Description: Sheffield, South Yorkshire ; Bristol, CT : Equinox Publishing Ltd, 2023. | Series: Studies in popular music | Includes bibliographical references and index. | Summary: "This collection brings together leading scholars of The Beatles to examine their origins, output and legacy. Interdisciplinary in its approach and international is its outlook, The Beatles in Perspective: A Carnival of Light showcases the latest research by historians, literary critics, musicologists, sociologists, poets and cultural critics bringing new perspectives on The Beatles and their milieu which will interest academics and fans alike"-- Provided by publisher.
Identifiers: LCCN 2023003414 (print) | LCCN 2023003415 (ebook) | ISBN 9781781791950 (hardback) | ISBN 9781800502420 (paperback) | ISBN 9781781791967 (pdf) | ISBN 9781800503991 (epub)
Subjects: LCSH: Beatles. | Rock music--1961-1970--History and criticism. | Rock music fans--History--20th century.
Classification: LCC ML421.B4 B4153 2023 (print) | LCC ML421.B4 (ebook) | DDC 782.42166092/2--dc23/eng/20230125
LC record available at https://lccn.loc.gov/2023003414
LC ebook record available at https://lccn.loc.gov/2023003415

Typeset by S.J.I. Services, New Delhi, India

Contents

Acknowledgements   vii

Introduction   1
James McGrath and Peter Mills

Part One: Culture and History   11

1   "Where You Once Belonged": Class, Race and the Liverpool Roots of Lennon and McCartney's Songs   13
James McGrath

2   Notes on The Beatles from a Black Liverpudlian Perspective   35
Mark Christian

3   From Liverpool to Tibet: 'Tomorrow Never Knows' and the Troubled Path to the East   43
Sharif Gemie

4   "Magical Mystery Tour": Suburbia and Utopia in Music and Films of The Beatles   59
Jon Goss

5   The Bohemian Beatles   85
Colin Campbell

6   Interlude 1: Growing up with The Beatles   108
Russell Reising, Peter Mills and James McGrath

Part Two: Audience, Fanhood, Interpretation   113

7   "My Name's Ringo and I Play the Drums": Being a Beatles' Fan in the Age of Interactivity   115
Stephanie Fremaux

8	The Beatles and Fandom *Richard Mills*	137
9	"Some kind of innocence...": *Beatles Monthly* and the Fan Community *Mike Kirkup*	159
10	"Misunderstanding all you see": Charles Manson Reading The Beatles at the End of the World *Gerry Carlin and Mark Jones*	185
11	Interlude 2: The Beatles, Interpretation and Influence *Russell Reising, Peter Mills and James McGrath*	202

Part Three: Savoy Truffles: Further Perspectives		**213**
12	Paul in the Picture: Anatomy of a Snapshot *Martin Malone*	215
13	The American Beetles: How a Fake Beatles Band Defined a Movement, Changed a Culture, and Beat The Beatles at Their Own Game *Ed Prideaux*	231
14	Interlude 3: Listening and Remembering *Russell Reising, Peter Mills and James McGrath*	249
Index		255

Acknowledgements

James McGrath and Peter Mills

We are grateful to the contributors for their work, commitment and patience during the completion of this book. We also thank the staff of Equinox for their guidance and support, in particular Val Hall, Janet Joyce and Sarah Lee, as well as Christopher Partridge and Alyn Shipton for their expertise. The editors also thank Sarah Norman for her expertise throughout the proofing stages of this book.

Colleagues at Leeds Beckett University kindly shared their expertise. Distinguished thanks are due to Adele Jackson for transcription work, for IT support, for arranging international interviews and for providing much-appreciated administrative support. This book also owes to the encouragement of Sally Cusworth and Rosamund Hoggard, and to the inspiration of two great scholars of 1960s culture and popular music, Matthew Caygill and Sheila Whiteley.

This book has its roots in a suggestion by Marcus Collins, which was developed by James McGrath, who was then joined in assembling and editing the volume by Peter Mills.

Introduction

James McGrath and Peter Mills

The Word

We know what you're thinking. Does the world need another book on The Beatles? Maybe. Maybe not. It is possible that the further away in time their era becomes, the more literature is going to emerge – consider, for example, their probable literary equivalent, William Shakespeare. That is the scale of what we are dealing with. The present volume is indeed part of that swelling tide – but it has plenty in it that the editors have never seen written about before, and in ways not seen before. So, it is certainly part of that firmly established field of study, but it is also something new.

Just before we delve into the contents of this book, it may be valuable to reflect upon the current state of "Beatle Studies".

At the most high-profile end, the world is still in the lengthy process of waiting for Mark Lewisohn's lifetime project, *The Beatles: All These Years*, which illustrates a key difference that has come into Popular Music Studies in the 21st century – those works that have an authorized gloss and use official archives and collections (e.g., Heylin 2021; Lewisohn 2013; Sandoval 2005) and those that pursue more closely focused lines of enquiry (Feldman-Barrett 2021; Niccolini 2021; Staley 2020; Woodhead 2013). This book occupies, maybe even carves out, a space between these approaches, linked but distinct.

But what is "Beatle Studies"? What are its characteristics? At a tremendously generous estimation the period in which the band were operative (in the sense that the work they produced endures) is a single decade. It is temptingly easy to see the end of the sixties as being inevitably the point at which the group had to break up; Beatles in 1971? It is hard to imagine. Reflecting on McCartney's *Ram* in 1971 for UK music weekly *Melody Maker* (31 July 1971), Ringo Starr observed "He seems to be going strange". So Beatle Studies is by necessity confined to a very brief period. Its cousin and corollary Bob Dylan Studies has in contrast had over 60 years of recording, performance and presentation to draw upon. It is also able to reach much further back into American cultural archetypes in a way that isn't quite the case for The Beatles – some work has focused on the dance craze, songwriting and music hall traditions in the UK but that is inevitably limited in range. Since the release of the "Red" and "Blue" double albums in 1973 (so many second-generation fans' gateway to the music) the band has lived on through a series of themed compilations (the neatly divided doubles *Rock and Roll Music*, 1976 and *Love Songs*, 1977 followed by *Ballads* in 1980), reissue campaigns (the 1976 blitz of picture sleeve singles, which spawned some new A-sides) with the 20th anniversary of 'Love Me Do' being marked with an early taste of what would arrive in the digital era with "lost" versions of the song issued for the already huge collectors' market. There was even a "Beatles Movie Medley" in 1982 to hook up with the craze for medleys with a thumping backbeat, popular at that time – it has been quietly forgotten (no reissues in any format at the time of writing) but was not such a terrible idea, not least in that it promoted the themed album *Reel Music* (1982). Indeed the movies have themselves proved an effective way of keeping versions and experiences of the group fresh, with remastering and reissues always emerging in succeeding formats. This is not unlike The Monkees, forever young on their TV show (two seasons, 1966–68) and fabulous movie *Head* (Bob Rafelson, 1968) all discovered anew by each new generation of pop fans. Similarly, how many Dylan scholars began to get hooked by marvelling at his style and sheer chutzpah as displayed in 1967's *Don't Look Back*? The elder co-editor of this book raises his hand.

If some of these repackaging campaigns felt industry-driven, it was with the *Anthology* releases of 1995–96 that the process of self-curation began. Decades of middling quality bootlegs were set aside as fans dug into the vinyl, cassette and CD sets while the television documentary version was screened in six one-hour parts in the UK on ITV, debuting on 26 November 1995. This whetted the more casual appetite for reviewing the group's achievements while also tempting the undecided to dive in deeper. The VHS set issued in 1996 added hours more material for the diehard, and the DVD box in 2003 provided even more. An LP sized coffee-table book covered more media bases. All sold very well. Since that time, the impression has been given of the remaining members and interested parties seeming highly attentive to arranging their own affairs, driving the critical and commercial narratives. The official version has also been established via friendly specialist music magazines acting as promotional vehicles and the story has been steered and deepened as a cultural archetype of its very own by the telling and retelling, the selling and reselling right up to 2022 – which brings us to what is arguably the most fulsomely immersive text and commodity yet to bear The Beatles' brand, Peter Jackson's eight-hour, three-part film *Get Back* (2021).

The Beatles "have three weeks to complete 14 new songs and a live show", begins *Get Back*'s official description (Jackson 2021), thus employing a narrative resonant of Jackson's *Lord of the Rings* extravaganza as well as video game plots – but also, of course, that of capitalism itself. It is perhaps this third strand that situates The Beatles closest to the everyday lives of their 21st-century audience. We see The Beatles working to an imposed deadline, under constant and monitored pressure, enduring various strains on their personal relationships, as well as on their health (and occasional chemical intake), that this creates. While *Get Back*'s focus on The Beatles' working lives is richly contrastable with that of *A Hard Day's Night* (made less than five years earlier), Jackson's film, in the absence of an actual writer, transforms Lindsay-Hogg's original footage from documentary towards something feeling more like reality TV. Reassuringly to many artist, academic and writer viewers, *Get Back* records The Beatles managing to miss a succession of small deadlines in order to realize the full potential of their work in the form of a final performance.

Like the *Anthology* a quarter of a century earlier, and *Let It Be* a quarter of a century before that, the 2021 *Get Back* project also yielded a corresponding official book of the same name, plus an album of "new" material via the expanded re-release of The Beatles' 1970 *Let It Be*. In a cunning twist of synergy, the 2021 reissue of *Let It Be* offers more than just a soundtrack to Jackson's film: it provides the missing *sound*. For across the whole eight hours of *Get Back*, not one song is heard in full. Multiple takes of each song falter, in ways that are by turns fascinating and frustrating. Yet when, as in for example Harrison's 'For You Blue', a "final" take is nailed, we watch and hear only a tantalizing segment before a caption announcing that this is the version featured on the *Let It Be* album appears on screen as if part-apology, part-advertisement. There is an aesthetic logic here: if the film contains a full performance of a song, then how many other takes, rehearsals and all would we also want? But that same logic holds less stably during the film's climactic rooftop performance. Instead of showing the culmination of all those rehearsals into a finished, live performance, each of the songs The Beatles perform on the rooftop is mixed with real-time interviews with passers-by at ground level. (The Rooftop Concert-only release of the film in Arts Theatres and IMAX cinemas duplicates this approach.) Jackson's *Get Back* remains, amongst much else, a promise of how this eight-hour film itself might act as a trailer for an extended or alternate versions still to come. The final words heard over the elongated end credits are Lennon's, declaring "We've got thousands of the bastards" – that is, takes of each song.

Its commercial gigantism aside, *Get Back* is a revelation and a joy. The discussion points it inspires are manifold. Most pertinently, Jackson's film shows the role in the sessions and the songs of the Black American keyboardist Billy Preston. In addition to becoming a fifth yet near-equally prominent instrumentalist, Preston seems to revitalize the previously fractured sense of The Beatles as a group. Preston is shown contributing throughout most of *Get Back*'s second half, albeit that no camera seems to have faced him directly during the rooftop performance.

Of comparable scope and perhaps also insight to the Apple-endorsed *Get Back* enterprise, an unofficial yet no less substantial text is the five-part, eleven-hour YouTube series *Understanding Lennon/McCartney* (2017), created by an individual or group known only as "breathless345". Comprising almost entirely of Lennon and McCartney's own words, the series juxtaposes interviews, songs, and archive footage galore to foreground the *love* the two subjects expressed for each other. While not seeking to reduce or define McCartney and Lennon's relationship according to any simple or single meaning of love, the work of breathless345 introduces the possibilities for Queer reflections on The Beatles: an area hitherto under-considered in the scholarship.

So, in relation to this kind of focus we might ask, is Beatle Studies actually John and Paul Studies? Check the indexes of the five Beatle studies on the nearest shelf. How much screen time is given to George and Ringo? In truth, this book doesn't devote complete sections to either of them, but what it does do is to reflect on The Beatles as a cultural entity. In this volume co-editor's book, *The Monkees,* Head *and the 60s,* Peter Mills reflected on the notion of collective identity in popular music, calling the magic formula "the John, Paul, George and Ringo of it" meaning that regardless of other considerations, in an effective band a kind of alchemy has to occur; in order for something to happen, it couldn't be just any four, it had to be *those four*. This book acknowledges this, and is concerned with the John, Paul, George and Ringo of it.

Another important presence in this volume is the city of Liverpool itself; a view of the Liver Building and four favourite sons graces the cover of the book and ghost footprints chase through the city's lanes and streets. When Peter Mills arrived in the city as a first-year undergraduate in 1981, the "Beatle Industry" in Liverpool was effectively the province of enthusiasts with long memories, who would show you where The Cavern once stood and ran private tours in the original Magical Mystery Tour bus to Menlove Avenue, Penny Lane and Strawberry Fields. Meanwhile a small room adjacent to the Armadillo Tea Rooms on Mathew Street displayed some local materials relating to the group and city. Now, as anyone who visits soon learns, The Beatles are a major factor in the city's public image and tourist offering, from souvenir shops to National Trust package tours. It is still difficult to understand The Beatles without knowing something about Liverpool, and not just in the sense of "where they came from" but the way the city shaped them, and the environments in which they grew up. This book reflects on such influences. The cumulative effect of these lines of enquiry is one of a fresh perspective on a familiar subject.

All Together Now: The Essays

Across 14 pieces we cover the waterfront with considerations of a wide array of topics and approaches. For tabular convenience, we have grouped the contributions into three main sections: "Culture and History", "Audience, Fanhood, Interpretation" and "Savoy Truffles: Further Perspectives". In the first, co-editor of this volume James McGrath opens proceedings with a keen enquiry into the early days of the group – not only the early days of the recording career, but the Liverpool roots of the band, including original research on The Beatles' first mentor and promoter Harold Phillips (1929–2000) aka Lord Woodbine, a Calypso singer who had come over from Trinidad in June 1948 on the *Empire Windrush*, on the same voyage as his friend Aldwyn Roberts aka Lord Kitchener. McGrath has already made a substantial public contribution to directing attention to the Lord Woodbine story, and adds much to it here. Mark Christian delves deeper into this hidden history, recalling his own encounter with Lord Woodbine and discussing the role of Black music and Black Liverpool on the young Beatles, reminding us of the derivation of a famous Beatle location and providing a pointedly Liverpudlian perspective on an act which has long belonged to the world.

We leap from Liverpool 8 to a mountain top in Tibet via Sharif Gemie's excursion into the soundworld of 'Tomorrow Never Knows' and how it connotes conscious and unconscious creativity and experience. We are reminded that for all its transcendental mystique, it was a deliberately constructed piece with plenty of connections to other musical forms, as well as exerting an enduring influence on pop – Phil Collins recorded it for *Face Value* (1981) and Vini Reilly and Bruce Mitchell (The Durutti Column) adapted it for a frustratingly unrecorded live highlight they called 'Revolver'. In fact, there are dozens of recorded covers of this apparently uncoverable song.

As noted earlier, the Beatle legacy is not only musical and Jon Goss looks at their films alongside the songbook, proceeding from the perspective of representations of suburbia and utopia in the work. It also acknowledges the role of humour in the work, something very particular to the Liverpool worldview. It is a culture of *craic*, certainly, but Scouse humour can also be a defence mechanism, sometimes even a strategy for survival. Lennon's post-Beatle description of himself as a 'Working Class Hero' is this brew at its most dark and bitter tasting. Colin Campbell's piece aligns with these themes and carries them into Central Europe, and a new state of mind, in his exploration of the bohemian

Beatles. Geographically, the term refers to a region now located within the Czech Republic; musically it calls to mind an opera by Michael William Balfe (1843) or a famous track by Queen (1975). This piece explores the idea of Bohemia as a way of being, in relation to the lives and works of The Beatles, and places them within subcultural moments of their own time – this is unusual in that they are usually viewed, correctly, as both being the instigators of such movements and also being "above" such transient pulses of culture.

The "Culture and History" section closes with the first segment of dialogue between this book's co-editors and renowned Popular Music and Beatles scholar Russell Reising. Each section contains one of these conversation pieces, and they provide a kind of third rail for the book overall. The opener looks at how one might "discover" The Beatles – the routes each individual listener takes to their initial encounter with the music and the folk narrative of the band.

The "Audience, Fanhood, Interpretation" section opens with evidence of the enduring nature of that wave upon wave of discovery, and fresh ways to explore engagements with popular music in general and The Beatles in particular. Stephanie Fremaux explores the nature of fandom, from the early, real-world museum in Hamburg through to the age of social media and fandom in virtual space. It then moves to a different kind of fan engagement via a study of the campaign to save and buy Ringo Starr's childhood home in Liverpool and onto virtually "joining the band" via the *Rock Band* game and virtual performances online generated by fan groups. Continuing this theme of fandom, Richard Mills looks at the phenomenon of Beatle fandom then and now, through reference to *Beatles Monthly* aka *The Beatles Book* magazine (1963–69, 1976–2003) and that quintessential fan event, the Convention. He necessarily considers the "dark side" of fandom; the reasons are terrible and sadly obvious. He also assesses the role of journalists and musicians as fans, fan fiction, tribute bands and The Beatles' presence on YouTube. Mike Kirkup's piece addresses *Beatles Monthly* directly and in great detail, revealing much about how the magazine functioned, using it as a means to explore the nature of fandom in the heated moment of its experience, with particular attention given to the letters the fans wrote to the magazine. These comments were of course much more subject to processes of labour and gatekeeping than the casually posted comment on social media – they had to be written, posted, received, selected, edited, printed. Yet they are not unrelated to their digital successors. Gerry Carlin and Mark Jones's piece explores how the dissociation of the artist from the art object can be blurred in the white heat of popular music cultures, how the "possession" of the recording via a personal copy can facilitate alarming readings, and how the music's audible power can inform negative interpretations. Appropriately, the second Interlude reflects upon the role of the listener and viewer in perceiving and frequently creating frameworks of interpretation and meaning.

The final section, "Savoy Truffles: Further Perspectives", wanders wider pathways. Martin Malone's piece extrapolates from a found object – a photograph of Paul McCartney taken in a Scottish dancehall at the beginning of 1963, published in this volume for the first time – and researches the band's secret history as an act on the dancehall circuit of northern Scotland, via the ebullient yet enigmatic figure of promoter Albert Bonici. John Lennon had loved his childhood holidays in Durness in Sutherland and it is surely no accident that he took Yoko Ono, Julian and Kyoko back to these very places on their hard-to-believe-it-happened road trip of June/July 1969, which ended with the car crash that hospitalized all four of them. It also delayed his joining the *Abbey Road* sessions. So, this part of the world had a role in the history of the band, even before Paul and Linda McCartney made it their main family home for most of the 1970s. Ed Prideaux's piece tells another untold story – in 1965, far, far away from Liverpool, London or Durness, a prototype of what would now be adjudged a tribute band engaged in an elaborate terpsichore of reality and fantasy. The piece tells the story of "The Beetles", a cover band, tribute act, shameless fake, according to your view, and how a brief period of welcome atrophied into disappointment and outrage amongst fans and eventually came to the attention of EMI. The karma comes in the way the band were described by contemporary Argentine media, taking the heat the military junta would have directed against the real band. It is an incredible story, researched and told highly engagingly. The final Interlude considers the duality of listening and remembering. We "remember" the first time we heard a song, or a band, and other reflections on our lives accrete around those sounds. The recording does not change, but the listener does.

Carnival of Light?

The one remaining unreleased Beatles composition is a largely form-free 13 minute 48 second improvisation titled 'Carnival of Light'. Instigated by McCartney, it was recorded on 5 January 1967 in one session (after The Beatles had completed work on 'Penny Lane'). Made as a favour to McCartney's musician friend Dave Vaughan, the piece was played as a soundtrack loop to a two-night arts event organized by the latter titled 'Carnival of Light Rave' and staged at London's Roundhouse on 28 January and 4 February 1967. Since then, The Beatles' 'Carnival of Light' has not been heard in public; it remains unreleased and (perhaps singularly amongst Beatles recordings) has never surfaced on a bootleg. Excluded from The Beatles' *Anthology 2* (1996), McCartney has since expressed his desire for 'Carnival of Light' to be released, though this would depend on approval from Ringo Starr, Yoko Ono and Olivia Harrison, which as yet appears to have been unforthcoming (see Thorpe 2008). Other than McCartney's biographer Barry Miles (1997), Mark Lewisohn is the only author known to have heard 'Carnival of Light', when given access to EMI's vaults to prepare his *Complete Beatles Recording Sessions* (2005: 92). Lewisohn's characteristically attentive summary of the 1967 recording, appropriately enough, reads almost like the instructions for a John Cage piece. For now though, perhaps the intrigue surrounding this track is in its own way more rewarding than the experience of actually listening to it might prove. The imagination itself is as good a place as any to enjoy The Beatles' 'Carnival of Light'.

In the meantime, here's our book; we hope you will enjoy the show.

References

breathless345. (2017) *Understanding Lennon/McCartney*. https://www.youtube.com/watch?v=RRZ7O0MZE7Y (accessed 15 July 2022).

Feldman-Barrett, Christine. (2021) *A Women's History of The Beatles*. London: Bloomsbury.

Heylin, Clinton. (2021) *The Double Life of Bob Dylan: Volume I: 1941–1966 A Restless, Hungry Feeling*. London: Bodley Head.

Jackson, Peter. (2021) *The Beatles: Get Back*. Apple Corps/Disney+.

Lewisohn, Mark. (2013) *The Beatles: All These Years: Vol. 1: Tune In*. London: Little, Brown and Company.

Lewisohn, Mark. (2005) *The Complete Beatles Recording Sessions: The Official Story of the Abbey Road Years*. London: Bounty Books.

Miles, Barry. (1997) *Paul McCartney: Many Years from Now*. London: Secker & Warburg.

Mills, Peter. (2016) *The Monkees,* Head *and the 60s*. New York: Jawbone.

Niccolini, Ilse. (2021) *How The Beatles Knew: A History of How They Wrote Their Songs*. USA: Tonal Publications.

Sandoval, Andrew. (2005) *The Monkees: The Day by Day Story of the 60s Pop Sensation*. San Diego: Thunder Bay.

Staley, Sam. (2020) *The Beatles and Economics: Entrepreneurship, Innovation, and the Making of a Cultural Revolution*. London: Routledge.

Thorpe, Vanessa. (2008) "Forty Years On, McCartney Wants the World to Hear 'Lost' Beatles Epic". *The Guardian* [online], 16 November. https://www.theguardian.com/music/2008/nov/16/paul-mccartney-carnival-of-light

Woodhead, Leslie. (2013) *How The Beatles Rocked the Kremlin: The Untold Story of a Noisy Revolution*. London: Bloomsbury.

Author biographies

Dr James McGrath is Senior Lecturer in English Literature and Creative Writing in the School of Humanities and Social Sciences at Leeds Beckett University, UK. He completed his doctoral thesis on the work of John Lennon and Paul McCartney, and his first book *Naming Adult Autism: Culture, Science, Identity* was published by Rowman & Littlefield International in 2017. His poems have been published in various literary periodicals.

Dr Peter Mills is Senior Lecturer in Media and Popular Culture in the School of Humanities and Social Sciences at Leeds Beckett University, UK. He has previously published on Samuel Beckett, Van Morrison and The Monkees. Peter is currently working on a series of short books on individual songs, a book chapter on the history of live music in Roundhay Park in Leeds, and an ambitious project looking to catalogue the history of live concerts at Leeds Beckett University since 1970.

Part One
Culture and History

1 "Where You Once Belonged": Class, Race and the Liverpool Roots of Lennon and McCartney's Songs

James McGrath[1]

While Lennon and McCartney's class affiliations are ambiguous to degrees that should remain debatable, the depth and the detail in which working-class life defines their work have been overlooked, thus misrepresenting The Beatles' cultural significance. As Collins (2012) critiques, initial New Left criticisms of The Beatles – almost exclusively in response to one composition, 'Revolution' (1968) – have recently been adapted by commentators eager to portray The Beatles as a culturally and politically conservative force. I argue that early left-wing and recent right-wing criticisms of The Beatles' legacy are misleading, because both overlook Lennon and McCartney's different relationships to working-class culture. I also emphasize an importantly related, even more marginalized aspect of The Beatles' history: the significance of Black musical and cultural influences from Liverpool. This chapter seeks to offer new interpretations of songs including 'Norwegian Wood', 'A Day in the Life', 'Revolution', 'Ob-la-di, ob-la-da' and 'Working Class Hero'.

In most official photographs of The Beatles, John Lennon and Paul McCartney are positioned apart, separated by George Harrison and Ringo Starr. Such images present The Beatles as a *group*, not just a band. Lennon and McCartney's visual distancing had a practical effect: these images could not be cropped to show only the two leaders. The subtle group emphasis counterbalanced a more eminently readable detail, variations on which adorn most pre-digital Beatles releases: "words and music by John Lennon and Paul McCartney". This chapter focuses on Lennon and McCartney as individuals. Harrison and Starr's importance is immeasurable, but sustained comparisons of McCartney and Lennon remain surprisingly rare in Beatles literature. The most extensive study of Lennon and McCartney's artistic partnership appears in Henry W. Sullivan's *The Beatles with Lacan* (1995), which compares the songwriters' upbringings (including the fact that both lost their mothers as teenagers) and discusses their work in Lacanian terms. In what follows, I hope to demonstrate new ways of conceptualizing and *hearing* McCartney and Lennon's work, together and apart: in class terms. I argue that although Lennon and McCartney's social origins were complex, their work is significantly tinged by working-class motifs. I also emphasize the overlooked significance of Black Liverpudlian influences on Lennon and McCartney. I illustrate how, culturally and economically, McCartney's upbringing was more typically working class, and how this shapes his work as a Beatle. I discuss how Lennon's work, like his upbringing, was more distanced from working-class existence, and how this distance corresponded with his critical, transiently radical, expositions on class both as concept and experience. Politically, Lennon emerged as the more left-wing, but only after The Beatles' 1969 split. Studies emphasizing Lennon's radicalism as an individual (Elliott 1999; Wiener 1984) pay little attention to this aspect of The Beatles. This chapter contends that while Lennon's complex working-class affiliations remain a vital part of his legacy, The Beatles' most culturally – and in this way, politically – radical work was mainly led by McCartney. The two artists' engagements with working-class life, culture and politics differed, but in these respects, their legacies remain complementary.

First, it is necessary to trace back a critical convention which, I argue, risks misrepresenting Lennon and McCartney's legacy. In December 1963, London's right-wing *Times* named them the year's "outstanding English composers", with classical music critic William Mann (anonymously) likening their compositions to Mahler's (Mann 1963). In 1967, the *New York Times* put Lennon and McCartney on an aesthetic par with T. S. Eliot (Goldstein 1967). Although valid, such critical responses inaugurated a tendency which remains problematic. These discussions legitimized their scholarly approaches to popular music by aligning Lennon and McCartney with canonized composers and poets, but in doing so, neglected working-class cultural influences on the songs. Though subsequent decades have yielded millions of published words around The Beatles, such focal points remain marginal. Mark Lewisohn's first volume of his three-part Beatles biography (2013) offers much exquisite detail, but because it is a work more of narrative than of reflection, and because it does not significantly address a less familiar aspect of the band's pre-1963 history – their links with Liverpool's Black musical scenes – Lewisohn's first instalment does not significantly challenge dominant representations of The Beatles.

Although, with critical nostalgia, Whiteley (1992) and MacDonald (1994) valuably emphasize The Beatles' countercultural significance, more recent studies seek to categorize or canonize the band as somehow fundamentally conservative (Fowler 2008; Heilbronner 2008, 2011). As Collins (2012: 2) notes in one of few recent studies to propose more radical interpretations of The Beatles, the recent conservative lines of critique actually derive from left-wing responses to the band following Lennon's ambivalent 'Revolution' (1968). However, the still-influential New Left critiques of The Beatles, and even more, the reactionary reappraisals, are drastically undermined by their methodology. These approaches to the politics of The Beatles' songs depend on literalist interpretations of lyrics alone, and the scarcity of overtly ideological language therein. While my primary focus is on lyrics, I also want to demonstrate how Lennon and McCartney's music can be debated politically, and how class and ethnicity are central to such discussions.

Lyricizing working-class existence created commercial advantages for The Beatles, as this class constituted the majority of a mass audience. Lennon and McCartney became millionaires partly by exploiting working-class experience. Here, however, the focus is on the songs they effectively exchanged for their wealth. In different ways, McCartney and Lennon's songs invoke backgrounds of austerity, maintaining significant, if not renewed, resonance in the present era.

"Where you once belonged"

Historicizing Lennon and McCartney's social and cultural roots

As Dave Laing shows, the issue of class and The Beatles' backgrounds presents considerable confusion for commentators (Laing 2009: 14–15). Indeed, the question of Lennon and McCartney's class origins is complex enough to yield a series of articles. In discussing "working-class" and "middle-class" identities here, I refer significantly to the occupations of the musicians' parents, and the implications of these regarding income and thus housing. As Gunn and Bell (2002) stress, definitions of class have always been both mercurial and debatable. However, distinctions between working-class and middle-class identities which persisted well into the 20th century concerned property-ownership; positions of power and subordination in the workplace; and divisions between "mental" and "manual" labour (see Gunn and Bell 2002: 7–8). Such considerations, as will be shown, highlight the complexities of Lennon and McCartney's class origins. However, this chapter gives particular attention to how, in different ways, both songwriters predominantly emphasized identifications with working-class life.

From aged five in 1946, Lennon was raised by his Aunt Mary ("Mimi") Smith at Mendips: a spacious, semi-detached house in Woolton, a south Liverpool suburb. The household income was precarious, especially after Mimi's husband George Smith (a dairyman) died aged 52 in 1955. Even before this, rooms in the house were rented to up to three student lodgers at a time. Lennon's widow, Yoko Ono, purchased Mendips in 2001 and donated it to the National Trust. Since its opening in 2003, it has become a critical cliché to deride Lennon's 1970 song 'Working Class Hero' by describing this suburban house (see Clayson and Leigh 2003: 15–16; Norman 2008: 29). McCartney's main Liverpool home, 20 Forthlin Road, Allerton, south Liverpool, was purchased by the National Trust in 1995, opening in 1998. Currently, Lennon and McCartney's homes are viewable only as a pair, making the immediate environs of their early lives instantly comparable in restored period detail. The contrast is powerful. To explore McCartney's smaller, darker, terraced council house minutes after the comfortable Mendips is to glimpse physical distinctions in the lives of the English working-classes and lower-middle classes circa 1960.

McCartney's mother, Mary, was a ward sister before Paul's birth (1942), later becoming a health visitor, then a midwife. These professions involved authority over other staff, as well as patients. As such, they were seldom associated with working-class identity. However, the McCartneys were never firmly middle class, signifiers of which were privately-owned property and the household's ability to manage on the husband's income alone (Gunn and Bell 2002: 194). Mary earned more than her husband, Jim McCartney: a lathe-turner and voluntary wartime fireman when Paul was born. He returned to his original job of cotton salesman after the War, but this paid insufficiently to support his family. The McCartneys lived in various rented homes before Forthlin Road and their moves indicate a degree of ambition. "My parents aspired for us, very much", McCartney remarks (cited in Miles 1997: 43). After Mary's death in 1956 when Paul was fourteen, Jim supported his two sons and himself on just £8 per week and worked in fear of redundancy (Lewisohn 2013: 99). Paul McCartney's class origins were complex but his descriptions of his parents foreground their most working-class occupations, naming his mother a nurse (cited in Miles 1997: 6) and father a fireman (cited in Odell 2008).[2]

Philip Norman places Mendips as the defining motif of Lennon's social formation (2008: 28, 50) and describes the house in detail in a *Daily Mail* article on "The Bourgeois Beatle" (2003). Yet Mendips also symbolizes Lennon's uprooting from far less privileged circumstances. He was moved there to live with his Aunt Mimi after Social Services ruled the rented one-bed flat where he lived with his mother Julia (a waitress) and her lover to be inadequate for a child (Baird 2007: 34). Lennon's first home, with Julia, had been her father's rented two-bedroom terraced house. Lennon's father, Freddie, a ship steward, was often absent without leave, providing the household no income, and he and Julia separated when John was two. From aged five, John remained with neither parent, but with Mimi. As Sullivan asserts, Lennon's upbringing involved a psychologically complex "class cleavage". Julia, who died when Lennon was seventeen, "never really rose above the working class, while Mimi's class ideals were those of the bourgeoisie" (Sullivan 1995: 61). Since uprooting into middle-class aspiration was synonymous with Lennon's traumatic separation from his working-class parents, it is unsurprising that his work was often bitterly hostile to notions of bourgeois identity. Mimi viewed McCartney, Lennon's chosen musical partner, as "common" (Baird 2007: 121); McCartney, conversely, recalls: "John's family was quite middle class and that was a lot of his appeal to me" (Howlett [broadcast], 2000).

A most ambiguous aspect of Lennon and McCartney's class identities is their grammar-school (and further) education. Lennon attended Art College but failed key components, leaving (as he had grammar school) without qualifications. McCartney gained five O-levels and one A-level in English. In 1964, Marxist scholar Terry Eagleton argued with tacit concern that Lennon and McCartney's educational backgrounds indicated a shift of popular music away from working-class culture (Eagleton 1964: 176–77; see also Harker 1980: 213). Yet their pursuit of popular music significantly represented a *rejection* of their education. While both teenagers experienced serious family traumas, it would be drastic to suppose music the primary cause of Lennon's failed and McCartney's incomplete O-levels, and both made noteworthy choices during further education. However, in 1960, when the fledgling Beatles were offered their first tour, Lennon and McCartney both missed their final exams for this opportunity. One of McCartney's sixth-form peers recalled that 'The conventional wisdom among my classmates was what a stupid idiot he was, ruining his career' (Ian Caulfield cited in Lewisohn 2013: 623).

Lennon and McCartney's cavalier attitudes to their education suggest little fear of future poverty; indeed, the consistent self-belief with which they pursued music as a profession suggests a degree of confidence enhanced by grammar-school education. Yet their choice of popular music as a career is riddled with class contradictions. Surviving as musicians as of summer 1960 (when they ceased receiving state support as students) placed them closer to the working classes both in wages and social circles. Nevertheless, biographies continue to gaze primarily towards established (if not middle-class) cultural reference points, focusing largely on The Beatles' bohemian affiliations. For instance, Norman (2008: 185–86) and Lewisohn (2013: 658–60) give ample coverage to English Beat poet Royston Ellis's 1960 stay with The Beatles in Liverpool. Such historical detail is insightful, but its foregrounding occurs at the expense of attention to The Beatles' links with more *socially* (not just culturally) marginalized individuals. Particularly significant here are the accounts of how, from 1958–1962, Lennon and McCartney keenly observed their home city's largely ghettoized Black music scenes, in and around Liverpool 8 (Toxteth).

George Roberts, a Toxteth-based manager of various Liverpool acts from 1959 to 1965, recalls the young Lennon and McCartney as "middle-class kids coming out from the suburbs, mixing with us working-class kids" in Liverpool 8, where Roberts managed the Starline Club. Located on Windsor Street, the Starline, Roberts explains, was "on the edge of our district, servicing mostly white people who had sympathies with the immigrant population" (interview, 19 March 2008). There, Roberts witnessed his main protégé, Somali-Irish Liverpool guitarist Vinnie Tow,[3] showing Lennon and McCartney various chords they were seeking to master, and how to tune a guitar "by pressing the ear against the instrument's body" (ibid.). This was not a singular occurrence. Roberts also saw Ismail "tutoring" Lennon and McCartney in the Cavern on "how to play a seventh chord in the Chuck Berry style. John in particular wanted to master the technique" (Roberts 2001). Key writers including MacDonald (1994) and Lewisohn (2013) emphasize the vital influence of American R&B on The Beatles. Nevertheless, the wider importance of R&B within Liverpool's own Black music scenes, and The Beatles' relationship to these remains largely unacknowledged in the dominant narratives, despite being outlined in numerous oral histories from below (Murray, dir. 1996; Henry 1998).

The Beatles' closest link with black Liverpudlian culture was Trinidad-born Lord Woodbine (Harold Phillips, 1929–2000).[4] Woodbine lived in Liverpool from 1949 onwards, where he led numerous steel bands. From 1958 onwards, Lennon and McCartney were often seen watching the All Caribbean Steel Band, led by Woodbine and based at Liverpool's Jacaranda coffee club (see Henry 1998). Together with The Beatles' first manager, Allan Williams, Woodbine co-owned the Cabaret Artists Club strip-joint, where the band briefly played (1960), and later the New Colony Club (1961–62), where they socialized. Woodbine also accompanied them to Hamburg in 1960. Lewisohn (2013) mentions that Woodbine (also a guitarist) was a calypsonian (2013: 518) but does not note his fuller significance: this Trinidadian was seemingly the first singer Lennon and McCartney encountered who performed his own songs. McCartney's 1980 comment on The Beatles' pre-EMI compositions is thus intriguing:

> we were trying to find the next beat – the next new sound. *New Musical Express…* was talking about calypso, and how [L]atin rock was going to be the next big thing. (Garbarini 1985: 56)

As Lewisohn discusses, Lennon's first composition (before meeting Woodbine) was 'Calypso Rock' (1957); one of only two LPs Lennon owned in 1959 was Lord Kitchener's 1955 compilation *Calypsos Too Hot To Handle* (Lewisohn 2013: 326, 797–98).

The substantial oral histories on black music in Liverpool and The Beatles, first initiated by Murray (dir., 1996) and Henry (1998), deserve greater recognition in the dominant narratives. What they indicate is that (and how) Lennon and McCartney's student-like readiness to assimilate an eclectic range of influences – a defining aspect of their work – began in their home city.

Lennon and McCartney's social origins were complex and eventful. As such, they can be narrated in multiple ways, particularly in terms of class. So far, I have focused on key elements of their backgrounds and how these have been historicized. I now turn to their actual work and how, while the artists' early lives were not without privilege, the content of their songs – not unlike their choice of rock 'n' roll as a career – significantly identify with working-class culture and, indeed, life.

'Eight Days a Week'
Work and culture in Lennon and McCartney's 1964–67 songs

It is easily overlooked that although Lennon's songs as a Beatle were often autobiographical, and although McCartney's vividly foregrounded themes of everyday life, the lyrics seldom indicate the singers' fame or wealth. Lennon drew inspiration from *The Daily Mail* of 17 January 1967 when composing 'A Day in the Life', but his lyric makes no allusion to the newspaper's (inaccurate) article about himself (*Daily Mail* 1967a), reporting that Lennon was writing a screenplay. McCartney's lines for the same song suggest not his London life but his Liverpool past and "what it was like to run up the road to catch a bus to school" (Aldridge 1967: 33). This discussion seeks to demonstrate that although there is artistic and biographical value in The Beatles' most overtly *confessional* songs, seemingly more routine experience also constitutes autobiography. This can be especially rich to discuss as cultural historical material.

MacDonald (1994: 126) reinforces the tendency to cite Lennon's first major autobiographical lyric as 'I'm a Loser' (Beatles 1964b). However, this complies with Lennon's post-Beatles inclination to emphasize only his melancholy lyrics as autobiographical (Wenner 2000: 9). An earlier lyric, corresponding more directly with Lennon's life, public and private, is 'A Hard Day's Night' (Beatles 1964a). Unlike the comparatively adolescent 'She Loves You' or 'I Want to Hold Your Hand' (1963), this lyric invokes a mature sexual (if not marital) relationship, centred on 'home'. Lennon ostensibly made his first wife, Cynthia Lennon, the subject of a passionate love song, much as he later would Ono. That 'A Hard Day's Night' is seldom considered autobiographical exemplifies how the (mostly male-authored) Beatles literature tends to dismiss Lennon's first wife, much as he himself would in retrospective interviews.

Although McCartney was more musically adept than Lennon, his lyrics prior to 1966 were confined to variations on a standard pop theme, love. Aptly, his first more complex lyric dealt with writing itself – and aspiration. Beneath the lyrical mask of a fictitious novelist, McCartney's 'Paperback Writer' (Beatles 1966a) is both pushy and pleading in expressing commercial ambition. Self-belief here depends on approval, and compromise is offered ("I can change it round"). It is as if, when composing the disjointed 'Paperback Writer' – a lyric, written as a letter, describing a book – McCartney discovered his songwriting priorities. Prefiguring his subsequent evocations of marginalized lives, the aspiring writer is the son of "a dirty man". But the song also suggests something of McCartney's past, in an ambitious yet impoverished family, and the linking of creativity with both economic and expressive urgency: "I need a job, and I wanna be a paperback writer".

McCartney's cultural aspirations during his years as a Beatle underscore his comments throughout Barry Miles's authorized biography. Indeed, *Many Years from Now* demonstrates McCartney's continuing cultural ambitions through its own, defensive reconstruction of his past – particularly when emphasizing his immersion in "avant-garde London" circa 1965–67 (Miles 1997: 220–21). However, 1960s sources concerning McCartney's cultural aspirations are more incisive, for these express a class-consciousness lacking in his later narratives. Profiled by Maureen Cleave for London's *Evening Standard* in March 1966, McCartney is reported to be "on a programme of self-improvement that he is embarrassed to discuss"; he stresses eagerness to "cram everything in, all the things I've missed", including Karlheinz Stockhausen's electronic compositions and Alfred Jarry's plays (Cleave 1966: 8). McCartney adds:

> I vaguely mind people knowing anything I don't know... what I feel most strongly about is... most people's attitudes to things like music and painting, culture with a capital C. If a navvy or a workie is seen coming out of an art gallery, it's a joke. Now, all a person wants to do is find out about something. (ibid.)

Vitally for The Beatles' artistic legacy, McCartney's 'self-improvement' corresponded with a will to bring mass audiences into new cultural territory. He told another interviewer in 1966 that "We can make a bridge… between us and Indian music, or us and electronic music, and we can take people with us" (cited in Reck 1985: 103). The Beatles' ventures into new cultural areas remained inclusive due to the gradualness with which these were introduced. Another key text – the Lennon-McCartney collaboration, 'Norwegian Wood' – records cynicism alongside fascination when faced with more elite cultural settings.

Lennon evasively commented that 'Norwegian Wood' (Beatles 1965) referred to "an affair I was having" (cited in Sheff 1981: 178). He did not reveal the other's identity, enabling commentators to mythologize the lyric. Bob Spitz repeats a longstanding assumption in Beatles literature, suggesting that Lennon was alluding to Maureen Cleave (Spitz 2005: 585). Norman, in one of his work's most publicized details, conjectures that the woman who inspired the song was Lennon's friend Sonny Freeman (Norman 2008: 418, 585). It has not previously been noted that 'Norwegian Wood' relates most consistently to Joan Baez's description of an awkward, ultimately abstinent night she spent with Lennon in August 1964 (Loder 1983: 20).[5] Lennon started the composition that month (Everett 2001: 313); it was completed a year later. The biographical intrigue spun by Lennon around this song has distracted from McCartney's co-authorship, which Lennon previously indicated (Wenner 1971: 85). McCartney claims the middle-eights and other lyrical contributions (Miles 1997: 270–71), and the focus on physical detail ("rug"; "wine") is most typical of McCartney; similar imagery recurs throughout his reminiscences of avant-garde London (Miles 1997: 216–18). McCartney proposed the image of "good Norwegian wood" furniture, inspired by the London house where he lodged with his actress girlfriend Jane Asher and her affluent family (cited in Miles 1997: 270). Asher introduced McCartney to London's elite artistic circles. Their relationship appears as pertinent to 'Norwegian Wood' as Lennon's liaison; yet, most compelling is not *who* the song represents but the cross-class encounter it narrates.

'Norwegian Wood' invokes a girl's minimally furnished room but the lifestyle is more bohemian than austere. Integral to the setting's otherness is the arrangement. At Lennon's request, Harrison replicated the former's guitar part with a sitar – and as discussed elsewhere, this Indian instrument's usage to establish otherness draws on Orientalist semiotics (McGrath 2011: 188). Lyrically, the song conveys disorientating fascination with the girl's home, through attention to detail unparalleled in The Beatles' earlier work. However, 'Norwegian Wood' culminates with the singer *seizing* the space which marked his exclusion. Waking alone in the girl's home, he "lit a fire". Ambiguously suggesting both comfort and arson, this inverts the singer's passivity. His entry into an elite cultural environment, precipitating eventual command over it, parallels much in The Beatles' legacy. Months earlier, with George Martin's aid, McCartney endowed 'Yesterday' with a string quartet: an arrangement associated with classical chamber music rather than mass cultural forms. The McCartney-led 'Eleanor Rigby' (Beatles 1966b) wholly dispensed with standard pop instrumentation, using a string octet.

It is significant that McCartney retrospectively claims "the idea to set the place on fire" in 'Norwegian Wood' (cited in Miles 1997: 271). It is often overlooked that McCartney's most audacious contributions to The Beatles' work surfaced in compositions led and sung by Lennon. McCartney-led songs employed adventurous yet respectable string arrangements (1967's 'She's Leaving Home' being a third example). His suggestions for more overtly experimental details – electronic music, and less structured orchestral passages – were reserved for Lennon's 'Tomorrow Never Knows' (1966), 'Strawberry Fields Forever' (1967) and 'A Day in the Life' (1967). It is therefore unsurprising that Lennon is still journalistically viewed as the risk-taking "clever" Beatle and McCartney, the crowd-pleasing "cute" one (Gilbert 2013: 73). Implicitly, this distinction positions Lennon as an innovator and McCartney as a follower of mainstream expectations. Part of this distinction's legacy, reinforced by Wiener (1984) and Elliott (1999), is that Lennon's reputation retains greater academic currency than McCartney's.

Although plentiful attention has been given to The Beatles' innovations in fusing popular music with far less mainstream Western traditions (Reck 1985; MacDonald 1994), what receives less recognition is how The Beatles' key innovations were adopted into their own, predominantly working-class cultural language. In the McCartney-led 'Penny Lane' (Beatles 1967a), classical adornments are no longer substitutes for The Beatles' instruments, as in 'Eleanor Rigby'. Woodwind and horn sections are now fully integrated into The Beatles' sound. The main instrumental passage (McCartney's suggestion) is led by Bach-inspired piccolo trumpet. In a song foregrounding working-class characters (plus an ostracized banker), The Beatles demonstrate their own cultural background – and moreover, *their audience* – to be worthy of musical language hitherto dominated by more privileged classes.

Heilbronner (2011) concludes that The Beatles "never attempted to undermine" the "aristocratic-bourgeois cultural hegemony" (Heilbronner 2011: 103). *Sgt Pepper's Lonely Hearts Club Band* (Beatles 1967b) contradicts this view. The content, while ambitiously experimental, is grounded in working-class cultural signifiers. Richard Hoggart's critique of working-class song traditions

(1957) is valuable here. The first two songs, while re-imagining The Beatles' identity, are overtly inclusive. The title track invites "you all to sing along", celebrating the tradition of working-class communal singing. 'With a Little Help From My Friends' celebrates the themes of love and friendship which Hoggart observed as permeating the most enduring working-class songs. A third theme noted by Hoggart, the near-sacred importance of home, recurs throughout the album, especially in McCartney's 'Fixing a Hole', 'She's Leaving Home' and 'When I'm Sixty-Four' (Hoggart 1957: 155–62).

Commencing with Lennon's 'A Hard Day's Night', The Beatles frequently celebrated working-class culture and, by extension, the resilience of working-class people. The problem here is that applauding the dignity of the oppressed risks excusing the system exploiting them. Indeed, reappraisals of The Beatles' relationship to Liverpool's working classes have stressed the band's increasing cultural distance from the city. Jon Murden's social-historical essay on Liverpool's post-war development stresses that 'Strawberry Fields Forever' and 'Penny Lane' imagined The Beatles' childhoods, not the city of 1967 (2006: 425). Fowler adds that the single ignored Liverpool's economic decline (2008: 172). Yet the *next* song The Beatles recorded presents their most scintillating critique of mass cultural existence and, indeed, oppression.

Although Lennon was often hostile to associations of middle-class identity, the frequently cerebral emphasis of his lyrics suggests privileges of his upbringing at Mendips, where he recalled in 1980, "the library was full of Oscar Wilde and Whistler" (cited in Sheff 1981: 156). In 'A Day in the Life' (Beatles 1967b), Lennon equates daily routine with easeful leisure time: reading, and philosophizing on the wider world. Yet here, it is through the latter activity – a luxury less accessible amidst the distraction and exhaustion of labour – that Lennon undermines agencies of authority. While national institutions invoke a notably English life, each is defamiliarized: not simply made strange, but *exposed* as abstract and detached. The daily news is laughable; nobody was sure if the man in the car was from the House of Lords; the English Army won the war in "a film"; the Albert Hall is full of "holes". The song's true national metonyms are the routines narrated.

McCartney's contrastingly quick-fire "day in the life" also suggests his Liverpool upbringing and less comfortable, more subordinated circumstances. Increasing from 77bpm in Lennon's sections to a more urgent 82bpm, insistent E-major piano chords invoke monotonous, externally imposed routine. McCartney's focus, contrasting with Lennon's national imaginings, remains on immediate, physical detail ("bed"; "comb"; "cup"). Although McCartney commented that the lyric recalls his schooldays, the adult vocal suggests "a modern everyman" (Riley 1988: 227). The ambiguity between adolescence and adulthood marks the singer's subordination.

Through Lennon's reflections on leisure, media and culture, and through McCartney's evocations of the mental and physical taxation of work, the universally titled 'A Day in the Life' exposes the vacuity of contemporary (indeed, capitalist) existence. Yet the song – only half of which consists of lyrics – is not defeatist. Again, McCartney suggested the most provocative detail in a Lennon-led song: the refrain, sung by Lennon, of "I'd love to turn you on". This exposes the dissatisfaction implicit in both narratives of daily life, and the subsequent twenty-four-bar orchestral intervention (again, McCartney's idea) –transcending established musical language through the largely improvised chromatic scale – hints at some notion of an alternative to regulated existence.

In 1969, left-wing journal *Black Dwarf* published an open letter to Lennon, proclaiming:

> The feeling I've go[t] from songs like 'Strawberry Fields Forever' and 'A Day In The Life' is part of what has made me into the kind of socialist I am. But then you suddenly went and kicked all that in the face with 'Revolution'. (Hoyland 1969)

"For this moment to be free"
Class, "race", and Lennon and McCartney's 1968–69 songs

By spring 1968, The Beatles' mass commercial success and critical popularity ostensibly made them a potential force in uniting workers with students. Yet, in late May, they recorded their seemingly most conservative song, Lennon's 'Revolution' (Beatles 1968a). Wiener, the most sympathetic radical scholar of Lennon's work, peruses the left-wing responses to 'Revolution' before conceding the lyric's "failure of intellect and imagination" in implying that "the most important feature of the May events was the violence of the students" (Wiener 1984: 59). *Black Dwarf* called the song "establishment propaganda" (Muldoon 1968: 8); *New Left Review* deemed it a "petty bourgeois cry of fear" (Merton 1970: 93). Although all three criticisms are valid, a facet of 'Revolution' which receives little recognition – arguably the most problematic aspect of this anti-revolutionary song – is that Lennon sings as though representing the working classes. The lyric's diction of "evolution", "constitution" and "institution", ascribed to what "you" say, implies a more educated (and decidedly *other*) recipient than any other Beatles composition.

The Left's responses to 'Revolution' nearly five decades ago have more recently been adopted by the Right with little further response from radical commentators. It is ironic that Lennon's most confrontational address to (his conception of) intellectuals should have yielded a tendency for The Beatles' lyrics at large to be read with superficial literalism. The scarcity of explicit political references in the songs enables 'Revolution' and Harrison's 'Taxman' (1966) to represent the sum of The Beatles' political legacy (Fowler 2008: 268; Heilbronner 2008: 102). As well as dismissing more subtle or debatable qualities of The Beatles' lyrics – and a mass audience's capacity to hear these – literalist interpretations often ignore the *music*.

The double album *The Beatles* (November 1968) increased the New Left's disillusionment with the band, largely *because* of its musical eclecticism. Jon Landau typified radical responses, asserting in 1969 that The Beatles were using parody as "a mask" behind which to "hide from the urgencies of the [political] moment" (cited in Wiener 1984: 64–65). More recently, postmodernist critiques have focused on parody itself in *The Beatles* (Whitley 2000; Roessner 2006). Despite utilizing Marxist-influenced models from Roland Barthes and Fredric Jameson, the postmodernist appraisals become somewhat trapped in hyper-real theoretical zones, effectively justifying the New Left criticisms by ignoring the album's more subtle political content. *The Beatles* is less a work of parody than a self-portrait, laying bare the band's influences. Here, Black musical influences are more prominent than on any Beatles album since the wryly named *Rubber Soul* (1965). While *Rubber Soul* substantially embraced American R&B, *The Beatles* bears more resonance of Britain's colonial legacy.

Although mostly composed in India, The Beatles' 1968 album is their first in three years on which the sitar is absent. The Beatles – most bitterly, Lennon – left Rishikesh personally disillusioned with their teacher, Maharishi Mahesh Yogi. However, their study of Transcendental Meditation reinvigorated both their productivity and diversity as songwriters. This renewed creativity continued flourishing on their return to England after a period abroad and coincided with newly urgent social-political concerns. While Britain's New Left, led by academics and students, sought to mobilize the working classes into revolutionary action, American historian Theodor Roszak sweepingly but pertinently wrote that the main cause inspiring the "fighting spirit" amongst Britain's workers was the "cry to drive coloured immigrants from the land" (Roszak 1969: 3). Conservative MP Enoch Powell was sacked from his shadow cabinet post when, in April 1968, his anti-immigration rhetoric equated West Indian immigrants with criminals. However, surveys indicated widespread support from Britons, and that many white working-class people supported Labour Home Secretary James Callaghan's tightening immigration policies (Hansen 1999: 812; Marwick 1981: 164–65). In April, dockers protested in London against Powell's dismissal. In May, when asked in New York about the controversy, Lennon commented "Britain is paying for what it did to all those countries". McCartney, responding to the suggestion that many Liverpudlians agreed with Powell, remarked defensively, if patronizingly: "they don't know anything else… they've got to agree with this fella" (*Newsfront* 1968). Although McCartney's answer is otherwise evasive, the immigration situation would, in 'Ob-la-di, Ob-la-da' (Beatles 1968b), shape one of his defining lyrical preoccupations: the everyday lives of working people.

'Ob-la-di, Ob-la-da' presents The Beatles' clearest, most celebratory foregrounding of Black musical and lyrical influences. Accentuated off-beats (also marking Starr's 'Don't Pass Me By', 1968b), complemented by a horn section, invoke ska: a Caribbean subgenre especially popular in Jamaica. McCartney selected the lead-character's name, "Desmond", because it sounded "Caribbean" (cited in Miles 1997: 419). Unlike most protagonists in McCartney's songs (for instance, 'Eleanor Rigby' or 'The Fool on the Hill'), Desmond and his wife Molly *belong* in the community imagined: "Desmond has a barrow in the marketplace, / Molly is the singer in a band". Alongside McCartney's recurrent theme of work, 'Ob-la-di, Ob-la-da' invokes his primary motif of belonging, here representing fulfilment unparalleled elsewhere in his Beatles lyrics: "In a couple of years, they have built a home, sweet home". The last verse sees the couple's children working with Molly; a second generation affirms this family's local belonging.

Stratton (2014) analyses this song as a positive diasporic narrative in response to Powellism, pointing out how the song has become part of British heritage. In one of the first academic considerations of Lord Woodbine's significance to The Beatles' music, Stratton outlines calypso influences in 'Ob-la-di, Ob-la-da', particularly its storytelling narrative (Stratton 2014: 12). Although Woodbine's lyrical relationship to 'Ob-la-di, Ob-la-da' can only be a matter of speculation, his musical influence is audible in Lennon's piano flourishes at 2'32 – 2'38, imitating steelpans. Asked by *Mojo* in 2008 about 'Ob-la-di, Ob-la-da' as a riposte to Powellism, McCartney acknowledged that the political situation was "in the background" but spoke more of Liverpool's influence and how The Beatles had been "very friendly with a lot of black guys", including Lord Woodbine; "they were just our mates we hung out with" (cited in Snow 2008: 58).

'Ob-la-di, ob-la-da' was a catchphrase of McCartney's friend Jimmy Scott, a London-based Nigerian musician. Although it is often stated that the title is Yoruba, its linguistic origins appear uncertain (Stratton 2014: 16). More significant here in the context of Britain in 1968 is the chorus's corresponding line, "Life goes on, *bra*": Jamaican-English for *brother*. When literalist interpretations are combined with political awareness, as in the standard critiques of

'Revolution', 'Ob-la-di, Ob-la-da', though less didactic, is equally pertinent to the political climate of 1968.

Diasporic community in 'Ob-la-di, Ob-la-da' is represented in radically benign ways but the song idealizes immigrant experience. Weeks later, McCartney and Lennon attempted a more explicit confrontation of crisis racism. What became 'Get Back' (Beatles 1969) began as a Beatles jam on 9 January 1969, based on newspaper headlines confirming Callaghan's refusal to ease immigration restrictions as more Asians were forced out of Kenya (*Daily Mirror* 1969). Aborted verses record McCartney's tendency to foreground isolated individuals, but here irony awkwardly blurs with an uncharacteristic element in McCartney's song writing: direct political comment. In 1995, *The Daily Mirror* sensationalized the "apparently racist" 'Get Back' outtakes but concluded that these were mocking, not expressing, racism, quoting lines including: "All the folks around don't dig no Pakistanis, taking other people's jobs" (*Daily Mirror* 1995). McCartney emphasizes that these lyrics were anti-racist (Miles 1997: 535), but for critics wishing to characterize The Beatles as right-wing, 'Get Back' is a core text. Heilbronner (2008) summarizes the released version as a "conservative response to the presence of immigrants in England's cities" (2008: 104). Such interpretations overlook one of The Beatles' key cultural-political gestures. Although other musicians on their releases included Ronnie Scott and Eric Clapton, these were uncredited. In April 1969, 'Get Back' was credited to "The Beatles with Billy Preston". The Beatles' proud recruitment of a Black American keyboardist – whom they met when he played in Liverpool with Little Richard in 1962 – says more than any discarded tapes.

"You're waiting for someone to perform with"

Lennon and Ono's turn to the radical

McCartney's 1966–68 work represents the most culturally and socially radical period of his (and arguably, The Beatles') career. In 1968, however, with Yoko Ono, Lennon began more fully embracing electronic composition, utilizing this more confrontationally. McCartney's experimentalism peaked with The Beatles' critically scorned television film *Magical Mystery Tour* (December 1967). The BBC received numerous complaints from viewers (*Daily Mail* 1967b). McCartney responded that The Beatles had attempted "something new" that "would not underestimate people" (Badman 2000: 333). Yet it is heartening that the public seemingly rejected this film, affirming that a mass audience's openness to new art includes, vitally, the capacity to discriminate. The Beatles' next release, McCartney's 'Lady Madonna' (March 1968), was contrastingly grounded, focusing on daily working-class domesticity. Its relatively straightforward arrangement, combined with the lyric's admiring but patriarchal celebration of motherhood, mark a turning-point towards the more conventional territory of McCartney's solo career. Lennon's work, however, was about to shift into the opposite direction.

Unlike McCartney, who emphasized his own affiliations with "the avant-garde", the art-college-educated Lennon used this term infrequently and cynically, expressing "reverse snobbery about *avant-garde*" (cited in Miles 2007). Lennon's ambivalence conveys resentment less of the avant-garde as aesthetic language than its eventual bourgeois connotations: a cultural fate historicized by Huyssen (1986). This pattern, however, is challengeable by the inclusion of Lennon and Ono's electronic composition 'Revolution #9' on *The Beatles* (1968). MacDonald, likening it to works by Stockhausen and Cage, asserts that while these "remained the preserve of the modernist intelligentsia", 'Revolution #9' was "packaged for a mainstream audience which had never heard of its progenitors" (MacDonald 1994: 230).

'Revolution #9' sonically equates mass political action with (to quote 'Revolution') 'destruction'. Its *musique concrète* sounds (echoing Jean-Luc Godard's film *Weekend*, 1967) include car-horns, fire, chanting crowds and breaking glass. However, while 'Revolution #9' is politically ambivalent, it presents Lennon's defining gesture of *cultural* revolt, reminiscent of Marcel Duchamp's challenges to the institutionalization of art. The track features cut-up, distorted recordings of classical works by Schumann and Sibelius. Yet, distributed as mass culture, the legacy of Lennon's gesture is different. Evaluating Duchamp's defaced *Mona Lisa* print *L.H.O.O.Q.* (1919) as the embodiment of Dadaist attacks on "bourgeois art-religion", Huyssen asserts that the twentieth-century avant-garde failed as "cultural revolt"; Duchamp's works were incorporated into private collections, and thus, bourgeois culture (Huyssen 1986: 147). 'Revolution #9' remains a commodity, but one marking the potency of mass culture to challenge the bourgeois seclusion of radical art. One year later, with Ono, Lennon applied a similar principle to what he viewed as the middle-class-led peace movement.

While 'Revolution' satirized the intellectualization of political frustration, 'Give Peace a Chance', Lennon's first non-Beatles single (Plastic Ono Band 1969), confronts the linguistic distance between peace advocates and the public they seek to convert. Lennon casts not the masses but intellectuals as illiterate, dismissing "this-ism, that-ism, ism-ism-ism" before declaring unity between all pacifists with the communally-sung chorus: "All we are saying / Is give peace a chance". Challenged by a *New York Times* journalist about the effectiveness of his campaign, Lennon angrily replied that the peace movement was dominated by "middle-class" manifestos by "half-witted intellectuals" (Solt, dir. 1988). Within weeks of this peace anthem's release, its chorus was being sung on anti-war demonstrations. The obverse of its transferability is its vagueness but Lennon's 1969 "peace" rhetoric began his trajectory towards political campaigns that were both more radical and more specific, with increasing focus on the working classes themselves.

As Wiener (1984) documents, Lennon and Ono endorsed a series of left-wing causes from 1969–72 through song, public demonstrations, interviews and financial support. Leaf and Scheinfield's 2006 documentary *The US vs John Lennon*, an impassioned if simplified testimony to Lennon's radical legacy, portrays his 1971–75 battle for US residency as the singer's victory. Legally, it was; Lennon received his Green Card in 1976. It is less often stated that the growing intensity of Lennon's immigration struggle by 1973 coincided with his general withdrawal from radical politics. However, in the week of his murder, Lennon and Ono were planning to attend a San Francisco rally supporting Japanese workers' rights in America and issued a statement of solidarity (Wiener 1984: 303–304). Unlike Lennon's radical commitments a decade earlier, this is unmentioned in his contemporaneous interviews. Nevertheless, the ways in which working-class loyalties and his Liverpool roots shaped Lennon's most enduring work remain pertinent.

The first major focus for Lennon's political radicalism was Black Power, initiated by approaches from Michael X (Michael Abdul Malik), London's most controversial Black political campaigner. He solicited funding from Lennon in 1969 after accusing him of having "stolen the rhythms" of Black musicians in Liverpool (Humphrey and Tindall 1977: 90–91). But Lennon's early black Liverpudlian links appear to represent less a point of political guilt than an influential backdrop to his multicultural ideals. Although, on becoming nationally famous, The Beatles grew shrewdly aware of politicians' opportunism, refusing to publicly associate with them after 1964 (Collins 2012: 4–5), Lennon willingly made an exception for a Black political leader. In January 1966, holidaying in Trinidad and Tobago, Lennon visited the islands' first Prime Minister, Eric Williams, with whom he was photographed.[6] Interracial solidarity is embedded in the musical content of Lennon and Ono's 1971 protest songs; gospel choruses lead 'Power to the People' and 'Happy Xmas (War Is Over)', while 'I Don't Wanna Be a Soldier' achieves its musical summit through the jazz saxophone of King Curtis. Black musical influences were also integral to occasional new directions in Lennon's later, otherwise largely conventional solo work, including funk ('What You Got', 1974) and steelpans in 'Borrowed Time' (1980), a reflection on his Liverpool youth.

As Norman (2008: 29) demonstrates, it is easy to mock Lennon's 'Working Class Hero' (1970) given his suburban upbringing. Yet the lyric itself implies Lennon's detachment from the working classes, despite his expressed identification with this group (Wenner 1971: 93). 'Working Class Hero', unlike most of Lennon's confessional songs, is narrated in the second person. However, this is not simple autobiography, but a protest song; and in Lennon's protest songs, the crucial figure is not the singer but "you". The arrangement flatters this, featuring Lennon alone on acoustic guitar. In a musical gesture akin to the lyrical directness of 'Give Peace a Chance', the song revolves around just two chords, easing its adoption by others.

The orthodox response to Lennon's 'Imagine' (Lennon 1971) is to quote "Imagine no possessions", then mention the singer's wealth. Lennon was the first person to indicate this irony, in the next line, "I wonder if you can"; unlike the preceding invitations, this is not "easy". Yet the possessions indicted are not material belongings but conceptual attachments: spiritual notions of an afterlife and nations and religions as dividing categories. The song's alternative to greed and hunger – "Sharing all the world" – may (or may not) sound unrealistic; but the title, too, hints at self-awareness not always recognized in dismissals of 'Imagine'.

There is symbolic value in the fact that Lennon never gave an entirely solo performance onstage of any song in his career. Others were crucial to his most innovative works – first McCartney, then Ono. However, the most vital of Lennon's collaborators is the one that remains: the audience. His most radical songs emphasize the listener's political power, not the singer's. Like McCartney's leading of The Beatles and their mass audience towards newer cultural territory, Lennon's attempts to promote political action proved transient. Yet the impermanence of these phases does not diminish their significance. Lennon and McCartney used their skills and positions to respond to various social, cultural and political undercurrents, amplifying and recording these for future audiences, and indeed, for history. In different ways, the artists' working-class loyalties were integral to this achievement.

McCartney's work, befitting his background, demonstrates greater engagement with working-class culture and, indeed, *experience*. Lennon's work, like his upbringing, is more removed from working-class existence, but this distance yields his critical engagement with class as a concept. McCartney's contributions to The Beatles' work were aspirational, but emphatically inclusive to audiences. His closeness to working-class culture ensured that he seldom overestimated a mass audience's openness to wider artistic areas – as The Beatles' popularity continues to suggest. Lennon's most radical work was often driven by cynicism towards bourgeois culture ahead of more direct identification with the working classes. Nevertheless, this position was crucial to how Lennon (with Ono) offered a democratizing of aesthetic and, more substantially, political engagement to listeners. McCartney and Lennon's work conveyed loyalty to working-class culture in different ways. In this, their legacies are mutually flattering. The Beatles' relationship to working-class and, especially, Black culture has been marginalized in most narratives. This chapter has sought to show how it need no longer stay the case.

Notes

1. This chapter was first published in *Popular Music History* 9/1 (2014).
2. A fireman and nurse feature in McCartney's play-like 'Penny Lane' (1967).
3. 1942–2007; Vinnie Tow later became Vinnie Ismail.
4. The name "Lord Woodbine" was not prompted simply by Phillips' love of cigarettes (and he did not smoke Woodbines, a popular and low-priced brand). "Lord" Woodbine's title referred to his status as a calypso singer-songwriter (one of his lyrics featured characters named after cigarettes). In 1947, he had toured Jamaica, sharing a bill with one of Trinidad's best-known Calypsonians, Lord Kitchener (Alwyn Roberts).
5. The lyric begins "I once had a girl"; Baez released versions of traditional ballads 'Once I Had a Boy' (1961) and 'Once I Had a Sweetheart' (1963).
6. Selections of these images (inaccurately dated 1968) appear on photographer Noel Norton's website: http://www.noelnortoncollectionltd.com/dignitaries.html (accessed 26 March 2023).

References

Aldridge, Alan. (1967) "A Good Guru's Guide to the Beatles' Sinister Songbook". *The Observer Colour Magazine*, 26 November: 26–33.
Badman, Keith. (2000) *The Beatles: Off The Record. Outrageous Opinions & Unrehearsed Interviews*. London: Omnibus.
Baird, Julia. (2007) *Imagine This*. London: Hodder & Stoughton.
Clayson, Alan and Spencer Leigh. (2003) *The Walrus was Ringo*. New Malden: Chrome Dreams.
Cleave, Maureen. (1966) "Paul All Alone". *Evening Standard*, 25 March: 8.
Collins, Marcus. (2012) "The Beatles' Politics". *British Journal of Politics and International Relations* 16/2: 1–19. https://doi.org/10.1111/j.1467-856X.2012.00545.x
Daily Mail. (1967a) "Back-Room Beatle?" 17 January: 4.
Daily Mail. (1967b) "Beatles on TV Baffle Viewers". 27 December: 1.
Daily Mirror. (1969) "Warning to the Premiers: No Extra Immigrants". 9 January: 1.
Daily Mirror. (1995) "The Banned 'Get Back' Revealed". 28 November: 3.
Eagleton, Terry. (1964) "New Bearings: The Beatles". *Blackfriars* 45: 175–78.
Elliott, Anthony. (1999) *The Mourning of John Lennon*. London: University of California Press.

Everett, Walter. (2001) *The Beatles as Musicians: The Quarry Men through Rubber Soul*. Oxford: Oxford University Press.
Fowler, David. (2008) *Youth Culture in Modern Britain, c.1920–c.1970*. Basingstoke: Palgrave Macmillan.
Garbarini, V. (1985) "Paul McCartney Interview [1980]". In *The Beatles Book*, 50–61. London: Omnibus Press.
Gilbert, Pat. (2013) "Don't Look Back in Anger". *Mojo*, November: 68–82.
Goldstein, Richard. (1967) "We still need the Beatles, but...". *New York Times*, 18 June: 24D.
Gunn, Simon and Rachel Bell. (2002) *Middle Classes*. London: Orion.
Hansen, Randall. (1999) "The Kenyan Asians, British Politics, and the Commonwealth Immigrants Act, 1968". *The Historical Journal* 42/3: 809–34. https://doi.org/10.1017/S0018246X9900864X
Harker, Dave. (1980) *One for the Money*. London: Hutchinson.
Heilbronner, Oded. (2008) "The Peculiarities of the Beatles: A Cultural-Historical Interpretation". *Cultural and Social History* 5/1: 99–116. https://doi.org/10.2752/147800408X267274
Heilbronner, Oded. (2011) "'Helter-Skelter'?: The Beatles, The British New Left, and the Question of Hegemony". *Interdisciplinary Literary Studies* 13/1–2: 87–107. https://doi.org/10.2307/41328514
Henry, Tony. (1998) "The Man who Put the Beat in the Beatles". *The Observer*, 2 August: 9.
Hoggart, Richard. (1957) *The Uses of Literacy*. Harmondsworth: Penguin.
Hoyland, John. (1969) "John Hoyland Replies". *Black Dwarf*, 10 January: n.p.
Humphrey, Derek and David Tindall. (1977) *False Messiah: The Story of Michael X*. London: Hart-Davis.
Huyssen, Andreas. (1986) *After the Great Divide*. London: Macmillan.
Laing, Dave. (2009) "Six Boys, Six Beatles: The Formative Years, 1950–1962". In *The Cambridge Companion to The Beatles*, ed. Kenneth Womack, 9–31. Cambridge: Cambridge University Press.
Lewisohn, Mark. (2013) *The Beatles – All These Years – Extended Special Edition: Volume One: Tune In*. London: Little, Brown.
Loder, Kurt. (1983) "Joan Baez: The *Rolling Stone* Interview". *Rolling Stone*, 14 April: 14–23.
MacDonald, Ian. (2005 [1994]) *Revolution in the Head*. London: Pimlico.
McGrath, James. (2011) "John, Paul, George and Richard: The Beatles' Uses of Literacy". In *Richard Hoggart: Culture and Critique*, ed. Michael Bailey and Mary Eagleton, 181–96. Nottingham: Critical, Cultural and Communications Press.
Mann, William. (1963) "What Songs The Beatles Sang". *The Times*, 27 December: 4.
Marwick, Arthur. (1981) *British Society since 1945*. Harmondsworth: Penguin.
Merton, Richard. (1970) "Comment". *New Left Review* 59: 88–96.
Miles, Barry. (1997) *Paul McCartney: Many Years from Now*. London: Secker & Warburg.
Miles, Barry. (2007) John Lennon/Yoko Ono interview, September 1969. http://www.rocksbackpages.com/article.html?ArticleID=723
Muldoon, Roland. (1968) "Subculture: The Street-fighting Pop Group". *Black Dwarf* 13/6: 8.
Murden, Jon. (2006) "City of Change and Challenge: Liverpool Since 1945". In *Liverpool 800: Culture, Character and History*, ed. John Belchem, 393–485. Liverpool: Liverpool University Press.

Newsfront. (1968) Lennon and McCartney interview, 14 May. http://www.beatlesinterviews.org/db1968.0514.beatles.html.
Norman, Philip. (2003) "The Bourgeois Beatle". *The Daily Mail*, 29 March: 36–38.
Norman, Philip. (2008) *John Lennon: The Life*. London: HarperCollins.
Odell, Michael. (2008) "Percy Thrillington, Magritte and Me". *The Guardian*, 29 November. http://www.theguardian.com/music/2008/nov/29/paul-mccartney-the-fireman-interview.
Reck, D. R. (1985) "Beatles Orientalis: Influences from Asia in a Popular Song Tradition". *Asian Music* 16/1: 83–149. https://doi.org/10.2307/834014
Riley, Tim. (1988) *Tell Me Why*. New York: Vintage.
Roberts, George. (2001) "Managing the Bands". http://www.triumphpc.com/mersey-beat/a-z/managingthebands.shtml.
Roessner, J. (2006) "We All Want to Change the World: Postmodern Politics and the Beatles' *White Album*". In *Reading The Beatles*, ed. Kenneth Womack and Todd Davis, 208–225. New York: SUNY Press.
Roszak, Theodor. (1969) *The Makings of a Counter Culture*. London: Faber.
Sheff, David. (2001 [1981]) *Last Interview: All We are Saying – John Lennon and Yoko Ono*. London: Pan.
Snow, Mat. (2008) "We Weren't Trying to Revive Rock 'n' Roll, We *Were* Rock 'n' Roll". *Mojo*, October: 57–59.
Spitz, Bob. (2005) *The Beatles: The Biography*. New York: Little, Brown.
Stratton, Jon. (2014) "Ob-La-Di Ob-La-Da: Paul McCartney, Diaspora and the Politics of Identity". *Journal for Cultural Research* 18/1: 1–24. https://doi.org/10.1080/14797585.2013.768473
Sullivan, Henry W. (1995) *The Beatles with Lacan*. New York: Peter Lang.
Wenner, Jann S. (2000 [1971]) *Lennon Remembers*. London: Verso.
Whiteley, Sheila. (1992) *The Space Between the Notes*. London: Routledge.
Whitley, Ed. (2000) "The Postmodern White Album". In *The Beatles, Popular Music and Society*, ed. Ian Inglis, 105–126. London: Macmillan.
Wiener, Jon. (1995 [1984]) *Come Together*. London: Faber.

Discography

Beatles, The. 1964a. *A Hard Day's Night*. Parlophone.
—1964b. *Beatles For Sale*. Parlophone.
—1965. *Rubber Soul*. Parlophone.
—1966a. 'Paperback Writer'. Parlophone.
—1966b. *Revolver*. Parlophone.
—1967a. 'Penny Lane'/'Strawberry Fields Forever'. Parlophone.
—1967b. *Sgt Pepper's Lonely Hearts Club Band*. Parlophone.
—1968a. 'Hey Jude'/'Revolution'. Apple.
—1968b. *The Beatles*. Apple.
—1969. 'Get Back' (with Billy Preston)/'Don't Let Me Down'. Apple.
Lennon, John. 1970. *John Lennon/Plastic Ono Band*. Apple.
Lennon, John. 1971. *Imagine*. Apple.
Plastic Ono Band, The. 1969. 'Give Peace a Chance'. Apple.

Filmography

Leaf, David and John Scheinfield, dirs. 2006. *The US vs John Lennon*. Lionsgate.
Murray, Derek, dir. 1996. *Who Put the Beat in Mersey Beat?* Inspiral Films/Granada TV.
Solt, Andrew, dir. 1988. *Imagine: John Lennon*, Warner Brothers.

Broadcasts

Howlett, Kevin. 2000. *Lennon's Legacy*. BBC Radio 2: 23 December.

Interviews

Interview with George Roberts, 19 March 2008.

Author biography

Dr James McGrath is Senior Lecturer in English Literature and Creative Writing in the School of Humanities and Social Sciences at Leeds Beckett University, UK. He completed his doctoral thesis on the work of John Lennon and Paul McCartney, and his first book *Naming Adult Autism: Culture, Science, Identity* was published by Rowman & Littlefield International in 2017. His poems have been published in various literary periodicals.

2 Notes on The Beatles from a Black Liverpudlian Perspective

Mark Christian

"The Beatles are a very important element in showing how the best of white musicianship has been influenced by African American musical heritage", Mark Christian importantly points out. In addition to publishing extensively on Africana Studies from both sociological and cultural studies perspectives, Christian (born in Liverpool in 1961) teaches undergraduate courses on The Beatles and has conducted tours of Liverpool for US visitors. In this online interview, Mark Christian reflects on the personal, musical and historical significance of The Beatles in his life and work. As a member of one of Liverpool's most distinguished musical families, and whose brothers formed the band The Christians, the author details here some of the many important links between The Beatles and Liverpool's various Black music scenes. Our discussion encompasses tourism in Liverpool; the value of listening to The Beatles' work chronologically; and the question of whether the band are overrated. Most importantly, however, Christian emphasizes the frequently overlooked influence of African American country/soul singer-songwriter Arthur Alexander on The Beatles. Taking Alexander's legacy as just one starting point for such discussion, Christian points out: "It is incredible how racism impinges on this history of a band, yet so much is owed from them to Black music". Christian also shares memories of knowing Harold Phillips (Lord Woodbine) during the later years of the Trinidadian-Liverpudlian musician's eventful life.

By way of an introduction, I was born on 16 April 1961 at 26 Osborne Road, Tuebrook, Liverpool 13. Two months prior to my birth, The Beatles played at St. John's Hall in Snaefell Avenue, almost directly across West Derby Road and less than a quarter of a mile from my home, on Friday 17 February. This was following the return to the city after their first season in Hamburg. During this period the band was booked into gigs largely by Mrs Mona Best, the mother of Pete Best. He was then still the drummer and by all historical accounts very popular with their Liverpudlian fans. The Beatles went on to play over ten gigs at St. John's Hall, a venue where I as a teenager would go to discos in the 1970s. Therefore I can state that in my life I have been closer to The Beatles than most, at least in a physical sense. To consider that a mere three years on from February 1961 The Beatles (minus Pete Best, with Ringo Starr now in place) would be playing on *The Ed Sullivan Show* in New York is rather incredulous. Indeed, only two years after those gigs in St. John's Hall they were taking the United Kingdom by storm. Lastly, my mother would often recall to me how I would literally do the twist to The Beatles' version of 'Twist and Shout' in my cot after the release of their first album *Please Please Me* in March 1963.

That stated, my family background also includes another interesting twist, no pun intended. With four of my brothers, Roger, Victor, Garry and Russell, I sang a cappella gigs around the city from 1977 to 1984. We called ourselves The Christians, simply because of our family name. To add more intrigue, Victor was a music teacher who taught at Quarry Bank school (later renamed Calderstones), John Lennon's former school, for about twenty years. Both Victor and I decided to stay in education, but in 1985 Roger, Garry and Russell joined forces with another local musician to form another version of The Christians. They went on to have some success in the late 1980s and early 1990s.

The 1989 Hillsborough tragedy, that would take the lives of ninety-seven Liverpool Football Club supporters, brought two of my siblings together with Paul McCartney and other Liverpool musicians to record 'Ferry Across the Mersey' to raise funds for the families. Garry sings lead parts, along with Paul McCartney, Holly Johnson and Gerry Marsden. The record reached No. 1 in the UK charts, and cemented my family again to the history of The Beatles, or at least to one of them.

Finally, again on a family note, my elder sister Pamela knew The Beatles socially from her lunch days at work spent at the Cavern when they played there in 1962. All being stated, we are a family that has been at times close to The Beatles' musical history.

The irony for myself in regard to The Beatles is that I did not study them seriously until I was in the United States as a graduate student in the early 1990s. Up until that time I listened to them periodically but never owned any CDs of their music. I had been brought up in my household back in Liverpool largely on rhythm and blues, plus soul, particularly emanating from the Atlantic and Motown labels. My favorite group was, and still is, The Temptations. All their albums were played by my elder siblings and therefore that is what I listened to as a child in the mid-1960s onwards. No Beatles albums were played by my siblings in my home in my youth. Yet we heard them on the radio and about town like everybody else.

I began to study The Beatles seriously because they were so popular in the United States, and because I was from Liverpool people would naturally associate me with them, "Oh you're from The Beatles' city, wow!" was the average response I received. With this kind of indirect pressure I decided to purchase a CD each month. I started with the *Please Please Me* album from 1963, and I would read about the group as I listened. I began to gain more respect for them as I delved deeper into their history. Yet what struck me profoundly was the way they had covered so many African American artists in their early years: Little Richard, Chuck Berry, Ray Charles, Arthur Alexander, The Coasters, The Isley Brothers, Smokey Robinson & The Miracles, Barrett Strong, The Marvelettes, Ritchie Barrett, and The Shirelles among them. Clearly, they were a band highly influenced by African American rhythm and blues. I was also struck by how closely The Beatles covered the original songs, in terms of melody and harmonies. One of my favorite songs on the *Please Please Me* album is 'Ask Me Why', which is clearly influenced by the era of Motown performers. It was surprising to me that this song was a B side (to the single 'Please Please Me') because it is so catchy and melodic; for me it was a clear hit had it been released as an A side single.

Have you used or referred to The Beatles in your own research or teaching? Does it seem that current students are still interested in The Beatles?

Yes, I focus on the early influences on The Beatles' catalogue before they became prolific song writers. I teach a class on African American music up to the 1960s and as a backdrop to the Civil Rights Movement. Students are always fascinated with the covers by The Beatles on various African American artists. With YouTube it is very convenient to show the class the original version and then the cover by The Beatles. Millennial students tend to be into hip hop music, but I have taught this class for nearly a decade and it is very popular. They also pick up the music samples hip hop artists take from past music. The Beatles are a very important element in showing how the best of white musicianship has been influenced by African American musical heritage. My classes are essentially about Africana history and culture and what I endeavor to do is show the influence across music. The Beatles were always honest about this fact; they openly stated their love for rhythm and blues.

Indeed, in a 1987 interview with Mark Lewisohn, Paul McCartney stated: "If the Beatles ever wanted a sound it was R&B. That's what we used to listen to, what we used to like and what we wanted to be. Black, that was basically it..." (cited in Younger 2000: 67). On the same point, John Lennon was a massive admirer of Arthur Alexander (1940–1993), the African American country/soul singer, and it is rarely acknowledged by mainstream commentators how much John Lennon took from this singer's styling and phrasing (Younger 2000). It is largely acknowledged how Little Richard influenced The Beatles' Paul McCartney, and the rendition of 'Long Tall Sally' by them is a worthy cover. Overall, yes, there is much to share with students in a contemporary sense when it comes to sharing the influences African Americans had on rock and roll music generally, but The Beatles were clearly a major employer of African American musical heritage. Research is rather thin, too, in just how deep this goes. 'Twist and Shout' by the Isley Brothers (first performed by the Top Notes) is another example of how The Beatles took from them and used for their act. The shaking of the heads and "Ooohhs!" was an Isley Brothers styling.

We've previously mentioned Lord Woodbine (Harold Phillips) and his significance as a mentor to the young Beatles, as well as his own work as a musician. Would you like to share any personal memories of Lord Woodbine, or comment on how he has been regarded in Liverpool?

I am happy to see a few works on Lord Woodbine. I actually met him when he worked in a store on Granby Street in Liverpool 8 in the late 1970s and early 1980s. I did not know the connection he had with The Beatles till much later, but he was always a smiling gentleman to me. Kind-hearted in a manner one can gauge from our interactions in his store. He seemed worldly and knowledgeable too with his conversation. However, not once did he ever mention The Beatles or his history with them to me. When I got into studying more deeply I came across the photo where he was once air brushed out; it is the photo of him with The Beatles traveling to Hamburg in a bus, sitting taking a break it looks like. What is sad is how his image was made invisible simply because he was a Black man. It is incredible how racism impinges on this history of a band, yet so much is owed from them to Black music.

Anyhow, Lord Woodbine worked with Allan Williams back in the early 1960s and that's how his connection with The Beatles was formed. He lived his life in the Liverpool 8 area, and three of his daughters, Pauline, Susan, and Barbara, were part of a girl group in the 1970s. Susan would also become the partner of my brother Garry, and have two children together, Miles and Pippa. So again, the connection to Liverpool musical heritage runs deep. In fact, Lee Mavers of the famous La's was the partner to one of my nieces, Nevada, and they have four children. We could say that all roads lead back to The Beatles in some manner!

Lord Woodbine would never benefit monetarily from having known and worked with The Beatles. He died in a tragic fire at his home in Liverpool 8 in July 2000. So, it really is a tragic story about a beautiful soul who brought so much to Liverpool's history of music and life. I hope one day he gets the credit he deserves and recognition from the city that owes so much to his existence. It is the unknown parts of The Beatles' story that need to be highlighted in the future. Lord Woodbine is a character that should never be forgotten to history.

In what ways, if any, are The Beatles overrated?

I do not believe they are overrated; I think they were a fabulous foursome with immense talent that grew as they got more experienced. They were innovative and their music is melodic and has a freshness to it each time one listens. When you study each album you see the development in their technique. Clearly, George Martin cannot be underestimated in his impact on them with his studious classical background and ability to manipulate whatever technology they had in the early 1960s to 1970. The question of them being overrated is rather moribund. Anyone who understands music, harmonies, and melody, and does not like The Beatles may have some deficiency in hearing because those four guys could make wonderful sounds together. John was clearly the leader, but Paul for me was the guy who kept them together and put forward ideas that were intelligent and innovative. For example, he's largely acknowledged as the inspiration behind the classic *Sgt Pepper*'s album. George is the deeply spiritual member, and a brilliant writer too in the latter albums, the "White" album, *Let it Be* and *Abbey Road*. Indeed, 'Something' is a song that Frank Sinatra once deemed the greatest love song in the last fifty years, and it never says "I love you" in it. Well, what better endorsement can you get musically? Ringo was important to the character of the group. Together they will be renowned until the earth stops spinning. They were never overrated, maybe underrated. Yes, they could not read music but clearly that does not mean anything when it comes to playing, singing, and writing songs that will live beyond many generations just as the works of Mozart, Beethoven, and other European classical musicians have done so for hundreds of years. No, The Beatles are not overrated, they grew to be a band that has proved their worth musically, socially, and generationally.

What aspects of The Beatles' history and legacy would you like to see addressed more often or more extensively in scholarship?

Well, this question I may have touched on above, but to emphasize I would hope that future scholars will give more credit to the impact African American artists had on their foundation as musicians. Because many of their idols did not benefit from the millions made by white rock and rollers. Not to sound righteous, but it seems unfair that the likes of Arthur Alexander ended his life driving a bus, after having such an impact artistically on John Lennon. Is this John's fault? Absolutely not, yet writers and scholars should do what they can to tell the stories of these facts and allow future generations to understand the depth of inequality that pervades all areas of music and life.

I would also like to have acknowledged the local scene in Liverpool and the Black musicians who may have impacted The Beatles: Derry Wilkie, The Chants, and possibly Lord Woodbine's generation of musicians that played in Liverpool as The Beatles were developing their skills. It is a missing piece in the history and one worthy of consideration for future scholars (Harry 2000; Leonard and Strachan 2010).

A topic of interest to Peter and myself is how The Beatles were regarded within Liverpool over the years. What are your memories of how The Beatles were regarded within Liverpool in the 1980s and 1990s?

I mentioned earlier that I grew to admire The Beatles when I left to study and work in the United States from 1992 onwards. I play acoustic guitar (not very well!) and I admire many of The Beatles' songs as a learning tool. I have also come to understand that the legacy of this group to Liverpool's history and cultural industry is immense. The tourism is obviously an area that will benefit the city and who can blame the council leaders for exploiting this? Clearly, they are an extremely relevant attraction to Liverpool visitors. I have taken visitors from the US on Beatle tours and I thoroughly enjoy it myself. If you admire music and history, then the tourism makes sense to me. If it benefits the local economy, then why not exploit this musical history? Liverpool is a great city to visit; it has a unique history that I share with my US students. For example, I tell them that the famous Penny Lane by The Beatles is a wonderful area, but the lane itself is named after a staunch slave trader, James Penny. This kind of historical parallel, a beautiful song with a horrific historical context unknown to most, is fascinating.

I believe the history of The Beatles will now be enshrined forever in the history of Liverpool. The story is actually fascinating, too: four guys, friends, who loved Black music, and developed their sound, built their unique style, and shook up the world. Anyone who does not like their story could be deemed rather mean-spirited. Tourism is good if it tells the true story and keeps it real, not faux.

In terms of the music itself, which is your favourite Beatles album, and why?

Like many admirers of The Beatles, it is hard to pin down a favorite album. I actually find their first one, *Please Please Me*, wonderful to listen to. *A Hard Day's Night* too. In *Rubber Soul* and *Revolver* you begin to get more innovation, I really like 'Norwegian Wood', 'Nowhere Man', 'I'm Only Sleeping', 'Here, There and Everywhere', and 'Got to Get You into My Life'. I could go on, as it is really difficult to choose a favourite album. *Sgt Pepper's* could be deemed the most innovative. 'A Day in the Life' represents their growth and talent as artists, as well as containing various features that would become 'Beatle-esque' in the sense of being adapted by others. *Abbey Road*, their last in the studio, has some exceptional tracks: 'Come Together', 'Here Comes the Sun' and 'Something'.

Overall, The Beatles are a group that will last through the annals of time. I am glad to have lived during their lifetime, too. We are blessed to have shared their story and to have been here to listen to them. Clearly, they will influence many future bands unborn, and songwriters who have yet to think about songwriting. I do hope too, that anyone who studies The Beatles goes to the roots of their beginnings and builds up from there as I did; it is a fruitful journey of discovery.

The Beatles were a unique group full of character and talent. No serious listener to popular music could seriously refute the depth of their talent. It is hard to realize that they were each 'retired' from the group well before the age of thirty. Their contribution to popular music will live on for many generations. Indeed, it could be argued that their popularity has never waned since the height of the fame they received in the 1960s. What can be stated with confidence is this: as long as music exists, then so will The Beatles.

References

The Christians, Holly Johnson, Paul McCartney, Gerry Marsden. (1989) 'Ferry Across the Mersey'. Stock, Aitken & Waterman.
Harry, Bill. (2000) *The Beatles Encyclopedia*. London: Virgin.
Leonard, Marion and Strachan, Robert. (2010) *The Beat Goes On: Liverpool, Popular Music and the Changing City*. Liverpool: Liverpool University Press.
Younger, Richard. (2000) *Get a Shot of Rhythm & Blues: The Arthur Alexander Story*. Tuscaloosa, AL: University of Alabama Press.

Author biography

Mark Christian is a full and tenured professor in the Department of Africana Studies, Lehman College – City University of New York, USA. His research focus is on the African Diaspora primarily in relation to the United Kingdom and the United States. His recent publications include *The 20th Century Civil Rights Movement: An Africana Studies Perspective* (Kendall Hunt, 2021) and *Booker T. Washington: A Life in American History* (ABC-CLIO, 2021). His latest book titled *Transatlantic Liverpool: Shades of the Black Atlantic* (Lexington Press, 2022) covers broader aspects of the Liverpool Black Experience.

3 From Liverpool to Tibet: 'Tomorrow Never Knows' and the Troubled Path to the East

Sharif Gemie

In 1966, 'Tomorrow Never Knows' closed The Beatles' seventh album Revolver, *suggesting spectacular new horizons not just within the group's own work, but in the musical and cultural outlook of The Beatles' audience. This chapter details John Lennon's various inspirations for the composition. More extensively, however, the author contemplates the fusion of Eastern and Western musical traditions within the song. Rather than marking some sort of cultural rupture, 'Tomorrow Never Knows' can instead be seen as an example of cultural continuity. It can be situated within the broad confines of "Orientalism" identified by Edward Said (1978). Orientalism could take many forms: sometimes a blatant racism; sometimes an articulate, pragmatic argument to rationalize imperialist expansion; sometimes an attitude resembling an admiration or even an affection for "Eastern" forms. The aspect which is most relevant here is the latter: those educated Westerners who looked eastward in search for some form of intellectual enlightenment.*

There is a photograph of the recording of 'Tomorrow Never Knows'.[1] It shows John Lennon in the corner of a studio, lying upside-down over a standard-issue office chair – the sort of chair that you might find in a university seminar room. His feet hang over the top of the chair, his chest is pushed out and his head rests on the floor. A guitar and various anonymous-looking pieces of studio equipment lie behind him. Lennon's hands are crossed over his stomach in an odd gesture, suggesting he was trying to get comfortable. Over his head is a large set of headphones, and an upside-down microphone hangs about six inches away from his mouth. Part of his face is visible in profile: rather than looking embarrassed, Lennon seems far-away, as if concentrating on something.

This bizarre image has a rational explanation. Like many singers, Lennon was sensitive about his vocal performance, and this led him to experiment with different techniques: for example, he tried lying on the floor to get a relaxed sound to his vocals for 'Revolution' on the "White Album" (MacDonald 1998: 282). However, this image of making 'Tomorrow Never Knows' has a force of its own: it evokes a grubby, untidy version of *Alice in Wonderland*, a strange upside-down world in which the singer is trying to contort himself into a new reality.

Was something magical produced by this exercise? Ian MacDonald makes some extraordinary claims for the song. According to him, its innovative use of the drone

> challenges not only seven centuries of Western music, but the operating premise of Western civilization itself....
>
> ['Tomorrow Never Knows'] launched the till-then élite-preserved concept of mind expansion into pop, simultaneously drawing attention to consciousness-enhancing drugs and the ancient religious philosophies of the Orient, utterly alien to Western thought in their anti-materialism, rapt passivity, and world-sceptical focus on visionary consciousness. (MacDonald 1998: 192)

While it is certainly a great song, it seems that – unusually – MacDonald has missed some important points about the track's content. This chapter will consider the context of the song, and question Lennon's inspiration to write it.

The end of the beginning

There can be no doubt about the tremendous power and originality of 'Tomorrow Never Knows'. It is marked by the introductory hypnotic drone of the tambura; by the near-absence of chord changes, a structure which mimics Asian musical forms; by the great rhythm hammered out by the drums and bass line, which also carry the main melody of the song – Harrison's guitars and Lennon's keyboards are almost swamped out in the wall of sound. The song resembles contemporary avant-garde music in its use of five tape-loops. There is even something distinctive about the vocal arrangement: for the first minute of the song, Lennon's voice is double-tracked in a curious, uneven fashion, with the dominant voice usually coming from the left-hand channel, but occasionally the right-hand voice sounding stronger. Then, after a brief instrumental break, and almost exactly half-way through the song, Lennon's voice returns in the centre of the mix, sounding more distant and distorted, but definitely singular. This goes against the traditions of Western pop songs, where vocal arrangements usually grow more complex as a song evolves, rather than simpler. One possibility is that the uneven double-tracking is meant to suggest an uncertainty, or a searching spirit, while the singular voice suggests the achievement of a unity: almost like a crowd throwing out questions, and then a single person answering.

'Tomorrow Never Knows' is also a great Lennon *and* The Beatles plus George Martin song. Like 'Strawberry Fields Forever', 'I Am the Walrus', or 'A Day in the Life', the contributions of the various Beatles and their producer are beautifully combined. While the inspiration comes from Lennon, one senses the extent to which the others got behind the song, pushing themselves to produce a highly distinctive sound: their contributions both transform and make the song. For example, Paul McCartney was far more familiar with *musique concrète* than Lennon: the distinctive tape-loops on 'Tomorrow Never Knows' were probably his idea (Norman 2008: 436). The key to all these landmark songs seems to be the manner in which Lennon's originality provoked the others to experiment, so one person's song becomes a field for a collective creativity. Arguably, none of McCartney's or Harrison's songs worked in the same way.

A further original element to the song lies in its creation of an odd logic through which beginnings and ends seem to be confused and even overturned. The song's position on *Revolver* even operates this way: the last song on the LP, it was actually recorded first, in April 1966, as if the group needed to know *Revolver*'s finishing-point before they could start the album. The *last* words of the song (and the LP) are "of the beginning", repeated seven times. In a sense, these words do take us back to another beginning: to Lennon's beginning. A point which often seems to be ignored by commentators is that John *Winston* Lennon was quoting Winston Churchill's speech of 10 November 1942, in which he warned his British audience that the recent decisive victory at El Alamein did not mark the end of the war, nor even the beginning of the end, but perhaps the end of the beginning.

Routes to the East

Over the centuries, there had been many previous points of contact between Western and Asian cultures: arguably such forms of interchange and exchange are a normal practice for performers, rather than something exceptional. One could cite countless examples of such borrowing: Mozart's opera *The Abduction of the Seraglio* (1781) featured sections of Turkish-inspired music. Two centuries later, in 1958, Dave Brubeck was touring with his quartet in Istanbul. He heard street musicians playing in 9/8 time, and was inspired by them to compose his 'Blue Rondo à la Turk' which appeared on his celebrated *Time Out* LP of 1959 (see Clark 2012).

If we turn to consider Britain specifically, one finds evidence of a range of connections and exchanges with other cultures. Even as the British Empire was formed, a minority of the Indian colonial administration – who became known as "Orientalists" – were charmed and fascinated by local cultures: principally by their religion, but also by their food and their music (see Allen 2002; Collingham 2005). The end of British rule in India did not end the links between the two countries: instead, various connections such as migration, tourism and cultural exchanges actually grew more frequent after 1947. Ravi Shankar appeared at the Edinburgh Festival in 1963: a soundtrack of Shankar's sitar-playing was then used as the soundtrack for Jonathan Miller's TV production of *Alice in Wonderland* in 1966 (see Robinson 2012). There is a plausible argument that Ray Davies's use of a drone (played on his 12-string guitar) on The Kinks' 'See My Friends' (1965) marks the first entry of Indian musical forms into modern Western pop music (MacDonald 1998: 195 n. 2). Rather less creditably, mock-Arab themes also formed a well-established if minor tradition in Western popular music. Ray Stevens had a hit with 'Ahab the Arab' in 1962, and Harrison sung 'The Sheikh of Araby' while playing with The Beatles in Hamburg in the same year (Reck 1985: 97). It would therefore be futile to attempt to search for a single 'first moment' of contact; the significant point is that there had been many East-West contacts prior to The Beatles' discovery of Asian musical forms.

A second form of contact between Western and Asian cultures was through drug consumption. In the early 1960s, drug-taking was still relatively rare in British society. The only regular dope-smokers in London were West Indians in Notting Hill and lascars, seaman from India, who lived near the docks (Green 1988: 10; Mills 2013: 63–75). Jazz musicians, an even smaller sub-group, also experimented with drugs (Roberts 2008: 72). Drug consumption changed dramatically during the mid-1960s. The bizarre history of LSD illustrates this point.

Aldous Huxley experimented with mescaline in 1953. His subsequent essay, *The Doors of Perception* (1954), suggested a new way of understanding and using certain drugs: not as cures in any obvious sense of the word, but as instruments to attain radically different states of consciousness. His hope was that he might be able to change his "ordinary mode of consciousness so as to be able to know, from the inside, what the visionary, the medium, even the mystic were talking about... the drug would admit me, at least for a few hours, into the kind of inner world described by Blake" (Huxley 1994: 5). Huxley referred to a short story by H. G. Wells, "The Door in the Wall", and suggested that humanity needed more "doors" (ibid.). At their most basic level, these routes provided necessary relief from the monotony of twentieth-century society, and it seemed illogical and inconsistent that while alcohol and tobacco were socially-acceptable "doors", other substances were discouraged or banned. Huxley noted the difference between the negative Western attitudes to such practices, and the more tolerant Taoist, Buddhist, Chinese and Tibetan approaches. In a complex passage he provided an explanation for this difference, arguing that Christianity had become a doctrine which condemned the mundane, outer world, and sought to escape into an inner world, while the various Eastern approaches were less judgemental: they allowed a sense of circulation, from dreamlike visions, to a recognition of "The Void", and then a return to the daily, mundane world, which could be seen with new eyes. Huxley cited the telling example of landscape painting, which in Western traditions was seen as a simple, secular art, but which in Eastern traditions was a branch of religious painting (Huxley 1994: 30–31). Certain drugs, argued Huxley, could function in the same, spiritual manner, allowing for a re-sacralization of daily life.

Huxley's arguments were vulgarized, wildly simplified and then popularized by Timothy Leary, Ralph Metzner and Richard Alpert. While Huxley's essay had been tentative, tantalizing and questioning, Leary, Metzner and Alpert's *The Psychedelic Experience* (1964) was a more formulaic text, almost like an instruction manual, albeit one written with a tremendous sense of excitement. Their claims were bigger. In part, Leary's ideas reflect some of the common themes that were circulating among the growing New Age networks: insights and wisdom can be found within the person, rather than from external authorities.

> These processes are a billion years older than the learned conceptual mind… Dozens of mythical and Darwinian insights flash into awareness. The person is allowed to glance back down the flow of time and to perceive how the life energy continually manifests itself in forms, transient, always changing, reforming. Microscopic forms merge with primal creative myths… a billion-year lesson in cosmology. (Leary et al. 2008: 28, 40)

The book's real originality lay elsewhere: *firstly*, with the claim that ingesting LSD was an effective means of gaining these insights, a kind of short-cut to Enlightenment, bypassing the need of years of tiresome meditation. But, *secondly*, Leary and his co-authors then made the wild claim that somehow the experience of taking LSD could be compared with the descriptions of death and re-birth described in an eighth-century Tibetan Buddhist text.[2]

With Huxley, the citation of certain Eastern traditions was part of an argument concerning the manner in which the Western mind understood reality. With Leary, Metzner and Alpert, the reference to Eastern traditions changes: it is never really clear why they decide that the *Tibetan Book of the Dead* has such a direct relevance to experiments with LSD, but its citation certainly provides their work with a sense of exotic grandeur. Put together, their various references made a winning combination: they invoked practical self-help, Eastern knowledge and Western science. Their ideas profoundly influenced some of those who experimented with new drugs. One memoir from the 1960s notes that: "The first acid trips were extremely serious. A day fasting before: reading *The Tibetan Book of the Dead*, *The Psychedelic Experience*; having Krishnamurti playing on record" (Green 1988: 177).

Such cultivated drug-takers may well have formed an elite, a small group of intellectually or spiritually orientated experimenters. Alongside them developed a larger group of drug-takers, sometimes just looking for a new type of thrill. For them, cannabis or LSD were simply new forms of intoxicants, to be treated like an evening in a pub. Twenty-five years later, Stephen Batchelor could see how such attitudes might seem funny: "What's it going to be tonight, lads, beer or acid?" (see Tomory 1996: 65). British society evolved in this curious, awkward manner. All these new ideas, habits and rituals added up to a new culture, a counter-culture which self-consciously broke with some of the imperial norms of British society, for cannabis was a drug that originated among the colonized, not the colonizers (Mills 2013: 118).

In a strange way, drug-taking turned consumers away from the UK. The most obvious explanation for this was simply the geographic origin of the most popular forms of cannabis resin: Morocco, Lebanon and Afghanistan. Sometimes cannabis was even marketed accordingly. But the association of drug-taking, alternative forms of consciousness and 'the East' seemed to be based on something more than mere geography. Huxley's mescaline came from Mexico, yet it led him to consider Taoism and Buddhism. LSD was manufactured in laboratories in Europe and the USA, not transported from Morocco or Afghanistan, yet Eva Douglas still found it carried her eastwards: "It was LSD that carried the idea of India to us all" (see Tomory 1996: 11).

But the most important transformation in the 1960s was that more Western people were travelling to the East: not as colonizers, missionaries or putative factory-owners, but – apparently – in order to learn from or to admire those cultures. In 1958, 33 British tourists went to Afghanistan; in 1968 there were 5,143; in 1961 some 139,800 tourists visited India; in 1971 about 301,000 made the same journey.[3] Among their number were beatniks, hippies, drug-takers and spiritual seekers, experienced travellers and drop-outs: all people who were expecting something special from their journey (see Gemie and Ireland 2017). While the numbers travelling still represent only a small minority of the European population, the *idea* of travelling eastwards was becoming more common, and – more generally – the idea of learning from the East was affecting more people.

Thus, rather than *initiating* an important cultural movement, The Beatles were *contributing* to an existing tendency. David Reck, in his article "Beatles Orientalis", presents a meticulous inventory of their points of contact with a vaguely defined "East". He identifies twenty-one songs by The Beatles in which there is some identifiable form of "Asian" influence, whether in lyrics, melodies, or instrumentation. Their first real contact with Indian music seems to have been entirely fortuitous, and owes more to the sub-genre of comic treatment of Asian themes than any serious attempt to study other musical cultures. *Help!* featured some comically grotesque Hindu cultists, and so a sitar was on the set. Harrison played with it during filming. He remembered it when The Beatles were in the studio in October 1965, and Lennon was looking for a solo part for 'Norwegian Wood'. Henceforth, all four Beatles grew interested – in different ways – in learning about Asian musical techniques. Harrison's and Lennon's compositions were the most marked by this search. The influences affected them in different ways. Harrison attempted something like a wholesale imitation of Indian forms (hence songs like 'Within You, Without You' and 'The Inner Light'): he used Indian musicians to record them, and studied how to play the sitar, practising two or three hours a day from 1965 to 1968 (Reck 1985: 107). For Lennon, Indian musical forms were more like another colour on the palette, to be used when effective in creating the effects that he was looking for.

The Beatles' visits to India were brief: they made one swift four-day visit to Delhi in July 1966, at the end of their disastrous tour of the Far East. All four bought sitars. They then had a longer stay in February 1968 in Rishikish in northern India, to learn meditation techniques from the Maharishi Mahesh Yogi. As has been well-documented, this trip ended in an acrimonious argument with the Maharishi and subsequent disillusionment with his teachings: see Norman (2008: 532–38). One might have expected that this second visit would have stimulated a series of Asian-inspired songs. Instead, rather than a beginning, the visit to Rishikish seems more like an ending. Reck comments:

> the stay in India did not produce a musical "travel journal" descriptive of the land or its people; there are no songs... of love in a mysterious or exotic setting, or (as in classical music) the picking up of "native melodies". The spectacular Himalayan scenery of Rishikish did not inspire a single song! (1985: 126)

The most faithful of The Beatles' attempts to reproduce Asian music – Harrison's 'Inner Light' – was actually recorded in January 1968, immediately before their flight out to India, as was Lennon's 'Across the Universe', probably his clearest attempt to articulate Buddhist-inspired ideas. The Beatles' most obviously Asian or Oriental music pre-dated and anticipated their most important contact with Indian society; Asia was re-constructed imaginatively before any real physical contact. 'Tomorrow Never Knows' clearly follows this paradigm: it attempts a kind of imaginative re-construction of Tibetan religious culture; it anticipates a journey not yet taken.

The process of the composition of 'Tomorrow Never Knows' is well-known. Lennon found a copy of Leary's *Psychedelic Experience* in the Indica art gallery and bookshop in London sometime in late 1965. According to one account, "he took the slim volume, curled up on the couch in the middle of the shop and read it from cover to cover" (Norman 2008: 430). He seems to have swallowed the book's arguments hook, line and sinker, and so came to understand LSD consumption as a quasi-religious practice, linked to Tibetan Buddhism. (Later he was to curse himself for having done so, referring to *The Psychedelic Experience* as "that stupid book of Leary's" (Wenner 2000: 53–54)). He followed Leary's instructions to the letter, recording himself speaking passages from the work to "guide" him while taking LSD (MacDonald 1998: 188). 'Tomorrow Never Knows' cheerfully plagiarizes phrases from *The Psychedelic Experience*, most notably the first line which is taken from Leary's repeated advice concerning what to do during upsetting psychological experiences while dropping LSD. "Whenever in doubt, turn off your mind, relax, float downstream" (Leary et al. 2008: 6).

'Tomorrow Never Knows' makes clear the differences between Lennon's and Harrison's reception of Asian musical forms. While Harrison imitates, with greater or lesser success, Lennon creates an original vision. And, if we concentrate on *Revolver*, Harrison's inspiration came directly from India, while Lennon was – briefly – captivated by an idea of Tibet.

Tibet

The first Westerners to see Tibet did so as part of a Hindu pilgrimage in 1624. In 1792 Tibetans closed their borders to Westerners for almost a century, during which a specific fascination developed for this faraway country, lost in the high mountains (Bishop 1989: 16). Tibet was imagined as "a land outside the grid of regulated space and time that seemed to be engulfing the rest of the globe" (Bishop 2001: 208). The very closure of the frontiers seemed a challenge to some, and a handful of intrepid explorers braved the extreme cold of its mountains to enter, illegally, into its lands. Their memoirs carry a variety of themes. One repeated topic was simply the dirt of the place. For example, Gabriel Bonvalot, writing in 1891, dismissively recorded that "the filthiness of the [Tibetan] women is only exceeded by their ugliness" (Bonvalot 2013: 338). Fernand Grenard, who travelled in Tibet in 1894, found the village of Naktchou to be "filthy, full of vermin, stinking, smoky and dark" (Grenard 2013: 405). The Swiss explorer Sven Hedin visited Tibet in 1906 and 1907. Describing the two Tibetans who served as his guides, he added the throwaway line "of course, they are disgustingly dirty" (Hedin 2013: 686). Sir Francis Younghusband led the largely pointless British invasion of Tibet in 1904. His memoirs of this expedition continued the same theme. Of Lhasa, he noted: "a sorry affair. The streets were filthily dirty, and the inhabitants scarcely more clean than the streets; the houses were built of solid masonry, but as dirty as the streets and inhabitants; and the temples we passed, though massive, were ungainly" (Younghusband 1910: 265).

However, other factors were in play. Firstly, an eighteenth-century and nineteenth-century interest in comparative religion led some to enquire about the nature of Tibetan Buddhism. One line of argument, compatible with the stress on the filth of Tibet, was to see it as an inferior form, a mere "Lama-ism", "a degeneration into a fossilized, despotic aberration", which was contrasted with the true, cultivated, humanistic Buddhism of China, India or Japan (Kvaerne 2001: 48). These relatively academic debates, however, were turned on their head by some weighty political considerations in the late nineteenth century. Tibet was caught between three empires: the Russian, the Chinese and the British. Despite the efforts of enthusiastic imperialists like Younghusband, the dominant British policy was to position Tibet as a buffer state between the three (see Bray 2001). (Younghusband was only able to justify his bloody intervention by arguing – wrongly – that there was evidence of a sustained Russian influence in Lhasa: see French 1995.) But if Tibet was to be preserved as separate from China, it made sense to note and publicize its differences from Chinese culture. Here, the eccentric, fraudulent but highly innovative Helena Blavatsky made a contribution. Her Theosophist Society, founded in 1875, proposed a type of spiritual unity of religions. She was originally interested in ancient Egypt as the source of the world's religions, but then moved to consider Tibet as the centre (see Pederson 2001). Her research suggested that Tibetan Buddhism was not a degenerate form, but that – on the contrary – the Tibetans had preserved a purer form of Buddhism than their neighbours.

After Younghusband's expedition of 1904, a small British colony of about a hundred people was first established in Gyantse and Yatung, and then in Lhasa itself. In the 1910s, one British official, Charles Bell, encouraged the Tibetan leaders to adopt some of the trappings of a nation state: to acquire a flag, a currency and stamps (McKay 2001: 78). Such innovations suggested how different Tibet was from China. This group of Brits was also the source of a new tone in descriptions of Tibet, which increasingly expressed an admiration for Tibetan religious cultures. Tibet was thus established as "the Land of Religion" (David-Neel 1997: 8).

This change in perspective was exemplified by the discovery of an ancient Tibetan text by an American Theosophist, Walter Y. Evans-Wentz (see Lopez 1998). While he could not read the Tibetan original, he worked with a Tibetan Lama, Kazi Dawa-Samdup. The two edited the Tibetan texts: the Tibetan doing the nuts-and-bolts of the translation, Evan-Wentz selecting, editing and organizing the material. The Tibetan title of one eighth-century text was "Liberation through Hearing"; Evans-Wentz altered it to "The Tibetan Book of the Dead", a reference to the older *Egyptian Book of the Dead*. The exact nature of the original text is still subject to question, but it certainly was not intended as a "how-to" guide; it was probably intended as liturgy to be read to mark the passing away of a dying person. The book was subsequently "re-discovered" for a Western readership via Leary (1964).

Tibet itself was also re-discovered, even celebrated, in twentieth-century Western culture. Alexandra David-Neel's *Magic and Mystery in Tibet* (first published in 1932, and then re-edited in 1967) presented readers with a description of a land in which magic was real, where miracles took place everyday, and where telepathy and telekinesis were practised – all due to the unique religious qualities of the land's Buddhist monks.

Marco Pallis, who visited Tibet in 1939, explicitly contrasted the spirit of the land with the "totalitarian materialism" which was dominating European society (Pallis 1949: 202). He presented a colourful, memorable picture of the omnipresence of the Tibetan chant of "Om mani padme hum":

> It figures not only on the innumerable Mani walls leading into and out of every town, village and monastery in Tibet, but also on many of the prayer flags, and inside prayer-wheels great or small, operated by hand or turned by wind or water power. Thus every person travelling in Tibet is continually in touch with the idea, bathed by its influence, whether he responds or not. It is wafted to him by all the breezes, in which also the birds are flying... So the whole country, from end to end, is pervaded with a devotional atmosphere; only the wilfully blind can altogether avoid responding to it, while wandering across the austere realm of the sacred landscape. (Pallis 1949: 202)

For Pallis, Tibet seemed to be a sort of Buddhist utopia.

Perhaps predictably, the Nazis were also interested in Tibet. They took one element of this new image of Tibet: the idea that this mountainous country had preserved some form of purity, but understood this as a racialized quality. Heinrich Himmler argued that this primordial Aryan virtue had then been challenged and weakened by the rise of Buddhism in Tibet (see Hale 2003). Himmler's sponsorship resulted in a German expedition to the country in 1939, and a film, *Geheimnis Tibet* [Secret Tibet], produced in 1942.

Heinrich Harrer, an Austrian PoW who escaped to Tibet from a British prison in India, produced a more rounded picture of Tibetan society, noting its backwardness, the effects of lack of adequate sanitation on its people, the "superstition" which reigned among some sectors and – above all – Tibet's dangerous weakness in the face of Chinese expansionism. But his *Seven Years in Tibet* (1955) also preserved important elements of the country's "Land of Religion" image. "The whole culture of Tibet is inspired by religion as it used to be in early days in our countries", he argued (Harrer 1955: 270). (*Seven Years* was then used as the basis for a film, starring Brad Pitt, produced in 1997.)

Another form of benevolent interest in Tibet came from climbers, who were captivated by the idea of Mount Everest. The numbers visiting Tibet increased in the twentieth century. The summit of the world's highest peak, Everest, was finally reached in 1953 by Edmund Hillary and Tenzing Norgay, and celebrated as part of the Royal Coronation in Britain. However, in the late 1950s and in the 1960s new, strict Chinese border controls prevented entry to Tibet. It has been estimated that until 1979, when the Chinese government finally began to permit tourists entry, only 1,250 Westerners had ever reached the Tibetan capital, Lhasa (see Bishop 1989: 240–45).

In the same year that The Beatles were recording 'Tomorrow Never Knows', a German Buddhist convert, Lama Anagarika Govinda, wrote another work idealizing Tibet. Govinda stressed the spiritual effects of the natural features of Tibet on the individual:

> In Tibet the capacity of concentration and self-observation, as well as our psychic sensitivity, is increased a hundredfold in the vastness, solitude, and silence of nature, which acts like a concave mirror that not only enlarges and reflects our innermost feeling and emotions but concentrates them in *one* focal point: our own consciousness. (Govinda 2006: 70)

However, there was a new, elegiac tone in this work. Govinda was already mourning a Tibet which no longer existed after the Chinese invasion.

These idealistic, romantic images and themes of Tibet were part of the culture of the hippy trail: it is almost certain that many of the Western hippy travellers to Kathmandu would have liked to have continued their journeys onto Tibet. "Once there was a land where the prayers never ceased", mourned the *Pilgrim's Guide to Planet Earth* (published in 1974). "The turn of the prayer wheels and the hum of chanting monks filled the icy air. The high mountain clarity was a fitting garment for the dharma. Everywhere there were golden monasteries, sacred shrines and holy places. This was Tibet before the 1950s" (Anonymous 1974: 225). Situated in the Himalayas, in the 1960s Tibet seemed to Westerners to be an inaccessible, semi-mythical place of magic and mountains which had contained, in the shape of the Dalai Lama, a living god (see Bishop 1989).

These new legends were inspired by ancient Tibetan and Hindu tales of mountain gods and utopian societies in hidden valleys, and by a series of Western evocations, of which the most popular was James Hilton's novel *Lost Horizon* (published in 1933, and subsequently made into films in 1937 and 1973). After a Tibetan revolt against Chinese rule in 1959, the Tibetan spiritual leader the Dalai Lama fled to Dharamsala, in India, which then became a Buddhist pilgrimage destination and another magnet for intrepid Westerners (Brox 2006: 89). Initially, the first sympathy for their plight came from the political right: it was not until after 1987 that Tibetan exiles made a conscious decision to appeal to the left (see Barnett 2001).

Interpreting 'Tomorrow Never Knows'

One plausible reading of 'Tomorrow Never Knows' might be to see it as a character portrayal: when Paul McCartney sang 'She's Leaving Home', he did not mean to imply that he was a teenage girl who had eloped with a man from the motor-trade. Perhaps Lennon merely meant to evoke the sensations of taking LSD in a striking sound collage? The supporting evidence suggests otherwise. Lennon's solecism is well-known, and he often proudly asserted it. "These stories about boring people doing boring things – being postmen and secretaries and writing home. I'm not interested in writing third-party songs. I like to write about me, 'cuz I know me" (Sheff 2001: 196–97). Lennon's remarks that he had wanted the song to be sung by hundreds of Tibetan monks also suggests the extent to which he was convinced of its authenticity (MacDonald 1998: 191). He had accepted Leary's extraordinary theses concerning the effects of LSD and their similarity to the ideas expounded by an eighth-century Tibetan religious text. This base gives the song its extraordinary power, for Lennon at once taps into the two great myths of "the East" which inspired so many of the hippy trail travellers: the myths of the "Land of Religion", but also the dope-otopia, the land where benign forms of drug consumption flourished.

The material surveyed above demonstrates some of the limitations of MacDonald's unusually naïve reading of this work. There is no portrayal of "the ancient religious philosophies of the Orient" in 'Tomorrow Never Knows': instead, it echoes a bowdlerized mis-reading of Tibetan culture, an interpretation that was much a product of imperial rivalries as an authentic representation of Tibetan religious cultures. While Buddhism does require a recognition of the smallness of individual lives, this is far from the catatonic passivity and complete withdrawal from active intellectual life which is preached in 'Tomorrow Never Knows'. (In terms of Buddhist doctrine, Harrison's 'Within You, Without You' is certainly on stronger ground, for many reasons: it presents a reasonably cogent philosophical stance; it does bear some meaningful relationship with recognizably Buddhist themes, such as the interconnectedness of life; and it avoids the dangers of Leary's preaching.)

As Lennon himself was later to recognize, for all its striking originality, the pretentions of 'Tomorrow Never Knows' drew attention to a dangerously gullible side to his own character. By 1970 he could recognize the dangers in Leary's teaching. "I got a message [that] on acid... you should destroy your ego, and I did... We were going through a whole game that everyone went through. And I destroyed meself [sic]... I destroyed me [sic] ego and I didn't believe I could do *anything*" (Wenner 2000: 53–54). However, his weakness was still active: after Leary, the Maharishi. After the Maharishi, Janov and primal scream therapy. After LSD, heroin. To this list of examples of Lennon's capacity to be influenced, one might also add Yoko Ono. With reference to Lennon's 'Julia', the song which seems to meditate on both Lennon's missing mother and his new love, MacDonald notes "the song suggests an offering to an ancestral spirit: an attempt to break an obsession by commending the supplicant's new earthly love in the hope of a blessing" (MacDonald 1998: 327). Certainly, it seems no exaggeration to speak of Lennon's "worship" for Ono. On the other hand, putting metaphors aside, Ono was not a chemical addiction, nor a "bad shepherd" like Leary. For all her eccentricity, she retained a sense of perspective and of ethics. What can be noted, however, is a type of continuity in Lennon's faith that his redemption would come from the East: whether from LSD-fuelled images of Tibetan Buddhism or from Ono's Japanese-inspired avant-garde approach to art and culture.

Rather than marking some sort of cultural rupture, 'Tomorrow Never Knows' can instead be seen as an example of cultural continuity. It can be situated within the broad confines of the "Orientalism" identified by Edward Said in his classic text from 1978. Orientalism could take many forms: sometimes a blatant racism; sometimes an articulate, pragmatic argument to rationalize imperialist expansion; sometimes an attitude resembling an admiration or even an affection for "Eastern" forms. The aspect which is most relevant here is the latter: those educated Westerners who looked eastward in search for some form of intellectual enlightenment.

In all these Western "readings" of Tibetan culture there is one consistency: the confidence by these readers that they can understand Tibetan religious culture with no significant conceptual problems. There is an arrogance here: Tibet is treated as a cipher to be positioned by the Western reader or listener. James Hilton, for example, never visited Tibet, yet his account of Shangri-La has been popularized so widely that it has acquired the status of truth.

The beginning of the end

Musically, 'Tomorrow Never Knows' did mark the end of the beginning. It was a way of explicitly and loudly saying goodbye to the catchy pop tunes produced by four lovable mop-tops, and a means of signalling a profound shift in the group's direction. This is probably the reason why the other three Beatles and George Martin pushed the song with such force: by establishing it as the end-point of *Revolver*, they were setting themselves the goal of a rupture in April, May and June 1966. But it interesting to pause to consider the resources they marshalled: a type of mobilization of different strands of cultural capital. McCartney's use of *musique concrète* established the Beatles as "serious" musicians, not purveyors of teeny-bop mush. The strange beats demonstrated both the Beatles' willingness to borrow from non-Western forms and their ability to imitate in competent fashion.

My argument is that we should also see 'Tomorrow Never Knows' as a direct descendant of Blavatsky and Hilton: Lennon himself later acknowledged his naivety about the effects of LSD. To this should be added his cultural and intellectual naivety in accepting *The Psychedelic Experience* as a work that accurately represented Tibetan religious culture.

Notes

1. A copy of the photo can be found at: https://www.yellowad.co.uk/it-happened-today-this-day-in-history-april-7-2/.
2. The most articulate account of this text and its bowdlerization in the West can be found in Lopez (1998: 46–85).
3. National Archives, FCO 47-429, document dated 24 February 1970. See also Kumar (1998: 27).

References

Allen, Charles. (2002) *The Buddha and the Saints: The Men who Discovered India's Lost Religion*. London: John Murray.
Anonymous. (1974) *A Pilgrim's Guide to Planet Earth*. San Rafael, CA: Spiritual Community.
Barnett, Robert. (2001) "'Violated Specialness': Western Political Representations of Tibet". In *Imagining Tibet: Perceptions, Projections and Fantasies*, ed. Thierry Dodin and Heinz Räther, 269–316. Boston, MA: Wisdom Publications.
Bishop, Peter. (1989) *The Myth of Shangri-La: Tibet, Travel Writing, and the Western Creation of Sacred Landscape*. Berkeley: University of California Press.
Bishop, Peter. (2001) "Not Only a Shangri-la: Images of Tibet in Western Literature". In *Imagining Tibet: Perceptions, Projections and Fantasies*, ed. Thierry Dodin and Heinz Räther, 201–21. Boston, MA: Wisdom Publications.
Bonvalot, Gabriel. (2013) "L'aventurier, le prince et le missionnaire". In *Tibet: Vers la terre interdite*, ed. Chantal Edel, 277–398. Paris: Omnibus.
Bray, John. (2001) "Nineteenth- and Early Twentieth-Century Missionary Images of Tibet". In *Imagining Tibet: Perceptions, Projections and Fantasies*, ed. Thierry Dodin and Heinz Räther, 21–45. Boston, MA: Wisdom Publications.
Brox, Trine. (2006) "Tibetan Culture as Battlefield: How the Term 'Tibetan Culture' is Utilized as a Political Strategy". *Buddhismus in Geschichte und Gegenwart: Gewalt und Gewaltlosigkeit im Buddhismus*. Online: https://www.buddhismuskunde.uni-hamburg.de/pdf/4-publikationen/buddhismus-in-geschichte-und-gegenwart/bd10-k06brox.pdf.
Clark, Philip. (2012) "He Got Rhythm". *The Guardian*, 7 December.
Collingham, Lizzie. (2005) *Curry: A Biography*. London: Random House.
David-Neel, Alexandra. (1997) *Magic and Mystery in Tibet*. London: Thorsons.
French, Patrick. (1995) *Younghusband: The Last Great Imperial Adventurer*. London: Flamingo.
Gemie, Sharif and Brian Ireland. (2017) "The Consul and the Beatnik: The Establishment, Youth Culture and the Beginnings of the Hippy Trail (1966–88)". *Twentieth Century British History* 28/3: 440–64. https://doi.org/10.1093/tcbh/hwx004
Govinda, Lama Anagarika. (2006) *The Way of the White Clouds*. London: Random House.
Green, Jonathan. (1988) *Days in the Life: Voices from the English Underground, 1961–1971*. London: Pimlico.
Grenard, Fernand. (2013) "La dernière mission de Dutreuil de Rhins. De Paris à Pékin, au Turkestan et au Tibet (1891–1894)". In *Tibet: Vers la terre interdite*, ed. Chantal Edel, 399–437. Paris: Omnibus.
Hale, Christopher. (2003) *Himmler's Crusade: The True Story of the 1938 Nazi Expedition into Tibet*. London: Bantam.
Harrer, Heinrich. (1955) *Seven Years in Tibet*. London: Reprint Society.
Hedin, Sven. (2013) "Le Tibet dévoilé, 1906–1908". In *Tibet: Vers la terre interdite*, ed. Chantal Edel, 677–789. Paris: Omnibus.
Huxley, Aldous. (1994) *The Doors of Perception* and *Heaven and Hell*. London: Flamingo.
Kumar, Subas C. (1998) "The Tourism Industry in India: Economic Significance and Emerging Issues". In *Tourism in India*, ed. Kartik C. Roy and Clement A. Tisdell, 21–46. New York: Nova Science Publishers.

Kvaerne, Per. (2001) "Tibet Images among Researchers on Tibet". In *Imagining Tibet: Perceptions, Projections and Fantasies*, ed. Thierry Dodin and Heinz Räther, 47–63. Boston, MA: Wisdom Publications.

Leary, Timothy, Ralph Metzner and Richard Alpert. (2008 [1964]) *The Psychedelic Experience: A Manual Based on the 'Tibetan Book of the Dead'*. Harmondsworth: Penguin.

Lopez, Donald S. Jr. (1998) *Prisoners of Shangri-La: Tibetan Buddhism and the West*. Chicago and London: University of Chicago Press.

MacDonald, Ian. (1998) *Revolution in the Head: The Beatles' Records and the Sixties*. London: Pimlico.

McKay, Alex C. (2001) "'Truth', Perception, and Politics: The British Construction of an Image of Tibet". In *Imagining Tibet: Perceptions, Projections and Fantasies*, ed. Thierry Dodin and Heinz Räther 67–89. Boston, MA: Wisdom Publications.

Mills, James H. (2013) *Cannabis Nation: Control and Consumption in Britain, 1928–2008*. Oxford: Oxford University Press.

Norman, Philip. (2008) *John Lennon: A Life*. London: HarperCollins.

Pallis, Marco. (1949) *Peaks and Lamas*. New York: Alfred A. Knopf.

Pedersen, Poul. (2001) "Tibet, Theosophy, and the Psychologization of Buddhism". In *Imagining Tibet: Perceptions, Projections and Fantasies*, ed. Thierry Dodin and Heinz Räther, 151–66. Boston, MA: Wisdom Publications.

Reck, David R. (1985) "Beatles Orientalis: Influences from Asia in a Popular Song Tradition". *Asian Music* 16/1: 83–149. https://doi.org/10.2307/834014

Roberts, Andy. (2008) *Albion Dreaming: A Popular History of LSD in Britain*. London: Marshall Cavendish.

Robinson, Andrew. (2012) "Ravi Shankar: Sitar Virtuoso and Composer Whose Work Introduced Indian Music to Western Audiences". *The Independent*, 12 December.

Sheff, David. (2001) *Last Interview: All We Are Saying – John Lennon and Yoko Ono*. London: Pan.

Tomory, David. (1996) *A Season in Heaven: True Tales from the Road to Kathmandu*. London: Thorsons.

Wenner, Jann S. (2000) *Lennon Remembers*. London: Verso.

Younghusband, Francis. (1910) *India and Tibet: A History of the Relations which have subsisted between the two countries from the time of Warren Hastings to 1910; with a particular account of the mission to Lhasa of 1904*. London: John Murray.

Author biography

Dr Sharif Gemie, independent writer and researcher, based in South Wales (UK), is co-author of *The Hippy Trail, 1957–78* (Manchester University Press, 2017), co-author of *Outcast Europe: Refugees and Relief Workers in an Age of Total War* (Continuum, 2011), and author of *French Muslims* (2010). He is currently writing a historical novel, *The Displaced*, about a British couple who volunteer to work with refugees in Germany at the end of the Second World War, due for publication in May 2023.

4 "Magical Mystery Tour": Suburbia and Utopia in Music and Films of The Beatles

Jon Goss

Taking Richard Lester's movie A Hard Day's Night *(1964) as The Beatles' definitive film and a centrepiece for discussing their legacy, this chapter explores converging influences on the band's career and image, including music hall, the Goons, and suburbia. Evolving themes are traced across The Beatles' recorded output, and the author considers the role of the group's retrospective comments in constructing a grand but nuanced narrative. The artistic impulse of the 1960s "to hold the moment, freeze it, show it and let it melt" (Melly 1970: 167) must be interpreted in a spatial as well as a temporal sense. Similarly, if rock is the music of growing up that promises the possibility of not growing up (Frith 1978: 209), it expresses the condition of containment and prospects of perpetual motion. The Beatles, then, exemplify the oppositional moment of youth, articulating precisely the impossible desire for the fully self-conscious experience of a temporal-spatial moment that is always already becoming another: for the pleasures of adulthood desired by youth, and the prospect of the city's freedoms viewed from the suburbs. Constantly reinventing themselves and on the move in response to a sense of social and spatial entrapment, The Beatles sought not to last in the establishment sense, but to escape reality and so sustain an intense experience of temporal and spatial transience.*

Introduction: "So, how long do you think you'll last?"

> ... a change to a new type of music is something to beware of as a hazard of all our fortunes. For the modes of music are never disturbed without unsettling of the most fundamental political and social conventions. (Plato 1984: 8)

Although there are numerous disagreements on facts in the vast material on The Beatles, attempts to make sense of their "scarcely-imaginable true story" (Norman 1981: xvi) generally rehearse what is basically a morality tale on growing up and the inevitability of accommodation to the "reality" of the adult world. The tale of these likely lads is told in terms of overreaching ambition, compromises between art and commerce, authenticity and mediation, and rebel and boy-next-door, and of a group progressively riven by personal and professional differences that eventually undermined the conditions of its existence. It is by now the "official" story, and one told by The Beatles themselves: as John Lennon put it laconically, "We killed ourselves to make it – and that was the end of it" (Wenner 2000: 20). This is also the dominant "pop" narrative, which now generally applies to individual artists and groups, the history of rock and roll, and even to the decade of the sixties.

If The Beatles are now the stuff of legend, it is significant that even from the onset of Beatlemania, that peculiar social hysteria first diagnosed in the fall of 1963, the establishment media speculated on the sustainability of the Fab Four (Braun 1964: 17), asking history to tell whether, in the words of the *Daily Mirror*, they would be more than merely "the pimple of the month" (quoted in Cohn 2001: 11) and asking the lads themselves, "What are you going to do when the bubble bursts?" (Wenner 2000: 69). Such questions suggest that the fate of The Beatles was already being incorporated into dominant discourse: first, by betraying a prejudice for the eternal values of high culture compared to the commercialized "fads" of popular culture; second, by implying that there was something undeserved about their success, because it was obviously too much fun for it to be called "work", and was all rather too sudden, something like showing that crime paid (Kureishi 1992: 364); and third by suggesting that their art and politics were merely temporary manifestations of youthful energy, ambition, and idealism, which would inevitably be compromised with adulthood and commercial success.

The Beatles brilliantly parodied media attempts to pin them down in both *A Hard Day's Night* (Lester, 1964) when the television director (Victor Spinetti) expresses professional paranoia, complaining that "once you're over 30, you're past it – it's a young man's game", and in *Help!* (Lester, 1965), when the police superintendent (Patrick Cargill) inquires "So, how long do you think you'll last?" At that time, they could not have foreseen that their prodigious artistic output would help permanently transform 20th-century culture; that it would be subject to continuous nostalgic reproduction, and rediscovered by each new generation of pop musicians and audiences. Rather, they rejected the ontological and socio-psychological premise of the question itself, as if meaning must seek ground, Becoming aspires to Being, and all motion come to rest. Indeed, The Beatles were fascinated by surrealism and nonsense poetry, and refused ultimate meaning in their lyrics; they resisted growing up, maintaining a childlike sense of fun, humor, and magic and exploiting their own childhood memories to suggest suspension within the flow of time and space; and they lived and acted in perpetual motion. Although they worked extraordinarily hard (the titles of *A Hard Day's Night* and *Eight Days a Week* are Ringo's characteristic malapropisms expressing his exhaustion) to make the money they so much desired, they refused to believe in deferred gratification, that the present moment in time and space must be lived towards another rather than experienced for itself. According to John Lennon, for example, "the whole Beatles' message was 'Be Here Now' and he likens himself to a chameleon, constantly adapting to changing times and places" (Sheff and Golson 1981: 70, 165). Paul McCartney similarly explains that "the most important thing to say to people is: 'It isn't necessarily so, what you believe'.... The whole thing being fluid and changing all the time and evolving" (McCartney 1967: 9).

The artistic impulse of the 1960s "to hold the moment, freeze it, show it and let it melt" (Melly 1970: 167) must be interpreted in a spatial as well as a temporal sense. Similarly, if rock is the music of growing up that promises the possibility of not growing up (Frith 1978: 209), it expresses the condition of containment and prospects of perpetual motion. The Beatles, then, exemplify the oppositional moment of youth, articulating precisely the impossible desire for the fully self-conscious experience of a temporal-spatial moment that is always already becoming another: for the pleasures of adulthood desired by youth, and the prospect of the city's freedoms viewed from the suburbs. Constantly reinventing themselves and on the move in response to a sense of social and spatial entrapment, The Beatles sought not to last in the establishment sense, but to escape reality and thus extend and sustain an intense experience of temporal and spatial transience.

The Beatles: the movie(s)

> It was as if we were all caught up in a big movie and we were the ones trapped in the middle of it. It was a very strange feeling.
> (George Harrison, in The Beatles 2000: 228)

Cinema and rock and roll took the lead in expressing the romantic spirit of the sixties, abandoning realism and narrative coherence for fantasy and the physical and emotional spontaneity of the moment. As Quentin Tarantino (1995: 125–26) argues, like rock and roll, cinema "opens your pores up, gets you all cut up and you're just into the excitement and emotion of it all". Rock and roll arrived in Britain in the form of a movie (Bradley 1992: 56), the musical *Rock Around the Clock* (Sears, 1956), and The Beatles were profoundly affected by the seminal *The Girl Can't Help It* (Tashlin, 1956). The Beatles were constantly involved in various aspects of amateur and professional film production during their careers, as well as in the five feature films and dozen or so promotional films they performed in together to showcase their music. There is a convergence in their own conceptions of the two arts, for with *Sgt Pepper...,* "making an album began to resemble the cumbersome, laborious process of making a film" (Curtis 1987: 129; George Martin in The Beatles 2000: 252), while *Magical Mystery Tour*, McCartney said, "was just like making a record album, that's how we did it anyway... A record is sound and a film is visual, that's the only difference" (Miles 1978: 111).

Rock music has always been intimately connected with visual images (Grossberg 1993: 188), but the sensuous combination of sound and vision around The Beatles was particularly remarkable, partly as a result of the saturated media coverage of the group's lives, but also their concerts, public appearances, films, cartoons, photography, and painting, artwork on their album covers and inserts, and the intense "visuality" of their music and lyrics. The visual appearance(s) of the four "mop-tops" was also vital to their success: it has been argued, for example, that *A Hard Day's Night* "probably more than their music, took The Beatles across social barriers, won them an audience among the intelligentsia, and broadened their hardcore base from teenage girls to rock and roll fans of every description" (Marcus 1980: 183). Part of the motivation for their production of *Magical Mystery Tour* (The Beatles, 1967), "the most expensive home movie ever made" (Lennon in Benson 1992: 174), was to respond to persistent requests for The Beatles to show themselves, and to reclaim control over their image (Fast 1968: 230).

In a sense, it could be argued that The Beatles' phenomenon was itself a "musical", if the genre is defined by the integration of music and narrative, enjoyable predictability, spectacle, and the fantastic combination of physical freedom and material abundance, spontaneous sociality and sexuality, and emotional transparency and intensity, that are characteristic of such entertainments' imagined utopia (Dyer 1992: 18–19; Marshall and Stilwell 2000: 2). In the musical, the establishment often frustrates "natural" desires to sing, dance, and love, but the talented heroes ultimately "break out" spatially and psychologically, making public their private desires, and temporarily taking over place and people with the sheer vitality of their music and dance. The Beatles, as ordinary northern lads with enormous talent, infectious enthusiasm for life, and what Walter Shenson called a "marvelous quality of disrespect" (quoted in Denisoff and Romanowski 1991: 134), certainly seemed the part.

As critics have noted, The Beatles possessed a "mercurial restlessness" (Bromell 2000: 28) and as a pop phenomenon, "simply refused to stand still" (Neaverson 1997: 117), characteristics that describe equally their constant artistic innovation and reinvention of identity, and their physical energy and endless mobility. It is a characteristic perhaps best represented by their musical and visual "leaps": first, the signature rise of the vocals and harmonies, such as the melodic leap of a fifth on the last syllable of 'I Want to Hold Your Hand', and other leaps of a fifth on 'Yellow Submarine', 'We Can Work It Out', 'Can't Buy Me Love', and 'Thank You Girl', as well as leaps of minor and major sixths in 'Day Tripper' and 'Rain', and the leap of an octave that occurs in 'Eleanor Rigby' (see Fitzgerald 2000: 60–61); second, is the image of The Beatles literally in mid-air, as in the famous Dezo Hoffmann photograph of the four lads jumping with youthful exuberance on the cover of the *Twist and Shout* EP, and the brilliant 'Can't Buy Me Love' sequence in *A Hard Day's Night*, where having momentarily escaped their "handlers", they cavort crazily on the playing fields at Isleworth. Dick Lester's jump-cut editing, unusual camera angles, and fast and slow motion perfectly capture the sheer exuberance of their response to Alun Owen's screenplay instructions simply to "play silly buggers" (Turner 1994: 53).

In the musical, the emancipatory moment is conventionally signified by the collapse of the distinction between diegetic and non-diegetic music as the realistic filmic narrative gives way to the "integrated number" and emotional tension is released in the collective "putting on a show", or an individual freely singing and dancing in natural or urban solitude (Dyer 1977; Laing 2000: 7). Ironically, The Beatles musicals challenged this convention, beginning with *A Hard Day's Night*. This was "arguably the first film of its kind to stage central musical numbers which are not tied to performance" (Neaverson 1997: 19) – the "silly buggers" scene, for example, was conceived as a means to visually express the emotional content of the song which Lester felt he could not do through the conventional integrated performance, an innovation that ultimately led to the music video. Nevertheless, a feature of the performance called "The Beatles" is their sustained blurring of the boundaries between art and daily life, and fantasy and reality, and above all the private and the public, as emotion, desire, and memory erupt into the everyday world.

Ticket to ride

Beatlemania was a phenomenon that literally "broke out", as The Beatles themselves exploded into public life and crowds of fans occupied airports and city streets, effecting unprecedented disruptions of urban life and providing thrilling spectacles of public emotion. On the Liverpool premiere of *A Hard Day's Night*, for example, 150,000 people thronged the streets, prompting

George to say, "after this, nothing matters. This is the ultimate" (*Life* 2001: 51). Although there was intense public interest in their personal lives, this was unlike the fandom of glamorous movie stars, for paradoxically it was the perceived ordinariness of The Beatles that gave them such extraordinary appeal. This image may also have been carefully contrived, Melly (1970: 73) even speculating that Pete Best's replacement by Ringo was not only on musical grounds, but precisely because he is "lovably plain, a bit 'thick' as a public persona, and decidedly ordinary in his tastes... reassuring proof that The Beatles bear some relation to normal people". Management and media combined efforts to create the impression of "ordinariness" most notably in *A Hard Day's Night*, and its effect is parodied brilliantly in *Help!* – where, as The Beatles walk up to the doors of four identical terrace houses in Twickenham, a vox pop character says "Lovely lads, and so natural... adoration has not gone to their heads", while inside, the houses form a vast interior fantasy world of modern furnishings, art, and gadgets. The appearance of ordinariness, however, was vital to their success, because it validated the collective experience of mundane routines and fantasies of escape from everyday life evoked in their music and films.

Although they played rock and roll and were called "working class", their wit and energy, as well as their enormous popularity and commercial success endeared them to the general public and even won over the establishment. For example, they appeared in a Royal Command Performance in April 1963, *A Hard Day's Night* received a Royal Charity Premiere in July 1964, and they received MBEs at Buckingham Palace for "services to British industry" in October 1965. While his business acumen has since been seriously questioned, Brian Epstein contrived the "wholesome" public image of his charges. Significantly, the contrast between The Beatles and the establishment's stereotypes of youth is made in gags involving "senile delinquents" in both *A Hard Day's Night* and *Yellow Submarine*. Queen Elizabeth II would later observe, "The Beatles are turning awfully funny, aren't they?" (Norman 1981: 306), and their unprecedented affair with America would turn sour as personal politics tested the tolerance of the establishment media. Nevertheless, in retrospectives they are typically forgiven their youthful transgressions: *Life* (2001: 99), for example, reminisces condescendingly that The Beatles are "a little like *our* children. It wasn't always fun as we watched them growing up.... We wince as they take off in some ill-considered direction but know there's nothing we can do. And then, when things work out better than we could ever have hoped, we're so happy for them."

The "progress" of The Beatles musically is also typically ascribed to growing up, so that changing music and lyrics "reflect the passage, perhaps, during this period, of a sizeable portion of Beatles fans from the self-obsession of adolescence to the greater objectivity of adulthood" (Cook and Mercer 2000: 92). While it is true that their songs abandoned a preoccupation with teenage love, their "mature" work still evokes memories and fantasies of childhood and ridicules the banality of adult lives. The Beatles retained their utopian desire for a future other than that promised by the establishment's idea of "growing up" and hence they displayed a childlike energy and commitment to physical fun. Their famous "one-liner" wit was derived from the playground; they maintained a sense of wonder at the world, investing the mundane with significance, and hence their infatuation with enchantment, magic, cartoons, circus and surrealism. They wrote children's songs, and incorporated into their work snatches of nonsense literature, nursery rhymes, lullabies, singalong, and schoolyard rhymes. They nostalgically recalled their own memories of childhood places and people to evoke lost freedom, innocence, and plenitude; and they used childlike enchantment as an ambiguous metaphor for alternative consciousness and psychedelic hallucination in songs like 'Lucy in the Sky with Diamonds', and in the movies, *Magical Mystery Tour* and *Yellow Submarine.*

Failure to grow up is a theme of *A Hard Day's Night*, a movie loosely based on the fact that The Beatles are treated as children on a school trip, their management making them answer their fan mail – "do their homework" – and go to bed on time, while desperately trying to keep them out of trouble. A key early scene in this movie involves the "pompous traveller" (Richard Vernon) who insists on closing the first-class compartment window and turning off Ringo's transistor radio. While The Beatles evoke their rights as fare-paying passengers – their "ticket to ride" – and obvious majority, he quotes British Rail regulations, insists he is a regular commuter, suggests that they belong on a different part of the train, and finally claims that he "fought in the war for your sort". The Beatles recognize that they cannot win and leave him alone, but they reappear in a surreal moment on the platform, mockingly calling the eternal refrain of street kids to property owners, "Hey, Mister, can we have our ball back?"

In the fictional films, The Beatles irreverently invade the spaces of the adult establishment: the first-class carriage, a gentleman's club, police stations, corporate offices, stage rehearsals, military recruitment offices, Asprey's (the Bond Street jewellers), Lambeth Palace Ecumenical Conference, Buckingham Palace, Stonehenge, game shooting, and military manoeuvres on Salisbury Plain. They are repeatedly harassed by the forces of institutional repression: in *A Hard Day's Night*, their management and the police; in *Help!*, sinister south Asians who adopt the cloak of establishment, such as military uniforms, clerical vestments, and colonial-era safari suits to capture Ringo, and ambitious scientists who seek the powers in his magic ring. In *Magical Mystery Tour*, an aggressive sergeant-major terrorizes the tourists until Ringo innocently asks "Why?"; and in *Yellow Submarine* (Dunning, 1968), the Blue Meanies resemble a fascistic police force, committed to eliminating music and colour from Pepperland. Even in the documentary *Let It Be* (Lindsay-Hogg, 1970), their impromptu rooftop concert disrupts business as usual among merchant bankers of Savile Row until the police arrive to put an end to their last live performance.

If the curious crowd gathering in *Let It Be* represents the last dispirited gasp of Beatlemania, at its height, it paradoxically imprisoned The Beatles and their music, while opening up a space for young women in particular to protest the double standards of adolescent sexuality and to publicly and collectively "lose control" (Ehrenreich et al. 1997: 524). It is now a commonplace that their "mop-top" androgyny challenged dominant gender relations, and that their boyish sexuality explains the attraction of pubescent girls towards them (Ehrenreich et al. 1997; Muncie 2000: 42; Marshall 2000: 168). However, it seems to me that their "pure" childishness and playfulness are perhaps as important to their identity, art, and sustained popularity.

Even if The Beatles resisted the establishment by refusing the necessity and desirability of its "growing up" story, their ordinariness and acceptability made them spokespersons for the youthful condition; both positions are brilliantly asserted in the trailer filmed for *A Hard Day's Night* where the four lads sit in pairs in antique prams addressing their audiences through radio mikes, while Ringo holds a phone and John a typewriter. The Beatles helped normalize "youth", transforming it from a problematic period of transition, acknowledged only from the disdainful perspective of establishment adulthood, into a permanent social space, a public spectacle where teenagers could share the experience of its contradictions. Unlike most mass displays of popular sentiment, Beatlemania was not organized as a celebration of tradition, but was a collective "happening" that provided a shared sense of participation in whatever new and different phenomenon The Beatles heralded. Although it may be an exaggeration, and certainly could not have been understood as such at the time, Beatlemania is thus interpreted as "the first and most dramatic uprising of *women's* sexual revolution" (Ehrenreich et al. 1997: 524; original emphasis), and as part of a youthful rehearsal of utopianism (Berman 1996: 16–17). Beatles' songs still play in teenage girls' bedroom shrines and at protest rallies of the youthful global justice movement: promising signs of the persistence of youthful desire and dissatisfaction with the platitudes of the adult establishment.

"Having a laugh"

> We're kidding you. We're kidding ourselves. We're kidding everybody. We don't take anything seriously except the money. (John quoted in Shaw 1968: 87)

In the fictional movies at least, The Beatles' subversive music, infectious humour, and disarming innocence take over the establishment and win the day. Their political praxis is perhaps best summed up by Ringo in *A Hard Day's Night*, when in the context of running battles between "delinquent" youth in the south of England, he is asked whether he is a Mod or Rocker, but replies "Neither – I'm a mocker", nicely illustrating their characteristically quick-witted responses to the "stupid" questions of the media, their "in-betweenness", and their persistent ridicule of convention. In fact, The Beatles succeeded in "domesticating" rock and roll by marrying the American music of youthful alienation to British comic traditions of music hall (vaudeville) and social satire.

Music hall is an urban working-class entertainment whose canny characters outwit new forms of authority in a modernizing and urbanizing world, and ridicule dominant bourgeois discourses of respectability and self-improvement. The Beatles thus operated at the interface of the post-war equivalent of Victorian double standard, exploiting "a kind of worldly hypocrisy which acknowledges things as they inevitably (and profitably) were, as well as things as they should be" (Bailey 1994: 163), by using double entendre, innuendo, and ambiguity in response to an oppressive moral authority. McCartney in particular "always had that sneaking respect for the old rooty-tooty music" (Martin in Turner 1994: 131), and music hall influences are apparent in songs such as 'Your Mother Should Know', 'Martha My Dear', and especially 'Honey Pie', which contains sounds of scratching to artificially age the recording (Whitley 2000: 111). John's 'Sexy Sadie' is also a music hall number, and The Beatles' collective effort on *Sgt Pepper* creates the illusion of a live performance on a music hall stage. Visual imagery of music hall imagery is apparent in early photographs such as those taken by Dezo Hoffmann on tour at Weston-super-Mare in 1963, The Beatles appearing in Edwardian bathing costumes with straw-boaters, and in their films, most obviously in the variety performance at the end of *A Hard Day's Night*, and in the "underground theatre" scene in *Magical Mystery Tour*.

The Beatles were also influenced by British television satire, especially the Goons, who specialized in slapstick, surrealism, sexual innuendo and camp send-ups of colonialism, the monarchy, government, public schools, and the military. This influence is most obvious in the films. Dick Lester developed his style of visual humour in television and film production for the Goons, and examples of his "Goonish surrealism" include the scenes in *A Hard Day's Night* with the "pompous traveller", the moment when a game of cards in the guard's van turns into a performance of 'I Should've Known Better', and George's wonderful shaving scene; and the constant anachronistic and out of place themes in *Help!*, a spoof on James Bond films that includes a battle scene between armies from the two world wars, dacoits in an ice-cream van, scientists on the beach, and a lawn mower cutting carpet. Satire is a symptom of social change (Walker 1974: 271), mocking traditions that are being lost and the uncertainty of what will be replacing them, as is nicely evidenced by the ambiguous relationship of The Beatles to modern technologies in these movies, such as hair-driers, automatic vending machines, tickertape machines, telephones, malfunctioning (British-made) machines, and the science fiction of "molecular loosening".

Magical Mystery Tour contains Goonish imagery too, parodying the establishment, popular performance, media censorship, and organized working-class entertainment – most obviously the "mystery tour" and games such as tug-o-war, sack race, blind man's buff. However, it also incorporates a more sophisticated surrealist aesthetic, for by then surrealism and nonsense literature had a profound effect on Lennon's writing (Neaverson 1997: 56) and McCartney had become an acknowledged patron of modern art. Apparently influenced by Luis Buñuel (Neaverson 1997: 56), the movie refuses conventional narrative logic and includes dream sequences such as Aunt Jessie's fantasy of gluttony and sexual desire, juxtaposed with the "reality" of the coach tour; distortions of time and space, such as a two-man tent that becomes a cinema, and of nature, such as when characters change into animals; and a host of surreal figures drawn from contemporary Beatles songs such as the walrus, eggman, and rubber man. The most sustained experiment in surrealism, however, is *Yellow Submarine* with its time-space transformations, visual and verbal puns, dreamlike characters and situations, and pastiche of modern visual art.

As rock and roll was appropriated by white teenagers, its concerns shifted from the economic insecurity and class *ressentiment* expressed in rhythm and blues, and lost much of its overt sexuality, exploring the joys and fears of meeting and dating, rather than infidelity and the pain of breaking up. Even as The Beatles progressively abandoned the "hard" style of their influences, they retained the powerful conflation of the "drive" of their early music created by the strong backbeat with the drives of the body, particularly in dance and sex – "rock and roll" was slang for sexual intercourse before expanding to cover a style of dance (Hudson 1984: 40) – and vehicular motion. This is exploited most obviously through playful ambiguity in song titles and lyrics, again evocative of music hall: 'Ticket to Ride', for example, was inspired by medical cards issued to prostitutes in Hamburg, and 'Drive My Car' and 'Helter Skelter' similarly exploit the sexual ambiguity of the word "ride"; while several songs contain sexual innuendo, such as 'Girl', where they sing the refrain "tit, tit, tit", and 'Penny Lane' which refers to "fish and finger pie". In movies, The Beatles, as characters, explicitly avoided love interest, but employ sexual innuendo and, in what seems to be something of a theme, denounce what 'Day Tripper' refers to ambiguously as "big teasers", such as when Ringo makes the joke in *A Hard Day's Night* that it "plays havoc with me drum skins". The Beatles expressed frustration at those who failed to "go all the way".

There is a double entendre in 'Day Tripper' too, as it also refers to "part-time hippies" or recreational drug users. The Beatles were serious drug users – how else could they sustain their energy, productivity, and creativity, let alone their sense of humour and the wonderful "skew" of their perspective on everyday life? "Having a laugh", in fact, was one of the various code words they used for smoking marijuana, and "flying" for the experience of psychedelic drugs, as they protected or fooled those who they took along for the ride.

The long and winding road

> We were told all the time: "You'll never do anything, you Northern bastards". It was that kind of attitude. So, although we didn't openly say, "Fuck you!" it was basically our thing: "We'll show these fuckers". And we walked right through London, the Palladium, and kept on going through Ed Sullivan and on to Hong Kong and the world.
> (John in The Beatles 2000: 103)

Gillett (1970: i) argues that "rock and roll was perhaps the first form of popular culture to celebrate without reservation characteristics of city life... [and] strident repetitive sounds of city life were, in effect, reproduced as melody and rhythm". In Britain especially, it expressed longing for escape from the strictures of middle-class suburban and provincial society, with its stasis, privacy, boredom and loneliness, through movement, public emotional expression, and spontaneous community of the imagined metropolis (Frith 1997: 276; Grossberg 1984: 238).

Interviews with The Beatles reveal their ambition to escape from lower middle-class suburban Liverpool, where they were trapped by geography and age, and the thrill they initially enjoyed as they "made it" to *Sunday Night at the Palladium*, number one in the charts, embassy parties, royal receptions, Hollywood, and Graceland. There is a persistent theme of physical escape:

Ringo says, "I felt Liverpool was dark and dirty; I wanted to get out... to escape Admiral Grove... I have an affinity with green, the sea and space... It's the space, I need to be able to look... I think that's all down to Liverpool being so closed in" (The Beatles 2000: 35). Similarly, John recalls that in childhood "some of my most vivid dreams were about me being in a plane, flying over a certain part of Liverpool.... You dream your way out until you actually, physically get out of it. I got out" (The Beatles 2000: 8).

Hamburg was their first stop, and according to Lennon, it was here that they "grew up" (*Life* 2001: 123), living the marginal existence of rockers, a nocturnal life of music, sex, drink, and drugs, which George Harrison, employing a favourite metaphor, recalls in cinematic terms as "like one of those black-and-white jazz movies of the Fifties" (The Beatles 2000: 78). As in the contemporary films now known as "British realism", however, London was the place to go and "catching the train south" – like The Beatles in *A Hard Day's Night* – was the means to escape the confinement of social class and geographical location in Britain (Walker 1974: 165). According to John (in Wenner 2000: 144), "London was something we used to dream of" and, says Ringo, "by the end of 1963, it was impossible to go home. And if you're in our business you go to London. The recordings are there, the places to be seen are there, where it's happening is there; it's just a natural move" (The Beatles 2000: 108). At first they "bombed around" the shops of King's Road, Fulham Road and Mason's Yard, where it always seemed to be sunny (Paul in The Beatles 2000: 254), or cruised London clubs with the Rolling Stones (Lennon in Wenner 2000: 65–66). Their freedom of the city was short-lived, however, as they were soon trapped by Beatlemania. Although "their defection to London" (Melly 1970: 83) caused resentment among Liverpool fans, leading to criticism in the *Liverpool Echo* and bitter letter exchanges in *Merseybeat*, it was only after they "made it" that they played up their Liverpool origins with their Scouse accents, dialect and idiom, and nostalgic reflections upon their childhood haunts. But still, they single-handedly transformed the geography of British rock and roll, establishing not only the possibility, but the desirability of social and musical origins outside of London (see Butler 1984: 19).

Beyond London lay America, whose popular culture – accents, language, music, dance, clothing, comic books and gum chewing – had long been adopted as a sign of resistance to the British establishment, particularly perhaps in Liverpool given the presence of "Cunard Yanks" (sailors associated with the trans-Atlantic trade), nearby American military bases, and regional phonetics (Paul in The Beatles 2000: 123). It was Hollywood, however, that most influenced The Beatles. As John puts it, "We all knew America, all of us. All those movies: every movie we ever saw as children, whether it was

Disneyland or Doris Day, Rock Hudson, James Dean or Marilyn. Everything was American" (The Beatles 2000: 10). To John, America "was the big youth place in everybody's imagination [because] America had teenagers and everywhere else just had people" and Hollywood movies showed that teenagers in America had money, sexual freedom and public presence denied to them in Britain (Paul in The Beatles 2000: 28; see also Melly 1970: 45).

The Beatles were particularly open about their materialist motivation – as George put it, "One thing we all agree on is that we like money. I've never heard of anyone who didn't actually" (in Fast 1968: 162) – and according to George Martin, commercial success in America was an overriding concern. Even if money "can't buy me love", it does buy diamond rings and fast cars, evidently something of an infatuation for, respectively, Ringo and Paul, and John and George. Nevertheless, America meant more than money: it stood for freedom and potential stardom. According to 'Honey Pie', for example, even "a working girl, North of England way" can "hit the big time in the USA", and in *A Hard Day's Night*, John confronts Paul's grandfather: "You know you're trouble – you should have gone west to America. You'd have wound up a senior citizen of Boston. As it is you took the wrong turning and what happened – you're a lonely old man from Liverpool". Ringo, in particular, was infatuated with America, especially the western aesthetic: in Hamburg he played for the Raving Texans, and had earlier planned to emigrate to live with Lightnin' Hopkins in Texas (The Beatles 2000: 37) or to become a cowboy (Cepican and Ali 1985: 111). On their tour of 1964 Ringo bought dozens of records, boots, shirts, ties, and garish souvenirs (Fast 1968: 171), while Paul recalls the thrill telling people at home of visiting Sunset Strip and Graceland, among other places (The Beatles 2000: 192). The Beatles souvenir albums contain colourful images of them, inevitably with pretty girls or armed police, on beaches, in swimming pools, water-skiing, on horseback, with guns, and above all in exotic cars, which generally contrast with the black and white images of them taken in Britain, on bicycles, in trains, at official receptions, in recording studios, or in bombed-out city locations.

John considers that even with the fame, power, money and playing to huge audiences, "conquering America was the best thing" (Hertsgaard 1995: 92) and he "regret[s] profoundly not being American and not being born in Greenwich Village", the center of it all in the late 1960s (Wenner 2000: 145). Again, however, once The Beatles had "conquered" America commercially, and experienced it for themselves, they abandoned American pronunciations they had affected, their songs became noticeably more British, and they thus effectively overturned the dominance of American artists and songs in British popular music. The irony expressed in 'Back in the U.S.S.R.' and the sense of entrapment in 'Blue Jay Way', for example, attest to the inevitable operation of the dialectic of desire and disappointment, escape and containment, in the context of The Beatles' youthful dreams and the reality of the United States.

Drive my car

> Why is the literature on pop music... so often empty of cars, not to mention elevators, offices, shopping malls, hotels, sidewalks, airplanes, buses, urban landscapes, small towns, northern settlements or satellite broadcasts?... Why is music so rarely conceived spatially... in relation to the changing production of spaces for listeners, and thus as an extension of the changing technologies that follow or draw their subjects into these spaces? (Berland 1992: 39)

Rock and roll originally expressed the ambiguity of mobility, as the source of both freedom and alienation, and The Beatles' music and films are similarly replete with imagery of transience, roads, vehicles, speed and space. Although Stu Sutcliffe's name, The Beetles, was originally inspired by the motorcycle gang in *The Wild One* (The Beatles 2000: 41), John changed the spelling to evoke the American "beat" aesthetic, and its mobility in dogged search of self and existential meaning (see MacDonald 1994: 5). Rather than world-weary, however, The Beatles are frantic: beginning in van trips all over the north of England and ending in whirlwind world tours, they performed no less than 1,400 live shows before their last show at Candlestick Park in 1966. Even after their last tour, however, they travelled extensively together, to India to see the Maharishi, for example, on shared vacations, and for their film projects. And even in the studio, John describes their musical progress in terms of a road analogy: "the whole thing was a gradual change. We were conscious that there was some formula or something – it was moving ahead. That was for sure, we were on the road – not physically; I mean 'on the road' in the studio – and the weather was clear" (The Beatles 2000: 212). Many Beatles songs refer to journeys, such as the childhood bus trips of 'Penny Lane' and 'A Day in the Life'; on the train in 'One After 909'; sailing in 'Honey Pie' and 'Yellow Submarine'; flight in 'Back in the U.S.S.R.'; and driving in 'Drive My Car'. Wandering and searching are themes of compositions such as 'Good Day Sunshine', 'Hey Bulldog', 'From a Window', 'Get Back', and 'Good Morning', and getting lost on the road in 'Two of Us', 'The Long and Winding Road', 'Blue Jay Way' and 'Magical Mystery Tour'. Themes of escape and/or flight are covered in 'Run for Your Life', 'She's Leaving Home', 'Flying', 'Free as a Bird', 'Blackbird', 'Everybody's Got Something to Hide Except Me and My Monkey', and 'I Am the Walrus'. Geographical separation and prospects of return and reunion are also persistent in 'Golden Slumbers', 'All I've Got to Do', 'All My Loving', 'I'll Be Back', 'I'll Be on My Way', 'When I Get Home', 'I'll Follow the Sun', 'It Won't Be Long' and 'Get Back'. The fantasy of escape is complemented by the experience of solitude and loneliness of the abandoned lover or one waiting alone in the suburban home in songs such as 'I Call Your Name', 'I Don't Want to See You Again', 'I Need You', 'I'll Cry Instead', 'Don't Pass Me By', 'Blue Jay Way', 'And Your Bird Can Sing', and 'Don't Bother Me'.

The Beatles' fictional movies involve journeys, chases, struggle for freedom, escapes, and moments of transcendence through musical performance, often reminiscent of music hall's "boys on a spree" (Bailey 1994: 157). In *A Hard Day's Night*, The Beatles travel by train to London for a television studio session pursued by adoring fans, and there are Keystone Cop-like chases, luxury cars, and a helicopter. A key scene occurs when Ringo "sags off" from rehearsals and wanders through London with a camera to the accompaniment of the instrumental 'This Boy', apparently oblivious of the passage of time and the concern this causes management. His wandering reveals the other side of "Swinging London": the derelict river area, the boys playing truant, the pub – ironically called the Liverpool Arms – where working-class men seriously play "childish" games like shove-halfpenny and bar skittles, and the threatening presence of the establishment in the form of a hostile policeman. It is reminiscent of Situationist's surrealist-inspired practice of derivé, as Ringo literally drifts dreamily through urban space rejecting rational, goal-oriented behaviour for imaginatively open engagement and chance encounters with people and places.

In *Help!*, The Beatles, and again particularly Ringo, wander aimlessly about London "being attacked by various plots" (Lester in Walker 1974: 268), and harassed by police. Apparently at the behest of the bandmates for an exotic location and skiing (see Neaverson 1997: 36), the film takes The Beatles characters to Austria and the Bahamas where they are pursued by an oriental conspiracy and mad scientists on bicycles, skis, a sleigh, a cable car, luxury cars, staff cars, ice-cream vans, sailboats, trains, tanks, passenger jets, and a zeppelin. The Beatles are "passengers" in their film (Lester in Neaverson 1997: 36), but enjoy greater freedom than in *A Hard Day's Night*. There are several variations on the theme of them cavorting crazily on the ski slopes of the Alps, on beaches in the Bahamas, and in military tanks on Salisbury Plain, and in their short promotional films, they invariably perform "silly buggers" in open space.

In *Magical Mystery Tour*, the 43 coach passengers set out from Allsop Place in London, where The Beatles began their first British tour (Fast 1968: 237) and head for Devon, where Paul and George hitchhiked as boys. The tour includes foot races, bicycles, motorcycles, and luxury cars as well as the coach, and mothers and vicars pursue the unmarried Beatles. As in *Help!* there is a huge set piece of The Beatles alternately cavorting and performing their music in the open, and similarly occupying military space (in this case an old US air base). The movie also includes "classic" surreal sequences such as Paul's daydream of 'Fool on a Hill' filmed in the south of France, and the 'Flying' sequence of colour-filtered landscapes and skies.

In *Yellow Submarine*, The Beatles are recruited in grimy, industrial Liverpool and transported on a "mind-blowing journey" to Pepperland in an effort to save this "tickle of joy on the belly of the universe" from the Blue Meanies, whose Blue Splotch has frozen in motion and drained all colour from its residents and whose anti-music missiles have silenced Sgt Pepper's brass band. With literally dozens of references to popular music and film, as well as modern art, science and philosophy, they travel through Seas of Music, Cinema, Personalities, Phrenology, Science, and Holes. Along the way they confront cartoon characters from Beatles songs, Paul engages in an aerial dogfight, George is caught in a crossfire between US and Japanese naval forces, and Ringo is captured by Indians and rescued by cavalry.

Even *Let It Be* is arguably about The Beatles running away, perhaps from themselves and each other (George really does temporarily leave), and while the original plans to present a world-wide live television concert on an ocean liner were scuttled, the poignant rooftop performance seems to echo their escape in the ascending helicopter at the close of *A Hard Day's Night*, which Dick Lester had used to suggest a "feeling of release, flight, mysticism, larger-than-life quality that seemed so necessary" (DiFranco 1977: 32). This scene is also evocative of a clichéd image in musical film, that is, the spontaneous number on an urban rooftop or music drifting over the cityscape (MacKinnon 2000: 40–41), representing a dream of escape from everyday life below, and in this case surely the bitter struggle over the running of Apple Corps, The Beatles' collective experiment in "western communism" (McCartney in Burrows 1996: 154). Here The Beatles are "playing virtually to nothing – to the sky" (McCartney in The Beatles 2000: 321), a fitting end, given the importance of celestial imagery in their music and movies, as well as in sixties pop in general, where it represents yearning for a spiritual and psychedelic experience beyond the banality of material life (see MacDonald 1994: 28).

If The Beatles, as persons, symbolically succumbed to the laws of the establishment at this moment, something about their performance escaped orthodoxy. John's remarks following the performance of 'Get Back' – "I'd like to say 'Thank You' on behalf of the group and ourselves and I hope we've passed the audition" – might be a testimonial to The Beatles, for they evoke their first trip to London, when they were driven by their talent and ambition to the capital and beyond, and imply a difference between the identity of "The Beatles" as a group and the individuals of which it was composed. John expresses the contradiction of freedom and constraint, escape and entrapment, in which The Beatles seemed paradoxically to find themselves, implying that the corollary of freedom is loneliness and that of fame and fortune is imprisonment, both extreme cases of the generalized socio-psychological predicament of suburban life, of growing up, and making it on establishment terms.

"Nothing is real and nothing to get hung about"

> Up until LSD, I never realized that there was anything beyond this normal waking state of consciousness. (George in Bromell 2000: 72)

After The Beatles gave up live performance, which had deteriorated into screaming "tribal rites" (John in Coleman 1992: 310), they were no longer four lads in a room and a car. Enclosed in the recording studio for long periods (four months in the case of *Sgt Pepper*), they were able to explore a variety of sounds, styles, musical instruments, and secondary recordings with stunning effect. As their music became more experimental and introspective, they similarly exploited artistic control over their visual image, particularly in *Magical Mystery Tour*, to explore the subconscious experience of memory, dreams, and psychedelic drugs. In these efforts, The Beatles retained physical motion as a metaphor for alternative consciousness in the form of the "trip", dramatically expanding the musical and filmic expression of temporality and spatiality.

It has been noted that part of The Beatles' popularity was due to their nostalgic tendencies (Frith 1987: 142; Neaverson 1997: 125); for them, emancipation did not involve a radical break from history, tearing everyday life out of tradition, but selectively suturing poignant moments of personal memory and history into contemporary everyday life. Their songs evoking journeys into their own childhood pasts – literally documenting their own childhood journeys in the case of the brilliant double-A side, 'Strawberry Fields Forever' and 'Penny Lane' – are consistent with a longing for simple innocence and an idealized community. The Beatles' fondness for anachronism is illustrated by their indebtedness to music hall, but also their adoption of Edwardian aesthetics, particularly in *Sgt Pepper* and *Yellow Submarine*, with their brass bands, flamboyant military dress, grandfathers on old penny-farthings, and servants and maids, consistent with a generational fascination-repulsion with Britain's imperial past, the leisured lives of the upper classes, and the youth of their grandparents. According to Ringo, The Beatles "loved dressing up" (The Beatles 2000: 257), but they seemed to have a particular fondness for camped-up military uniforms, beginning in *A Hard Day's Night* in the make-up room scene where Ringo, reading *Queen*, jokes about joining the guards in order to wear a bearskin hat and the grandfather accuses them of being "powdered gee-gaws" and "a bunch of cissies". Their appropriation of military clothes in subsequent movies exemplifies what de Certeau (1984: xiii) calls the "tactics of subversion", whereby subordinate cultures appropriate imposed rituals, representations and laws: "subvert[ing] them not by rejecting or altering them, but by using them with respect to ends and references foreign to the system they had no choice but to accept". Their delight in vintage uniforms is a symbolic rejection of the militarized discipline of work and sartorial functionality, as well as contemporary configurations of class, gender, and generational relations.

Dream and sleep images occur in several of songs of The Beatles, including 'I'm Only Sleeping', 'Good Night', and 'Golden Slumbers', and there are two dream sequences in *Magical Mystery Tour*. More important, however, is the imagery of psychedelia, for as Curtis (1987: 190) notes, there is a correspondence between internalization of awareness through drugs and internalization of music through the recording studio. Music and drugs share "closely related phenomenologies", stretching time and distorting space, as both rhythm and meaning "reverberate" through our being (Bromell 2000: 73). Given censorship and the difficulty of verbally communicating the effect of drugs – the subject of 'I Want to Tell' – The Beatles thus resorted to allusion in lyrics, and innovative musical and visual imagery. There are numerous drug references in Beatle songs, of course, even if the "real" meaning of 'Lucy in the Sky with Diamonds' is still debated. At the same time, electronic sound effects "denaturalized" music analogous to the effects of drugs on sensory experience, such as their borrowing of reverberation from surf music (where it stood for the vastness of oceanic space) to evoke the interior spaces of the mind (Bromell 2000: 96; Hicks 1999: 65). Perhaps also partly in response to actual confinement, they used the studio to create imaginary space within the music, such as sound moving across speakers and creating the illusion of depth and scale through "elongation" of the signal, layering, and the "wall of sound" effect. They pioneered and became "masters of what might be called musical architecture" (Hertsgaard 1995: 163), reproducing for mass consumption in bedrooms a world of sound, space, and movement that existed only in the studio.

The movies also reflect The Beatles' lengthy experience with illicit drugs. Dick Lester recalls that the manic-paced *A Hard Day's Night* was made on amphetamines and *Help!* on marijuana, while both *Magical Mystery Tour* and *Yellow Submarine* explicitly evoke sustained psychedelic experience, which John significantly likens to "real life in CinemaScope" (The Beatles 2000: 180). Although of very different cinematic style, each of these movies involves The Beatles characters travelling from one surreal situation into another. *Magical*

Mystery Tour was made on LSD and knowingly combines the traditional British working-class charabanc outing with Ken Kesey and the Merry Pranksters' trip from San Francisco to the World's Fair in New York in 1965 (immortalized in Tom Wolfe's *Electric Kool-Aid Acid Test*) – "a psychedelic journey to zap America with acid, music and happenings" (Chambers 1985: 93). The Beatles are four musicians whose music casts spells and transforms An Ordinary Coach Trip into a Magical Mystery Tour. In the 'Flying' sequence, the host, Jolly Jimmy Johnson (Derek Royle), contrasts the scene of the English countryside on one side of the coach, with the artificially coloured exotic landscapes on the other, suggesting that it is all a matter of perspective. 'Yellow Submarine' refers to a narcotic pill (and allegedly to John's image of George's house during his famous "dental treatment", his first experience of LSD) and the cartoon uses primary colours, throbbing and strobe effects, and distortion of perspective to simulate the exaggerated visual sensitivity of an acid trip. The characters evoke the shape-shifting effect and paranoia of LSD, and the puns and scattered code words mine the drug lexicon. This work also exploits the effects of synesthesia, the aural-visual sensory crossover that The Beatles sought in their music, as in John's injunction in 'Tomorrow Never Knows' to "listen to the color of your dream" and his description of 'Being for the Benefit of Mr. Kite' as "cosmically beautiful... pure, like a painting, a pure watercolor" (Turner 1994: 128).

One of the effects of the playful verbal, visual, and musical ambiguity in The Beatles' work was to allow the establishment to turn a blind eye to its subversive intent, while (again as in music hall) creating a "potent sense of collusion" (Bromell 2000: 22) with their primary audience. Their intense use of drugs was for a long time the industry's best-kept secret, and apparently even George Martin was not aware of their LSD consumption until Paul publicly advocated its use in interviews in *Life* and *Queen* magazines, even though they had already recorded *Revolver* (1966), the album that introduced the world to what became known as "psychedelic" music (The Beatles 2000: 242). The Beatles thus exploited the "knowingness" characteristic of working-class entertainment, which relies on familiarity with language use and meaning, sexual knowledge, and particular social competencies to create a sense of corporate subjectivity (Bailey 1994: 138). When The Beatles sang "Oh I'll tell you something, I'll think you'll understand" ('I Wanna Hold Your Hand'), "Well, she was just seventeen, You know what I mean" ('I Saw Her Standing There') and 'Do You Want to Know a Secret?', they publicly express illicit sexual desire, even perhaps closeted gay love, by creating a conspiracy of meaning among "knowing" listeners (see Cohen 1991: 178). A similar conspiracy effect is obtained in their movies, such as *A Hard Day's Night*'s use of Liverpool slang like "grotty" (grotesque) and "gear" (de rigueur), John sniffing (snorting) a Coca Cola (coke) bottle, and the gag about the bellboy in the closet.

Another innovation that drew audiences into The Beatles' world involved ironic distancing from direct personal expression, a general rock and roll characteristic, particularly compared to its musical progenitors, in the form of stylistic performances, dressing up, and group identity (Grossberg 1984: 232). In the case of The Beatles, however, this included the brilliant innovation on 'She Loves You', which incorporates a conversation about a lover, a simple trick which shifted focus from the traditional confession of love to collective experience of sexual relationships and so "enormously expanded the emotive spatiality of pop" (Bromell 2000: 28).

The filmic equivalent to this strategy is to take the audience behind the scenes into the confined space of The Beatles' world. *A Hard Day's Night* establishes the precedent: we are chased with them down narrow alleyways, travel with them on a train, where we join them performing in the cage of a guard's van, and are closeted with them in various small rooms. Dick Lester introduces two key innovations: first, the cut-in between performance and close-up of audience, reducing the social and psychological distance, and communicating the music and emotion shared between them (Laing 2000: 7); and second, the deep focus shot behind the stage simultaneously capturing performance and audience response (Sarris 1964). This movie is the "most seminal of all pop films" (Melly 1970: 161) and while such cinematic innovation cannot be claimed for the other movies, the effect of our spatial confinement with The Beatles is maintained in *Help!* (The Beatles share a home and various gangs of conspirators attempt to penetrate their hermetic world); in *Magical Mystery Tour* (the coach and the underground theatre); in the yellow submarine in *Yellow Submarine*; and recording their last album at Twickenham Studios in the documentary *Let It Be*. If The Beatles were in constant motion for the best part of the sixties, their music and film enable us all vicariously to go along for the ride.

"I don't want to spoil the party"

> The Beatles were better than good actors. They were brilliant at playing themselves. (Walter Shenson in Pritchard and Lysaght 1999: 25)

Although I have followed convention in treating "The Beatles" as plural, Paul (in Hertsgaard 1995: 135), at least, suggests that The Beatles possessed some kind of gestalt, that "We're individuals, but we make up together the Mates, which is one person".

Under the influence of Astrid Kirchherr who modelled them on the Exis of Hamburg, and later, Brian Epstein, who had them wearing box jacket suits, shirts and ties, they rejected the model of individual and predatory sexuality for an androgynous fraternity. Their look evolved but uniforms remained essential to their collective identity, as McCartney explains: "The thing about suits was that they always made us feel part of a team. When we arrived we were in our civvies, but once we put those on we were The Beatles!" (The Beatles 2000: 216). According to Nik Cohn, describing their appearance on *The Ed Sullivan Show*:

> They seemed to possess a secret shared understanding, some kind of instinctive group strength… [T]hey look like the four limbs of a single anatomy. Their whole power was in their unity. (Cohn 2001: 13)

Epstein in particular was determined to keep the group "together", even to the extent of refusing solo songwriting credits to Paul on 'Yesterday' (written and performed without other members of the group), and trying to maintain the "pressure cooker" effect by having them buy neighbouring houses in the stockbroker belt outside London. At one point, they collectively investigated a Greek island where they could all live with their families. The fear of dissolution certainly seems a theme in The Beatles' movies, and especially the loss of Ringo, symbolic of their "common touch": this motivates action in *A Hard Day's Night* as he "parades" through London and is arrested on a series of trumped-up charges; in *Help!*, when a sinister oriental sect seeks him for human sacrifice in order to bring youth back to religion; and in *Yellow Submarine*, when his cartoon character experiences an "arrowing" capture by Indians. Ringo was in fact the first to leave the group (albeit temporarily) during the recording of *The Beatles* (the "White Album") in 1968.

The Beatles were a group without obvious leadership, in contrast to the dominant model of lead-singer and backing band (see Inglis 2000: 99), and the problem for media, the music industry, and perhaps also some of their audience, was to put The Beatles in their respective places within the band. Audiences needed individual personalities on which to project their desires and wanted to know how the interpersonal relations worked among "the Mates". Ehrenreich et al. (1997: 525), for example, note the concern of female fans over the identities of the individual Beatles, quoting one fan who "especially liked talking [about] the Beatles with other girls. Someone would say, 'What do you think Paul had for breakfast?' 'Do you think he sleeps with a different girl every night?' Or… 'Is George really more sensitive?'"

The Beatles' films helped to establish their individual public personas, beginning with *A Hard Day's Night*. According to Richard Lester, part of the intention of the film was to create distinct public personalities for the individual Beatles:

> Paul was the sexy one, John was clever and sarcastic, Ringo was lovable, and George was mean.... We were trying to separate their characters officially, so we were desperately trying to give them separate characteristics... (in DiFranco 1977: 20)

In both this film and *Help!* The Beatles paradoxically "play themselves", suggesting again the idea that The Beatles were always already "an act", caught up in Beatlemania and the sixties, for a moment occupying the *gap* between art and life (Melly 1970: 138).

Even as their roles evolve, they played what John called "Beatles-by-numbers" (*Life* 2001: 53): media-mediated caricatures, easily assimilated as complementary dimensions of a single ego, hence perhaps the serious intent behind the pun in *Rubber Soul*. Perhaps their most obvious self-conscious performance was as Sgt. Pepper's Lonely Hearts Club Band, a concept that involved imaginary alter egos "emancipating [The Beatles] even from themselves" (Everett 1999: 67). Neaverson (1997: 68), however, notes how *Magical Mystery Tour* similarly subverts the "The Beatles" as they each play multiple characters and appear as themselves; in some cases the distinction is unclear, frustrating any clear identification, least of all in terms of the images constructed for them in previous films and in the popular media.

By the time of *Let It Be*, the act is practically over, and although some have claimed "John spends most of the 'Get Back' sessions hiding behind the façade of 'the witty Beatle'" (Sulpy and Schweighardt 1997: 2), the documentary is a sometimes brutally honest exposure of the disintegration of legendary artistic synergy and interpersonal harmony. The film was originally conceived as a project for The Beatles to "Get Back" to their roots in live performance and rock and roll; in the words of the song, to "get back to where they once belonged". But The Beatles had finally gone too far, and as George bitterly put it, the film should be called "Let it Rot" (Benson 1992: 205). The explanation of the break-up is complex and contested, but it involves, amongst other things, what John (in Wenner 2000: 20) describes as the implosion of the myth of The Beatles, as each member of the band discovered their own identities, and what George diagnoses as the need to escape the "stifling" experience of the "small place" that The Beatles had become (in The Beatles 2000: 352).

Conclusion: "Revolution"?

> The Beatles' feel for history conveyed as much through their music as their lyrics, obliged them to be more worldly than revolutionary, more witty than angry, more comedic than tragic. They sang that things were getting better all the time. (Bromell 2000: 111)

There is no shortage of overt political statement in The Beatles' music: for example, 'Back in the U.S.S.R.' alludes to the Cold War; 'Piggies' mocks middle-class consumption; 'Revolution' expresses opposition to violence; and 'Come Together' was originally written as a campaign song for Timothy Leary (running for governor of California against Ronald Reagan). In public appearances, they promoted Transcendental Meditation and legalization of marijuana; advocated the use of psychedelic drugs and supported draft dodgers; they protested their own commercial exploitation – hence *Beatles for Sale* – and with Apple, pioneered "people's capitalism" (Kureishi 1992: 368); and in each of their movies, even the documentary *Let It Be*, The Beatles confront the repressive forces of the establishment represented by the police and/or military. For The Beatles, however, the personal is the source of the political, and social transformation will only come through enhanced self-consciousness and capacity for compassion – hence 'All You Need Is Love'.

Since the 1970s, The Beatles have been viewed as hopelessly romantic, and as with their songs and movies (continually re-released for enormous profits), together with the whole library of coffee-table books, we can nostalgically replay the emotional roller-coaster ride and its predictable ending, as reality finally penetrated the fiction and brought it to a juddering halt. The message of The Beatles, however, should not be that of inevitable failure of utopian dreams in necessary compromises of everyday reality, but that emancipation can only be but a momentary experience of the possibilities of freedom, always realized within a situation of constraint. Emancipation is not the material realization of utopian dreams, but the moment in place and time where utopian fantasy and everyday life meet, where dream and reality intersect. It is thus like adolescence and musical performance, a moment always conscious of its ephemerality, lived in the intensity that accompanies knowledge of transience. And that is why it is always "musical", in the sense that Lefebvre (1991) means when he describes music as the junction of the erotic and political, but also in the sense of the filmic genre which combines diegetic and non-diegetic soundtrack, for music itself always only exists in performance: even in mass-produced recordings its consumption uniquely occupies every everyday space anew, and potentially makes new meanings. The Beatles' phenomenon briefly created a utopian moment, a space and time of which their music and film still provides a fleeting glimpse, where and when in John's words (in MacDonald 1994: 7), "rock-and-roll was real. Everything else was unreal".

References

Bailey, Peter. (1994) "Conspiracies of Meaning: Music-hall and the Knowingness of Popular Culture". *Past and Present* 144/1: 138–70. https://doi.org/10.1093/past/144.1.138
Beatles, The (2000) *The Beatles Anthology*. San Francisco: Chronicle Books.
Benson, Ross. (1992) *Paul McCartney: Behind the Myth*. London: Victor Gollancz.
Berland, Jody. (1992) "Angels Dancing: Cultural Technologies and the Production of Space". In *Cultural Studies*, ed. Lawrence Grossberg, Cary Nelson and Paula Treichler, 38–55. New York: Routledge.
Berman, Paul. (1996) *A Tale of Two Utopias: The Political Journey of the Generation of 1968*. New York: W. W. Norton.
Bradley, Dick. (1992) *Understanding Rock 'n' Roll: Popular Music in Britain 1955–1964*. Buckingham: Open University Press.
Braun, Michael. (1964) *Love Me Do: The Beatles' Progress*. Harmondsworth: Penguin.
Bromell, Nick. (2000) *Tomorrow Never Knows: Rock and Psychedelics in the 1960s*. Chicago: Chicago University Press.
Burrows, Terry. (1996) *The Beatles: The Complete Illustrated History*. London: Carlton.
Butler, Richard W. (1984) "The Geography of Rock, 1954–1970". *Ontario Geography* 24: 1–33.
Cepican, Bob and Waleed Ali. (1985) *Yesterday...Came Suddenly: The Definitive History of the Beatles*. New York: Arbor House.
Chambers, Iain. (1985) *Urban Rhythms: Pop Music and Popular Culture*. Basingstoke: Macmillan.
Cohen, Sara. (1991) *Rock Culture in Liverpool: Popular Music in the Making*. Oxford: Oxford University Press.
Cohn, Nik. (2001) "Introduction: Remember". In Editors of Time Life (eds), *The Beatles: From Yesterday to Today*. *Life* 1.4 (25 June): 8–17.
Coleman, Ray. (1992) *Lennon: The Definitive Biography*. New York: HarperCollins.
Cook, Guy and Neil Mercer. (2000) "From Me to You: Austerity to Profligacy in the Language of the Beatles". In *The Beatles, Popular Music and Society*, ed. Ian Inglis, 86–104. Basingstoke: Palgrave Macmillan.
de Certeau, Michel. (1984) *The Practice of Everyday Life*. Berkeley: University of California Press.
Curtis, Jim. (1987) *Rock Eras: Interpretations of Music and Society 1954–1984*. Bowling Green, OH: Bowling Green State University Popular Press.
Denisoff, R. Serge and William D. Romanowski. (1991) *Risky Business: Rock in Film*. New Brunswick, NJ: Transaction Publishers.
DiFranco, J. Philip. (1977) "An Interview with Richard Lester". In *The Beatles in Richard Lester's A Hard Day's Night: A Complete Pictorial Record of the Movie*, ed. J. Philip DiFranco, 17–34. London: Chelsea House.
Dyer, Richard. (1977) "The Colour of Entertainment". *Sight and Sound* 5/11: 28–31.
Dyer, Richard. (1992) *Only Entertainment*. New York: Routledge.

Ehrenreich, Barbara, Elizabeth Hess and Gloria Jacobs. (1997) "Beatlemania: A Sexually Defiant Consumer Culture". In *The Subcultures Reader*, ed. Ken Gelder and Sarah Thornton, 523–36. London: Routledge.

Everett, Walter. (1999) *The Beatles as Musicians: Revolver through the Anthology*. Oxford: Clarendon.

Fast, Julius. (1968) *The Beatles: The Real Story*. New York: Putnam and Sons.

Fitzgerald, Jon. (2000) "Lennon-McCartney and the Early British Invasion 1964–6". In *The Beatles, Popular Music and Society: A Thousand Voices*, ed. Ian Inglis, 53–85. New York: St. Martin's Press.

Frith, Simon. (1978) *The Sociology of Rock*. London: Constable.

Frith, Simon. (1987) "Towards an Aesthetic of Popular Music". In *Music and Society: The Politics of Composition, Performance and Reception*, ed. Richard Leppert and Susan McClary, 133–49. Cambridge: Cambridge University Press.

Frith, Simon. (1997) "The Suburban Sensibility in British Rock and Pop". In *Visions of Suburbia*, ed. Roger Silverstone, 269–79. New York: Routledge.

Gillett, Charlie. (1970) *The Sound of the City: The Rise of Rock and Roll*. New York: Outerbridge & Dienstfrey.

Grossberg, Lawrence. (1984) "Another Boring Day in Paradise: Rock and Roll and the Empowerment of Everyday Life". In *Popular Music 4: Performers and Audiences*, ed. Richard Middleton and David Horn, 225–56. Cambridge: Cambridge University Press.

Grossberg, Lawrence. (1993) "The Media Economy of Rock Culture: Cinema, Postmodernity and Authenticity". In *Sound and Vision: The Music Video Reader*, ed. Simon Frith, Andrew Goodwin and Lawrence Grossberg, 185–209. London: Routledge.

Hertsgaard, Mark. (1995) *A Day in the Life: The Music and Artistry of the Beatles*. New York: Delacorte Press.

Hicks, Michael. (1999) *Sixties Rock: Garage, Psychedelic, and Other Satisfactions*. Urbana: University of Illinois Press.

Hudson, Kenneth. (1984) *The Language of the Teenage Revolution: The Dictionary Defeated*. London: Macmillan.

Inglis, Ian. (2000) "'The Beatles are coming!': Conjecture and Conviction in the Myth of Kennedy, America, and the Beatles". *Popular Music and Society* 24/2: 93–108. https://doi.org/10.1080/03007760008591769

Kureishi, Hanif. (1992) *London Kills Me*. Harmondsworth: Penguin.

Laing, Heather. (2000) "Emotion by Numbers: Music, Song and the Musical". In *Musicals: Hollywood and Beyond*, ed. Bill Marshall and Robynn Stilwell, 5–13. Portland, OR: Intellect Books.

Lefebvre, Henri. (1991) *The Production of Space*. Malden, MA: Blackwell.

Life. (2001) *The Beatles: From Yesterday to Today*. Boston, MA: Little, Brown and Co.

MacDonald, Ian. (1994) *Revolution in the Head: The Beatles' Records and the Sixties*. London: Fourth Estate.

Marcus, Greil. (1980) "Rock Films". In *The Rolling Stone Illustrated History of Rock & Roll*, ed. Jim Miller, 177–89. New York: Random House.

Marshall, Bill and Robynn Stilwell. (2000) "Introduction". In *Musicals: Hollywood and Beyond*, ed. Bill Marshall and Robynn Stilwell, 1–4. Portland, OR: Intellect Books.

Marshall, Philip D. (2000) "The Celebrity Legacy of the Beatles". In *The Beatles, Popular Music and Society: A Thousand Voices*, ed. Ian Inglis, 163–75. New York: St. Martin's Press.
McCartney, Paul. (1967) "I'm Trying to Take People with Me". *International Times* 6: 8–10.
Melly, George. (1970) *Revolt into Style: The Pop Arts*. Oxford: Oxford University Press.
Miles, Barry. (1978) *The Beatles in Their Own Words*. London: Putnam Publishing.
Muncie, John. (2000) "The Beatles and the Spectacle of Youth". In *The Beatles, Popular Music and Society: A Thousand Voices*, ed. Ian Inglis, 35–52. New York: St. Martin's Press.
Neaverson, Bob. (1997) *The Beatles Movies*. London: Cassell.
Norman, Philip. (1981) *Shout! The Beatles in Their Generation*. New York: Simon and Schuster.
Plato. (1984) "Republic". Excerpted in *Music in the Western World: A History in Documents*, ed. Piero Weiss and Richard Taruskin. New York: Schirmer Books.
Pritchard, David and Alan Lysaght. (1999) "The Fab Four Frolic Again". *Box Office* 135/2: 24–26.
Sarris, Andrew. (1964) "Films: Bravo Beatles!" *Village Voice* 9/45: 13.
Shaw, Arnold. (1968) *The Rock Revolution*. London: Crowell-Collier.
Sheff, David and G. Barry Golson. (1981) *The Playboy Interviews with John Lennon and Yoko Ono*. New York: Playboy Press.
Sulpy, Doug and Ray Schweighardt. (1997) *Get Back: The Unauthorized Chronicle of The Beatles' Let It Be Disaster*. New York: St. Martin's Press.
Tarantino, Quentin. (1995) "What is a Pop Movie Anyway?" Interview in *Celluloid Jukebox: Popular Music and the Movies since the 50s*, ed. J. Romney and A. Wootton, 125–26. London: BFI.
Turner, Steve. (1994) *A Hard Day's Write: The Stories Behind Every Beatles Song*. New York: HarperCollins.
Walker, Alexander. (1974) *Hollywood UK: The British Film Industry in the Sixties*. New York: Stein and Day.
Wenner, Jann S. (2000) *Lennon Remembers*. London: Verso [1973].
Whitley, Ed. (2000) "The Postmodern White Album". In *The Beatles, Popular Music and Society: A Thousand Voices*, ed. Ian Inglis, 105–125. New York: St. Martin's Press.

Author biography

Jon Goss is Professor of Geography in the Department of Humanities and Social Sciences at Clarkson University in Potsdam, New York, USA. His research and publications in cultural geography focus on landscapes of consumption, tourism and film, and he is currently working on a project examining images of mimetic desire in the billboards of midtown Manhattan.

5 The Bohemian Beatles

Colin Campbell

Although, in post-Leary psychedelic parlance, The Beatles had "tuned in" and "turned on" by 1967 (as was apparent in their interest in drugs and their modes) they had in various ways "dropped out" of the mainstream years earlier. This chapter considers The Beatles' relationship to various counter-cultural influences and the broader definition of the term "bohemian". The group's relationship to scenes and movements, including the Beats, hipster-rockers and, later, the Continental avant-garde, is discussed. However, as Colin Campbell argues, it is something of a mistake to conceive of The Beatles as having become bohemians. Rather it is suggested that, to a significant extent, they always were bohemians, or at least that bohemianism was a crucial part of their identity, and what is more, that this helps to account for their phenomenal success.

Introduction

At first sight the idea that the members of the most successful rock band of all time could be thought of as bohemians might seem strange. For bohemian is a name generally applied to young people who have artistic pretensions and yet whose work is little recognized or valued (at least in their lifetimes), and who – since they reject bourgeois values and are consequently generally disinclined to get a proper job – live a hand-to-mouth existence in poor and squalid surroundings. Hardly a picture that is easily reconciled with the popular image of the Fab Four. Yet a little reflection quickly reveals a possible connection, for in the latter stage of their career, The Beatles did become what one might call the unofficial leaders of a popular youth movement, one that was generally known as the counter-culture, whose members – the hippies – would indeed fit such a stereotype. For these were young people, who although mainly the sons and daughters of well-to-do professional parents, were busy following Timothy Leary's injunction to "tune in", "turn on", and "drop out". Leary's slogan became widely known following his 1966 *Playboy* profile (see Leary 1970: 117). And although the Beatles themselves couldn't be said, in the late 1960s, to be actually "dropping out" (in reality this was something they had done many years earlier), they had indeed "tuned in" and "turned on"; something that is apparent in their interest in drugs and in their mode of dress if nothing else. Consequently, it would seem acceptable to suggest that, in the last few years of their career at least, the label "bohemian" might be applicable. However, it will be suggested here that it is something of a mistake to conceive of The Beatles as having *become* bohemians. Rather it is suggested that, to a significant extent, they always were bohemians, or at least that bohemianism was a crucial part of their identity, and what is more, that this helps to account for their phenomenal success.

Bohemianism

Bohemianism is a term that stands for an unconventional and irregular way of life, one that is voluntarily chosen and frequently involves artistic pursuits, amongst romantic individuals in revolt against what they see as a utilitarian and philistine society. It is recognized as being a modern phenomenon, making its first appearance in Paris in the 1840s and thereafter spreading to all major cities of Europe and North America, where it has remained a feature of cosmopolitan life, periodically flourishing and dying back, but never actually dying out (see, inter alia, Grana and Grana 1990; Lipton 1959; Parry 1960; Ransome 1907). It was the romantic myth of the unhappy and neglected genius, that is to say the impoverished artist whose talent goes unrecognized by society and who consequently dies in squalor, which helped to bring Bohemia into being; for its currency and appeal led many young artists to embrace suffering, and even "martyrdom", in order that it might serve as proof of their greatness. By the time that The Beatles were growing up in the 1950s the Beat movement in the USA, together with the Existentialist movement on the continent of Europe, were the principal forms in which the Western bohemian tradition manifested itself, and it was The Beatles' good fortune that, during their early career, they were to come into close contact with both.

The Beatles and the Beat movement

The Beat movement first appeared in the 1950s in both New York and California, the centre of the movement moving to San Francisco when Allen Ginsberg and others followed Jack Kerouac there in 1953. It was both a literary and a social phenomenon, the principal Beat writers in addition to Ginsberg and Kerouac being Gregory Corso, Gary Snyder, William S. Burroughs, Lawrence Ferlinghetti, Philip Whalen, and Neal Cassidy (Parkinson 1961). The key texts were Kerouac's novel *On The Road* (1957) and Ginsberg's poem, *Howl*; the trial and eventual acquittal of Ginsberg (on charges of obscenity) for publishing the latter in May 1957 being the principal event that brought the Beats to public attention (Marwick 1998: 32). This publicity in turn gave a boost to the movement, encouraging disaffected youngsters across America to adopt a Beat way of life. These Beat youngsters became dubbed "beatniks" by the media, a term coined by San Francisco columnist Herb Caen amidst the cultural shockwave following the successful launch into orbit in 1957 of the Russian spacecraft, Sputnik I and II. This term was then generally used to distinguish the literary "elite" (such as Ginsberg, Kerouac, and the others, who were still referred to as "Beats") from the larger population of youngsters with little or no literary ability or pretension, yet who aped the Beat way of life. Although the centre of the Beat movement was undoubtedly the United States, Beats, or at least beatniks, could also be found in Britain in the late 1950s.

Like the situation in the United States, beatniks in the UK could be found in the low-rent quarters of large cities, such as Birmingham, Manchester or London. However, they could also be found in St. Ives and Newquay in Cornwall, attracted by the mild climate, where they were often banned from pubs and shops because of their unconventional scruffy and generally unwashed appearance. The beatnik image was one of duffle coats, sandals, polo-neck sweaters, berets, longish hair and, for the girls, very pale make-up. Critically, Beats and beatniks could also be found in Liverpool in the 1950s, especially in the Liverpool 8 district. This was an area where, as Ray Connolly explains, "students, actors, artists, prostitutes and priests would gather in the two famous pubs, The Crack and The Philharmonic" (Connolly 1981: 38). It was in the former of these, The Crack (or Ye Cracke) that John Lennon, together with fellow students Bill Harry and Stu Sutcliffe, would "sit for hours... discussing Henry Miller and Kerouac and the 'beat' poets, Corso and Ferlinghetti" (Norman 1981: 52). For it was at Liverpool College of Art that John Lennon was introduced by fellow students Stu Sutcliffe and Bill Harry to the work of the American beat generation, such that, as Dave Laing puts it, "the Sutcliffe-Harry-Lennon circle occasionally overlapped with a nascent British beat scene…" (Laing 2009: 17).[1]

Beatnik horror[2]

Intriguingly it was The Beatles' first manager, Allan Williams, who was instrumental in assisting in a media exposé of bohemian – that is to say, beatnik – life in Liverpool in the 1960s. He was the owner of a small club called The Jacaranda, in Slater Street, which was where The Beatles, who at that time consisted of John Lennon, Paul McCartney, George Harrison and Stuart Sutcliffe, liked to hang out. Significantly, Paul described it as having "the kind of bohemian atmosphere that they liked" (Miles 1998: 53). For in July 1960 *The People* newspaper ran an article entitled "The Beatnik Horror, for though they don't know it they are on the road to hell." This article was illustrated with a carefully posed photograph, arranged by Williams, of the flat below Sutcliffe's at 3 Gambier Terrace; a photograph that shows an out-of-focus young man, possibly John Lennon, sitting on the floor. It detailed the decadent lifestyle of bohemians around Liverpool 8. The article commented: "Most beatniks like dirt. They dress in filthy clothes, their 'homes' are strewn with muck... this is a flat of a beatnik group in Liverpool" (Forbes 1960: 3). Whether the photograph in question shows Lennon or not, he did move into the Gambier Terrace flat with fellow art students Stuart Sutcliffe and Margaret Chapman sometime in late 1959 or early 1960, where he and Sutcliffe – in typical bohemian fashion – painted the rooms yellow and black.[3] We also have Paul McCartney's description of this flat, or at least, of the kind of "art-school flats in... [the] run-down district of Liverpool 8" where Lennon hung out while an art student. He describes these as "bare, bohemian places, with naked bulbs, dirty floorboards and a mattress in the corner, where the curtain was an old blanket tacked over the window and the furniture was sometimes burned to provide warmth" (Miles 1998: 50), noting that these flats were the scenes of "intense all-night talks and as much debauchery as could be managed on a meagre art-school grant" (ibid.).[4] Paul McCartney has also asserted that he believes he got a better education from John and Stu than he got at school. This was because they led him into "a world of poetry, beatniks, Bohemians and art school parties" (Sutcliffe and Thompson 2002: 47).

Liverpool College of Art

That Paul McCartney should link beatniks, bohemians and art school parties in this way is no accident for, in the period immediately after the Second World War, local colleges of art in the United Kingdom, such as that in Liverpool, played an important role, as Frith and Horne document, in disseminating unorthodox ideas and cultural practices. Indeed, they could be described as bohemian hotbeds given that typically, "Art students in those days distanced themselves from both the respectability of their varied middle-class backgrounds and from the 'trivial' commercial pleasures of the masses" (Frith and Horne 1987: 75). The fact that Lennon and Sutcliffe were both art students is therefore crucial to an understanding of the processes that led to The Beatles developing a bohemian identity. Even more significantly, the two of them were not just fellow art students but close friends, for as Frith and Horne observe, "art school friendships... offer a way for students to apply the tenets of Romanticism... to everyday life" (Frith and Horne 1987: 84). Added to this was the fact that Sutcliffe resembled the classic image of the bohemian, for he did indeed lead the life, as Ray Connolly says, of "the sensitive, vulnerable artist in a garret" (1981: 39). Indeed, Pauline Sutcliffe says that for art students like Lennon and her brother, the heroes were painters and poets like Modigliani and Rimbaud, artists who suffered for their art. She comments that the "starving-artist-dying-young-for-his-art fantasy" appealed to them, even though she does go on to say that she didn't think that Stu and John were ever "the true starving-in-a-garret types" (Sutcliffe and Thompson 2002: 39), albeit she does admit that "Stu was the romantic artist" (Sutcliffe and Thompson 2002: 45). He was also someone whom Lennon admired greatly, being attracted to precisely this romantic image. But then, significantly, it was because John believed firmly that "an artist was an artist, whether he held a paint brush or a guitar", that he insisted on Stuart being a member of the band, finding it difficult to believe that the same person could not do both (Sutcliffe and Thompson 2002: 39). In the event, Stuart proved John to be wrong in this belief, and yet his contribution to the development of The Beatles was considerable nonetheless. Pauline Sutcliffe has said that her brother wanted to "elevate rock and roll to an art form" (Sutcliffe and Thompson 2002: 63), while Shelagh Johnston (general manager of The Beatles' Story museum in Liverpool) has said – in a letter to Pauline Sutcliffe – that she believed Stuart to have been "an immense influence on the Beatles, highly inspirational: his own artistic style and fashion consciousness was terribly strong and affected all of them, especially John" (Sutcliffe and Thompson 2002: 227–28), who was in turn "the conduit to the others" (ibid.).[5] More specifically, Philip Norman suggests that John learned from Stu "of the French Impressionists, whose rebellion against accepted values made that of Rock and Roll seem marginal" (Norman 1981: 52).

Royston Ellis

In fact, all of the Beatles and not just Lennon and Sutcliffe were, at that time, closely associated with the Beat or beatnik-bohemian movement, while also associated, if informally, with the College of Art.[6] As Frith and Horne put it, "The Beatles... were part of the Liverpool 8 art scene", with its "bohemian cafes, pubs, clubs and pads" (1987: 85). For, not only did they hang out in bohemian cafes and pubs but, more significantly, they were professionally involved with a Beat poet. His name was Royston Ellis and although British, he was heavily influenced by the American beat generation. Ellis called himself "The King of the Beatniks" while also acting as the *Record Mirror*'s teenage pop pundit. By 1960 he had published two collections of poetry, *Jiving to Gyp* and *Rave*, and in

June, he travelled to Liverpool to perform a poetry reading at the University. Since he usually read his poetry to a jazz backing, he searched among locals for suitable musicians to accompany him. He met Sutcliffe and persuaded him to allow the Silver Beetles, as they were then called, to back him. Ellis bonded in particular with Lennon, both of them sharing an enthusiasm for the American beat poets, and he spent a week at 3 Gambier Terrace with Lennon, Sutcliffe and the other art student "beatniks", while also giving readings of his poetry, appropriately enough, at The Jacaranda coffee bar (Sutcliffe and Thompson 2002: 68). Ellis introduced The Beatles to Benzedrine – obtained from a Vick inhaler – as well as telling them all about the London demi-monde of "drugs and queers and the bohemian lifestyle".[7] The importance of Ellis is that he straddled pop and literature, while recognizing the artistic potential of rock 'n' roll. Given his background and experience, it was inevitable that The Beatles would be impressed by him, while Ellis claimed that it was he who convinced John to leave art college and follow his dream of becoming a rock 'n' roll performer. Ellis also claims that he convinced The Beatles to change the spelling of their name, suggesting that as he was a beat poet and they were going to back him with beat music they should call themselves the "Beatles".[8]

The Beatles as Teds and rockers

If there is a difficulty with accepting that, in the early years, The Beatles could be thought of as bohemians, which in this case really means Beats or beatniks, it is that one is accustomed to thinking of them at this time as identifying with a very different youth sub-culture, that which comprised the principal audience for rock 'n' roll; in other words the teenage delinquents who, in Britain in the 1950s, were generally known as "Teddy Boys" because of their vaguely Edwardian style of dress. This consisted of drape jackets with velvet collars, drainpipe trousers, crepe-soled shoes and bootlace ties. They also wore their hair long with side-whiskers, while a great deal of grease generally supported a quiff at the front and a D.A. or duck's arse, at the back. As an overall image it has been compared both with the Regency buck and the Mississippi riverboat gambler (Melly 1970: 35; Brake 1980: 73).[9] Now there is little doubt that two of The Beatles at least emulated this style; indeed it is reported that the Quarrymen "all wore Teddy Boy clothes, had their hair piled high and sleeked back like Elvis... [with] John [being]... the biggest Ted of them all" (Davies 1978: 35), while George Harrison was described as "a real out and out Teddy Boy" (Davies 1978: 50).

However, given that rock 'n' roll originated in the USA, it was actually a rather different image of the youthful delinquent or rebel that came to displace that of the Teddy Boy in the eyes of many rock and roll aficionados. This was the rocker, or the menacing biker hipster, as classically portrayed, for example, by Marlon Brando in the film *The Wild One*.[10] Like the Teddy Boy image, this too was essentially a butch macho cultural style in which the core value was – in addition to the central place occupied by the search for kicks – solidarity with one's mates or gang. However, unlike the Teddy Boys, their typical dress consisted of studded leather jacket, heavy boots, broad studded belt and oil-stained denims. An identification with this image, as far as The Beatles are concerned, largely displaced that of the Teddy Boy. Indeed, it is doubtful whether the earlier identification was ever substantial; Lennon said, "they all thought I was a Ted at Art College when I arrived… But I wasn't really a Ted, just a Rocker. I was only pretending to be one" (Davies 1978: 64). Certainly, it is noticeable that, although when they first arrived in Hamburg it would appear that The Beatles were still wearing the "classic teddy boy uniform" (Inglis 2012: 33), the photographs taken later by Astrid Kirchherr reveal five young men dressed in classic rocker garb, much indeed like the majority of their audience at that time. That is to say, they were dressed in black leather jackets, black jeans, and pointed cowboy style shoes for, as Paul said, by this time they had adopted "the Marlon Brando look" (Roylance 2000: 50).[11]

Yet it is possible that the assumption that The Beatles had adopted this image could be a little misleading for there was an alternate male image to that of the arrogant, brutal, even destructive, delinquent rocker to be found in this youth sub-culture. This alternative represented the more adolescent side of the teenager, the aspect associated with the turmoil of puberty and the struggle for independence. This was the image immortalized in the person of James Dean. As George Melly describes him, he was serious, moody, sensitive, and incoherent – the genuine victim of adult misunderstanding (1970: 38). It was this image that was most clearly exemplified, during their time in Hamburg, by those who can be thought of today as the two largely-forgotten Beatles, Sutcliffe and Pete Best. As Hunter Davies puts it, "Stu wore his sunglasses on stage and looked very defiant. Pete never smiled or jumped around… but simply looked sullen and menacing. Both of them were looked upon as James Dean figures by the audience, moody and magnificent" (Davies 1978: 95). Later, when George Martin met him, he thought that Pete was, in appearance, "rather like James Dean" (Inglis 2012: 139). However, according to his sister, it was Sutcliffe who was known as "the James Dean of Hamburg" (Sutcliffe and Thompson 2002: 80).

The Beats and the hipster-rocker

It is important at this point to say something about the nature of the relationship, as it developed in the late 1950s and early 1960s, between the two different youth sub-cultures that The Beatles were involved with at this early stage in their career, that is to say the Beat-bohemians and the hipster-rockers (the latter in both their Marlon Brando and James Dean forms). On the face of it, these were not merely different but opposed forms of youthful counter-cultural deviancy or dissent, for while the bohemians had distinct aesthetic and intellectual interests, with a special taste for modern jazz, the hipster-rockers' interest did not extend much beyond gang loyalty, the search for kicks, and of course rock 'n' roll. Consequently, one would expect there to be little love lost between the two groups, with each despising the other's values, tastes, interests and indeed general outlook on life. However, there were points of contact, notably a common interest in amphetamines, coupled with a dislike of authority, especially given that both were frequently subject to police harassment. Critically there was another factor at play, one that worked during the 1960s to not exactly bring them closer together but rather to cause bohemians to admire if not actually idolize the rocker. This was the populism, or more especially, primitivism, that was such a marked feature of the bohemian worldview (Matza 1961: 112). Because of the enormous value placed on spontaneity and the simple, unselfconscious enjoyment of experience, bohemianism had tended, from its earliest beginnings, to elevate the "primitive" or "noble savage" above that of the civilized man or woman. The gypsy had been the original model for this idealization of the primitive – hence the origin of the label "Bohemian" – but successive generations had found alternative models. For the Beat generation in the United States, the primitive they tended to idealize was the "hipster" of the Northern cities. Originally this had been a young, black, urban, working-class male who, not having what most people regarded as "a proper job", tended to live off his wits (which, according to some uses of the term "hipster", could involve association with criminal underworlds). However, in the 1940s some disaffected whites had begun to imitate the quasi-outlaw lifestyle of the hipster. Hence the "white hipster", or "white Negro", was born. One consequence of this was that, by the end of the 1950s, representatives of this kind of hipster had begun to replace the original black hipsters as the ideal-type Beat folk hero. One clear sign that this was happening is revealed by the fact that both James Dean and Marlon Brando had become added to the Beats' list of "saints" by 1959 (Rigney and Smith 1961: 34). In other words, in bohemian iconography, by the time we get to the early 1960s, the "noble rocker" had come to replace the black working-class hipster as the dominant image of the idealized "natural man [sic]".

Against the background of this development, it becomes possible to understand the reaction of Hamburg bohemians Klaus Voorman, Astrid Kirchherr and Jürgen Vollmer when they first encountered The Beatles in autumn 1960. That they came across them at all was, as is generally known, something of an accident given that, under normal circumstances, none of them would have ventured near the Reeperbahn where the Kaiserkeller Club was situated, let alone have gone into the club. However, Hamburg itself, and especially the St Pauli district was, rather like Liverpool 8, something of a bohemian quarter, with a rich mix of both long-term and temporary residents.

Despite this the Kaiserkeller where, in autumn 1960, The Beatles were playing, was most certainly not a natural haunt for bohemians given that it was a hang-out for rockers. Indeed, as Klaus Voorman put it, it was "a very rough scene down there" (Davies 1978: 97), with an audience that was largely made up of "punchers" or "real toughs" as Astrid Kirchherr described them (Davies 1978: 99). Yet, given their character as German bohemians, or Exis, it becomes possible to understand the appeal that these wild and somewhat over-the-top rock 'n' roll performers might have had for these young art students. As Hunter Davies expresses it, The Beatles had a "rough, natural, undisciplined vitality" which Klaus, Astrid and their friends "were attracted to" (1978: 102). Indeed they described themselves being mesmerized by The Beatles, with Kirchherr later recalling that, "they looked absolutely astonishing" (Spitz 2005: 223), while Jürgen Vollmer said that "five mesmerizing musicians appeared before me like an explosive revelation. Each of them incarnated the image of the 'rebel without a cause' who rumbled also in my soul" (Inglis 2012: 54). Thus it was in Hamburg that The Beatles projected a rocker image of the kind that was so beloved by the bohemians. Yet of far greater significance was the fact that, as Kirchherr, Voorman and Vollmer were about to discover, the reality behind the image was that The Beatles were actually bohemians much like themselves.

The Exis

Kirchherr, Voorman and Vollmer were friends who had attended a German art college, the *Hamburg Meisterschule für Mode, Textil, Grafik und Werbung* (now the University of Applied Sciences), and just like many art students back in the UK had, as a consequence, adopted something approximating a bohemian lifestyle. They were called Exis because they regarded themselves as existentialists and consequently, as Barry Miles puts it:

> Modeled themselves on the habitués of the St-Germain-des-Pres, the Paris Left bank literary crowd that centred on Jean-Paul Sartre, Simone de Beauvoir, Juliette Greco and Albert Camus. The Exis read Beckett, Genet, Artaud and Marquis de Sade. They were students and artists; anti-establishment in a cerebral, intellectual way. They wore dark clothes, black turtleneck sweaters, tight-fitting corduroy, [and] tight black trousers. (1998: 60)

This description is endorsed by Astrid Kirchherr herself, for in 1995 she told BBC Radio Merseyside:

> We got inspired by all the French artists and writers... and we tried to dress like the French existentialists... We wanted to be free, we wanted to be different, and tried to be cool, as we call it now.[12]

In her case, "being cool" involved taking drugs – mainly Preludin, which the three of them also supplied to The Beatles – as well as painting her bedroom black, with silver foil on the walls and a large tree branch suspended from the ceiling.

The Beatles were, in their own way, equally fascinated by Klaus, Astrid and their friends. For John they were "the first Germans I ever wanted to talk to" (Davies 1978: 99), while Paul said "we were so into them and they were very artsy. They were not the first artsy people we'd seen, but they were the first unique artsy people we'd seen" (Inglis 2012: 54). None of which, as Miles observes, is in the least surprising, given that not only were Stuart and John also art students, but given their prior experience of Beats and beatniks in Liverpool, "The Exis seemed like an extension of a scene with which they were already familiar" (1998: 65). Crucially, when the Exis discovered that Stuart was not just an art student but a serious painter, while John was also an art student, there was, as McCartney put it, "this great connection" (Roylance 2000: 50). One reason that the Exis made such an impact on The Beatles was due to the fact they were older than they were. Consequently they were not meeting German art students so much as practising "bohemian artists".

It was an affinity that, significantly, led to a change in The Beatles' appearance, as for all their apparent commitment to a rocker image, they were all-too-ready to adopt elements that constituted aspects of the Exis' bohemian style, specifically the long, or longish, hair – very different in its styling from that of the Teddy Boys – the leather trousers, and the collarless jackets. In fact, as Paul put it, "we got a lot of our look from them", the Exis (Roylance 2000: 50): a look they took with them back to Liverpool and which was still part of their trademark appearance when they became internationally famous in 1963, and which would remain part of their visual identity until 1966. As Pauline Sutcliffe notes, when Brian Epstein first saw The Beatles playing at the Cavern in November 1961, wearing their leather biker jackets, leather trousers and black T-shirts, they looked "Hamburg exi (sic) rather than Liverpool Teddy" (Sutcliffe and Thompson 2002: 149).

However, crucially, it was not simply their appearance that had changed as a consequence of their time in Hamburg. For, in addition to the fact that the long hours of practice had helped them develop what Inglis calls "an independent musical identity" (Inglis 2012: 85), their contact with the Exis had also changed them as people, and hence as a group.[13] While the experience clearly had more of an effect on some than others; for example, when Stu returned to Liverpool in 1961, his friend Bill Harry thought that he had "turned into an existentialist", as he talked about Kierkegaard rather than music (Sutcliffe and Thompson 2002: 120), all were affected to some degree. What Paul has said is that the underlying feeling they had after Hamburg was that it was as if they were "an art group", that is to say being a member of The Beatles was like "being in an association with a few artistic friends", more specifically, as he notes, like a group of Beat poets, an image they were happy to present to others, if only in the form of a joke (Miles 1998: 83). Significantly, however, Paul also added that, "There was *always* an underlying ambition to go in a slightly artistic direction, whereas a lot of our fellow groups didn't have that" (Miles 1998: 84; italics added). So, one might conclude that The Beatles' contact with the Exis in Hamburg did not so much change them as give them the inspiration, and indeed the confidence, to be what, underneath, they had always been, that is to say artists of a romantic-bohemian disposition.

The Beatles become "artsy"

The extent to which The Beatles could give expression to their romantic-bohemian disposition was, however, severely curtailed by commercial realism, more specifically by the need to give their audiences, both in Hamburg and back in Liverpool, what they wanted. Hence, as Miles puts it, while they "were attracted to the Exi style... [they] didn't want to alienate either their tough Liverpool audiences or the Hamburg Rockers". Consequently they sought to combine "both Rocker and Exi in one style [as in the case of] the famous Beatles haircut" (1998: 78). Although of course it wasn't simply in the matter of their appearance that compromises of this kind were necessary. Indeed, it would appear that The Beatles realized that there were a number of hoops that they needed to jump through if they were to become successful, let alone "the toppermost of the poppermost" (see Kramer 2009: 70). Given the nature of the entertainment business in the late 1950s and early 1960s, to make it big one had to "come through show business", or as Ringo put it, "We had to go through the Shirley Bassey School, that was our battle" (Roylance 2000: 103). By this he seems to mean that they had to go through what was at that time the conventional route to success as popular performers, one that culminated in featuring on the bill at such established pinnacles of popular entertainment success as *Sunday Night At The London Palladium* and *The Royal Command Performance*. Hence, although at first they were rather reluctant, or at least some of them were, to follow Brian Epstein's dictats and smarten up their act, they nonetheless acquiesced. For, as John put it, they realized that they were faced with a choice between either, "making it or still eating chicken on stage" (Roylance 2000: 67).[14]

Evidence of artistic commitment

However, none of this meant that their bohemian artistic tendencies were necessarily suppressed. Whilst they were clearly ready, up to a point, to do whatever was necessary to become successful, they still insisted on a high degree of artistic integrity. It would seem, post Hamburg, that the idea that they were first and foremost artists rather than merely musicians or rock 'n' roll performers, was firmly fixed in their minds. It is significant in this respect that the first question McCartney put to Epstein when the latter first offered to manage them was to ask if this would mean making a difference to the way they played. Reassured that it would not, they agreed to his proposal (Epstein 1964: 51). Consequently, although Epstein took control of many aspects of their career from then on, the actual process of music making wasn't one of them. What is more, unlike many aspiring pop groups of their day, The Beatles would not agree to record all the material suggested to them, increasingly insisting on only recording their own. For, as Paul put it, when refusing to record the song 'How Do You Do It', "We're students and artsy guys – we can't take that song back to Liverpool, we'll get laughed at" (Roylance 2000: 77). Clearly, as far as John, Paul, George and Ringo were concerned, they were – as Kenneth Womack puts it – "artists, not a mere 'stage act'" (2009: 49).

It is revealing, in this context, to see precisely how often, in the years from 1964 up to their eventual break-up in 1970, one or other of The Beatles asserted that they were first and foremost "artists". For example, Paul said – apropos of just getting a fee for *A Hard Day's Night* rather than a percentage – that "we didn't really care: We're artists, we don't look back..." (Roylance 2000: 130). Sometimes the reference is to an intellectual or even a student identity, as when Paul says that as time went by, they got more and more, "into ourselves. Our student selves rather than the 'we must please the girls and make money' [selves]" (Roylance 2000: 160). Unsurprisingly, this difference soon became apparent in their lyrics, as John explained: "I had a sort of professional song-writer's attitude to writing pop songs... I'd have a separate song-writing John Lennon who wrote songs for the meat market, and I didn't consider them [the lyrics] to have any depth at all: to express myself I would write" (Roylance 2000: 157). Lennon's more introspective lyrics, clearly emerging by the second half of 1964, were in fact preceded by his first book, *In His Own Write* (1964). John himself said that he never really thought about writing a book but being a success as a Beatle gave him the confidence to do it. He said, "If I hadn't been a Beatle, I wouldn't have thought about having the stuff published. I would have been crawling around broke and just writing it and throwing it away." Intriguingly, he then adds the comment, "I might have been a Beat poet" (Roylance 2000: 134). This distinction between two types of writing quickly changed, especially after meeting Bob Dylan in August 1964. For then, as he says, "I started being me about the songs, not writing them objectively, but subjectively" (Roylance 2000: 157). John may not have become a Beat poet – although some of his lyrics might well be considered to have a poetic quality – but The Beatles themselves certainly were interested in poetry, as is revealed by McCartney's story about the volume of Yevtushenko's poetry he had been given when in Hamburg: "We were always interested in that kind of thing. We were slightly studenty. We used to make fun of the other bands that weren't... The point was that we *had* a book of poetry, it was part of our equipment. It was part and parcel of what we all liked – art" (Roylance 2000: 158; italics in original).

Bob Dylan's influence

John Lennon's comment to the effect that he might have been a Beat poet casts something of a new light on The Beatles' meeting with Dylan in August 1964. That encounter is now part of rock folklore, with special attention usually given to the fact that Dylan offered them marijuana (something they had seldom encountered before). What has not perhaps received the attention it deserves is the fact that Dylan himself was greatly influenced by the Beats, especially by Allen Ginsberg, who was a close friend. In 1985, Dylan commented that the work of the Beats "had as big an impact on me as Elvis Presley" (Wilentz 2010: 3). Moreover, Al Aronowitz, who helped to introduce The Beatles to Dylan in August 1964, had published numerous journalistic pieces on the Beats. McCartney refers to Aronowitz as having been "on the fringes of Beat generation circles since the late fifties" (Miles 1998: 187), while

George Harrison refers to both Aronowitz and Dylan as "part of a beatnik crowd", tellingly adding: "We had always liked Bohemians and beatniks. I still do – I like anyone who is not run of the mill" (Roylance 2000: 158).

Commercial success versus artistic integrity

As far as the tension between focusing on commercial success or artistic integrity was concerned, the balance had changed significantly by 1967 (the year of Epstein's death). George Martin had already commented on the fact that it was The Beatles' determination to experiment that really marked them out as "artists" (Roylance 2000: 196).[15] Giving up touring was the key step in gaining full artistic control. For as long as they were performing live there was an obvious emphasis on giving the audience what they expected to hear, while opportunities to innovate were necessarily limited. However, abandoning touring and consequently having more time to spend in the studio meant that they were free to experiment.

Intriguingly, Paul, in describing what it felt like to have been given this new freedom, compares it with another art form altogether. He says that giving up touring and spending time in the studio felt "as if we were painters who had never really been allowed to paint – we'd just had to go selling our paintings up and down the country. Then, suddenly, we had someone telling us, 'You can have a studio and you can paint and you can take your time'" (Roylance 2000: 198). This analogy, that is, the comparison of composing with painting, is made more than once. For example, John refers to 'Revolution 9' as being like "an action painting" (Roylance 2000: 307), while Paul, talking about his style of songwriting, observes that although some of his songs are based on personal experience he likes to disguise these a little. He continues, "If I were a painter, I'd probably mask things a little bit more than some people" (Roylance 2000: 339). But then it would appear that, for The Beatles, and especially for Paul and John, music was never seen as divorced from other art forms; as John expressed it, they saw themselves as "artists... [and] nothing else" (Roylance 2000: 328).

The Beatles as avant-garde artists

Bohemians are not simply people who dedicate their lives to art and are consequently prepared to make any kind of sacrifice in the process. They are also typically young people who believe in challenging the artistic standards and conventions of their time. In that respect they do not so much create works of art as engage in experimental or avant-garde art. That this was true of The Beatles in the years from 1965/66 onwards is indisputable. We have already seen that this could be said of Lennon's writings, but it was also the case with the film *Magical Mystery Tour* (1967), a film that, according to Paul, Steven Spielberg took notice of when he was in film school. Paul simply refers to it as "an art film" while George Martin called it an "avant-garde video" (Roylance 2000: 274).

Understandably perhaps, The Beatles appear to have felt a certain sense of embarrassment at the suggestion that they were seriously into the avant-garde, given their purported public identity as simple rock 'n' rollers; an embarrassment that they attempted to cover with jokes – hence John Lennon's famous comment about avant-garde being "French for bullshit", as well as George Harrison's reference to "the Stockhausen kind [of] 'avant-garde a clue' music" (Roylance 2000: 210).[16] Nonetheless, the truth was that, by 1966 at the latest, this was clearly the case, and of the four of them it was McCartney who, as Martin said, was "more avant-garde than the other boys. We always think of John as being the avant-garde one... but at that time (1966) Paul was heavily into Stockhausen and John Cage and all the avant-garde artists" (Roylance 2000: 210).

Paul McCartney and bohemian London in the 1960s

Crucially, from 1964 through to 1968, while Lennon was living a domestic family life in Weybridge, McCartney was living a bachelor's life in central London. At first, he lived in the attic room of the parents' house of his then girlfriend, Jane Asher, at 57 Wimpole Street, only moving into a house of his own, in Cavendish Avenue, in 1965. It was during this period that Paul came into contact with what Miles calls "the London avant-garde scene", or more specifically, "a demi-monde of writers, jazz musicians and junkies" (1998: 211). His main "conduit" into this scene was, as Miles calls him, a "student and intellectual" friend of Asher's brother Peter, John Dunbar (1998: 212). Dunbar's flat in Lennox Gardens was, as Miles recounts it, a meeting place for "a scurrilous counter-cultural gang of beatniks, artists and drug-takers" (1998: 216). Coming into contact with such people clearly affected Paul, who seems to have revelled in the new freedom it afforded him:

> I finally had time to allow myself to be exposed to some of the stuff that had intrigued me for a long time, since my mid-teens really, when I'd started to read about artists' experiences and that kind of culture, an inquiring culture. I might have just been reading about Madame Blavatsky or André Breton, whatever it was... but it started to awaken in me the sense that this kind of bohemian thing, this artistic thing was possible. So I used to take a lot of time for those

> pursuits... and it was nice for this to leak into the Beatle stuff as it did. (Miles 1998: 221)

Among the many things that could be said to have "leaked" in this way was Paul's interest in the music of such modern composers as Stockhausen and Cage, and yet the "inquiring culture stuff" that Paul was exposing himself to at this time embraced much more than music.

Essentially this was because of Paul's involvement with the Indica bookshop and art gallery, which was opened by Miles, Dunbar and Peter Asher in the autumn of 1965 in Mason's Yard, St James's. The bookshop concentrated mostly on "American small-press imports, books by Beat generation writers, and more serious avant-garde literature" (Miles 1998: 224), while the gallery contained art of a distinctly "way-out" variety (1998: 228). Paul was not only the bookshop's first customer but actively assisted in its initiation and promotion, while frequently providing financial support. Not surprisingly it was through the bookshop and its co-owner, Miles, that Paul was introduced to the work of the Beat poets and especially Burroughs and Ginsberg (1998: 233). Indeed, when Lennon visited the shop (in March 1966), he ended up talking about Ginsberg and the Beats with Miles (1998: 229). Paul even worked with a Beat poet, Harry Fainlight, in drawing a half-page psychedelic ad for the bookshop that was to appear in the *International Times* (1998: 238). This magazine was a crucial factor in kick-starting the underground movement of the 1960s. Finally, it is worth noting that during his period of association with Miles and the Indica bookshop, McCartney helped with the development of an experimental studio, a demo studio intended to be "available for poets and avant-garde musicians to record their work" (1998: 238). Although nothing really came of this idea it was, as Miles notes, just one of the many projects that later helped inspire The Beatles to launch Apple, or in this specific case, Zapple (1998: 239). While, as we have just seen, Paul could be said to have been the lead bohemian and experimenter in the years 1964–66, this was about to change, following the meeting between John Lennon and Yoko Ono that took place, appropriately enough, in the Indica gallery in November 1966. Yoko's importance, in this context, being the fact that she was an avant-garde conceptual artist, and it was as an experimental artist that John was attracted to her, observing that she was, in effect, "me in drag" (Wiener 2006: 136).

The Beatles and the counter-culture

With the emergence of the counter-culture in the late 1960s The Beatles' identity as bohemians becomes obvious for all to see, no longer in part disguised by their nostalgic attachment to the rocker image. Their dress, behaviour and interests show this in no uncertain terms. After all, LSD is manifestly a bohemian drug, not a teenage delinquent's drug, while interest in Eastern spirituality (as evidenced by their involvement with the Mahesh Maharishi Yogi) and the determination to engage in artistic experimentation and, if possible, shock the bourgeoisie in the process (see the Butcher album cover, and later, the 'Two Virgins'), are all classic hallmarks of a bohemian-romantic outlook on life. As too is the experiment that was Apple. This was intended as a vehicle to "help young artists so they wouldn't have the trouble we had with all the tramping around being undiscovered" (Roylance 2000: 287). In other words, this was a naïve utopian mission to provide funding for unknown artists, a kind of charity for bohemians. And typically, when the experiment descended into chaos, they indulged in exactly the kind of grand gesture that earlier bohemians would have appreciated. They gave everything away. As for The Beatles' involvement in the bohemian counter-culture and the emergence of hippies, The Beatles weren't merely catering for that movement. They were, as Paul says, "*just being part of it*", adding – significantly – "as we had always been". That is to say, they were only doing "what the kids in the art schools were all doing" (Roylance 2000: 253; italics in original), or as John expressed it, "we were just reporting what was happening to us" (Roylance 2000: 201).

The importance of art colleges

As noted earlier, of crucial importance in understanding how it was that bohemianism lay at the heart of The Beatles' sense of identity is the role of the art college, specifically the Liverpool College of Art but also, indirectly, that of the art college in Hamburg. For in the 1960s, as Frith and Horne make clear, art colleges were breeding grounds both for bohemianism and romantic attitudes to art and life. Indeed, it was because in the 1960s so many art students became rock and roll musicians, that pop music itself became "inflected... with bohemians dreams and Romantic fancies" (Frith and Horne 1987: 73). This was certainly true of The Beatles, for as Frith and Horne go on to say, "the Beatles' importance... was to keep a sense of Bohemia alive in the club [The Cavern], even as it drew a younger, lower class, more casually hedonistic crowd, and to apply an artistic attitude to these youths' concerns for style and rock 'n' roll" (1987: 85). It was this artistic attitude that differentiated The Beatles from so many of their contemporaries, for it meant they brought into the business of making music attitudes that could never have been fostered under the pressures of professional entertainment. It is for this reason that, as Frith and Horne emphasize, The Beatles prospered when virtually all their "Merseyside colleagues" were creatively stagnating, "doomed to play out their careers in performances of their old 'entertaining' hits night after night on the working men's clubs and cabaret circuit" (1987: 86). For, in their eyes, "Rock... unlike pop, was to be serious, progressive, truthful, and individual, a cluster of terms whose significance lay in the Romantic self-image of the 1960s art student" (1987: 90).

The Beatles' academic and artistic background

The very fact that The Beatles were associated with art college was itself an indication that their educational background was itself rather different from these "Merseyside colleagues". For although they were not generally regarded as especially outstanding by their teachers, Stuart Sutcliffe, John Lennon, Pete Best, Paul McCartney and George Harrison had all been quite successful in the British educational system, all five succeeding in qualifying for a place at a grammar school. This distinguished them not only from four-fifths of their age-group, who would have gone to the less academic and consequently less prestigious secondary modern schools, but from the educational background and experience of the majority of their fans. In addition, Sutcliffe and Lennon went on to further education having gained places at Liverpool College of Art, while Best passed up an opportunity to go to a training college to be a teacher in order to play with the group in Hamburg; furthermore it is very probable that Paul McCartney, if only he had had the appropriate help and advice, would have gone on to university.[17]

With educational backgrounds like these the odds were in favour of these five young men going on to a moderately successful career in a profession of some kind, which was indeed what their parents hoped – and, in so far as they could, intended – to be the case. Yet in the event this was not to be, as they either failed to go on to further or higher education, or, as in Lennon's case, dropped out before completing the course. And they did so in order to devote their lives to an unstructured and uncertain career in the arts, much against their parents' and guardians' better judgement, most of whom would have echoed John's Aunt Mimi's warning to the effect that, "The guitar's all right for a hobby, John, but you'll never make a living out of it" (Roylance 2000: 11). The fact that the majority of The Beatles dropped out of a system in which they may have been relatively successful in order to pursue what their parents and guardians clearly considered a hobby marks them out not only from most of their rock and roll predecessors on the other side of the Atlantic but also most of their contemporaries in the emerging Liverpool music scene. For, as Mike Evans observed, "John Lennon was an art student – not a truck driver like his hero Elvis Presley" (Evans 1984: 5). Billy Fury, for example, was a deckhand, Freddie Garrity a milkman, Johnny Gentle a carpenter, Billy J. Kramer an engineering apprentice, and Teddy Taylor of Kingsize Taylor and the Dominoes, a butcher's boy (Sutcliffe and Thomson 2002: 69). That the other Liverpool groups saw The Beatles as different in this respect is clear from Johnny Gustafson's dismissive reference to them as a "Bohemian clique" (Laing 2009: 22).

It is hardly surprising that John, Paul and George did better in the educational system than many of their contemporaries in the rock 'n' roll scene, since they all appeared to have had an interest in literature and the arts from an early age, an interest that, in general, seems to have predated their "discovery" of rock 'n' roll. At grammar school, Lennon neglected his class work to make obscene drawings, invent rhyming couplets and generally concentrating on his "magazine", the *Daily Howl*. It is not surprising therefore that he later remarked that he was "always a sort of poet or painter" (Roylance 2000: 56). Paul also wrote poetry at school, and had an interest in modern art (which he later indulged fully when he could afford to). Then when he was in the sixth form he discovered an interest in literature, delighting in Chaucer and reading plays by Sheridan and Shaw, as well as attending the Liverpool Playhouse and the Royal Court theatres (Miles 1998: 42). He even went to lectures at Liverpool University (Miles 1998: 43), and contemplated becoming a teacher.

Conclusion

The Beatles' career can be seen as conforming to the classic bohemian life-trajectory apart from the not inconsiderable difference that they ended up becoming phenomenally successful rather than experiencing failure and dying young. They rejected the prospect of taking up respectable middle-class professional careers, a prospect for which their backgrounds and educational experience could be said to have been preparing them, in favour of the life of itinerant musicians. By making this choice they ensured that they would experience the typically insecure, peripatetic, hedonistically inclined, yet frequently impoverished and squalid, life of the bohemian, both in the UK and in Hamburg. A life marked by a close-knit communal fellowship, as well as conflicts with authority. However, as emphasized above, unlike so many of their contemporary Merseyside rock and rollers, this decision was not made out of the simple calculation that the prospect of commercial success, no matter how remote, was better than a poorly paid manual job. Rather it followed from a pre-existing intellectual and aesthetic sensibility, evidence for which is to be found in both their personal interests as children and adolescents and in their experience of growing up in what was a bohemian quarter of Liverpool and spending their impressionable years in its cafes and bars. For this was an environment in which the local art college played a significant role and where one of their earliest engagements was as a backing group for a Beat poet. They then moved to Hamburg only to immediately fall in with another group of bohemians; in this case existentialist ex-art college students who played a major role in moulding their appearance as well as their attitudes. Finally, having been influenced by both the Anglo-Saxon Beat movement and Continental existentialism, they became the unofficial spokespersons for a new, more widespread and powerful bohemian movement, moulding it through their music, while exemplifying it in their appearance and conduct.

A superficial consideration of The Beatles' career suggests that they started out on their journey to stardom as straightforward rock 'n' rollers only ending up as fully-fledged bohemians once they had attained their life's ambition. But this is clearly not the case. For intellectual and aesthetic concerns were central to The Beatles from the very beginning, while at all stages of their career they were in close contact with either representatives or advocates of either the Beat bohemian or existentialist bohemian tradition. Consequently, for The Beatles, and especially for Paul and John, music was never divorced from the other art forms, but integral to it. Right from the early years the composing and performing of music was an activity that was integrally connected with poetry, drama, philosophy and the fine arts, while throughout their career they thought of themselves as artists and not simply as musicians, and certainly not as just performers or entertainers. And it was this basic commitment that enabled them to retain their artistic integrity even when apparently conforming to commercial requirements, just as it was this same fierce commitment to artistic integrity that largely helps to explain their phenomenal success.

Notes

1. Another important venue for Beatnik "happenings" was the basement of the Everyman Theatre, referred to by Paul Du Noyer as "the Cavern's artier cousin" (2014: 28).
2. This was the title of an article in *The People* newspaper in July 1960 that 'exposed' "the decadent lifestyle of bohemians around Liverpool 8".
3. https://www.beatlesbible.com/people/stuart-sutcliffe/
4. Lennon himself has said of the Gambier Street flat that, "it was in a terrible condition. There was no furniture, just beds" (Roylance 2000: 14).
5. McCartney has said that Sutcliffe contributed "an intellectual spirit to the group" (Sutcliffe and Thompson 2002: 98)
6. The Quarrymen regularly rehearsed in one of the Art College's life rooms and performed in the basement (Sutcliffe and Thompson 2002: 51), while the Beatles

actually performed at the Liverpool College of Art in 1959 and 1960 (Schultheiss 1980: 14).
7. http://www.dmbeatles.com/forums/index.php?topic=12852.0 (accessed 22 March 2014).
8. Ibid.
9. Intriguingly, Pauline Sutcliffe refers to Lennon wearing a long frocked black jacket "like a Mississippi gambler" (Sutcliffe and Thompson 2002: 35).
10. Brake refers to the image of the rockers as "a kind of motorized cowboy, loners and outsiders, contemptuous of authority" (1980: 77).
11. According to his sister Sutcliffe was a huge fan of Marlon Brando, regarding him as "cinema's primitive modern male" (Sutcliffe and Thompson 2002: 60).
12. Kirchherr's interview with Spencer Leigh on BBC Radio Merseyside's 500th *On The Beat* programme, Saturday 26 August 1995.
13. Interestingly, Jurgen Vollmer describes the "prefame Beatles" as "Rockers by looks and Exis at heart" (2002: 5).
14. Epstein, in addition to insisting that they wore matching suits, smiled at the audience and performed set-list of songs, also banned smoking, drinking, eating and swearing on stage.
15. The Beatles were also unusual in trying to influence the presentation of their work, for example in relation to the album sleeves for their records. For now they wanted photographs of themselves that were similar in quality to those taken by Astrid and Jürgen in Hamburg; for fundamentally, as George put it, by now they had decided to "get artistic" (Anthology 107).
16. John later admitted that he had been guilty of "intellectual reverse snobbery about avant-garde" (Miles 329).
17. Richard Starkey is of course the exception here. He does not appear to have taken the 11-plus examination, and so naturally he went to a secondary modern school.

References

Brake, Mike. (1980) *The Sociology of Youth Cultures and Youth Subcultures: Sex, Drugs and Rock 'n' Roll?* London: Routledge and Kegan Paul.
Connolly, Ray. (1981) *John Lennon 1940–1980: A Biography*. Glasgow: Fontana Paperbacks.
Davies, Hunter. (1978 [1968]) *The Beatles: The Authorized Biography: Updated to include the Beatles' solo careers*. London: Granada Publishing.
Du Noyer, Paul. (2014) "Sight and Sound: When Neighbourhoods Spawn New Genres". *Observer New Review*, 27 April: 25–28.
Epstein, Brian. (1964) *A Cellarful of Noise*. London: Souvenir Press.
Evans, Mike. (1984) *The Art of the Beatles: Exhibition Catalogue*. Liverpool: Merseyside County Council.
Forbes, P. (1960) "This is the Beatnik Horror". *The People*, 24 July: 2–3.
Frith, Simon and Howard Horne. (1987) *Art into Pop*. London: Methuen.
Grana, Cesar and Marigay Grana, eds. (1990) *On Bohemia: The Code of the Self-Exiled*. New Brunswick, NJ: Transaction Books.
Inglis, Ian. (2012) *The Beatles in Hamburg*. London: Reaktion Books.

Kramer, Howard. (2009) "Rock and Roll Music". In *The Cambridge Companion to The Beatles*, ed. Kenneth Womack, 65–74. Cambridge: Cambridge University Press.

Laing, David. (2009) "Six Boys, Six Beatles: The Formative Years, 1950–1962". In *The Cambridge Companion to The Beatles*, ed. Kenneth Womack, 9–32. Cambridge: Cambridge University Press.

Leary, Timothy. (1970) *The Politics of Ecstasy*. London: Granada.

Lennon, John. (1964) *In His Own Write*. London: Jonathan Cape.

Lipton, Lawrence. (1959) *The Holy Barbarians*. New York: Julian Messner.

Marwick, Arthur. (1998) *The Sixties: Cultural Revolution in Britain, France, Italy and the United States, c.1958–c. 1974*. Oxford: Oxford University Press.

Matza, David. (1961) "Subterranean Traditions of Youth". *Annals of the American Academy of Political and Social Science* 338: 102–118. https://doi.org/10.1177/000271626133800112

Melly, George. (1970) *Revolt into Style: The Pop Arts in Britain*. London: Allen Lane.

Miles, Barry. (1998) *Paul McCartney: Many Years from Now*. London: Vintage.

Norman, Philip. (1981) *Shout: The True Story of the Beatles*. London: Elm Tree Books.

Parkinson, Thomas, ed. (1961) *A Casebook on the Beat*. New York: Thomas Cromwell.

Parry, Albert. (1960 [1933]) *Garrets and Pretenders*. New York: Dover.

Ransome, Arthur. (1907) *Bohemia in London*. New York: Dodd, Mead.

Rigney, Francis J. and L. Douglas Smith. (1961) *The Real Bohemia: A Sociological and Psychological Study of the "Beats"*. New York: Basic Books.

Roylance, Brian, ed. (2000) *The Beatles Anthology*. London: Cassell.

Spitz, Bob. (2005) *The Beatles: The Biography*. London: Little, Brown,

Sutcliffe, Paul and Douglas Thompson. (2002) *The Beatles' Shadow: Stuart Sutcliffe & his Lonely Hearts Club*. London: Pan Books.

Wiener, Jon. (2006) "May '68: Rock against Revolution". In *Read the Beatles: Classic and New Writings on the Beatles, Their Legacy, and Why They Still Matter*, ed. June Skinner Sawyers, 135–41. London: Penguin Books.

Wilentz, Sean. (2010) "Bob Dylan, the Beat Generation and Allen Ginsberg's America". *The New Yorker*, 13 August. http://www.newyorker.com/online/blogs/newsdesk/2010/08/sean-wilentz-bob-dylan-in-america.html

Womack, Kenneth, ed. (2009) *The Cambridge Companion to The Beatles*. Cambridge: Cambridge University Press.

Websites

http://www.beatlesbible.com/people/stuart-sutcliffe/ (accessed 14 May 2014).
http://www.dmbeatles.com/forums/index.php?topic=12852.0 (accessed 14 May 2014).

Author biography

Colin Campbell is Emeritus Professor of Sociology at the University of York, UK. He is the author of a dozen books and over one hundred articles dealing with issues in the sociology of religion, consumerism, cultural change, and sociological theory. He is probably best-known as the author of *The Romantic Ethic and the Spirit of Modern Consumerism* (Macmillan, 1987; Palgrave-Macmillan, 2018). His other major publications include *Toward a Sociology of Irreligion* (Macmillan, 1971; Alcuin Academics, 2013), *The Myth of Social Action* (Cambridge University Press, 1996), *The Easternization of the West* (Paradigm Publishers, 2007), *Has Sociology Progressed? Reflections of an Accidental Academic* (Palgrave Macmillan, 2019) and *Consumption and Consumer Society: The Craft Consumer and Other Essays* (Palgrave-Macmillan, 2021). Colin has also written extensively on The Beatles; see *The Continuing Story of Eleanor Rigby: Analysing the Lyric of a Popular Beatles' Song* (Leicester: Troubador, 2018).

6 Interlude 1: Growing up with The Beatles

Russell Reising, Peter Mills and James McGrath

Professor Russell Reising is one of the leading Beatles scholars in the USA, he has written, edited and contributed to multiple volumes focusing upon or relating to the band and their times. This volume's editors, James McGrath and Peter Mills, conducted a long and winding conversation with him via the internet during lockdown. We make use of segments of it throughout this book.

In this first Interlude, the conversation begins by considering how one might 'discover' The Beatles – the routes each individual listener takes to their initial encounter with the music and the folk narrative of the band, and how innovation sounds when you hear the work as a whole rather than experience it over a decade in real time.

PM: So, Russ, you are a leading Beatles scholar but we were wondering how you got to that point. I know from my own experience that the acknowledgement of pop in academia as a legitimate subject for study is a very recent one. In fact, I kind of helped put it there. To start off, what do we think about the current reputation of the group among young music lovers?

RR: Considering their enduring influence, I just had one of my students drink some coffee with me and I asked her, I said "do you think your children will be Beatles fans?" You know my children are, because we were first-generation Beatles people and so my kids grew up hearing The Beatles all the time. Of course, there's a lot of water under the bridge now but my student said yes, she thinks so, because she absorbed The Beatles and other sixties stuff so thoroughly via her parents that it doesn't seem like fleeting or time bound to her. I've often thought that we might be the first generation to share a musical culture with our children in terms of popular music.

PM: Yes, in the same way generations of a family might all love Shakespeare or Hitchcock.

RR: My kids liked Oasis and a lot of stuff that was influenced by The Beatles so there's much more of a continuation between the music I was listening to when I was twelve, thirteen, twenty, fifty, sixty-six, but she was saying that she thought absolutely that The Beatles have that kind of staying power. She didn't speculate on why but did say among her ilk, kind of dreadlock hippy people in their early twenties, The Beatles stand up to whoever else they're listening to.

PM: My children listen to them too; I haven't really forced them on them, when they were younger I did try it actually, "here's some Lovin' Spoonful, just go away and see how happy that makes you" and they would say "yeah it's alright but I'm gonna go back to One Direction now" or whatever it was they were listening to.

RR: I have two daughters and a son so I went through the gamut. I like to say to people I started my life arguing with my parents about Bob Dylan's voice and now I'm arguing with my son about Bob Dylan's voice. I say "son, he wrote 'Blowin' in the Wind'" and back comes the reply "yeah but his voice, Dad", although my son is a hipster in every other imaginable way. It took me until *Revolver* (1966) to really make the shift from Dylan to The Beatles, to really get on board with them. Before that I thought it was great and exciting of course, but the songs weren't very different from pop music in general: my baby done left me and I feel so bad – so I thought they were the best at what they were doing but they didn't really jump out at me until I first heard 'Love You To'.

I went holy Christ, what is *this*. I was already interested in Buddhism and when I first heard that, that weird exoticism, through the whole song, not just for effect as in 'Paint It Black' (Rolling Stones, 1966), so when I first heard that I thought that these guys really have something to say now. It was that ineffable quality, the mysterious impact of the sound, and that is how I've always gravitated towards music. This is odd because I can't write about music in the formal sense – I'm not a musicologist – I write about lyrics, so I end up writing about music as poetry, yet it was never the lyrics that really captured me even if I could understand them. I never understood early Dylan stuff or early Stones stuff you know, because you could hardly hear or make out never mind understand them – but then that was part of the appeal to me.

JM: In my case growing up in the eighties it was the children's Beatles songs that brought me in – 'Yellow Submarine', song and film – and although I don't like it so much now 'Maxwell's Silver Hammer' was why I first listened to *Abbey*

Road, 'Octopus's Garden' as well, so I think that's part of this wide appeal, even for very young children there are kind of ways in.

RR: I don't know why but *Abbey Road* has always been near the bottom of my top ten Beatles albums. I think it was songs like 'Maxwell's Silver Hammer', 'Octopus's Garden' and 'Oh! Darling' that I just thought clever and humorous but they aren't 'Here Comes the Sun' or 'I Want You (She's So Heavy)'.

JM: I've enjoyed hearing the extra songs on the reissued *Abbey Road* deluxe release, especially when you hear Billy Preston more on 'I Want You'.

RR: Oh nice, nice. Well, he kind of was that sixth Beatle for a while, after George Martin. I always thought that the fifth Beatle was really the studio.

JM: I know what you're saying. But the alternate takes really showcase the input of Billy Preston.

RR: While I think Jimi Hendrix was the first person to learn to play the electrical system, that actually uses the sonic power of electricity, I think The Beatles were the first to learn and to really exploit the possibilities of the studio. By which I suppose I mean some of the accidents – you know the feedback at the beginning of 'I Feel Fine' (1965) was an accident. Parlophone had a policy forbidding feedback on any of their recordings and so they sort of had to downplay that for a while! Yet something that might have been a mistake, The Beatles were able to turn it into gold. Similarly in 'Long Long Long' you have that wine glass or a bottle vibrating on the amplifier, and you know at the end of 'A Day in the Life' you wait to hear that chair creaking and somebody going "shush!" So, these things that were accidents in the studio environment sort of become highlights of Beatles songs, I'm not sure that anybody else was ever able to give themselves the freedom to do that.

PM: Well of course, because they were at the top of the tree, they had less restrictions on studio time and could approach recording in a different spirit: the way that *Abbey Road* was made, I imagine most pop or rock albums in 1969 weren't made in that way with that kind of unlimited time. What it isn't though is the Steely Dan model – let's spend three months on four seconds of trumpet.

RR: Yeah [laughs] I was going to say one song but that was generous.

PM: So, it's understanding the environment and the environment sort of meshing with the material really: an undimming modernity.

RR: Yeah, I think that was it, in a sense. Looking at it from our perspective that was a form of the postmodern, with their own sort of surreal reflections on musical history and styles –something like 'Rocky Raccoon' or 'Oh! Darling', some of those songs were definitely looking backwards to go forwards. It almost reminds me of early Roxy Music. It was really hard to tell what era they were from. It was just really really difficult to tell where they were coming from, sort of Bryan Ferry channelling that suave Elvis thing: is it dance hall stuff or is this space music? Listen to that first Roxy album, I swear you can't tell what era the music is from.

It's not 'transhistorical', it's just so full of historical resonance that it's really difficult to pin down and I think that's one of the things that will enable The Beatles to endure long after we're all gone: The Beatles were never of their time! I mean they created the time but they were never 'of' it. A group like The Animals were, Burdon and Price, whom I loved and still love, even the Stones. Nobody defined the time and understood the future long before it happened like The Beatles did and I think in some respect people are still catching up.

PM: Yes, but the interesting thing is when you're talking about early Roxy Music, with that very deliberate sort of twining together of avant-garde techniques and a thoroughgoing knowledge and immaculate execution of historical musical styles, the mixing up of those things, there was an art agenda for them – Bryan Ferry had that 'retrofuturist' flair and signature style which was applied across the band's output. The Beatles' records had some of that but did not pursue such a deliberately crafted policy of musical and visual presentation. But in both cases, the avant-garde element flowed from much more familiar sources and means. Yet now the songs are so familiar it's harder to hear and feel the shock of the new. Take 'Tomorrow Never Knows'. Not that it's lost its power to amaze because every time I hear it I'm still stunned, but it is familiar to everyone and some of its innovations are mainstream devices now. I've known that song since I was a boy, first on a really scratched copy of *Revolver* in about 1976 and so the first time I heard it without all the noise I thought oh wow that's incredible because I didn't know what the hell were the clicks and pops and what was actually on the track.

RR: Yeah, plus I mean it was very hard for a little hifi that I had in 1967 to do anything like justice to that. Now my speakers cost fifteen thousand dollars and I get my money's worth.

Author biographies

Russell Reising is Professor emeritus at the University of Toledo, Ohio, USA. Professor Reising has taught, spoken, and published widely on topics in American literature and culture, Japanese literature and culture, popular culture and popular music. He has lived, studied, and taught all over the world, including Taiwan, Japan, Finland, England, and the United States. Russ's academic work has also resulted in his being commissioned to present workshops and lectures in England, Italy, Spain, Finland, Estonia, Bulgaria, Poland, the Czech Republic, Austria, Australia, and Japan. He was also an original member of the Educational Advisory Board at the Rock and Roll Hall of Fame and Museum. In 2008, Russ was one of only thirty Americans invited to participate in the People's Republic of China's first international literary conference.

Dr Peter Mills is Senior Lecturer in Media and Popular Culture in the School of Humanities and Social Sciences at Leeds Beckett University, UK. He has previously published on Samuel Beckett, Van Morrison and The Monkees. Peter is currently working on a series of short books on individual songs, a book chapter on the history of live music in Roundhay Park in Leeds, and an ambitious project looking to catalogue the history of live concerts at Leeds Beckett University since 1970.

Dr James McGrath is Senior Lecturer in English Literature and Creative Writing in the School of Humanities and Social Sciences at Leeds Beckett University, UK. He completed his doctoral thesis on the work of John Lennon and Paul McCartney, and his first book *Naming Adult Autism: Culture, Science, Identity* was published by Rowman & Littlefield International in 2017. His poems have been published in various literary periodicals.

Part Two
Audience, Fanhood, Interpretation

7 "My Name's Ringo and I Play the Drums": Being a Beatles' Fan in the Age of Interactivity

Stephanie Fremaux

The 21st century has seen various public initiatives and digital projects led by Beatles fans utilizing both low-tech and high-tech approaches. Examples range from the online crowdsourcing campaign in 2008 to save Madryn Street in Liverpool 8 (the location of Ringo Starr's birth home) from demolition, to the high-tech success of Rock Band: The Beatles *(2009), and fan-generated sites such as* The Beatles: Live At The Internet. *To study the effects of user-generated opportunities provided by digital media on audiences and fandom, an interdisciplinary approach is required, drawing on celebrity and popular music research, as well as performance theory and digital media studies. By using the above examples as case studies of the many ways in which Beatles fandom is manifesting itself in a digital age, this chapter argues that digital media has allowed music audiences a new sense of ownership created through performance and user-generated content.*

Introduction

Since 2012, there have been a number of 50th anniversary commemorations around key milestones in The Beatles' career as unprecedented pop stars (1962–1970). While these events have been celebrated both in public and through a slew of consumer products available for fans to complete their ever-growing collections of Beatles memorabilia, there have also been several interesting public initiatives and digital projects led by fans utilizing both low-tech and high-tech approaches. Such examples include the ways in which fans have interacted somewhat unconventionally with the metal outline Beatles statues at Beatles-Platz (Square) in Hamburg, Germany, and the "do it yourself" (DIY) campaign using a crowd-sourced funding platform to save Madryn Street in Liverpool – the location of Ringo Starr's birth home – from demolition by the city council. Other, more high-tech examples of Beatles fandom include the popularity of the *Rock Band: The Beatles* (2009) video game and fan-generated websites such as *The Beatles: Live at the Internet* in which fans are either able to become their heroes through the virtual reality of game play or experience a virtual performance by a band no longer able to play live. These initiatives demonstrate that even in the age of digital media, a band from a time of analogue that broke up decades ago is still relevant to fans' sense of identity and self. Much of the work that has previously examined popular music and fandom has drawn on the invaluable work produced by Simon Frith's research on popular music history and the relationship between the industry and young consumers' consumption habits (see Frith 1981, 1988, 1996, 2007). This research, along with P. David Marshall's (1997, 2000) work on the meanings of popular music performance and celebrity, has been the inspiration and foundation of this author's work and teaching over the past decade. However, with more recent developments in the way that present-day audiences and fans have started engaging with all media as content creators, it has become increasingly difficult to draw on Frith and Marshall without considering the work around fandom by scholars such as Henry Jenkins (2006a, 2006b), Jonathan Gray et al. (2007), and Cornell Sandvoss (2005). Their respective works on participatory culture, new definitions of fandom, and the ways in which audiences have become active and interactive (rather than passive) contributors and authors of content to the changing media landscape have opened up new dimensions when applying Frith and Marshall's research to the analysis of popular music texts. The effects of user-generated opportunities provided by digital media on audiences and fandom have prompted this chapter's research to incorporate an interdisciplinary approach that draws on celebrity and popular music research as well as that of performance theory and digital media studies with the objective of building on these cornerstones of popular music scholarship to open up new avenues for discussion and enquiry.

Arguably, easy-to-use software and social media platforms have created a paradigm shift from a largely consumer-based mode of fan consumption to one where the new currency is exchanged in user-generated content developed through knowledge and skill. For fans sharing their fandom on the internet, labour is considered to have the same value as money in the marketplace (see Lessig 2004; Barton and Lampley 2013). By using the above examples as case studies of the many ways in which Beatles fandom is manifesting itself in a digital age, this chapter argues that digital media has allowed music audiences a new sense of ownership created through performance and user-generated content. In this way, an interdisciplinary approach can help to achieve a clearer understanding of how Beatles fandom has continued to thrive as well as how, through strong ties to identity and (performance of) the self, Beatles fans are not identified merely as "fanatic" consumers, but as having a vested interest in inserting themselves more equally into the Beatles' story. Beatles fandom is not just a reaction or element of Beatlemania, but instead fans are co-owners in keeping the Beatles' legacy alive and relevant.

Context: Popular music and fandom

One of the concepts in Frith's work on popular music is the examination of music in young people's lives. Frith has charted the developments in the music industry from the 1960s onwards alongside the evolution of the teenager into the youth culture and associated subcultures (1981, 1988, 2007). In particular, Frith's work has examined the link between teenagers and youth and how they spend their leisure time and disposable income, stating how the dance halls in the early 20th century, for example, were "an early recognition of teenage culture in which pop music and youth consciousness were integrated in a process eventually symbolized by rock 'n' roll" (1981: 203). From this example, Frith (1981) acknowledges that youth and popular music have a long, shared history but argues that many sociologists before him ignored why the two have gone hand in hand. In *Sound Effects* (1981: 205–206), Frith addresses this by conducting interviews with samples of young people; he found that although tastes differ, what the students listened to represented a strong sense of individualism. Furthermore, Frith (1981: 208) notes how these individual tastes "become a group of individualists and need the symbols and friends, and institutions, to assert themselves as a group". While this basic principle would prove to be true for years to come, focusing on the impact of digital technology and the shifts in celebrity culture, the case studies presented in this chapter highlight the new ways in which audiences "assert themselves as a group" and the effect this has had on the relationship between audience and artist. For example, Kerr et al. (2004 cited in Crawford and Rutter 2007: 276) argue that the importance of digital media for fans has allowed them the opportunity to experiment "with alternative identities". Not only does this reinforce the performativity afforded by new media, but it also suggests that a person's identity is no longer fixed by how they dress and the music genre associated with that style. The examples chosen for this chapter each illustrate the performative nature of interactivity on either a low-tech or high-tech scale that invites the ordinary, everyday fan to "become", if briefly, their favourite artist. This idea can be supported by once again considering Marshall's (2000: 164) definition of celebrity in which he suggests that "celebrities are sites for the play of identification and identity". Taking this into account, these examples of fan interactions represent opportunities to vicariously try on that artist's public persona with potential layers of meaning integrated into the performance depending on that fan's depth of knowledge about that particular artist. In addition, Frith (1988: 12) argues that "songs and singers are fetishized, made magical, and we can only reclaim them through possession, via a cash transaction in the marketplace". While there is no argument against singers and their songs being fetishized and mythologized, this idea is problematized by what is meant by reclaiming these singers through "possession".

As evidenced by the high levels of pirating of media content online, and an increased awareness by the public around copyright law and intellectual property infringement, it is clear that digital media and social network spaces no longer value the traditional monetized currency system under which capitalist society operates. Rather, these online spaces trade in knowledge and creativity whether the law deems it legal or (as is often the case) not. This idea is evidenced in Pierre Lévy's (1994) thesis on collective intelligence, with Jenkins (2006b: 18) arguing that collective intelligence is used by consumers through the use of "different media technologies to bring the flow of media more fully under their control and to interact with other consumers". The participatory culture brought about by digital media has created a shift in importance from possession as ownership of a physical artefact (record, t-shirt, gig ticket) to possession as (in)vested interest in the artist's copyrighted material. For instance, contemplating how "technological changes raise issues of power and manipulation", Frith (2007: 82) asks, "how does the ownership of the technical means of production relate to the control of what is produced? Do technological developments threaten or consolidate such control?" Arguably, it is no longer enough simply to express fandom or solidarity via the marketplace, as audiences are now placing a more equal status on their role in an artist's success – and easy-to-use, readily accessible technology is a major factor in giving audiences a more equal footing in that relationship.

This shift from a monetary currency in the physical marketplace to one of a knowledge-based currency in the digital sphere could also be a result of the changing and often problematic definitions of fandom. Most fan scholars point to Abercrombie and Longhurst's (1998) work on audiences to set up a base definition for fandom to work around (see Gray 2003; Hills 2002; Ross and Nightingale 2003; Sandvoss 2005). While Hills (2002: ix), for example, notes the importance of that work which designates audiences as "fans", "cultists" and "enthusiasts", he also argues that it is not particularly helpful to spend too much time proposing "rigorous definitions" (Hills 2002: xi). There are also scholars such as Sandvoss (2005) and Grossberg (2006) who write about the tendency for fans to evoke negative connotations – those people who are obsessed or seen as "cultural dopes" (Grossberg 2006: 582). While such research does not propose an all-encompassing definition of fans, it does operate on the basis that fans are a positive and influential factor in the relationship between media production and media consumption. In addition, it also works on the basis that a large part of being a fan and expressing fandom relies on the ability to use media artefacts as "an expression of their own lived experience" and as a way "to construct new identities for themselves" (Grossberg 2006: 582). In this way, fandom is "always performative" and fluid (Hills 2002: xi). As these case studies will show, whether the activity is low-tech or high-tech, fans can no longer rely solely on the traditional modes of fandom which have included purchasing merchandise or attending a live performance/gig. Instead, fans' conditioning brought on by the internet and social media toward personalized experiences and greater opportunities for "performing" different (and sometimes new) aspects to their personality are influencing how they interact with media artefacts. The effect is not to achieve close proximity to or an acknowledgement by the object of fandom, but a realized opportunity to try on the identity of the object of fandom – to become, if briefly, that object of fandom.

Arguably, in the case of Beatles fans, this opportunity existed as early as 1963 when merchandise such as artificial mop-tops, boots and sweaters could be purchased to replicate The Beatles' look. What has changed is the relationship between performance and the self, and how we have become curators of our digital self through social media. There is also a mainstream acceptance of and growing popularity in costume play (cosplay), which acts as a physical extension of an aspect of the participant's identity. Furthermore, where mop-tops and Beatle sweaters were arguably marketed to a younger audience, today's cosplay is not restricted to a particular age group. Grossberg (2006: 590) differentiates between consumer and fan, noting the worth of a fan's investment of energy, as this energy "always returns some interest on the investment through a variety of empowering relations" including ways in which fans feel "control over his or her life" and can "be someone". Perhaps what is most important to emphasize is Grossberg's (2006: 590) argument that fans can truly feel "empowered in the sense that they are now capable of going on, of continuing to struggle to make a difference", which is arguably amplified by the effects of a celebrity focused culture and the "broadcast yourself" nature of social media.

The second concept (the first relating to the means of technical production), relevant to this re-evaluation of Frith and Marshall is the scholarship centred on the live music performance. Both scholars place importance on the live performance as a way not only of promoting new material, but of connecting fans and the artists performing due to the physical proximity of being in a shared performance space, and due to a set of codes that dictate actions performed by both parties present. Frith (1988: 135) argues that "the most important rock event is the *live* performance, where performers and audiences genuinely react to each other" (original emphasis). In addition, Marshall (2000: 166) states that live performance creates "a form of solidarity with the performing group", citing The Beatles' 1965 performance at New York's Shea Stadium as the time when "the moment of the crowd was ultimately more significant" than the physical proximity to the stage or even the quality of The Beatles' performance. Furthermore, Marshall (1997: 159) defines the pop music concert as "not an introduction to the music for the fans, but a form of ritualized authentication of pleasure and meaning of the records through a 'lived' experience". Marshall (1997: 159) continues by noting the emotive value of live performance, asserting that the live performance gives an opportunity for "display and expression by the audience" to create a "celebration of the performer". After The Beatles resolved to cease playing live following their last scheduled concert on 29 August 1966, at San Francisco's Candlestick Park, an unprecedented challenge was faced by the band's manager Brian Epstein, as well as for their label EMI, as to how The Beatles were to remain in the public eye and also remain connected to their fan base. Live performance had become not just the tool that helped The Beatles to hone their musical chops in the seedy clubs in Hamburg or in the underground Cavern Club in Liverpool; it also became a key element of their Beatlemania image, as evidenced by George Harrison's famous comment after the Candlestick Park gig, "Well, that's it. I'm not a Beatle anymore" (Julien 2009: 1). By the time the band left behind Hamburg and the Cavern to play to larger venues full of screaming fans, the band felt that live performance was starting to have an adverse effect on their musical development. There was never an official announcement that they would stop touring or playing live, but as a result of the increased aversion to live performance and its close association with Beatlemania, Harrison would continue to resist Paul McCartney's attempts to convince the band to play live, even if it was just a one-off gig, until the band took to the Apple Corps rooftop in January 1969 as depicted in the documentary *Let It Be* (Michael Lindsay-Hogg, 1970). Marshall's (1997: 161) assessment of the function of live performance continues:

> The star's cultural power depended on a very close affinity with a specific and loyal audience. The star, then, was actively engaged in the construction and differentiation of audience groups, in terms

of style and taste, and in authenticating their elevated position. The popular music star, more than other forms of celebrity, had to be a virtual member of his or her own audience in order to sustain his or her influence and authenticity, and the commitment of the fan.

Arguably, the Beatles stopped performing live because it hindered them from "authenticating their elevated position"; indeed, much of the music they began producing from 1966 onwards proved to be too complex to play onstage without the help from other musicians not officially part of the collective. While The Beatles maintained their popularity after they stopped touring, when they did reappear for their final aforementioned live rooftop performance, it is clear to see that the onscreen audience's reaction from the streets below is mainly subdued and prompted out of curiosity. Although the 1969 performance was not given advance publicity, it is symbolic that the mere curiosity shown by passers-by does not come close to replicating the scenes of hysteria with the throngs of screaming girls blocking traffic in the streets of London five years earlier. In this way, The Beatles had not sustained their influence or their authority, during which the commitment of the fans had begun to wane.

For many music fans, the live performance is a rite of passage not only in terms of age and maturity, but in terms of crossing over from admirer to dedicated fan. Recall the scene in *Almost Famous* (Cameron Crowe, 2000) for example, when Billy's mother nervously drops him off at his first rock concert and instructs him of the exact time and location that she will be back to collect him. Her view is that the rock concert is a venue for all the hedonistic pleasures stereotypically associated with popular music and rock in particular. Nowhere is the importance of attending a gig and the communal experience it provides truer than in today's increasingly popular three-day music festivals; the price of gig tickets often soars into the hundreds of pounds. Yet, what happens when a popular band refuses to continue touring or is no longer able to perform live, as is the case with The Beatles? How are fans able to equal the solidarity on display at a rock show when the public displays associated with live performance (the cheering, clapping in time, the sing-a-long, personal acknowledgement by the lead singer to the crowd, the air guitar, and the shared emotions conveyed in the crowd setting) no longer have an official space to be displayed acceptably? Writing about the role of technology in theatre performance, Christie Carson (2006: 181) explains that it is "digital technology and the Internet" that are now bridging the gap between performer and audience today by allowing for "a two-way form of communication which extends beyond polite applause" and that it is through this use of digital technology that performers can "redefine their relationships with their audiences... and as a result, [redefine] their public image". However, this can raise some questions over how many times that public image can be redefined and what effect that may have on an artist's history. This is an issue relevant to all of the examples presented here. Those previous models of fandom offered by Frith and Marshall are arguably limited due to the focus on live performance which is often led by the artist. Instead, what Carson (2006: 181) points to is a relationship that becomes more "participatory [and] non-hierarchical" by embracing, rather than dismissing or fearing, the developments allowed by technology that allow fans to become producers and performers themselves.

Mop-tops at the ready: Becoming a Beatle, Step 1

While conducting primary research on the function of the now closed Beatlemania museum in Hamburg, Germany in 2010, it was surprising to observe not only how interactive the museum was in terms of replicating the Beatlemania experience for visitors, but how fans were interacting with displays in rather low-tech ways (Fremaux and Fremaux 2013). One of the more poignant examples was the interaction observed at Beatles-Platz just outside of the museum. The square features metal silhouette outlines of the five original members including drummer Pete Best and bassist Stuart Sutcliffe. Passers-by, young and old, were placing their bodies within the metal outline of their favourite Beatle while pretending to perform as their photograph was taken. These actions were repeated throughout the day without any prompting or instruction. Witnessing these interactions immediately prompted questions around performativity and the idea of playing with identity as part of pop music celebrity. Marshall's definition of celebrity includes elements that are applicable not just to the rich and famous, but to the average person as well. For example, celebrity can be "a presentation of the self for public consumption which accommodates something private and personal" (Marshall 2000: 163). Since The Beatles are no longer able to perform live as a collective and the chances to see the surviving members of the group are becoming increasingly more expensive and difficult, are ordinary, everyday music fans filling the concert experience void by taking on the performance role once filled by their favourite artist(s)? As Jenkins (2006b: 144) attests, "knowledge cultures" will "gradually alter the ways that commodity culture operates". Though the Beatlemania museum was part of the commodity culture, the low-tech opportunities to interact allowed fans to create meaningful and personalized connections to the long defunct band.

The Beatlemania museum was located in the heart of the Reeperbahn area, where The Beatles performed in clubs such as the Kaiserkeller, the Star Club, and the Top Ten Club at various points between 1960 and 1962. The museum contained five floors of memorabilia, artefacts, and opportunities for interactivity in an attempt to recreate a sense of the heady and liberating spirit of rock 'n' roll in the Reeperbahn of the 1960s and to reinforce the mythology of the band once they made it big as the Fab Four. The journey the museum visitor took was a chronological one, starting on the fifth floor by going through an "immigration process" that included a passport photograph booth in which the visitor could have the mop-top of their choice superimposed over their photograph. This was the first low-tech step in the visitor "becoming" their favourite Beatle. After strolling along the reconstructed Große Freiheit, the visitor walked the steps down to the next floor, which contained a mock-up of a recording studio complete with a karaoke-style machine that allowed the visitor to select a Beatles song and to record their own vocals over the backing track. While many may argue this activity is merely a glorified version of a karaoke night at the local pub, the replica studio booth setting and the journey motif of the museum's layout helped to lend a sense of "value, meaning, purpose, personal identity, and (em)power(ment)" to this musical performance (Peters 2008: 4). These signifiers are achieved through the importance of music placed on the visitor's life. As Bloustien et al. (2008: xxv) note, "Performing someone else's music allows us to express our feelings although we are different people". In this way, the consumer can also be considered a producer by creating something that is distinctively unique. For instance, the visitor who interacted with the recording booth was able to inject the performance of their chosen song with their own experiences and personal style, as well as the chance to mimic key patterns or styling used by the lead singer on the original recording. Once the take had been captured, the visitor later had the opportunity to purchase their effort on a memory stick in the gift shop for €15, thereby creating a scenario where the producer once again becomes the consumer.

As Frith (1988) and Marshall (1997) rightly pointed out, new recordings need to be promoted through touring. The visitor to the museum was prompted to move along to the next section of the exhibition – a section called "Beatlemania" which consisted of a large rectangular white space with two chairs in the middle facing a blank wall. When seated, the concert footage from The Beatles' Shea Stadium concert was projected on the wall in 4:3 aspect ratio before the aspect ratio began to widen to the point where the footage was projected on the surrounding walls and ceiling, while the audio of screaming fans became louder. In this way, the visitor was given some sense of the overwhelming and deafening experience of what it was like to attend a Beatles' concert with the visitor being immersed both visually and sonically. The clip deconstructed the elements of a classic Beatles' performance to illustrate how the performer-spectator interaction central to live performance had broken down (Kelly 2007: 105–106). There is a lack of physical proximity for fans onscreen as they are kept far from the stage by large metal barriers, and there is also a lack of proximity for the audience of the footage as The Beatles are replaced by extreme close ups of screaming fans. The screams from fans completely drown out the band's performance, giving the visitor an understanding of The Beatles' increased frustrations with playing live (the band argued that their development as musicians was being hindered and that the quality of their playing had diminished due to the inability to hear each other through the onstage monitors [Rodriguez 2012]). Like The Beatles, escaping into their *Sgt Pepper* personas, the museum visitor could then retreat to a *Sgt Pepper*-themed area on the next floor down, in a space that was highly interactive on a low-tech level. In addition to the usual video monitors that play interviews with key members in the Beatles' entourage and display archive footage, there was a very large replica of the *Sgt Pepper's Lonely Hearts Club Band* (1967) album cover. There was no instruction on how to interact with this piece, so the visitor could seemingly be free to either place themselves in the space at the back between Edgar Allan Poe and Fred Astaire or pose at the front of the cover holding one of the instruments on display. Strategically placing oneself in front of a chosen Beatle could block them out entirely from the photograph, changing The Beatles' line up to John, Paul, George, and… [insert your name here].

The last element of interactivity found at the Beatlemania museum and that still exists today is the row of five metal statues outside Beatles-Platz. Because the statues are outlines, passers-by can easily pose with these works of art in a new and engaging way that allows one to briefly "try on" a different persona – that of their favourite Beatle. Not only does this present an opportunity for fans to interact with the statues, but it also enables them to interact with each other, even when those also posing are complete strangers. Of all the passers-by posing with the statues observed over the course of a day, none simply stood next to a statue or placed their arm around it. Instead, everyone observed placed their body within the outline of a chosen statue and in many instances pretended to strum the guitar or grasp the drumsticks. This low-tech "performance" creates the greatest sense of closeness and physical proximity afforded to Beatles fans replicating some of the basic conventions of attending a live performance (Kelly 2007; Marshall 2007). In addition, it was interesting to note that no one posed with the statue of Stuart Sutcliffe, the original bass player of The Beatles who left the group in 1961 to stay in Hamburg and who later died of a brain haemorrhage in 1962, a day before The Beatles' return to the Reeperbahn. While the museum attempted to provide insight into Sutcliffe's life, work as a painter, and role within The Beatles, outside at Beatles-Platz the casual Beatles fan and passer-by is left unaware of Sutcliffe's history. If the consumer as producer/creator has a platform not only to act out different identities, but to share them as well, there is a risk for "the potential breakdown of the real and the fictional as distinct categories" (Auslander 2006: 196). In this way, The Beatles as the "Fab Four" are further mythologized by fans' prior knowledge and limited experience of The Beatles' legacy in a way that could potentially rewrite elements of the band's history.

What was most noticeable about the Beatlemania museum's layout and exhibition space was the lack of physical barriers and floor staff, allowing visitors to touch and interact with displays without feeling restrained or uncomfortable about what the "rules" might be. Even when it was not completely certain if some aspects were designed to be interactive, or when it was not clear how to interact, the museum left the visitor to experiment with play and performance in a way that allowed the visitor to question their sense of identity by exploring their relationship with The Beatles and their music and to share those thoughts with fellow companions/visitors. Often the ability to interact in a way that lets the user/visitor/consumer play and perform in some way greatly outweighs the "quality or significance of the interactions taking place" (O'Grady 2011: 146). The focus for this type of interaction is on interpretation and meaning created by that visitor, which is informed by their knowledge, making the experience more personalized. Being given the opportunity to explore and interact "provides an additional layer to how we experience and shape our own existence and identity" (ibid.). Gibson and Connell's (2007: 175) research on Graceland, Elvis Presley's former home in Memphis, Tennessee raises issues in the use of the audio-guided tour, noting that "the mood is sombre, bodies stop in the space... visitors resist the temptation to talk or laugh". Increasingly, that type of experience will arguably be a thing of the past as users' engagement and interaction with digital media begin to dictate new social codes of conduct. As Jenkins (2006a: 24) asserts, "audiences, empowered by these new technologies... are demanding the right to participate within the culture". This right is being asserted not just within the marketplace but also in digital and virtual spaces where the user is empowered through performance to tell/experience the story on their terms.

Own Ringo's house: Becoming a Beatle, Step 2

Another key example of an initiative which takes control of Beatles heritage and the Beatles' story out of the museum and into the hands of the ordinary fan is the Save Madryn Street campaign. 9 Madryn Street in the Dingle, an area in Toxteth, Liverpool, was the birth home of Ringo Starr, who resided in the property until he was five. His aunt had also lived a little further down the short street in number 21. However, in 2005, Liverpool City Council first announced the intention to demolish the rows of streets in the area known as the Welsh Streets, which included Madryn Street. The proposal was part of a regeneration plan associated with the regeneration of Liverpool leading up to the city's year as European Capital of Culture in 2008. On 18 September 2010, a formal demolition order was posted on Madryn Street and local tour guide Phil Coppell became the chairman of the Save Madryn Street campaign. The campaign gained momentum in working with Save Britain's Heritage and a reprieve came from then Shadow Housing Minister, Grant Shapps. It was thought in 2012 that Madryn Street had been saved. However, in 2014, Save Britain's Heritage were still fighting a public inquiry to try to overturn the city council's decision to demolish Madryn and other nearby streets (Save Britain's Heritage 2014).

Beatles fandom on the internet has become more sophisticated since the days of free web-hosting services like Geocities, where like-minded "neighbourhoods" of web-based fans created pages of Beatles-related GIF animations, screen grabs, MIDI sound files, and wallpapers. The development of social media has now superceded Geocities as a form of interaction. There are only a handful of worthwhile, fan-run (and regularly maintained) Beatles sites on the internet today, including the British Beatles Fan Club where members receive four high-quality magazines a year (as well as discounts and other member benefits); another valuable resource is the *Beatles and Beyond* weekly internet radio show produced and hosted by Peter Dicks which is available for free on iTunes. These are examples of fans' knowledge and time being spent as capital investment into the larger pool of Beatles' fandom. Costs are kept low or generated through advertisement space in order to finance the production of the media artefact. However, the Save Madryn Street campaign, in conjunction with Save Britain's Heritage, takes this notion of ownership a step further by harnessing the participatory culture and politically active nature of social media to set up a crowdfunding solution encouraging Beatles fans and conservationists to step in where the city council, private sector, and public sector initiatives like the Heritage Trust have refused. Since the success of crowdfunding platform Kickstarter, which launched in 2009, a number of similar crowdfunding platforms have sprung up on the internet to encourage a public sphere inspired community to help fund a variety of projects and initiatives. From supporting budding artists to raising funds for film projects by established Hollywood stars, crowdfunding projects like those on Kickstarter have funded tens of thousands of creative projects (see "Seven Things..." 2014). Not only does the Save Madryn Street campaign represent the ways in which do it yourself (DIY) fandom has moved to a global platform, it also represents the idea of fans as part investors in a real piece of (in this instance) Beatles history. With most crowdfunding, there are different levels of benefits awarded to investors based on how much is donated. For a mere £50, those donating to the Save Madryn Street campaign will receive a special postcard and poster, as well as an invitation to the campaign party at the Empress Pub (featured on the cover of Starr's first solo album, *A Sentimental Journey*, 1970). The added bonus for donations at this level is to be named in the official report on the public inquiry as an acknowledged campaigner.

Save Madryn Street proved a successful campaign. Most of its houses, including the former home of Starr, still stand.[1] Referring back to Grossberg (2006: 584), there are still "consumer sensibilities" at play in the Save Madryn Street campaign. However, these are not marketplace transactions under a traditional business model. For example, these investments will not directly benefit The Beatles or their Apple Corps empire. Furthermore, fans investing knowledge, time and money in this way are no longer dependent upon an industry or celebrity figurehead to "embody the power of the audience members" (Marshall 2006: 636). Even Marshall (2006: 642) admits that the old commercial-based "economic models have been challenged" as commercial products are no longer at the centre; the "production of the self" has taken over due to "new media forms of presentation over representation" (2006: 644). Arguably, this emphasis on performance and presentation of the self through social media elevates the fan to a more equal footing with the artist, rather than the previous pressures on fans to show their level of fandom by owning every piece of Beatles related merchandise (officially released or otherwise). Even at the 2014 International Business Festival, which took place in Liverpool and included a "Business of the Beatles" Symposium at Liverpool Hope University, the emphasis was on sharing knowledge rather than sizing up collections. For instance, those in attendance had the opportunity to have conversations with Roag Best (Pete Best's half-brother and son of former chief executive of Apple Corps Neil Aspinall), Martin King (managing director of The Beatles Story museum), and Bill Heckles (of Cavern City Tours). These examples of direct fan involvement reinforce the authority that fans gain through their investment. According to Grossberg (2006: 587) there is also a link between this investment and the construction of a fan's identity.

Get blisters on your fingers: Becoming a Beatle, Step 3

Jenkins's (2006a: 24) assertion that empowered audiences are increasingly demanding to participate within an artist's career in more substantial ways is represented in the rising mainstream popularity of the video game culture. *Rock Band: The Beatles* was developed by Harmonix shortly after its acquisition by MTV Games, and the development of the project was carefully overseen by Apple Corps with input from the surviving Beatles and representatives of the deceased members' families. The release of the game and bundle packages which included the game cartridge plus a choice of replica instrument controllers used by one of the band members (Lennon's Rickenbacker rhythm guitar, McCartney's Höfner bass, Harrison's Gretsch electric guitar, or Starr's Ludwig drums) on the memorable date of 09.09.09, coincided with the release of the band's entire back catalogue of official UK album releases re-mastered in stereo and mono audio formats. Coinciding with the releases, Apple Corps added a variety of products to satisfy the demand and buzz generated by the marketing campaign, and the nature of these products firmly establish the band's adaptability to the new digital landscape. Arguably, The Beatles had always been at the forefront of technological experimentation within the recording studio, even when such ventures received a lukewarm response from fans and critics. It is rare for The Beatles franchise to authorize the use of the band's licensed material for "out of house" use but the success of the *Guitar Hero* and *Rock Band* series was too great to ignore. Both McCartney, and Lennon's widow Yoko Ono, have commented on the association between video games and the younger generation. McCartney noted how the idea to get involved with the *Rock Band* project was through Harrison's son Dhani "who's a gamer and he's of the generation", while Ono felt it was a way of getting The Beatles' music and "message" to "the current generation – and beyond", citing video games as "an incredible revolution" (M. Miller 2009: 42). Throughout their career, The Beatles have been able to engage with fans of all ages on different levels. For example, their carefully constructed mop-top image enabled the band to be deemed acceptable by parents and the establishment, and their mature and thoughtful lyrics along with their wit and humour contributed to their popularity with older audiences. Similarly, The Beatles' version of the *Rock Band* series is constructed in a way that is appealing to loyal fans who might not be gamers as well as newer audiences familiar with the *Guitar Hero* format.

For those unfamiliar with the *Guitar Hero* and *Rock Band* titles, the premise is based around rock musicians, represented by onscreen avatars who build their career from playing small bars and clubs to working their way up to rock stardom in "tour" mode. What differentiates *Guitar Hero* from *Rock Band* is that *Rock Band* allows for multiple players as well as vocalists. Players of both series can also choose training or practice modes in which single songs can be selected from lists categorized as "easy", "medium" and "expert". This option gives those fans new to gaming the opportunity to enjoy game play while feeling a sense of progression and achievement as they learn the controls and finger techniques required. On the other hand, more seasoned gamers are satisfied by the challenges of the levels which "provide exciting situations to experience, stimulating puzzles to engage with, and interesting environments to explore" (Birringer 2006: 48). The more skilled the player becomes, the more they are rewarded with rare archive content that becomes unlocked throughout the game. Both titles and their sequels rely on permission from the license holders to use original versions of classic rock tracks by artists such as Metallica, Van Halen, Foghat, Kiss, Alice Cooper, and many, many more. However, *Rock Band: The Beatles* was the very first to feature a sole act and selections spanning their entire back catalogue. The Harmonix developers not only worked closely with the Beatles but also with producer Giles Martin, son of original Beatles' producer George Martin, to overcome the technical hurdles required to separate out the different tracks on each recording in order to be able to make playing along work in the game. As a result of the care and attention to detail at each stage of the development process, *Rock Band: The Beatles* provides an accurate portrayal of the Beatles' history and legend. For example, both McCartney and Starr were asked to verify and approve the trivia unlocked by adding up bonus points during the levels. For McCartney, it was a chance to clear up misconceptions that had become fan mythology (M. Miller 2009: 42). This attention to detail provides a more authentic experience for the player to be transported into, "thus producing a sensation of being 'in the scene'" (Birringer 2006: 46). Represented within the game are accurate depictions of locations such as the Cavern Club in Liverpool, the set of *The Ed Sullivan Show*, Shea Stadium in New York, the Budokan arena in Tokyo, and the rooftop of the Apple Corps building in London. The Beatles' post-touring years are represented by a mixture of scenes from Abbey Road studios and fictional psychedelic dreamscapes inspired by the band's later recordings.

In creating an authentic visualization of The Beatles' history, the game fills (and perhaps capitalizes on) the void left by the fact the Beatles will never again perform live, in the flesh. Instead, the function and codes associated with live performance are left to be adopted by the identity assumed by the player(s) and the way in which they interact with the controller, onscreen gameplay, and where relevant, with other players participating in the performance. Video game theory scholars such as Smith (2004), Newman (2005), Kelly (2007) and K. Miller (2009) have all considered the significance of not only how game players interact with the onscreen narrative or action, but also what happens to the players' sense of self and identity during game play. For example, Munday (2007: 55–56) notes the importance of the player(s) feeling immersed, "cocooned" even, in order to "lose themselves in the game" and that it is music "that contributes to the player's sense of immersion". This is conceivably made all the more easier due to the game player's familiarity with at least the earlier tracks and undeniable hits included in the Beatles edition of the series. Once the player is immersed into the virtual game world, interactivity arguably allows the player to feel as though they have become their chosen Beatle. As Marshall (2006: 640) notes, the sophistication of the development of these games where players can choose their avatar and customize that look enable the player to "conjoin the game identity with their own". In terms of proximity, audience and performer have become one by sharing the same performance space and by making the same movements to (re)create music. While the player cannot design their own avatar with this specific title, they can choose which replica controller to use, physically self-identifying as their chosen Beatle. In this way, "the avatar becomes the extension of the physical self" (Wood 2011: 18). The television commercial released by MTV Games to promote *Rock Band: The Beatles* reinforces this notion that players can, if not feel like their favourite Beatle during game play, be on a more equal level with their musical heroes in a way that they are not able to fulfil in real life. The 30-second spot begins by showing The Beatles walking across the Abbey Road pedestrian crossing as immortalized on their 1969 release of *Abbey Road*. The song chosen as a soundtrack for the advertisement is 'Come Together' which acts as a sonic cue for the multicultural throng of people young and old who appear at the crossing with the band members. But rather than simply walking across the street mimicking the event, the camera focuses on particular members of the crowd interacting with and talking to each Beatle as if on an equal level. For example, one little girl hands Harrison the replica Gretsch guitar as he proceeds to examine it with great curiosity. The tagline "meet the Beatles, rock the world" is voiced over the end of the advertisement. Moltenbrey (2010: 34) argues that being able to buy upgraded reissues is one thing, but the video game means "fans can accompany the stars on a virtual stage and enjoy the music in a way that was unheard of" during the height of The Beatles' popularity. In addition to the sense of equality conveyed, the advertisement provides a real sense of The Beatles' music and to some extent the video game gives audiences a communal experience not to be replicated in real life.

It is through these game worlds and their authentic representations or their fantastical creations that players are allowed "to take on different representations of self" (Wood 2011: 18). This is further evidenced by the affinity players feel to certain characters or avatars, how some players engage in cosplay while performing, and the ways in which players often refer to actions made on screen by their avatars in the first person. In the original series of *Guitar Hero* and *Rock Band*, the players are able to choose their avatar and the game play not only replicates the established garage band to rock god mythology of popular music, but also rewards the players' use of common physical motions associated with playing the guitar. As *Guitar Hero* designer Rob Kay states, through "gestures associated with rock guitarists", players are able to stop "pretending to be a rock star" and instead put "themselves in the shoes of a rock star" (K. Miller 2009: 413). Therefore, it is not so far-fetched to take the argument of a video game providing fans with the opportunity to become their music hero or for players to become a celebrity, however minor or short lived, for the audiences they are performing to, whether that be a group of friends in their living room or thousands of viewers on YouTube.

Conclusion: Virtual performance, real fandom

What is perhaps most important to take away from Frith (1996) and Marshall's (1997, 2006) work is the emphasis on the role of performance. As this work has shown however, there needs to be a greater focus on the relationship between the fan and performance, especially when performative opportunities are becoming more personal, individualized experiences led by fans rather than led by musicians. Arguably, even the music festival has become less about the musical performance and more about the performative experiences created by festival-goers. As O'Grady (2011: 171) argues, "Any work that involves interactivity is, by its very nature, going to blur and bring into question the relationship between audience and performer". Once the formal structures of the live concert performance and the traditional business model of physical commerce being bought and sold in the marketplace are no longer the dominant forms of consumption, audiences begin experimenting with new ways of demonstrating their loyalty as fans. The ease and access of celebrities by fans through social networking sites such as Twitter and Facebook and the recognition of user-generated content by celebrities and the media industries highlight how the very nature of the performer-audience relationship has begun to change into something different, signalling that the formal barriers once instated by the establishment have begun to crumble. Thanks to this acknowledgement by the more progressive of the artists and musicians out there, they "have a closer relationship with their audiences than ever before" (Brown 2011: 184). Again, as evidenced by these examples from The Beatles, this is a testament to the band's lasting legacy, especially as there are no documented examples of Apple Corps taking fan creations to court over copyright infringement.

While the world will never experience a real-life Beatles reunion concert, one site on the internet is proposing a way of experiencing the excitement and collective nature of a Beatlemania era performance. *The Beatles: Live at the Internet* is an interactive performance website, created by a group of university students, which brings fans together to experience famous Beatles performances at venues including the Cavern Club, *The Ed Sullivan Show*, and the London Palladium.[2] The performances are taken from footage found on YouTube and the site relies on those with "virtual tickets" (which also include a "Beatle-ize Me" mop-top to affix your photograph to) to communicate via a forum on Twitter. On a designated day and time, the audience meet at the site to experience the performance together. In addition, there is an advertisement for a Beatles Britain app where users can access trivia facts, participate in quizzes, and find out where and when Beatles tribute bands are performing in their area. Whereas we have seen in the previous section how fans can perform versions of Beatles' songs through video games, and those performances can be loaded onto YouTube, this idea of a virtual performance elevates the role of the fan as communication between fans about the performance and The Beatles' significance in their lives becomes possible, making the representational field of the gig secondary. This communication is a key difference. For instance, when watching footage of old Beatles' performances such as their 1965 gig at New York's Shea Stadium, the nature of the live concert performance is such an entrenched discourse that the fans are seen communicating to the stage through screams and applause. Communicating with each other is nearly impossible due to the noise and mesmerizing reaction to being in the presence of their idols. Similarly, when one has been to gigs where the seating is arranged around dining-room tables, once the main act steps on stage there is a collective shifting of chairs to face the stage with backs turned against those friends or fellow fans behind them. Again, *The Beatles: Live at the Internet* is the type of user-generated content that represents "the breakdown in control of mediated culture by the major players in the entertainment industry" (Marshall 2006: 641). By allowing fans to participate in a "live" performance in this way, opening up channels of communication, and creating an event on the fans' terms, arguably, the former discourse dictating live performance has been challenged to transcend the obstacles preventing The Beatles from ever playing again.

The pace at which media producers are beginning to recognize the importance of participatory culture is high, while the advancements being made through 3D and holographic technology are rapidly becoming more convincing and sophisticated. These developments may, in the future, provide audiences with more platforms to transform their image or identity in a virtual space – think of the Holodeck on *Star Trek: The Next Generation*, or more plausibly of deceased rap star Tupac Shakur's "live" appearance as a holographic image at the Coachella Festival in California in 2012, sharing a stage and interacting with the very real Snoop Dog. A more recent example is the Michael Jackson holographic performance of his posthumous single 'Slave to the Rhythm' at the 2014 Billboard Awards (see Gallo 2014). It was a performance that, in order to accomplish, required developments in new technology. Was this a reaction by the entertainment industry and the Jackson estate to keep up with fan-generated content? Jenkins (2006a: 24) warns that those old guards of the media industries who refuse to engage with the increasing demands for interactivity and participation by consumers will "face declining goodwill and diminished revenues". What is certain though is the direct impact that interactivity through the more digitally sophisticated outlets and platforms has had on how fans interact with older, traditional media. Bands such as U2, with their "Claw" stage for their 2009–2011 360° tour (Michaels 2011), and St. Vincent, are representative of the constant re-evaluation of the role of live performance in an increasingly participatory digital culture. Annie Clark (who performs as St. Vincent) recently discussed the need to "democratize" her concerts in order to get people dancing and moving – a key element that she believes will make the performance experience complete (Weiner 2014: 74). This element of democracy again changes the discourse of live performance as the fan/audience member is recognized on a more equal footing to their rock idol, whether physically or symbolically. Because the Beatles empire has continued to remain open to experimentation and to the interests of the youth culture forty years after they disbanded (see "Beatles Brand…" 2010), the band can remain relevant and co-exist next to contemporary artists that continually challenge traditional notions of live performance.

Notes

1. See the Save Britain's Heritage press release of 23 July 2022: https://www.savebritainsheritage.org/news/item/285/Press-Release-Pathfinder-continues-in-Liverpool-where-planning-permission-is-granted-to-demolish-440-terraced-houses-on-the-Welsh-Streets-SAVE-demands-Public-Inquiry

2. The website is still available but has not been updated for several years.

References

Abercrombie, Nicholas and Brian Longhurst. (1998) *Audiences: A Sociological Theory of Performance and Imagination*. London: Sage.

Auslander, Philip. (2006) *Liveness: Performance in a Mediatized Culture*. Abingdon: Routledge.

Barton, Kristin M. and Jonathan M. Lampley, eds. (2013) *Fan CULTure: Essays on Participatory Fandom in the 21st Century*. Jefferson, NC: McFarland and Co.

"Beatles Brand 'Advances with Technology'" (2010) *BBC News* [online], 17 November. http://www.bbc.co.uk/news/entertainment-arts-11774269 (accessed 23 March 2023).

Birringer, Johannes. (2006) "*Saira Virous*: Game Choreography in Multiplayer Online Performance Spaces". In *Performance and Technology: Practices of Virtual Embodiment and Interactivity*, ed. Susan Broadhurst and Josephine Machon, 43–59. Basingstoke: Palgrave Macmillan.

Bloustien, Gerry, Susan Luckman and Margaret Peters. (2008) *Sonic Synergies: Music, Technology, Community, Identity*. Aldershot: Ashgate.

Brown, Ralph. (2011) "Performance, Culture, Industry". In *Performance Perspectives: A Critical Introduction*, ed. Jonathan Pitches and Sita Popat, 180–86. Basingstoke: Palgrave Macmillan.

Carson, Christie. (2006) "Technology as a Bridge to Audience Participation?" In *Performance and Technology: Practices of Virtual Embodiment and Interactivity*, ed. Susan Broadhurst and Josephine Machon, 181–93. Basingstoke: Palgrave Macmillan.

Crawford, Garry and Jason Rutter. (2007) "Playing the Game: Performance in Digital Game Audiences". In *Fandom: Identities and Communities in a Mediated World*, ed. Jonathan Gray, Cornel Sandvoss and C. Lee Harrington, 271–81. New York: New York University Press.

Fremaux, Stephanie and Mark Fremaux. (2013) "Remembering the Beatles' Legacy in Hamburg's Problematic Tourism Strategy". *Journal of Heritage Tourism* 8/4: 303–319. https://doi.org/10.1080/1743873X.2013.799172

Frith, Simon. (1981) *Sound Effects: Youth, Leisure, and the Politics of Rock 'n' Roll*. London: Pantheon.

Frith, Simon. (1988) *Music for Pleasure: Essays on the Sociology of Pop*. Cambridge: Cambridge University Press.

Frith, Simon. (1996) *Performing Rites: On the Value of Popular Music*. Cambridge, MA: Harvard University Press.

Frith, Simon. (2007) *Taking Popular Music Seriously: Selected Essays*. Aldershot: Ashgate.

Gallo, Phil. (2014) "Michael Jackson Hologram Rocks Billboard Music Awards: Watch & Go Behind the Scenes". *Billboard.com*, 18 May. http://www.billboard.com/articles/events/bbma-2014/6092040/michael-jackson-hologram-billboard-music-awards (accessed 23 March 2023).

Gibson, Chris and John Connell. (2007) "Music, Tourism and the Transformation of Memphis". *Tourism Geographies* 9/2: 160–90. https://doi.org/10.1080/14616680701278505

Gray, Jonathan. (2003) "New Audiences, New Textualities: Anti-Fans and Non-Fans". *International Journal of Cultural Studies* 6/1: 64–81. https://doi.org/10.1177/1367877903006001004

Gray, Jonathan, Cornel Sandvoss and C. Lee Harrington, eds. (2007) *Fandom: Identities and Communities in a Mediated World*. New York: New York University Press.

Grossberg, Lawrence. (2006) "Is There a Fan in the House? The Affective Sensibility of Fandom". In *The Celebrity Culture Reader*, ed. P. David Marshall, 581–90. Abingdon: Routledge.

Hills, Matt. (2002) *Fan Cultures*. Abingdon: Routledge.

Jenkins, Henry. (2006a) *Fans, Bloggers, and Gamers: Exploring Participatory Culture*. New York: New York University Press.

Jenkins, Henry. (2006b) *Convergence Culture: Where Old and New Media Collide*. New York: New York University Press.

Julien, Olivier. (2009) *Sgt. Pepper and the Beatles*. Aldershot: Ashgate.

Kelly, Jem. (2007) "Pop Music, Multimedia, and Live Performance". In *Music, Sound, and Multimedia: From the Live to the Virtual*, ed. Jamie Sexton, 105–120. Edinburgh: Edinburgh University Press.

Kerr, Aphra, Pat Brereton and Julian Kücklich. (2004) *New Media: New Pleasures?* STeM Working Paper: Final Research Report of a Pilot Research Project. http://eprints.nuim.ie/426/1/NMNP_IJCS_final05b.pdf (accessed 23 March 2023).

Lessig, Lawrence. (2004) *Free Culture: The Nature and Future of Creativity*. New York: Penguin Books.

Lévy, Pierre. (1994) *Collective Intelligence: Mankind's Emerging World in Cyberspace*. Translated from French by Robert Bononno, 1997. London: Perseus Books.

Marshall, P. David. (1997) *Celebrity and Power*. Minneapolis, MN: University of Minnesota Press.

Marshall, P. David. (2000) "The Celebrity Legacy of the Beatles". In *The Beatles: Popular Music and Society*, ed. Ian Inglis, 163–75. London: Macmillan Press.

Marshall, P. David. (2006) "New Media – New Self: The Changing Power of Celebrity". In *The Celebrity Culture Reader*, ed. P. David Marshall, 634–44. Abingdon: Routledge.

Michaels, Sean. (2011) "U2 to Sell 360° Tour 'Claw' Stages". *The Guardian* [online], 29 June. http://www.theguardian.com/music/2011/jun/29/u2-360-tour-claw-stage-set (accessed 23 March 2023).

Miller, Kiri. (2009) "Schizophonic Performance: *Guitar Hero*, *Rock Band*, and Virtual Virtuosity". *Journal of the Society for American Music* 3/4: 395–429. https://doi.org/10.1017/S1752196309990666

Miller, Mitch. (2009) "*The Beatles Rock Band*: Around the World with the Fab Four". *Game Informer* 197 (September): 38–47.

Moltenbrey, Karen. (2010) "Sound Effects: Harmonix Re-Creates the Sights and Sounds from the Beatles for its Latest *Rock Band* Title". *Computer Graphics World* 33/2: 30–34.

Munday, Rod. (2007) "Music in Video Games". In *Music, Sound, and Multimedia: From the Live to the Virtual*, ed. Jamie Sexton, 51–67. Edinburgh: Edinburgh University Press.

Newman, James. (2005) "Playing (with) Videogames". *Convergence: The International Journal of Research into New Media Technologies* 11/1: 48–67. https://doi.org/10.1177/135485650501100105

O'Grady, Alice. (2011) "Interactivity" and "Interactivity: Functions and Risks". In *Performance Perspectives: A Critical Introduction*, ed. Jonathan Pitches and Sita Popat, 146–47; 165–72. Basingstoke: Palgrave Macmillan.

Peters, Margaret. (2008) "Introduction to Part 1". In *Sonic Synergies: Music, Technology, Community, Identity*, ed. Gerry Bloustien, Susan Luckman and Margaret Peters, 3–6. Aldershot: Ashgate.

Rodriguez, Robert. (2012) *Revolver: How the Beatles Reimagined Rock 'n' Roll*. Milwaukee, WI: Backbeat Books.

Ross, Karen and Virginia Nightingale. (2003) *Media and Audiences: New Perspectives*. Maidenhead: Open University Press.

Sandvoss, Cornel. (2005) *Fans: The Mirror of Consumption*. Oxford: Polity.

Save Britain's Heritage (2014) http://www.savebritainsheritage.org/ (accessed 23 March 2023).

Save Britain's Heritage (2022) https://www.savebritainsheritage.org/news/item/285/Press-Release-Pathfinder-continues-in-Liverpool-where-planning-permission-is-granted-to-demolish-440-terraced-houses-on-the-Welsh-Streets-SAVE-demands--Public-Inquiry (accessed 15 September 2022).

"Seven Things to Know about Kickstarter". (2014) *Kickstarter* [online]. https://www.kickstarter.com/hello?ref=footer (accessed 23 March 2023).

Smith, Jacob. (2004) "I Can See Tomorrow in Your Dance: A Study of *Dance Dance Revolution* and Music Video Games". *Journal of Popular Music Studies* 16/1: 58–84. https://doi.org/10.1111/j.0022-4146.2004.00011.x

"The Beatles: Live at the Internet" [online]. http://beatlesinternet.wix.com/beatlesinternet (accessed 23 March 2023).

Weiner, Jonah. (2014) "The Dream World of St. Vincent". *Rolling Stone*, 3–17 July: 72–75.

Wood, Jessica. (2011) "Gaming and Performance: Narrative and Identity". In *Performance Perspectives: A Critical Introduction*, ed. Jonathan Pitches and Sita Popat, 15–22. Basingstoke: Palgrave Macmillan.

Author biography

Stephanie Fremaux is Lecturer in Media Theory at Birmingham City University, UK. In addition to Beatles scholarship, her research expertise includes popular music on film; 1960s British cinema; and popular music heritage touring. Dr Fremaux's book *The Beatles on Screen: From Pop Stars to Musicians* was published in 2018 by Bloomsbury Academic.

8 The Beatles and Fandom

Richard Mills

The roles of fans, both collectively and individually, have been crucial to the cultural mediation and even construction of The Beatles. This chapter chronologically discusses key manifestations of such processes. The Beatles Monthly *fanzine commoditized The Beatles as four lovable mop tops, while letters from girls as published in the magazines carried a highly sexualized subtext.* Beatles Monthly *also provided a space where original meanings of The Beatles' image and music were translated into various sexual meanings. With Beatles conventions, beginning in 1974 in New York, fans began to take their own forms of ownership over The Beatles' legacy (at a time when the group itself seemed uninterested). The Beatles phenomenon has also produced the curious hybrid of the journalist/fan, and with further forms of creativity, the work of slash fiction and innovative remixes as disseminated on YouTube, thus experimenting with form itself in new ways of hearing – and, in an important sense, "owning" The Beatles' music.*

All Beatles scholars and fans will be familiar with the 'Hey Jude' video: a promotional film first broadcast on *The David Frost Show* on 8 September 1968. This film is a visual illustration of The Beatles and the concept of fandom. The film reminds us that The Beatles' work, and in fact, all art is a profound negotiation between artists and their followers.

The Beatles have been singing 'Hey Jude' for three minutes and nine seconds when there is a frisson of excitement in the audience. Paul McCartney is jostled by fans, who then invade the stage and sing along to the refrain, as familiar now to British people as the national anthem. In reality, the stage invasion was rehearsed in Twickenham Film Studios four days earlier; the overflow of communal emotion is, in fact, rehearsed spontaneity. As the song is interrupted, the eye is drawn away from the four familiar faces to the fans. The Beatles are no longer the focus of the viewers' attentions. The 'Hey Jude' promotional film is a reminder that there is an alternative history of the Beatles phenomenon: a fans' history of The Beatles that runs concurrently with the popular story we all know.

One significant problem with a chronological approach to this subject is the danger of creating a canon of Beatles fandom, and new orthodoxies in the process, but because there is such an endless stream of fan activity concerning The Beatles, it is the only organizational method that makes sense when dealing which such a huge subject matter as The Beatles and their audience.

Since the beginning of Beatlemania in 1963, numerous subcultures have built up around The Beatles. The most significant of these fan cultures surrounding the band have been the *Beatles Monthly* fanzine, which started in 1963; fan conventions which began (four years after The Beatles' official split) in 1974; the cult of journalists/super-fans, who have built careers writing partial and biased accounts of the band; dangerous Beatles fanatics such as Mark Chapman; fans who use YouTube to re-invent the Beatles' canon of work in innovative and exciting ways; fan fiction and slash fiction which give fans control over their fictional re-imaginings of The Beatles, often placing their idols in the most unusual, surreal and erotic dream scenarios; and, lastly, fans who want to be The Beatles and form tribute bands as the ultimate act of devotion.

"She Loves You": *Beatles Monthly*

The fanzine *Beatles Monthly* was produced by The Beatles' fan club (mostly female) and it ran from 1963 to 1969. *Beatles Monthly* was founded in 1963. It was first published in August 1963 and continued for 77 editions until it stopped publication after the December 1969 edition. It was revived in 1976, and ceased publication in 2003. *Beatles Monthly* was the first official fanzine on The Beatles. However, a more accurate title of the fanzine might have been "She Loves You", as *Beatles Monthly* (in its original run) showed The Beatles' image and music being re-appropriated, primarily by female fans.

In early 1963, publisher Sean O'Mahony asked Brian Epstein if he could publish a magazine devoted to The Beatles. Epstein and the group agreed, and the title launched in August 1963 with a print run of 80,000. By the end of the year circulation had grown to 330,000 copies per month. O'Mahony edited the magazine under the name of Johnny Dean.

The magazine's photographer, Leslie Bryce, had unrivalled access to the group throughout the 1960s, travelling the world and taking thousands of photographs. In addition, Beatles roadies Neil Aspinall and the late Mal Evans wrote many of the articles, and artist Bob Gibson created numerous cartoons and caricatures of the Fab Four on a regular basis.

In May 1976, O'Mahony revived the publication and republished all 77 original issues including new Beatles news and articles. The reissue programme was completed in September 1982. Finally, the decision was taken to continue the magazine with all-new content. Publication continued until January 2003, when it once again ceased to exist.

In this long history, the fanzine commoditized The Beatles as four lovable mops tops or boys next door, but from issue one the girls were aggressive fans and considered The Beatles as sex objects. The meanings created by girl fans were all to do with a sexual participation in this image: even the most asinine comments or letters from the fans had a highly sexualized subtext. For instance, in the section "Letters from Beatle People", "Marie Selander from Hasselquistvagen 1, Johanneshov, Stockholm" describes the fan hysteria surrounding The Beatles. In the letter entitled "Beatles in Sweden", Selander's letter describes Beatlemania in a sexualized manner:

> I sat there calmly talking to my friends. Then suddenly they came up on the stage! I found myself jumping into the air, then crawling on the floor with my tongue hanging out of my mouth like a red tie and my eyes nearly fell out of my head! (recognise yourself girls?) After the show I flew home singing "You really got a hold on me". (Dean 1995: 78–79)

This is a typical letter from a girl fan in 1963–64: The Beatles are objects of sexual desire; however, an explicit expression of female sexuality was impossible in the censoriously patriarchal 1960s. It was the 1990s before Beatles scholarship caught up via the feminist work of Barbara Ehrenreich, Elizabeth Hess and Gloria Jacobs. And as we shall see, this is tame stuff compared to online Beatles slash fiction in the noughties. Ehrenreich, Hess and Jacobs show the extent to which girl fans made their own erotic agenda when it came to their idols.

> For the girls who participated in Beatlemania, sex was an obvious part of the excitement. One of the most common responses to reporters' queries on the sources of Beatlemania was, "Because they're sexy". And this explanation was in itself a small act of defiance. It was rebellious (especially for the very young fans) to lay claim to sexual feelings. It was even rebellious to lay claim to the active desiring side of sexual attraction: the Beatles were the objects; the girls were their pursuers. (Ehrenreich, Hess and Jacobs 1992: 90)

Here, the girl fans are described as active pursuers; without them The Beatles music and art ceases to have significant meaning. As *Beatles Monthly* demonstrates, artistic credibility always has to be tempered with the chase for an audience. Once the audience is found, it chases the performers back, and the pursuers begin to produce their own work and responses to The Beatles.

Beatles fans were empowered by creating *Beatles Monthly*: a cultural space where the original meanings of The Beatles' image and music are translated into a series of sexual meanings beyond the intentions of the original text. Taking The Beatles' work and changing it is a feature that has recurred throughout The Beatles' career (the "Paul is dead" rumours that were read into the *Abbey Road* and the *Sgt Pepper* albums are an example of this).[1] In *Textual Poachers*, Henry Jenkins described this process as "poaching" meaning away from the creators to the audience: "Fans construct their cultural and social identity through borrowing and inflecting mass culture images" (1992: 23). *Beatles Monthly* was a forum where the fans appropriated The Beatles into their own private sexual fantasy.

As early as 1963, teenage girl fandom was re-circulating The Beatles' image and work into the fans' own products such as *Beatles Monthly*, as well as further magazines and, indeed, subcultural groups. From the beginning, the teenage girl hysteria surrounding The Beatles wrested control from The Beatles' organization:

> In its intensity, as well as its scale, Beatlemania surpassed all previous outbreaks of star-centred hysteria. Young women have swooned over Frank Sinatra in the forties and screamed for Elvis Presley in the immediate pre-Beatle years, but the Fab Four inspired an extremity of feeling usually reserved for football games or natural disasters. (Ehrenreich et al. 1992: 86)

The screaming of Beatlemania was the sound of teenage girl fans creating their own identity, and *Beatles Monthly*, especially the "Letters from Beatle People" section, was the written expression of this fan intensity. Ehrenreich et al. recognized the social and cultural implications of this expression:

> Yet, if it was not the 'movement', or a clear-cut protest of any kind, Beatlemania was the first mass outburst of the sixties to feature women – in this case girls... To abandon control – to scream, faint, dash about in mobs – was, in form if not in conscious intent, to protest the sexual repressiveness, the rigid double standard of female teen culture. It was the first and most dramatic uprising of *women's* sexual revolution. (Ehrenreich et al. 1992: 85; original emphasis)

What is most notable about *Beatles Monthly* fandom is that it occurs within The Beatles' marketing machine – in a particular socio-economic framework. Lennon and McCartney deliberately wrote 'She Loves You' to appeal to teenage girl fans, and their manager Brian Epstein dressed The Beatles in suits to tidy up the image for girl fans. *Beatles Monthly* was about the fans appropriating The Beatles for sex. Epstein's image of the group at the time was clean, safe, take-me-home-to-dad, but the fans usurp this with sex. In a sense, the fans were targeted by The Beatles and the machinery of the music business, and it is, therefore, ironic that female empowerment is visible in the pages of *Beatles Monthly*. The fanzine is a site of fan emancipation, as

> Empowerment of textual poachers… does not occur within a transhistorical or essentialist space. Rather, it occurs quite precisely within the economic and cultural parameters of niche marketing whereby fan-consumers and producers are more closely aligned with a common 'reception sphere' or interpretative community. (Hills 2002: 40)

Beatles Monthly was the first significant step that Beatles fans took to interpret The Beatles in the context of their own lives. In the next five decades, there would be many more strategies fans would adopt to weave the music, films and image of The Beatles into the web and weft of their own lives. The next attempt at Beatles appropriation came after *Beatles Monthly* had been discontinued and the band had broken up in 1970.

(Un)conventional: Beatles fan conventions

The home of Beatles fandom in the 1960s was *Beatles Monthly*. Apart from screaming at concerts, it was one of the few cultural spaces where fans could express their opinions on The Beatles. In 1974, fan conventions replaced the magazine as a space where Beatles' fandom continued to flourish. The continuing popularity of the band in this decade was due, in large part, to these fans who met and swapped memorabilia, dressed as The Beatles, played in cover Beatles bands, had trivia quizzes on The Beatles, viewed Beatles fan art, hosted Battle of the Bands competitions, and swapped memorabilia.

The Beatles conventions began in 1974 when Mark and Carol Lapidos created America's first Beatles celebration in New York. It had the blessing of John Lennon, who said to the couple, "I'm all for it, I'm a Beatle fan too" (Lapidos 2011). Since the 1970s, these events have become generic and a typical convention will have major and minor players in Beatles history who give talks and sign autographs for the fans at annual Beatles conventions all over the world. These figures range from Pete Best (their original drummer) to the English actor Victor Spinetti (who appeared in every Beatles film). Las Vegas has run the longest Beatles fan convention. The running order of the Las Vegas event, on 21 May 2007, is typical of Beatles fan conventions:

> Highlighting the virtually round-the-clock activities are several set-piece events commemorating the Fab Four anniversaries:

- A special live performance of the entire "Sgt. Pepper" album
- A re-enactment of the legendary "All You Need Is Love" happening
- Performance of songs John & Paul played the day they met
- Live performance of songs from the "Love" show & album

The other Beatles-related activities in several ballrooms include concerts, photo & art exhibits, reminiscences by close pals and associates of the Beatles, Q&A panels, autograph sessions, talent contests for bands and individuals, trivia gameshows, Beatles memorabilia assessment (by a top "Antiques Roadshow" appraiser), merchandise marketplace, screenings of rare Beatles videos, exhibit and sales of fine art created and signed by the Beatles. There will also be the first-ever Vegas online Beatles auction – conducted by famed auctioneers ItsOnlyRocknRoll.com. The Mirage is set to become a veritable treasure trove for Beatles fans!

Nine of the Beatles' friends who socialized and worked with them have already signed-on to be Special Guests throughout the three days. They will be reminiscing in special on-stage discussion sessions, performing concerts, signing autographs and interacting with the fans:

Peter & Gordon – Good friends of the Beatles who also had 10 US Top 40 hits! ("Peter" is legendary record producer Peter Asher – whose sister Jane was Paul McCartney's mid-1960s girlfriend.)

Pete Best – The Beatles' first drummer will attend with his own band.

Victor Spinetti – Actor & very close Beatles pal – co-starred in three of their films!

Denny Laine • Laurence Juber • Denny Seiwell – three members of Paul McCartney's band Wings. Also played music and socialized with the other Beatles.

Mark Hudson – Beatles pal who became record producer for Ringo Starr (as well as Aerosmith, Bon Jovi & Ozzy Osbourne).

Larry Kane – The only US broadcaster/journalist to have accompanied the Beatles on BOTH their 1964 & 1965 US tours – becoming a trusted road companion. (Mills 2019: 39–40)

The significance of fan conventions is that consumers have control over the presentation and dissemination of Beatles-related activity. This is ironic, as

Apple Corps, representing the former Beatles, struggled from the early 1970s to the 1990s to exert a semblance of control over the Beatles' franchise, their finances and their publishing. Fan conventions represent a cultural shift away from The Beatles to their fans; and the fans have equal autonomy over The Beatles' music and image as the band themselves. The conventions are similar to *Beatles Monthly*, in that the meaning of The Beatles' legacy resides with the fans as much as Apple. It is also important to note that The Beatles' "friends" and ex-colleagues such as Pete Best, Victor Spinetti and Denny Laine, and tribute acts, emphasize this paradigm shift away from the band to everybody who ever had any involvement with the band, no matter how tenuous the link. Fan conventions are important in the history of Beatles fandom, as they demonstrate the extent to which the caesura of The Beatles' split caused such trauma and shock and opened up such a gap in people's lives that ex-colleagues, fans and business associates, all felt a need to fill this Beatle-shaped hole with a constant supply of Beatles tribute acts, Beatles musicals, Beatles art and Beatles memorabilia.

'Paperback writer': Journalists as fans

The Beatles phenomenon has produced a curious hybrid which is the journalist/fan. The three main obsessives in this category are: Hunter Davies (the only authorized Beatles biographer), Ian MacDonald (sixties proselytizer, who has written an acclaimed book which has an essay on every Beatles song ever released) and Philip Norman, a Lennon obsessive, who has courted controversy with his opinionated work on The Beatles.

Norman and Davies are super-fans and have clear agendas in their writing. Davies, when researching *The Beatles: The Authorised Biography* (Davies 1968), found John Lennon an uncooperative subject and produced a book that heavily favoured McCartney: in short, a highly impressionistic and subjective take on The Beatles. Norman, too, fell into a similar trap, favouring Lennon in his opinionated writing on The Beatles. The reason for this bias in both writers is the simple fact: they are fans just as much as they are "objective" journalists: their work is very subjective, hence the term, journalist/fan. All three journalist super-fans write about their own life and experiences as much as they do about The Beatles.

As mentioned above, Hunter Davies found Lennon an uncooperative subject when he was researching his authorized biography, *The Beatles* (1968). In 1967–68, by all accounts, Lennon was in an LSD induced torpor and could not summon up much personal interest in Davies's project. McCartney, on the other hand, was eager to talk and was a much more willing participant in

Davies's research: the result was a very flattering portrait of McCartney and a very negative and partial account of Lennon's contribution to The Beatles.

Philip Norman's book *Shout* (1981) took the same basic facts as Hunter Davies, and came to a vastly different conclusion. Throughout the text, Lennon is lauded as the errant artistic genius of The Beatles and McCartney is depicted as a Machiavellian schemer, who rides to success on Lennon's coat tails. The reasons for such a subjective account are that Norman's book was published a year after Lennon's murder and Norman deifies Lennon post-tragedy, as did most of the Western mainstream media; it is also quite clear from the book that Norman had been writing about The Beatles since the 1960s, and his work had a tendency to hero worship Lennon. James McGrath identifies Norman's subjectivity as verging towards the extreme:

> Norman's florid prose and disdain for McCartney render his narrative impressionistic and biased. Though he later retracted the statement, Norman commented upon the book's 1981 publication that "John was three-quarters of the Beatles". (McGrath 2010: 309)

With *Revolution in the Head* (1995), Ian MacDonald has written the most scholarly mainstream book on The Beatles: it was instantly held up as a classic by fans and critics alike. However, his account is again biased and partial. For example, MacDonald's interest in Hinduism and Buddhism coloured his account of The Beatles significantly. He believed passionately in an after-life having read widely on Eastern religions: this may be seen in his essay on Nick Drake, for example. This bias is explicit when he writes about The Beatles' and especially Harrison's spiritual interests. In fact, before MacDonald's suicide in 2003, he was planning to re-write *Revolution in the Head* to give more scholarly attention to Harrison's contribution to The Beatles' canon. We get an insight into this unfinished project in his collected journalistic work *The People's Music* (2003). In the "The Psychedelic Beatles: Love and Drugs", he suggests that it was "Harrison who inspired the West's mainstream acquaintance with Hindu religion and created the late sixties spiritual revival" (MacDonald 2003: 96). It is this religious theme which informs most of his published work with an anti-materialist spiritual quality. MacDonald was a writer who was a proselytizer for the 1960s counter-culture and *Revolution in the Head* is as much a paean to 1960s idealism and spirituality, as it is a work of praise for The Beatles. It is a book as much about MacDonald's religious convictions (which are similar to Harrison's) as it is a book about The Beatles. MacDonald's journalistic voice is often the argumentative tone of an opinionated hippie: a 1960s evangelist for the counter-culture.

MacDonald's essay on the Lennon song 'Glass Onion' epitomizes this tendency: his writing here is not objective journalism, but the hectoring of a super-fan. Here, MacDonald overstates Lennon's taunting of the fans, unrealistically suggesting that this irresponsible teasing of his audience in the songs and his love of chaotic random word-play led to his murder:

> Chaos draws psychopaths.... Listeners were left to generate their own connections and make their own sense of what they were hearing, thereby increasing the chances of dangerous misinterpretation along Mansonian lines.... the aleatory philosophy of derangement associated with the Sixties counter-culture, obsessions such as those which beset Charles Manson, and later Lennon's assassin Mark Chapman, were inevitable. As prominent advocates of the free-associating state of mind, The Beatles attracted more crackpot fixations than anyone apart from Dylan. While, at the time, they seemed like harmless fun for Lennon to make them the subject of the present sneeringly sarcastic song, in the end they returned to kill him. (MacDonald 2008: 313–14)

The 'Glass Onion' essay shows MacDonald's worst subjective traits. It is *his* contention that The Beatles' random and chaotic attitude to their art was in some way responsible for fan violence and murder. There is no way to quantify such a bold claim; in fact, if anyone is to blame, it is more likely to be journalists and the media for disseminating fantasy and myth. Nevertheless, a strength of MacDonald's essay is it underlines the special relationship between the Beatles and their fans. The song 'Glass Onion' is addressed to the fans and acknowledge them in a similar manner to the camera in the *Hey Jude* and *A Hard Day's Night* films, but it was a massive overstatement to suggest that Lennon's jokes led to his murder. James McGrath's words on MacDonald describe his biased tendencies accurately (and his words can be inadvertently applied to Hunter Davies and Philip Norman's partial writings). To McGrath, MacDonald is "subjectively passionate" and "asserts arguments without solidly constructing them" (McGrath 2010: 312).

Although Davies, MacDonald and Norman produced three excellently researched books, they are journalists whose fandom subsumes their supposed "objective" journalistic integrity. Their subjectivity shines through, and is a perceived strength or weakness depending on the extent to which readers are credulous about their opinions. In sum, then, all three are fans as much as they are journalists.

Fanaticism and The Beatles

On the darker side of Beatles fandom are fans who become dangerous fanatics. The two fans that reached this tipping point are John Lennon's murderer Mark Chapman and Michael Abram, who attempted to murder George Harrison in a knife attack in 1999. Both were Beatles obsessives, and both felt that they were on missions from God. In fact, each "fan" explained their obsession in religious terms, Mark Chapman suggesting that "a small part of me must be the Devil" (Jones 1992: 98).

These Beatles "fans" give us an insight into schizophrenia, mental illness and the inability of fans to distinguish between fantasy and reality. The Beatles became such a huge cultural phenomenon that they attracted extreme reactions to their celebrity. By 1966, their tours had become dangerous; when they had to flee the Philippines, after snubbing the first lady Imelda Marcos, they were attacked in the airport and bullet holes were found in the rear of their aeroplane.

Mark Chapman is currently serving twenty years to life in Attica Correction Facility in New York City. Denied parole for the eleventh time in 2020, *The Guardian* quoted Chapman stating, "I felt that by killing John Lennon I would become somebody and instead of that I became a murderer, and murderers are not somebodies" (Beaumont-Thomas 2020). In 1980, his celebrity hit list included David Bowie, Elizabeth Taylor and Johnny Carson.

The Michael Abram story is equally upsetting and tragic. Abram (from Huyton on Merseyside) broke into George Harrison's home in 1999, brutally stabbing him seven times in front of his wife Olivia and son Dhani. In 2000, Abram was cleared of attempted murder and served nineteen months in a mental health facility. After his release, Harrison's widow was distraught and implied that the attack had hastened her husband's death (in November 2001) from cancer: the attack sapping his will and physical strength to fight the disease. In both examples, celebrity fandom has led to delusion, obsession, violent attack and murder.

However, there is an important caveat about over-simplifying the unhinged fan thesis. Mark Duffett correctly points out that Mark Chapman's fandom was

> Far more complex than those of a supposedly normal fan... Chapman suffered from a major personality disorder which did not spring from his fandom. By the time he began to think about killing John Lennon, Chapman had been sectioned in a psychiatric hospital, prayed to Satan in the nude... When Chapman became fixated on the singer he posed as a fan in order to get close. By that time he

was therefore not a fan driven insane, but an insane man pretending to be a fan in order to meet John Lennon. (Duffett 2013: 108)

It seems likely that the violence of Chapman and Abram are a complex psychological cocktail of religious fundamentalism, envy and paranoia. However, it is very difficult to build a psychological profile of Chapman and Abram without understanding that their identification with Lennon is not simply "a psychical process whereby dangerous or disavowed aspects of the self are projected onto somebody else"; this is a complicated mental process where "inner and outer self" exist "at the level of unconscious fantasy: we are not aware of their dynamics" (Hills 2002: 97). Even with access to the psychological reports, it is nigh-on impossible to understand the motivations of Chapman and Abram. Perhaps it is a moot point whether they were fans or not when they carried out their murderous intentions. What is clear, however, is that both "fans" represent fandom when it tips from harmless obsession into psychotic narcissism and violence.

'Images of broken light:' The Beatles on YouTube

Beatles fandom is such a sharp *volte-face* away from the creators and towards the audience that any top-down prescriptive dissemination of The Beatles' image and music is very unlikely in the future. The essence of how information is spread and shared has been radically changed by YouTube. New cultural products have been created by this participatory culture:

> This development takes us toward an interesting future where the ratio between the amount of professionally generated content and the amount of user-generated content available online is asymptotically approaching zero. In other words, almost all content available online is user-generated and only a small fraction is created by those people who actually write texts, make movies or sing songs professionally. In a world coloured by virtues of the remix culture it will become virtually impossible to charge users for simple access to content. It is interesting to speculate how such a development will affect the professional development of popular culture. Probably it will be increasingly difficult to create profitable entertainment projects such as full-length motion pictures or traditional music albums. In order to survive, the producers should rather focus on providing tools and building blocks for users to create their own material. (Wikstrom 2009: 159)

YouTube is the forum where fans have aggressively "poached" The Beatles' work (Jenkins 1992). Here, through "fanvids", the fans have radically mashed

The Beatles' songs, films, interviews and still photography into new texts. Fanvids is the phenomenon of fans making their own tribute videos of The Beatles and posting them on YouTube.

YouTube was started in 2005 by Chad Hurley, Steve Chen and Jawed Karim, who were employees of PayPal. It grew rapidly, becoming the third most used internet site after Google and Yahoo. By July 2006, the site was receiving 65,000 new videos every day and the site was receiving 100 million video views per day. YouTube now has a market share of approximately 44 per cent and more than 5 billion videos were viewed in July 2008. On 13 November 2006, Google bought YouTube for a reported 1.65 billion dollars. YouTube's ubiquity and its participatory nature made it ideal for disseminating the Beatles canon of work and for re-interpreting or "mashing" this canon.

For the first time, there was a forum where ordinary consumers could post and share their own videos. In a very real sense, cultural clout now lay with the consumer and nowhere did this pay more dividend than with the image and music of The Beatles. A very carefully controlled and packaged cultural phenomenon was now virtually unrecognizable.

The free exchange of videos has kept the music and images fresh. Not only are pieces of music augmented with video and comment, but the forum has provided a wealth of original material that has rarely been seen or heard before. YouTube also shows rehearsals and outtakes that mainstream media organizations have not broadcast.

YouTube gives us access to a dizzying variety of "new" Beatles texts. Every song, film, interview or public appearance is available online in a new form. YouTube quite simply changes any preconception about The Beatles or their work. It is a digital cubism, capturing The Beatles from many new angles. A project to list, review and archive this material would be a lifetime's work and, unlike the old canon, it is a constantly shifting visual text. The participatory nature of YouTube has replaced experts with amateurs:

> Thus far the commercial media and entertainment industries have pursued an industrial or expert-system model of production, where professionals manufacture stories, experiences and identities for the rest of us to consume. This system is representative, both in the sense that 'we' are represented onscreen and in the sense that a tiny band of professionals 'represents' us all. The productivity of the system is measured not by the number of ideas propagated or stories told, but by the number of dollars earned per story. Thus, over the past century, cinema, radio, and television have all organised and scaled human storytelling into an industrial system, where millions watch but mere hundreds do the writing. Broadcast media

speak to and on behalf of us all in anonymous cultures. (Burgess and Green 2009: 132–33)

The result of the YouTube generation is a dynamic process where fans (amateurs) have offered an alternative to an "industrial system" of experts. YouTube is a forum where "bottom-up (DIY consumer-based)" fan activity has superseded "top-down industrial expert based knowledge" (Burgess and Green 2009: 133). The creation of YouTube signals a period in history when experts have been replaced by fans.

Paul is undead: Slash and fan fiction

Fan fiction grew out of *Spockanalia*, a fanzine started in 1967 by *Star Trek* obsessives. The first edition had a letter of encouragement from Leonard Nimoy (Spock from the television series). Here is the birth of fan fiction: by definition, a genre of amateur works of fiction. Of course, it didn't take Beatles fans long to catch up. Girl fans had been writing romantic stories about The Beatles in notebooks since 1963. Beatle fan fiction evolved from this science fiction genre, and by 2006, Rooftop Sessions (one of the main online forums) had collated thousands of stories. This has become known as "slash fiction": that is, highly eroticized sexual fantasies by fans, which often star The Beatles in homoerotic stories.

Slash fiction and fan fiction have much in common: both fulfil fans' wildest fantasies and both completely re-appropriate The Beatles' work, image and personalities to the fans' needs. Notable classics of the genre are Mark Shipper's *Paperback Writer* (1978), *Beatles* by Lars Saabye Christensen (1984) and Zombie Beatle fiction *Paul is Undead* by Alan Goldsher (2010). In Alan Goldsher's novel, Jesus agrees with John Lennon that The Beatles are bigger than him. The plot of the novel develops with The Beatles being attacked and turned into zombies. *Paul is Undead* epitomizes slash, and for that matter fan fiction, as The Beatles are placed in fantastic circumstances (which could be in the romantic, pornographic or horror genre). These fan spaces completely transgress and re-interpret The Beatles' music and image.

There are hundreds of online forums that have thousands of stories with the four Beatles as central characters. For instance, Across the Universe: Fan Fiction Archive, produces unprofessional work published by the fans for the fans, with titles including "Going to the Moon" and "Meeting an Alien Beatles". The internet teems with sites of this type: Angelfire: stories, poetry and essays about The Beatles; Bungalow Bill's Beatle Fan Fiction; Nothing is Real: A Beatles Fan Fiction Site; and Beatlegirl's World.

There is a need in fan books and slash fiction to take control of The Beatles phenomenon. Mark Shipper's book, published in 1978, presents an alternative Beatles history. The book's subtitle, *The Life and Times of the Beatles: The Spurious Chronicle of Their Rise to Stardom, the Triumphs & Disasters Plus the Amazing Story of Their Ultimate Reunion*, indicates that the intention of many Beatles fans is to control the Beatles story to such an extent that they force the band to reform.

Fans wanting to control or appropriate the Beatles legend is key to understanding fandom, and this is especially true in the case of such unregulated activity as slash fiction. *Beatles! Slash: All You Need Is Love* is a fan site dedicated to slash. The site is described as "a community for writers and fans of Beatles slash (fan fiction featuring male/male romantic pairings, though we also welcome female/female pairings)" (BeatlesSlash n.d.). The site recognizes that fans feel so passionately about The Beatles that even in such an unrestrained and liberal online environment, fans still manage to go too far: personal attacks, cyber-bullying and generally extreme behaviour. It has become such a problem that in September 2014, the site feels it has to warn all participants about "trolling", as it "has experienced a lot of trolls and drama recently... measures must be taken to protect the rest of the members" (BeatlesSlash n.d.). The site also reveals warnings about the explicit nature of the postings: "All Adult / R-rated / NC-17 rated posts (whether they are pictures, fic, stories, etc.) *must* be flagged as 'Explicit Adult Concepts' when you post them" (BeatlesSlash n.d.).

The highly sexualized fiction available in Beatles! Slash is an electronic version of The Beatles as a fetishized love object that we saw earlier in my description of *Beatles Monthly*. This online participatory culture has the same sensual intimacy and ego-driven narcissism as *Beatles Monthly* (an Oedipal desire for The Beatles which we saw in the murderous urges of Mark Chapman and Michael Abrams) but the main difference being that this technology is an "affinity space", "a world where knowledge is shared and where critical activity is ongoing and lifelong" (Jenkins 2006: 192–93) and where the exchanges between fans are fast, urgent and almost immediate unlike the "snail mail" print media of *Beatles Monthly*.

"I play the part so well": Beatles tribute bands

A fan's desire to write sexual fiction about The Beatles is an act of dedicated fan worship, but, in a sense, the tribute bands are the ultimate fans. The tribute acts inhabit the musical habitus of The Beatles. They try their best to be The Beatles; they mimic their songs note for note and their personalities down to the last glottal stop. It is method acting, and they take the characters home at night. The website thewordislove.co.uk provides an archive on Beatle tribute bands. Like slash and fan fiction, the list is endless and it would be an daunting task to delineate the history of each group. The most successful tribute acts, such as The Bootleg Beatles, The Kazakhstan Beatles, The Apple Pies, The Return, The Roaches, The Scarabs, The Cheatles, The Nowhere Men, and Rain, are so obsessed with The Beatles that they not only want to play their music, but they also want to speak in their accents, wear their clothes, adopt their mannerisms and devote their lives and careers to imitating The Beatles. Journalist Ian Herbert, reviewing the annual Beatles week in Liverpool in 2000, shows the international flavour of the acts:

> Next year the Bombay Beatles, the convention's first Indian band, will be putting in an appearance (largely on the basis of their novelty factor). Both will have the most obscure band yet to live up to – the Kazakhstan Beatles, enigmatically known as Museum, who appeared two years ago. The band comprised four shepherds who lived 70 miles from the nearest town. The founder member bought a guitar, formed a band and within a few years was covering "Yesterday" and "Hey Jude" in a local factory. The locals loved it. "They weren't great, but they weren't awful," said [Cavern City Tours Manager Bill Heckle], ambiguously. He's taken a few punts on tribute bands in his time. "At least they (the Kazakhstanis) went down better than The Punkels (from Hamburg, Germany) who covered everything punk-style at a hundred miles an hour. We had some very angry letters about them." Such is the desperate lot of those given the apparently impossible job of making their Beatles sound original. "Some are look-alikes, some are sound-alikes, some are none," said Mr Heckle. "They're all seeking a new take but there aren't too many novelties left." The bands' names reflect this painful quest for something a little different. Known variations of the original have included The Beagles, the Beetles (both from Japan), The Buttles (Walsall), The Beats (Argentina), as well as the Fab Four, the Fab Faux (both USA) and the Fab Two, an Irish band lacking in numbers. (Herbert 2000)

Georgina Gregory makes a serious contribution to the understanding of such a diverse group of tribute bands in her recent study of "ghost" acts. Gregory identifies tribute bands as uber-fans, existing due to the trauma felt by The Beatles' split in 1970. The fan activity from the 1970s Beatle conventions to tribute acts has been a desire to fill the gap in fans' lives when the object of their obsession no longer exists as a functioning unit producing new music and film. This production was now left up to the consumers, and certainly the most theatrical and dramatic act of fandom plugging the gap in this loss was Beatles tribute acts. In *Send in the Clones* Gregory writes that,

> Reasons for the appearance of three of the earliest tribute bands, The Bootleg Beatles, Rain and The Beatnix, can be attributed to an emotional vacuum created by the original band's break up in1970.... The Beatles demise should not be underestimated – fans reeling from the shock of the split –continued to hanker for a reunion, but despite rumours their wishes were to fulfilled and no outlet was available for the pent-up emotions.... The process of grieving is not restricted to death [...] their desire to be united with the lost loved one may lead them to experience and sometimes welcome hallucinations of the deceased. It is easy to see how, in the process of coming to terms with the loss of the Beatles, their tributes fulfilled an important role in representing a tangible link with lost loved ones, allowing the grief feelings to be discharged. (Gregory 2012: 41)

Another feature of grief is a desire to return to fond, early memories before the trauma. This is another reason for fans to escape into the past. This impulse is an *en mal d'archive*: a desire to return to a childhood Eden before the fall – in this case, a time when Beatles music and The Beatles' image flickered across nascent minds (see Reynolds 2011: 28). The Beatles themselves were not immune to this sickness and a Paul McCartney concert in 2014 is an unusual spectacle, as he is as prone to the allure of fandom as his fans. In fact, Paul McCartney is the ultimate Beatles tribute act because his sets are almost entirely comprised of Beatles cover versions: his shows are a Beatles retrospective complete with video montages of the band in their heyday, and McCartney dressed in Cuban-heeled Beatles boots and a mop-top hair style.

Conclusion – Paul is dead: A fan's story

Beatles fans have re-interpreted and appropriated The Beatles' cultural phenomenon to their own ends. Fandom has produced a wealth of archival material which is shifting constantly and reconfiguring Beatles' art at a speed difficult to capture. Beatle history is frozen, trapped in aspic to many cultural commentators and journalists, who consigned The Beatles to a series of clichés synonymous with the 1960s. Fans keep The Beatles' art alive because they have adopted the songs and iconography from the sixties and changed these media clichés into something that has relevance to their own lives. What fans see and hear on television or listen to on records or watch on film is sucked into fans' heads; once there, it becomes translated into a private, personal and unique experience for the individual. In other words, art is changed into a fresh idea by the receiver of information: popular culture is as much about the fan as the artist who creates the product. My survey of fandom captures the dynamism and creativity of Beatles fans that customize their own Beatles videos. They illustrate a famous Beatles song with a subjective selection of imagery that has relevance to them: fans re-theme The Beatles' work.

Beatles fandom has resulted in new hybrid forms produced by the consumer: mashed fanvids, slash fiction, *Beatles Monthly* letters, and tribute acts. Fans have posted outtakes and unreleased performances of songs on YouTube. For example, the song 'India' has been available to a mass of people for the first time. For many years demos of songs, recorded on their return from the Maharishi's ashram in Rishikesh, circulated on bootleg – now, most are commercially available. In 1968 in Rishikesh, The Beatles recorded songs such as 'Brian Epstein's Blues', 'Child of Nature' and 'Spiritual Regeneration' which had never before been heard beyond a niche of hardcore Beatles fans. On YouTube, their songs in general have been augmented by the fans' own creativity: they post video images to accompany these songs. As we have seen, fans use the raw material of Beatles music, film and iconography to make their own pop videos: it is the fans' art, they are cultural pop cultural magpies, and although the results vary in quality, they never cease to be original and interesting.

The creative consumerism of YouTube has resulted in The Beatles' work being reinvigorated by fans' input. The appearance of re-worked Beatles songs is seemingly endless. The consequence of this is a celebration of the transitory. Their canon is removed from its old signature in space and time. Their work has been cut loose from its sixties' event and context. Fans and musicians have radically altered The Beatles' canon.

Many contemporary musicians such as Danger Mouse have posted their own re-working of classic Beatles songs, mashing The Beatles' canon adding a hip hop and dance dimension to their music. They and many other contemporary artists use innovative techniques to produce "new" material and in fact much of it is so convincing that it is often difficult to distinguish the imitators and the satirists from The Beatles themselves. Fandom, and particularly YouTube, translates their work in a variety of texts which tell us about our present day. As Benjamin put it, "The mass is a matrix from which all traditional behaviours toward works of art issues today in a new form" (Benjamin 1999: 232).

What we are left with is a dual interpretation of old and classic works of art. The traditional canon of The Beatles' songs opens a vista on the 1960s while a reinterpretation of their work by a contemporary audience conveys society as it is today and creates a new consumer-led form of art. The cultural ramifications of this are immense: the empowerment of fans and their ability to control Beatles product for further audiences keeps alive the optimism and power of those beautiful songs. The songs are now our property: they are the product of the consumer.

To apply Benjamin's 1936 observations on changes in mass consumption of art in *The Work of Art in the Age of Mechanical Reproduction*, YouTubers "brush aside a number of outmoded concepts, such as creativity and genius, eternal value and mystery-concepts whose uncontrolled application would lead to a processing of data in the Fascist sense" (Benjamin 1999: 212). New technology is a limitless vista of imaginative possibility. For instance, the multifarious rare outtakes, rare press conferences, lost studio tapes, Beatles parodies (The Rutles, Peter Serafinowicz; a slew of spoofs by unknown fans such as the Teables and the Rutbeats and even a Sesame Street parody), along with posting of the home videos of John, Paul, George and Ringo, demonstrate how technological innovation has translated The Beatles' work anew, and how this material is a necessary resource for Beatles scholars and a riposte to Beatles mythology. YouTube refutes Beatles mythology because it offers fans an interactive smattering of new and dynamic Beatles related material.

User-generated content on YouTube has permanently dented the monolith of The Beatles' cultural industry. It has promulgated an interactive forum that deconstructs and translates The Beatles' image and music anew. Simultaneously, it puts an alternative cyber canon into effect. This canon may not exist in the physical manner of previous cultural artefacts of the 1960s and 1970s; but it is an alternative canon nonetheless. Jean Burgess and Joshua Green discussed the archival possibilities of YouTube in 2009:

> In fact, if YouTube remains in existence for long enough, the result will be not only a repository of vintage video content, but something more significant: a record of contemporary global popular culture (including vernacular and everyday culture) in video form, produced and evaluated according to the logics of cultural value that emerge from the collective choices of the distributed YouTube user community. YouTube is thus evolving into a massive heterogeneous, but for the most part accidental and disordered, public archive. (2009: 88)

This alternative archive differs in many significant ways to the traditional Beatles canon. The user participates in the meanings of the text and decides when the canon is reviewed, changed and updated: it doesn't have to go through the officials of the music business (in the case of The Beatles, the Apple organization). In a real sense, we have a constantly shifting archive, the pace of which is dictated by audience interaction, not established record companies. The way The Beatles' work is disseminated has been completely reconfigured by YouTube. Their work is now more random, more fragmentary and creatively evolving into a public sphere that is dictated by the audience. YouTube has radically changed how we spread and receive information.

YouTube and Beatles fandom is predicated on individualism and entrepreneurism like the 1960s counter-culture which produced The Beatles and their work. Subcultures in the 1960s and the noughties were the result of "doing your own thing.... they were uninhibited examples of private enterprise" (Marwick 1998: 17).

From fanzines in the 1960s, through fan conventions in the 1970s, journalist super-fans such as Davies, Norman and MacDonald, dangerous fanaticism, YouTube, fan fiction and tribute bands, The Beatles' story is about fandom and the extent to which fans have manipulated and appropriated the Beatles phenomenon and music to their own ends.

Fandom is a narrative thread running parallel with the Beatles phenomenon. It is The Beatles' story told (and owned) by their fans: an unofficial history which challenges the official history of The Beatles and Apple. Beatles' fan activity is the story of The Beatles told by the fans and this chips away at The Beatles' cultural monolith, whose deconstructed fragments reveal a story that would bemuse even the surviving Beatles. Fandom has developed into a life of its own as a way for fans to deal with the loss of The Beatles' cultural phenomenon. The spread of Beatles fandom has been so vast that any attempted survey of its development is redundant as soon as fingers hit the keyboard. Jenkins's pioneering work on fandom commented on this seemingly endless production of alternative archive:

> Fan culture is a complex, multidimensional phenomenon inviting many forms of participation and levels of engagement. Such an approach also traces a logical progression from the immediate reception of a broadcast toward the construction of alternative texts and alternative social identities. (1992: 2)

By participating in and studying this parallel history, our knowledge of Beatles fans continues to expand and diversify into new areas. In 'Within You Without You', George Harrison sang that "with our love we could change the world" (The Beatles, 1967). Even Harrison could not have anticipated to what extent The Beatles' music and iconography could have been re-interpreted by the fans.

The beginning of Beatles fandom is captured in the final concert scene of *A Hard Day's Night*. The closing scene is similar to the 'Hey Jude' film in that its apparent spontaneity is in fact rehearsed. The film's director, Richard Lester, shot the scene in an attempt to capture Beatlemania. Many of the shots in this scene are taken from behind Ringo's drum kit and the camera repeatedly focuses on the fans. The majority of the shots in this closing sequence are directed at the audience. The camera placement was a deliberate act to acknowledge the importance of the fans. In fact, the original title of the film was going to be "Beatlemania", such was the debt The Beatles' organization felt to the fans. Onstage, The Beatles are saucer-eyed in awe of what the fans are going to do next: scream, sing along or invade the stage. These scenes chronicle the birth of Beatles fandom and visually testify to the fact that The Beatles have no control over how the fans are going to react. From fanzines to "mashed" fanvids, the fans continue to innovate and shift The Beatles' canon into fresh and exciting cultural spaces.

My first Beatles memory was from 16 October 1969. It was the day the rumour broke that Paul McCartney had died. On my fifth birthday, a few weeks earlier, I had been given a blue budgerigar which I called Paul. I loved this bird and spent hours doting on it. My elder brother also seemed to like it. He rattled its cage and shouted "who's a pretty boy then". Paul looked at my brother, and fell off his perch dead. I was in floods of tears. "Paul's dead, Paul's dead", he shouted to my mother, who was downstairs, listening to the news. "I know, I just heard it on the radio", she replied. This personal recollection shows the extent to which audiences misinterpret, appropriate and change the meanings of a cultural phenomenon. The rumour of McCartney's death was obviously false, and our reaction was what I would call fandom: a personal or communal re-appropriation of a performer's music and image. Since the release of The Beatles' first single, 'Love Me Do', an address to the fans to buy Beatles records according to Lennon and McCartney, Beatles fans have been reacting to The Beatles through devotion, and obsessive, eccentric and occasionally psychopathic behaviour. In sum, then, a definition of Beatles fandom is an instance when The Beatles are translated anew by fans, into constantly changing and unexpected areas. Fandom is an active and participatory act: as 'Hey Jude' instructs, "Take a sad song and make it better".

Notes

1. On 22 November 1969 a rumour was circulated by fans that Paul McCartney had been killed and replaced by a Scottish musician William Campbell. The most extreme example of fans appropriating Beatles' texts are the "clues" on the *Abbey Road* album cover. The prosaic cover of four Beatles crossing Abbey Road is given symbolic meaning by fans. The iconic picture is read as a funeral procession. John, in white, is the priest leading the procession, Ringo in a black suit is supposed to

represent the undertaker, George in denim is the gravedigger and Paul, who is barefoot, signifies the corpse.

References

Beatles, The. (1967) 'Within You Without You'. *Sgt Pepper's Lonely Hearts Club Band*. Parlophone.
BeatlesSlash. (n.d.) http://beatlesslash.livejournal.com/profile#/profile/ (accessed 3 September 2014).
Beaumont-Thomas. (2020) "John Lennon Killer Mark David Chapman Denied Parole for 11th Time". https://www.theguardian.com/music/2020/aug/27/mark-chapman-john-lennon-killer-parole-denied-yoko-ono (accessed 5 April 2023).
Benjamin, Walter. (1999) *Illuminations*. London: Routledge.
Burgess, Jean and Joshua Green. (2009) *YouTube: Digital Media and Society Series*. Cambridge: Polity.
Christensen, Lars Saabye. (1984) *Beatles*. Oslo: Cappelen Damm.
Davies, Hunter. (1968) *The Beatles: The Authorised Biography*. London: Heinemann.
Dean, Johnny. (1995) *The Best of The Beatles Book*. London: Beat Publications.
Duffett, Mark. (2013) *Understanding Fandom: An Introduction to the Study of Media Fan Culture*. London: Bloomsbury.
Ehrenreich, Barbara, Elizabeth Hess and Gloria Jacobs. (1992) "Beatlemania: Girls Just Want to Have Fun". In *The Adoring Audience: Fan Culture and Popular Media*, ed. Lisa A. Lewis, 84–106. Abingdon: Routledge.
Goldsher, Alan. (2010) *Paul is Undead: The British Zombie Invasion*. New York: Gallery Books.
Gregory, Georgina. (2012) *Send in the Clones: A Cultural Study of the Tribute Band*. Sheffield: Equinox.
Herbert, Ian. (2000) "Love Me Too: The Fab Faux Industry Support over 200 Beatles Tribute Bands (and That's Just in Liverpool)". *The Independent*, 18 November.
Hills, Matt. (2002) *Fan Cultures*. Abingdon: Routledge.
Jenkins, Henry. (1992) *Textual Poachers*. Abingdon: Routledge.
Jenkins, Henry. (2006) *Convergence Culture: Where Old and New Media Converge*. New York: New York University Press.
Jones, Jack. (1992) *Let Me Take You Down: Inside the Mind of Mark David Chapman*. New York: Villard.
Lapidos, Mark. (2011) "And So It Began – Beatlefest '74: 9/7-8/1974". *The Fest.com*. https://www.thefest.com/and-so-it-began-beatlefest-74-97-81974/ (accessed 5 July 2014).
MacDonald, Ian. (2003) *The People's Music*. London: Pimlico.
MacDonald, Ian. (2008 [1995]) *Revolution in the Head: The Beatles' Records and the Sixties*. London: Vintage.
McGrath, James. (2010) "Cutting up a Glass Onion: Reading The Beatles' History and Legacy". In *Fifty Years with The Beatles: The Impact of The Beatles on Contemporary Culture*, ed. Jerzy Jarniewicz and Alina Kwiatkowska, 303–325. Lodz: Lodz University Press.
Marwick, Arthur. (1998) *The Sixties*. Oxford: Oxford University Press.
Mills, Richard. (2019) *The Beatles and Fandom: Sex, Death and Progressive Nostalgia*. London: Bloomsbury Academic.

Norman, Philip. (1981) *Shout! The True Story of The Beatles*. New York: MJF Books.
Reynolds, Simon. (2011) *Retromania: Pop Culture's Addiction to Its Own Past*. London: Faber and Faber.
Shipper, Mark. (1978) *Paperback Writer: The Life and Times of the Beatles. The Spurious Chronicle of Their Rise to Stardom, Their Triumphs & Disasters Plus the Amazing Story of Their Ultimate Reunion*. Los Angeles: New English Library.
Wikstrom, Patrik. (2009) *The Music Industry: Music in the Cloud*. Digital Media and Society Series. Cambridge: Polity.

Author biography

Dr Richard Mills is a Senior Lecturer in Literature and Popular Culture at St Mary's University, London, UK. He has been programme director for the Film and Popular Culture, Cultural Studies and Irish Studies degrees. He has published extensively on popular music, Irish literature and culture, film, fashion and British television. Mills is the author of *The Beatles and Fandom: Sex, Death and Progressive Nostalgia* (Bloomsbury, 2019). He is co-editor of *Mad Dogs and Englishness* (Bloomsbury, 2017) and the author of the forthcoming *The Beatles and Black Music: Post-colonial Theory, Musicology and Remix Culture* (Bloomsbury, 2023) and *The Beatles and Humour* (Bloomsbury, 2023). Richard is a regular contributor to BBC4's Last Word, Sky News, RTE and BBC Live.

9 "Some kind of innocence...": *Beatles Monthly* and the Fan Community

Mike Kirkup[1]

The Beatles Book *(better known as* Beatles Monthly*) has been overlooked in both academic research and popular biographies of The Beatles. Over 77 monthly issues between 1963 and 1979, the magazine told the Beatles story as it happened, giving modern readers a unique chance to follow the story without hindsight. This chapter looks in detail at the content of the magazine and its historical and social context: its beginnings as a form of "pop propaganda", issues of fandom and the communication between fans and the band and the treatment of the change in The Beatles' image in early 1967.*

> We turned into Beatles because everybody seeing us sees The Beatles. We're not The Beatles at all. We're just us.
> John Lennon (1967, cited in Frontani 2007: 130)

> My world evolves (sic) around him, is plain to see for all,
> I'd rather die than be untrue to my Beatle Paul.
> Last two lines from an anonymous poem (BB56, March 1968: 19)

Introduction

In a *Look* magazine interview from 1967, John Lennon's comment highlights The Beatles' view that being in one of the most popular pop bands at the time was a performance, a carefully stage-managed act. Indeed, The Beatles' story has become as familiar to fans as an ancient folk-tale or fable, and details of the lives of the Saints John, Paul, George and Ringo are etched into public consciousness through decades of films, books, news reports, re-released music, and magazines. Even the band's name, "The Beatles" (with the raised, copyrighted "T" of course) was a discussion point at the Business of The Beatles symposium as part of 2014's International Festival of Business in Liverpool, England. The symposium's convenor Mike Southon argued that through that logo, The Beatles were "the biggest brand in the world". In addition, 2014 saw the re-release of a number of re-mastered box sets including the US Albums (£112), the Japan Box (£96), and the mono albums on vinyl (£300), all compiled from the re-mastered tracks from the 9 September 2009 mono and stereo CD box sets. In this way, Apple Corps Ltd are able to keep The Beatles brand thriving by creating products to coincide with 50th anniversary commemorations, but also fans are able to purchase a set that most closely represents their own nostalgic journey with the Fab Four. Inglis (2000: xv) describes The Beatles as "prominent across a variety of categories – historical, sociological, cultural, and musical" and their continued popularity over fifty years after they disbanded is evidence of this. Arguably, The Beatles' music, which has remained fresh-sounding, relevant, and an inspiration to fans and new bands alike, is "greater, ultimately, than the men who created it or the empire they built it around" (Doggett 2009: 350). Yet, despite such an accolade, one area of The Beatles' tale that has been overlooked by fans and scholars is a publication that started just as they were on the cusp of national fame in the summer of 1963 and ended when The Beatles, as a working group, were already disbanded.

The Beatles Book[2] (also known as *Beatles Monthly*) was first published in August 1963 and ran for 77 issues until December 1969. It contained news, song lyrics, letters from fans, interviews, and a wealth of incredible photographs of the band. Original reissues were reprinted from April 1976 with a new wrap-around mini magazine called *The Beatles Appreciation Magazine* and included up-to-date information about solo releases and band re-releases. These reissues ran until September 1982. With the 20th anniversary of the release of 'Love Me Do' in October 1982, original *Beatles Monthly* publisher Sean O'Mahony decided to re-launch the magazine with issue number 78. By following on directly from the last original issue, O'Mahony was able to create the idea of continuity, as if The Beatles' career had not ended. Indeed, in terms of interest from the public and the media, and through continued VHS, vinyl compilations, and the birth of the CD format in the mid-1980s, it had not ended. These new issues (subtitled "The Original Official Monthly Magazine") ran until the final issue in January 2003, reaching number 321.

Through *Beatles Monthly*, a publication created by fans for fans (publisher Sean O'Mahony has consistently stated he was an unabashed fan of the band), fans had one constant medium to communicate to each other and to the band itself, from the release of 'She Loves You' backed with 'I'll Get You' ("John and Paul stayed up until three in the morning... writing both numbers!!" BB01, August 1963: 25) to the final edition (BB77, December 1969) where the tone was more sombre ("Ever since Apple started everything seems to be so very, very serious. Nothing is just plain fun anymore". BB77, December 1969: 15).

Beatles Monthly was about *the fans'* Beatles and through a content analysis across the 77 issues, this chapter will explore the role the magazine had in communicating their career journey to the fans, how fans were able to communicate directly with the band and each other, and how the magazine continues to be an invaluable and poignant social and cultural artefact even in these days of new digital media. Through content analysis, this research will consider how the magazine transmitted such ideas as the changes of style (music and fashion) between 1963 and 1969, how controversial subjects such as Paul McCartney's admission of taking LSD in 1967 and John Lennon's relationship with Yoko Ono from 1968 onwards were tackled, as well as analyse the reaction from fans ("Beatle People" – a phrase created by the magazine) included in the letters page and from fan contributed articles. The content analysis will also include an examination of graphics, reports, and perhaps most crucially, the regularity of appearances of each Beatle in photographs in order to interrogate how *Beatles Monthly* portrayed the cultural and social aspects of the time. For example, just a comparison of the front and back covers of the first and last issues tells a great deal about how The Beatles changed physically. Initially, The Beatles are professionally photographed as grinning, identikit pop "artistes" (BB01 August 1963, front cover) but by BB77 December 1969, the photographs are rather grainy and amateurish, capturing the world-weary images of rustic men on their last ever group photo session at Tittinghurst Park, Lennon's estate in Ascot, in August 1969. Arguably, *Beatles Monthly* metamorphosized into a much more complex form of fan communication than merely a channel for pop propaganda, and despite being overseen by The Beatles' management it was a forum where even fans' dissenting voices could be heard. In addition, this research also draws on interviews I have conducted with the fans that had letters published in the magazine about their thoughts on the changing image of the band, and an interview with the publisher Sean O'Mahony who has discussed his thoughts with me around the magazine's function and content. Arguably, all of these aspects contained in the magazine over its initial run came to be not only endorsed by The Beatles, but added elements to The Beatles' story.

The original run of the magazine is not only a unique collection of information and images of the band, but also allows fans to follow the career of The Beatles as if from the *inside* rather than solely from second-hand sources such as news footage or documentaries. Revising these artefacts provides a fresh perspective into how manager Brian Epstein and the band were able to control their image and promote and reinforce a specific ideal of a family-friendly pop group that became mythologized as the mop-topped Fab Four. Henry Jenkins notes that: "there is a new kind of cultural power emerging as fans bond together within larger communities, pool their information, shape each other's opinions, and develop a greater self-consciousness about their shared agendas and common interests" (cited in Gray et al. 2007: 362).

Jenkins may have been speaking about the rise of community through social media and the internet, arguing that the fan is not just a consumer, but producer, shared a valid authorship with the origins of their fandom. Yet, when considering the function of *Beatles Monthly*, this statement brings insight into the unfolding dramatic narrative of The Beatles' story – one in which the original readers had no idea, for example, that the planned *Get Back!* album would never be released, nor would the band ever play the London Roundhouse in 1969 as rumours suggested. By examining the original run of these magazines, we can experience the innocence and unknowingness of the young fans all those years ago. In addition, a closer investigation of these magazines uncovers a tension, on the one hand using the magazine simply as pop propaganda by keeping the images of The Beatles as clean as possible in an attempt to not upset their massive audience who believed them to be single, clean-living "boys", and on the other hand being the first attempt to treat a young pop audience with respect by providing an inside perspective behind the reasons and possible explanations for the change in their idols, documenting the journey from innocence to maturity.

In an age of social media, interactivity, and participatory culture aided by increasingly easy-to-use, portable "smart" technology, scholars such as Jenkins (2013) and Shirkey (1999) argue that fandom is the future. Jenkins (2013: 363) flies the flag for the study of fandom, noting the changes in definitions of fandom, fan activity, and the ways in which academics are exploring their own fandom through scholarly research. Similarly, Shirkey (1999: np) states, "no one is a passive consumer anymore because everyone is a media outlet". He discusses fan tastes ruling the box office and dominating television ratings, as well as the increased popularity in the games industry. However, this chapter will instead focus on the past to argue that these modes of fandom and communication between fan and celebrity were already in operation in the 1960s.

One key point Jenkins makes about fans that is relevant to this study, is the definition of the word fan itself, shortened from "fanatic". There are many levels of fandom of course, and with regards to The Beatles he makes the point that Charles Manson and Mark Chapman were both Beatles fans who became fanatics (Jenkins 2013: 12–13). But if we consider the anonymous fan quoted at the beginning of this chapter, who would rather die than "be untrue to my Beatle Paul", there is an interesting dimension of obsession to consider, not just of Beatles fans, but of all followers of specific cultural artefacts or individuals. When Jenkins (2013: 12–13) mentions that the root of the word fan is "fanaticus... of belonging to the temple, a temple servant, a devotee", there is a real connection to the spiritual and religious comfort, sense of belonging and fervour that believers experience from their chosen religion. Certainly, in some of the communication in *Beatles Monthly*, the language of fans does suggest the worship of deities, the sense of congregation, the praising of individual Beatles, and the sense they are "followers" or "devotees" who cannot hear negative things said against *their* idols.

"And in the beginning…" 1963

Before proceeding with the content analysis, it is first necessary to establish a context around 1963 as arguably *the* most important year for The Beatles when events in their career started to move unbelievably fast even by today's standards of instant celebrity. At the beginning of January 1963, The Beatles were about to embark on a short tour of the ballrooms and town halls in Scotland, far removed from the impending Beatlemania that would soon hit in the summer of that year with the release of the 'She Loves You' single. They played towns such as Keith, Elgin, Dingwall, Bridge of Allan, and Aberdeen, and up to then the band's media success only included a No. 17 single and a scattering of radio appearances. Their one national television appearance until then had been a mimed performance of 'Love Me Do' and almost a whole minute of 'P.S. I Love You' on the ITV children's show *Tuesday Rendezvous*.[3] By August 1963, The Beatles had undertaken three national tours between February and June, as well as a 22-date UK seaside tour, had appeared on 35 radio shows (11 being their own BBC Light programme show, *Pop Go The Beatles*), and were seen on 17 TV shows, ten of which were national. By the end of August, The Beatles had recorded two No. 1 singles (with the third, 'She Loves You', showing promise at No. 12), a No. 1 album that had been at the top of the charts since 11 May, and the 'Twist & Shout' EP at No. 1 throughout July and August (British Chart Archive). Michael Braun (cited in Evans 2009: 64) talks about how the national press began to use the band to sell papers around the time that 'She Loves You' was released in June 1963 after realizing very quickly that headlines including "Beatles" or catchy song lyrics like "Yeah Yeah Yeah" would sell.

Within this short period of time, The Beatles had become a show business phenomenon with a core demographic of teen and pre-teen girls, as well as a wider audience of families due to their seemingly non-threatening image, likeable personalities, and constant exposure across television, radio, and the mainstream press media that made them "entertainers" on the show business/variety act circuit. In reality The Beatles, spurred on by their hedonistic and gruelling experiences in Hamburg between August 1960 and 31 May 1962, were young men who had experienced the sex and drug culture of rock 'n' roll in the sweaty and dingy clubs along the Reeperbahn in Hamburg's red-light district. They had girlfriends, and in Lennon's case, he was already married to Cynthia Powell who gave birth to his first child Julian in April 1963. However, maintaining a fan- and family-friendly image was thought to be crucial to The Beatles' success. Epstein and his small collection of trusted staff (many of whom were employees under him at his North End Music Stores, NEMS, in Whitechapel Street, Liverpool) knew that the best publicity needed to be created and controlled by themselves. This started with the usual music business PR staffers producing press releases, writing sleeve notes for albums and EPs, ghosting newspaper articles in the name of individual Beatles, cleaning up negative news stories, or simply hiding anything that could potentially be seen as putting fans off the band (Barrow 2005: 44). Furthermore, Epstein saw the group as part of the British show business establishment in the vein of variety shows such as *Sunday Night at the London Palladium*, *The Royal Variety Show*, *Big Night Out*, and *Morecambe and Wise* with Lennon and McCartney as "professional" songwriters in the style of Leiber and Stoller, or Rogers and Hart. Informed by his stint at the Royal Academy of Dramatic Arts (RADA), Epstein had The Beatles at the top of his NEMS tree along with other acts he managed including Cilla Black, Gerry and the Pacemakers, and Billy J. Kramer and the Dakotas. Brian Mulligan (cited in Southall 2007: 31) says that The Beatles "were (Epstein's) babies and were the source of most of the money". Perhaps Epstein's premonition for The Beatles' success and the way in which the band quickly surpassed the other NEMS acts was the reason for Epstein's undivided attention and devotion? At any rate, with increasing success, Epstein arguably needed a vehicle to keep control of the news and image surrounding The Beatles, as well as a way to get information direct to the core audience without the filter of the news media. *The Beatles Book* became that vehicle.

"Will you read my book?": The origins of *The Beatles Book*

Sean O'Mahony, publisher of *Beat Monthly*, first met Epstein in the spring of 1963 to discuss a magazine dedicated entirely to The Beatles, and by the time O'Mahony met the band in June 1963, The Beatles were on the brink of national fame (Harry 1992: 498). Paul McCartney joked, "what on earth are you going to put in it?" (BB88, August 1983) and this comment has an amusing irony now as of course O'Mahony managed to find something to "put in it" for 321 months! Photographer Philip Gotlop was used for the first issue (BB01, August 1963) while the band was recording 'She Loves You' on 1 July 1963. Gotlop is not credited and allegedly the band did not want him to be their photographer (Dean, BB88, August 1983). This demonstrates that The Beatles wanted to feel relaxed in the studio, surrounded by people with which they felt most comfortable, and perhaps they were even beginning to think about their image by this point in terms of how they would be perceived from the "outside". The photographs from issue 2 (September 1963) onwards were taken by Leslie Bryce right up to mid-1967. After that, other photographs were used by non-professional insiders of the band's inner circle such as roadie Mal Evans and Tony Bramwell, who would be CEO of Apple Corps in 1967, the year when The Beatles became more insular in the studio focusing on their musicianship rather than public appearances.

Beatles Monthly was a perfect marketing tool for Epstein and the band largely due to the control of access they retained over O'Mahony and the relationship that was formed could be described as endorsing the product. The magazine sold for one shilling and sixpence, and The Beatles were given a 33 per cent share in the profits. 80,000 copies of issue 1 were sold and "at its height... sold 350,000 copies per issue" (Harry 1992: 498). The magazine brought in a steady income in regard to sales and advertising, and most importantly it was mailed directly to the fans allowing Epstein the chance to control not only information about the group and their plans, but also the visuals that became vital to the press and the fans. Pictures taken at recording sessions or photo shoots were used almost immediately in the next issue, with only two or three weeks in between. Tony Barrow, press officer for NEMS, certainly saw the potential for the magazine to help create and maintain the desired image of the band with a "good news policy; being adopted where they could deny unsavoury rumours and dismiss tasteless gossip" (Barrow 2005: 44). Barrow adds, "We had one or two news pages we used at least in part for propaganda purposes, publicizing those aspects of the group's latest adventures that we wanted to get across to fans" (ibid.). He also talks about the "perfect timing" of the first issue on 1 August 1963 as 'She Loves You' was released on 23 August and The Beatles were in the middle of a series of concerts around the seaside towns of Britain where the family audience of mum, dad, sister, brother would all be available to watch them (see Creasy 2010 for details of fans' reactions before and during the birth of Beatlemania).

Contributors to the magazine ranged from O'Mahony and Barrow, as well as Mal Evans and Neil Aspinall – both road managers and pre-fame friends to the band. These insiders, along with fans, would contribute in terms of writing articles about their experiences meeting the group, or even give opinions on the latest Beatles record. Through the magazine, Barrow coined the phrase "Beatle People" to describe the loyal fans and used it as the title of the fans' letters page, "Letters from Beatle People". The heading was used throughout the magazine's run, up until the last issue of the new series in January 2003.[4] In the first issue, the fan club page also welcomes fans with a cheery "Dear Beatle People...". The phrase is simple but memorable, again making a link between the group and the fans; a subset of fans who were not just casual listeners or fair-weather followers, but the *real*, dedicated fans – the "Beatle People". Subscribing to *Beatles Monthly* provided a strong sense of authenticity.

While it may not be surprising that a fan magazine endorsed by the band themselves, and including contributions from The Beatles' inner circle, would hide a thinly veiled authenticity for behind-the-scenes, insider information, there was another layer reinforcing the propaganda nature of the publication: many of the contributors and names within the magazine are fictitious. The two fan club secretaries, "Bettina Rose" and "Anne Collingham", were actually NEMS employees Maureen Payne and Valerie Sumpter. One regular contributor, Billy Shepherd, was Peter Jones, editor of *Record Mirror* magazine, the name Billy creating a hip feeling of linking him to the young, Liverpool-born singers of the day, including Billy J. Kramer and Billy Fury. Tony Barrow, who unofficially contributed to and edited the magazine, worked under the pseudonym of Frederick James. The use of these full names rather than using "Fred" or "Jim" gives the pseudonym an air of authority, one whom the fans could still trust despite being their parents' age. The editor was named as "Johnny Dean" but was in fact the publisher Sean O'Mahony. The slightly hipper name does conjure links to James Dean and the crop of "Johnny" singers (Burnett, Gentle, Goode, Johnny and the Hurricanes). It was also a sign that someone younger had editorial control and was talking directly to the fans, with a cheery "Hi" at the beginning of each issue.

During its original series running from August 1963 to December 1969, *Beatles Monthly* kept to a basic content/layout template that would become familiar to fans each month. Fans would know where to go for fan club information, news about "the boys", and letters from fans. Regular features included:

- Front and back cover photos, including a centre photo spread showing individual or group portraits evenly spread between each individual Beatle. A full breakdown of image percentages is included below.
- Editorial: written by Johnny Dean in a chatty, informal style. Fans were told of specific information about (or in later issues commenting on) news of the day that had involved The Beatles.

- Fan Club newsletter: written by Anne Collingham or Bettina Rose.
- "A Tale of Four Beatles": written by Billy Shepherd, this section examined how the band had met and the details behind when they started touring and recording. This column ran from BB02, September 1963, to BB09, April 1964.
- "This Month's Beatle Song": the lyrics to a Beatles album track or single, illustrated by a Bob Gibson cartoon, with details of authorship and publishing information, and up to and including BB07, February 1964, a brief piece of copy describing the song, its source recording and its success in the charts.
- "Behind the Spotlight": written by Dean and Shepherd, this column was a behind-the-scenes look at a day in the lives of The Beatles. It eventually morphed into a "Two Years Ago" retrospective series looking back at the events in the band's career , and this section ran from BB13, August 1964 until BB62, September 1968 with some poignant words to fans in the final paragraphs: "we leave them with no hint into what direction they'll be heading in two years time" (BB62, September 1968: 22). While this was in fact referring to when The Beatles stopped performing live in 1966, it was just as relevant in September 1968 because we now know the band were beginning to fracture.
- "Letters from Beatle People": this was the major forum for fan communication in the magazine with names printed along with full addresses. Up to mid-1967, comments after some letters were even "written" by a particular Beatle. This emphasized the personal connection between the group and the fans as some fans received a reply from "Paul" or "John". A similar dynamic is experienced in social media when a message to a celebrity gets re-posted or replied to. It reinforces a kind of parasocial relationship, a feeling of intimacy between celebrity and fan.
- "Beatles News": containing information about tour dates, record release dates, track listings, cover versions, general news, and news that would today be termed "celebrity gossip".

In terms of coverage, O'Mahony set out to give the group equal representation. This demonstrated the importance of democracy within the group as The Beatles had always maintained there was no single leader. It also demonstrated that all of the fans were loved and appreciated equally; there was no one favourite fan. In the very first issue of *Beatles Monthly*, Johnny Dean pledges:

> I'll always try and give each of them one quarter of the Book. In some issues this may not be possible and you will find that one of the boys hasn't got as many pics as the others. But don't worry because I'll make it up to him in the following edition. (BB01, August 1963: 3)

And in addressing potential concerns about the frequency of each Beatle to be featured in the centre spread, Dean states, "I always give the boys the big spread in turn" (BB09, April 1964). The following is a list of the number of appearances for each Beatle on the covers and centre spreads from BB01 to BB77:

Total front covers:
- Group: 19 (25%)
- Paul: 19 (25%)
- John: 15 (19%)
- George: 14 (18%)
- Ringo: 14 (18%)

Total centre spread:
- Paul: 20 (26%)
- John: 18 (23%)
- Ringo: 17 (22%)
- George: 16 (21%)
- Group: 9 (12%)

Total back page:
- George: 18 (23%)
- Ringo: 18 (23%)
- John: 16 (21%)
- Paul: 16 (21%)
- Group: 11 (14%)

Total tally for the above figures:
- Paul: 55 (71%)
- John: 49 (64%)
- Ringo: 49 (64%)
- George: 48 (62%)
- Group: 39 (51%)

From these statistics, Paul seems to be the most favoured in terms of numbers of single photos, with John and Ringo coming second, and George just behind them, challenging the familiar "John, Paul, George and Ringo" line-up used by the media and fans over the last fifty years.

"P.S., We Love You...": Letters from Beatle People

The letters element of the magazine was the central method of communication between the fans and the group, and also between fans themselves, and was a feature that was retained throughout the run of the new *Beatles Monthly* up to its closure in January 2003. The letters page was headed by a cartoon by Bob Gibson of The Beatles opening mail (a message to fans that the letters mattered to them, and that they personally read them perhaps) with the title "Letters from Beatle People", another element that remained until the final issue of the renewed magazine. The sense of being able to communicate directly to the group, or an individual member, on a one-to-one basis, is crucial in building up a relationship between the fan and the object of the fandom. In the first four years, letters were regularly "answered" by a named Beatle, with a comment underneath the printed letter. For example, a letter from a fan thanking The Beatles' parents for answering fan mail had the following reply from Harrison: "I think my Mum and John's Aunt Mimi are great for helping us out with our mail. In fact, I'd like to thank all our relations for being so wonderful about everything" (BB10, May 1964: 18). Certainly, in the early years and up to mid-1966, the letters were almost 100 per cent positive and included declarations of love, lists of favourite tracks/longest tracks/shortest tracks, requests for pictures, and poems and songs written by fans. Some were answered by Anne Collingham, Johnny Dean, or an individual Beatle, but individualized replies stopped around mid-1967, and from August 1967 until the last issue in December 1969, there were no replies printed.

Sean O'Mahony states that certainly in the early days of the publication, the group responded to fan mail and questions enthusiastically, and that "if we knew the answer to a fan's question, we would give it" (email correspondence with the author, June 2014). However, increasing pressure on their time for tours and recording from 1964 onwards meant that replies had to be added by editorial staff. The last issue (BB77, December 1969) had some uncredited lines as an ironic sign-off, without any names against the comments; there were no longer any "Beatles" to write them.

An example of the intimacy between group and fans is shown in letters sent to fans from Lennon during 1962 and 1963. One from October 1963 reads:

> Dear Sandra
> Thanks for your letter, and the praise. In reply to your question, yes, I am married and my wife's name is Cindy. We also have a baby son. I hope this won't stop you liking me. Must finish here.
> Love to you always,
> John Lennon
> xxxxxx
> Just for you. (Davies 2012: 69)

The idea that being married would put fans off the band was certainly a concern for Epstein; his marital status is not mentioned in the profile of Lennon in the first *Beatles Monthly*, and Lennon hopes "it won't stop you liking me" (ibid.).

The letters page of *Beatles Monthly* is a fascinating historical archive where fans praise, argue and comment about the changing times of that decade. Each month moves on through what are now familiar landmarks in the narrative arc of The Beatles' story and popular culture including the films, the release of *Revolver* and the end of touring in 1966, the appearance of facial hair, *Sgt Pepper's Lonely Hearts Club Band* and the death of Brian Epstein in 1967, the "White Album" in 1968, the proposed live show at the Roundhouse in 1969, Lennon meeting Yoko Ono, McCartney getting married to Linda Eastman, and the release of *Abbey Road* in 1969. Over the time of the magazine, there were some negative letters, and certainly during the last two years of the run, O'Mahony was not afraid to print cutting comments about certain songs, albums, their dress sense, and their girlfriends, Jane Asher in particular .The idea of Beatles fans being critical of, and in some cases, openly hostile, to members of the group, is a new phenomenon, a side of Beatles fandom not usually seen. What follows is a selection of extracts from critical fan letters to *Beatles Monthly*, ranging from complaints about screaming at concerts, to attacks on individual songs and Beatle fashions.

Fans' behaviour

This a plea from a fan for quiet at concerts.

> In your next newsletter, couldn't you tactfully ask members to check their screams when going to one-nighters, etc. I know the yells must upset The Beatles – they looked very worried when they played Walthamstow (24th May 1963)... their heartthrobs don't spend all their time perfecting a routine – for the benefit of fans – just to be drowned out when they come to put their act into practice. (Valerie Payne, Leyton. BB02, September 1963: 16)

Anne Collingham replies, "I know The Beatles are disappointed when their act is drowned out by certain sections of the audience". Valerie shows concern for the group both in a personal sense (she does not want to see them look worried), and as professionals (having their stage act ruined). The idea of members of The Beatles' audience *not* screaming seems bizarre today, given the familiar (perhaps over-familiar) images of black and white newsreels showing every single member of their audiences screaming, shouting and weeping in close up. This early letter is a good example of how *Beatles Monthly* worked as a communication tool between fans as well as between the group, their management and their audience, and the press. Valerie wants fans to understand and respect The Beatles by not screaming, and she uses the medium of the magazine to do it.

The next extract, from BB06 January 1964, is a fascinating glimpse into the social mores of the early 1960s, where the writer is concerned about unruly behaviour reflecting on herself, her parents, and their friends.

> ... where the hardship comes in is when a few unruly youths decide to make a show of themselves and go wild *to attract the newspaper cameras* [emphasis added]. Then we all get a bad name and people start using the word "Beatlemania" as a smear rather than as a compliment. (Anthea Wellington, Birmingham, BB06, January 1964: 18)

Anthea links the bad behaviour with the media, which brings to mind Stanley Cohen's (2011) work on moral panic which focused on the violence between Mods and the Rockers at Clacton and Hastings in 1964. She also has a concern about family image: "Some of my parents' friends said things like 'Do you really associate with those roughs and hooligans?'" (Cohen 2011: 18). Then, Anthea appeals to fellow fans not to behave badly outside the theatres, as well as not to scream "pointlessly" inside (ibid.). Anne Collingham replies that The Beatles say, "They've paid their seat money and if they want to scream they should be allowed to", adding, "my mail proves that there are thousands of Beatle People WHO DON'T WANT TO SCREAM. Personally, I hope that thousands more will make a New Year resolution to join the non-screechers..." (BB06, January 1964: 18).

Surprisingly, given the seemingly worldwide acceptance of Beatles music in a positive way, the most interesting aspects of fan letters in *Beatles Monthly* was criticism from fans, particularly from mid-1967 onwards with the biggest volume of critical letters appearing throughout 1969. Specific targets for criticism were 'Yellow Submarine' (1966), the *Sgt Pepper* (1967) album, 'Revolution 9' (1968), 'Get Back' (1969), and the solo albums of Lennon and Ono – *Unfinished Music No. 1: Two Virgins* (1968) and *Unfinished Music No.*

2: *Life With the Lions* (1969) – and Harrison's *Wonderwall Music* (1968) and *Electronic Sound* (1969). 'Yellow Submarine' is the first Beatles song to be specifically criticized by fans in the magazine, albeit humorously where it is described as a "Sally Army bash on a Saturday afternoon" (BB38, September 1966) but two serious points are brought out by the letter. One, the idea that anything The Beatles record will sell, no matter what it sounds like, and two, the reference to the press attacking them, something that had not been seen in almost three years of blanket coverage. Pauline from Aldershot wrote,

> Could you please tell me if you recorded 'Yellow Submarine' to see if it would sell because YOU were singing it? Let's face it, it sounds like the Sally Bash Army on a Saturday afternoon. I just don't believe you take this recording seriously because your (sic) usually such perfectionists. Please, please, we want our Beatle music, not a third rate, amateur tin pot band. For pity's sake don't give the newspaper's a real chance to tear you to pieces. (BB38, September 1966)

The next stage of musical criticism focuses on the album *Sgt Pepper's Lonely Hearts Club Band* (1967) and perhaps the key piece that related to The Beatles music printed in *The Beatles Book* was an article called "Is *Sgt Pepper* too advanced for the average pop fan to appreciate?" (BB49, August 1967: 24–27) by "Frederick James", which purports to be a "cross section of opinions" reflecting the feelings towards the album. For an album praised for decades as the peak of The Beatles' artistic powers, and appearing top in countless "Best of..." polls, it is actually rather refreshing to hear the opinions of true fans *at the time*, without the benefit of hindsight, particularly the criticism. In his re-examination of the album and its cultural influence, Clinton Heylin (2007: 202) examines the comments of *Beatles Monthly* and mentions specific criticisms in the article, suggesting in regard to the fans that the band had "overplayed their hand" with *Sgt Pepper*. He also points out that the negative criticism is overwhelmingly female.

Below is a sample of negative and positive comments about the album, which by then had been released for around two months and had been top of the album charts for almost two months. Starting with the negative comments, Karen from Long Eaton wrote, "I really enjoyed everything The Beatles recorded before *Revolver* but it's impossible to understand half the stuff they do today". This comment is followed by similar sentiments from Joanne in Welling:

> I was one of the first Beatle People in my neighbourhood to buy the new LP. I can't tell you how disappointed I was when I played it

through. Out of all the songs only 'When I'm 64' and 'Sgt. Pepper's Lonely Hearts Club Band' itself came up to standard. Everything else is over our heads and The Beatles should stop being so clever and give us tunes we can enjoy. (BB49, August 1967)

These comments present the idea of the "past" Beatles compared favourably to "current" Beatles – "the stuff they do today", "give us some tunes", and "everything they recorded before *Revolver*" – with these fans looking back to simpler, more tuneful songs. The clichéd parental refrain of "the old songs are the best, they were all melody" versus modern pop songs is in play here, but now said by the younger generation themselves. There were targeted attacks against Harrison's contribution to the album, 'Within You, Without You', an Indian influenced track with no Western instrumentation or other Beatles playing on it. As Jean from London wrote, "It's dreadful, just a crazy lot of noises with no tune at all". Echoing this perhaps more vehemently was Claire from Bebbington, "Atrocious! Horrid! I can't hear the words and there isn't a tune at all. Let George make an album of his own instead of wasting 5 minutes of Beatle Time!" Such a personal attack on a particular Beatle and their song was unprecedented. After the release of Harrison's first full Indian style song, 'Love You To' on *Revolver*, there was no such criticism. Indeed, on the *Beatles Monthly* letters page after its release, there were numerous supportive comments including a fan requesting that Harrison create a sitar sonata (BB42, January 1967: 19), and a disappointed American fan who wanted him to play his sitar on the 1966 American tour. For some fans, such as Judy from Leytonstone, there was a sense that The Beatles were passé because of their more experimental sound and that the band's replacements had already arrived. As Judy wrote, "The records I used to play most were *Help!*, *A Hard Day's Night*, and *With The Beatles*. Now I've put these away and I love the Monkees". This is certainly seen by fans today, with interchangeable boy bands taking their places in the hearts of teenage girls, for example One Direction being toppled by Five Seconds of Summer in the UK charts. Ironically, the Monkees took on the "Beatlemania" aspects of The Beatles such as screaming fans, mop-top hair, and individualized personas given to each member (cute Davy, serious Mike, dumb Pete) just as The Beatles were losing theirs.

Other negative comments echoed not only the emotional investment made by fans to buy into The Beatles' music, but also the financial investment. Ann in Bognor Regis wrote, "I spent £2 (including the train fare) to buy *Sgt Pepper* and there are only three songs on it worth hearing". Similarly, Jan in Caernarvon wrote: "I was looking forward to *Sgt Pepper* but the title song is the only one I really like. It's like The Beatles we used to know before they went stark raving mad and started to write rubbish". From these fans' comments, it can be argued that despite the investment, they were receiving little or nothing in return. The mention of the band going "stark raving mad" and now writing "rubbish" is a sharp indication that The Beatles' development of their image was not just experienced as a *physical* change by some fans, but a cultural and emotional shift that they did not want to be a part of. They were losing their Beatles and were not happy hearing them play new sounds or sing strange new words with opinions on controversial "adult" topics such as politics, drugs and religion.

Obviously, there was praise for the album, too. Most fans were taken along with the music, as for example Sylvia from Bristol wrote: "I disagree very strongly with a lot of The Beatles' personal opinions but I respect their great talent as composers and performers". Sylvia separates the music from the personal in order to appreciate The Beatles as a group while disagreeing with what they think or say. This possibly refers to Lennon's comment about The Beatles being more popular than Jesus which was widely reported in the summer of 1966, but more likely it could be about McCartney's admission in *Life* magazine that he had taken LSD. This was also discussed in a television interview broadcast on ITV News on 19 June 1967. A feature about this event, with McCartney's statement, was published in BB48, July 1967 – the issue before the article on *Sgt Pepper* was printed. In addition to letting the music speak for itself over The Beatles' personal views, the article in BB49 August 1967 also includes comments from fans that reveal a deep emotional response to the music, arguing that this new material was so mature that fans had to unpick the layers in order to fully appreciate it. Peggy from Essex noted, "*Sgt Pepper* contains words and ideas which are far above anything anyone else is capable of creating", while Valerie from Chertsey notes:

> ... I listened again and again. Finally I was overwhelmed by what I heard. Not just impressed but overpowered. It's all marvellous music. Particularly 'A Day in the Life' and 'Lucy in the Sky with Diamonds'. But it's no good just half-listening. You've got to concentrate hard and let The Beatles hypnotise you...

The mention of these two songs in particular is worth noting as they are two key examples of The Beatles (specifically Lennon as chief songwriter on both) using psychedelic imagery and musical experimentation such as the orchestral swell at the end of 'A Day in the Life' climaxing with the final E major chord that ends the song and the album. Comments also reflect the ways in which fans referred to the band's past musical legacy as an important part of The Beatles' identity but that they also needed to appreciate the band's maturing style. As Wendy from Ealing noted, "I, for one, wouldn't want to hear *Please Please Me* re-hashed a hundred times over the years". Jackie from Chesterfield argued that actually *Sgt Pepper* had something for everyone with a variety of "simple, catchy little numbers like The Beatles used to do" as well as the "more advanced" numbers. There were even those fans that really loved Harrison's 'Within You Without You' such as Brenda from Morecambe ("It's the most beautiful music George has ever made...") and Marianne from Edinburgh ("Of all the new LP's songs I love George's the best because it's haunting"). In the previous issue, Johnny Dean mentions in his editorial that "95% of Beatle People were completely happy with what the boys" were doing (BB48 July 1967: 2). Of the 5 per cent who did not like *Sgt Pepper*, Dean stated that "they would have liked a few more early-Beatle-type-numbers to be included" (ibid.). In interviews with the author for this chapter, two Beatles fans who grew up with the group during the 1960s discussed their differing points of view on the band's change of image. Cath Westerbrook wrote to *Beatles Monthly* in February 1968 praising the *Magical Mystery Tour* film, describing it as a "fantastic success... a change only The Beatles could execute... I'm sure you would find the majority of the public appreciated your work of art". However, 44 years later she admitted that because her then boyfriend hated it, she felt she had to write in to defend the film. She recalls, "I had no idea what it was about, but I distinctly remember thinking that I SHOULD like it because it was The Beatles" (interview with author, 10 August 2012). The concept of not being able to criticize the subject of her fan worship also comes into play when The Beatles experimented with drugs and different spiritual aspects. Cath, like many other fans at the time, felt a loyalty to the band which is evidenced in some letters to *Beatles Monthly*. Cath goes on to say, "I would never admit to myself that they were druggies because they were my heroes... I also thought the clothes were ridiculous and quite embarrassing" (ibid.) Like Jan in Caernarvon writing into *Beatles Monthly* about *Sgt Pepper*, Cath also admitted at the time that she "didn't get" a lot of the later music and thought they were writing "rubbish". By the time of the White Album in 1968, she, like many no doubt, "felt they were just trying to see what they could get away with and put out any kind of tripe" (ibid.).

Another fan, Linda Taylor, had the opposite point of view with reference to The Beatles' changing image:

> Looking back, I felt that as I changed fashion, they [The Beatles] followed me. We were walking around Newcastle in late 1966 in Afghan coats, and then I saw them on TV with their hippy gear on and thought "they're like us". I always liked them so their change didn't bother me. (Interview with author, July 2013)

In *Beatles Monthly*, the next phase of critical letters came after the release of *The Beatles* (the White Album) in November 1968. Much of the criticism was around the avant-garde sound collage 'Revolution 9'. However, demonstrating that some of The Beatles' fans had indeed grown with them, there were some words of praise for the experimental piece. Other fans still felt alienated by the track, but one fan is almost apologetic for not being able to understand it. Elaine from Gillingham wrote:

> The first time I heard the complete LP, I thought it was good. However, I feel disappointed that the boys chose to include 'Revolution No. 9'... I listened to this particular sound and kept asking myself what the purpose of it was, but I came to no logical conclusion... Maybe if someone could enlighten me I'd be able to understand and therefore appreciate it more. (BB66, January 1969: 18)

Criticism of the more obscure Beatles' releases was also evident in later issues of *Beatles Monthly*, particularly those by Harrison, and Lennon and Ono's new work together. The majority of letters at this time, and indeed from the first issue onwards, were enthusiastic and praiseworthy of the band and their music. However, these defiant fans, putting their point of view across, are refreshing to read in a fanzine. It was not just the positive letters that were printed, something O'Mahony makes a point of reiterating in editorials. The fans seem to be angry or disappointed in a number of ways. One, a realization that the old Beatles have gone, and two, the new experimental Beatles are not being understood; they are a "bit too way out" as Ann states in her letter. The expectations of some of The Beatles' fan base have not been met by the band themselves; they are not "being Beatles" as the fans had come to know them.

Towards the end of the magazine's run, and The Beatles' career, the criticism got more vicious, with one fan daring O'Mahony to publish his letter, as he wants to attack Lennon for being a greedy rock star:

> I know this letter will never be published, but I must fill you in... They have reported what the fans want to hear instead of the truth. The truth is quite evident: John is a wise and shrewd man. He is out for money first and to please his fans second. He wanted to stop touring because there's more money in recording and now he wants to tour America (not Britain) because that's where the money is. I guess he could use the extra "pocket money" after buying a new home, Tittenham (sic) Park, for $360,000. Only John could produce something like *Two Virgins*, call it art, and cart his money off to the bank laughing. (Bob, Rhode Island, BB72, July 1969)

"The Void": September 1966–April 1967

Between their last American show on 29 August 1966, until the broadcast of the 'Strawberry Fields Forever'/'Penny Lane' promo films in February 1967, The Beatles were almost completely out of the public eye for the first time in over three years. They spent some time apart – Lennon was acting in *How I Won the War* (Richard Lester, 1967), McCartney was working on *The Family Way* (John and Roy Boulting, 1966), Harrison was in India, and Starr was at home with his wife Maureen. However, in terms of public image, they were still seen as the "Mop Top" Beatles by the world at large. They were not seen live or on TV, and there were no new singles to promote between August 1966 and February 1967; they were invisible to the general public, and also to their fans. During this time, in the press, contemporary images of the band were largely absent – there were some of John getting his hair cut for the film, and also some of the first of him wearing his infamous "granny glasses" for Peter Cook and Dudley Moore's *Not Only But Also...* sketch show broadcast on Boxing Day 1966. However, in December 1966, the country saw a very different looking Beatles from the mop tops of the past five years.

An ITN television special, *Reporting 66*, was broadcast across the country, on 28 and 29 December, and included a section about what the group was up to; specifically, what was their future, and questioning if they were breaking up. Lewisohn (2000: 234) states "this edition was at first subtitled 'Beatles Breaking-Up Special', but then became, more correctly, 'End of Beatlemania'". The group were filmed individually entering Abbey Road on 20 December, all with moustaches (Harrison sporting a beard), all dressed very differently, with John wearing his "granny glasses". They looked a totally different group of individuals. This was the first real contemporaneous public view of the group since their final show at Candlestick Park, San Francisco, on 29 August 1966, four months earlier. For a group that had been constantly in the national eye since the summer of 1963, the image of the familiar mop tops changed to four whiskered adult musicians, talking about not performing again in public, must have been a shock. The brief ITN interviews aside (which were screened across the ITV regions at different time slots and dates, so it cannot really be seen as a "national" event), the first real global unveiling of the "new" Beatles was the screenings of the 'Strawberry Fields Forever'/'Penny Lane' promo films, shot in January and February 1967. Apart from the promo clips, visual appearances of the band at this time were sparse, certainly on TV. On television, the only major appearance was McCartney interviewed on 18 January for *Scene Special: It's So Far Out It's Straight Down* (ITV, Granada region) screened in the North West only on Tuesday 7 March, 10.25pm–10.55pm (Lewisohn 2000: 355).

The appearance of the group with facial hair may seem trivial now, but at the time, it was rather shocking, and the group themselves were aware of the changes to their image. McCartney, speaking in a *Sunday Times* interview (23 January 1967) said, "We Beatles are ready to go our own ways... I'm no longer one of the four moptops" (Frontani 2007: 126). He called his recently debuted moustache "part of the breaking up of The Beatles. I no longer believe in the image" (ibid.). Similarly, Harrison in 1967 commented, "a moustache on a Beatle was kind of unexpected" (Badman 2000: 266).

Readers of *Beatles Monthly* who usually were kept up to date with photos of the band no more than a month old, did not get to see the new "official" Beatles look until the April 1967 issue. That was over three months after the ITN screening, and two months after the release of the 'Strawberry Fields' single cover shoot and promo videos. Their last real contemporaneous photos as a group were from the US tour in August, eight months earlier, but the magazine did print some recent images, unveiling Lennon in his glasses (BB42, January 1967: 28), pictures of a moustached Harrison in India (BB40, November 1966: 6), and McCartney sitting with George Martin (BB43, February 1967: 11). However, in BB43, February 1967 and BB44, March 1967, there were many more pictures of moustached Beatles, but ones that were rather different. They seem to be contemporary pictures of the band with facial hair, but looking carefully, it is obvious that hair has been added to previously existing photographs, mainly from photo sessions in late 1964.

Breakdown of The Beatles' airbrushed photos, and their sources

Airbrushed photo	Photo session source
BB43, February 1967	
George, page 8	Photo shoot at George's house, early 1966 (see also BB31, February 1966: cover and p. 10).
George, page 30	UK Autumn tour 1964 (see BB17, December 1964: 14). NB: he has a moustache in his reflection in the mirror, but not on his face.
Paul, back cover	Suggests 1965 due to hair style and similar photographs from that year.
BB44, March 1967	
Paul, front cover	Suggests 1965 due to hair style and similar photographs from that year.
Ringo, page 3	Suggests 1964 *Beatles for Sale* sessions.
George, centre pages	UK Autumn tour (see BB17, December 1964: 25).
George, page 27	Suggests *Help!* sessions.
Ringo, page 28	Suggests summer tour, 1966.

It is hard to believe that *Beatles Monthly* did not have access to contemporary material from late 1966 to early 1967 to place in the photo spreads. Future editions of the magazine had dozens of stills from the *Sgt Pepper* sessions and the epic 'A Day in the Life' session was actually filmed on 10 February 1967. The band had also worked on a number of songs for the album at Abbey Road Studios between November 1966 and April 1967 when BB45 officially unveiled the new look. In an email conversation with the author, publisher Sean O'Mahony admitted that hair had been added because it had been hard to obtain many up-to-date photographs of the band at that time. As a result, earlier photographs, some of which had been used in previous editions (see table above), had been touched up. However, looking back, one could argue that this was a way for the fans to slowly become acclimatized to the new Beatles look, this move from boys to men via their growing of moustaches and beards. As Harrison pointed out above, a new look Beatles was "unexpected" to say the least. Once again, *Beatles Monthly* became a sound piece for fans to comment on this new look. Margaret from Hull (BB44, March 1967: 18) stated her preferences in a forceful way:

> I think you're fab, gorgeous and lovable; I always have done, but please shave off those nasty moustaches. I keep seeing my wide-eyed innocent cherub-faced Paul behind those horrid whiskers, it doesn't make any of you look any better and I, along with thousands of others think you look fabulous enough without them. Please don't take it too hard but take it from me, an ever-loving Beatle maniac, they DON'T suit you.

Interestingly, at that time *Beatles Monthly* had only printed one "official" moustache picture of McCartney in BB43, February 1967 (p. 11) so Margaret must have seen newspaper pictures and the 'Strawberry Fields Forever'/'Penny Lane' promotional films. What is also worth considering is that as The Beatles' image changed, Bob Gibson's *Beatles Book* cartoons eventually morphed, but this happened very slowly. Arguably, this was a way of trying to keep the mop-top image dominant for as long as possible. For the "Beatles News" section, a more up-to-date picture was eventually used in BB65, December 1968, showing longer hair and Lennon with his glasses on, but only Starr was drawn with a moustache. The letters page kept the mid-mop-top look until the very last issue. In this way, the mop top and mid-mop-top images were kept in *Beatles Monthly* longer than The Beatles did in real life. In the very late issues of BB75, October 1969, and BB76, November 1969, the band are presented as clean shaven with slightly longer mop tops, taken from the more innocent days.

"And in the end…": Publisher as fan

The final issue of the original *Beatles Monthly* was published in December 1969, and featured a lengthy piece written by publisher Sean O'Mahony under his own name. Titled "The End of an Era", with the subtitle "*The Beatles Book* belonged to the Sixties – it can't do the right job for the Seventies", it is written directly to the fans, discussing how the magazine started, and brings together several strands of opinion about the group, their career, their image, and the press. O'Mahony is refreshingly honest about each Beatle, acknowledging for example that Harrison disliked the magazine. O'Mahony also admitted he preferred The Beatles before what he called "their hairy period", stating that they were "tremendously photogenic, or at least they were in the days when you could see all of their faces" (BB77, December 1969: 14). In addition, O'Mahony is very honest about what he describes as "the drug problem". He gives a passionate account of his personal feelings towards drug use, directed *against* The Beatles, but aimed *at* the fans, warning them about the "pro-pot brigade" and describing drug takers as "stupid" (ibid.). It is the magazine's final communication to the readers that have grown up with it, and who are still in the thrall of their heroes – the message is clear: do not slavishly copy The Beatles in this particular regard.

O'Mahony ends the piece regretting the lack of humour around "the modern Beatles", and we now know with hindsight that this was a bitter time in The Beatles' career, largely hidden from the fans, with legal arguments rife around financial affairs, contracts, and control of publishing rights. He signs off with a poignantly brief "Bye", a sign that there was little more to say about the band which, in reality, had ceased to exist at this time. O'Mahony writes as his alter ego, Johnny Dean, in the final editorial where he specifically mentions the fans, describing them as "retain[ing] a sense of proportion, and most important of all, a sense of humour about the world around them", again hinting at the seriousness of the legal situation at Apple Corps. Dean continues by mentioning he has enjoyed the Beatles era, but "that it has given me many problems". Not going into any more detail, O'Mahony could mean the later years of the magazine, where comment from the group became non-existent and in some cases rather hostile, as was the case with Harrison's thoughts on the magazine (BB77, December 1969: 2).

Arguably, The Beatles created the first modern pop mass fan-base, with the full power of the press, the record industry, television and radio. Even non-fans knew them, their story and their music, and the force of that fandom even had a name ("Beatlemania") that likened it to a disease, contaminating a nation, and that is still a global phenomenon, 54 years since the band last played in a studio together. In "The Future of Fandom", Clay Shirkey (cited in Gray et al. 2007: 364) asks the question "who *isn't* a fan?" and in this age of hyper mass media, where audiences are saturated by every latest popular group/sound/dance routine/TV show/film franchise not only by the traditional media channels, but through media actually produced and distributed by fans themselves, the idea that "there may no longer be a normal way of consuming media" is valid (Gray et al. 2007: 364). It is impossible to escape being a fan of anything, even if one wanted to. For Beatles fans, from August 1963 to December 1969, *Beatles Monthly* was the only direct line between fans and the group. It began as an information service, a way of getting messages to the fans in the way the management wanted, but very quickly it developed into the voice of the fans themselves; they are the dominant feature of the original *Beatles Book*, with their delight, their fears, their humour, their obsessions and their fanaticism. Looking at it now, *Beatles Monthly* is a social document showing the true nature of the times, unfiltered by time, cynicism, and The Beatles themselves to provide a unique window into a world where the story is told *as it happened* rather than after it happened. We think of hindsight as a positive element in our lives. However, in this case, reading each issue of *Beatles Monthly*, one by one, it is vital *not* to use hindsight, to actively forget that when we are reading BB39, October 1966 that they will never tour again, and their next album will be *Sgt Pepper's Lonely Hearts Club Band*, or that after August 1969, the four Beatles will never again be in a recording studio at the same time. In this way, we are not seeing The Beatles' story through the eyes of historians or popular culture academics, but through the eyes of those original fans. As we are all fans too, it is arguably an invaluable experience to reflect on the nature of that fandom and our relationship to that band, over fifty years after they last played together.

Author's note

I am interested in continuing research into *The Beatles Book* with one idea being to publish an index to accompany not just the original series, but also the reprints with the wrap-around *Appreciation Society Magazine*, and the new version, beginning in October 1982 until January 2003, as there is a wealth of excellent material buried within those pages from writers such as Pete Doggett and Mark Lewisohn, as well as specific articles by Tony Barrow about key events in The Beatles' careers.

If anyone is interested in possible collaboration, please get in touch at m.kirkup62@gmail.com

The Beatles Book Photo Library

This is a unique archive of photographs of the band from 1963 to 1969, some of which featured in *Beatles Monthly* and some unseen. It is planned to digitize the material, and for more information, please contact Jo Adams at joadams1@btinternet.com / http://www.beatlesbookphotolibrary.com/

Acknowledgements

Thank you to Dr Stephanie Fremaux – colleague, friend, and fellow Beatles fan who read, proofed, advised, and suggested above and beyond. Thank you to Beatles fans Cath Westbrook and Linda Taylor for their time and memories, to Sean O'Mahony for very kindly answering my questions, and Jo Adams for her assistance.

Notes

1. A version of this chapter was first published in *Popular Music History* 9/1 (2014).
2. Note that, for the sake of clarity, *The Beatles Book* will be referred to throughout as its better-known title of *Beatles Monthly*. Quotes and any textual references to each issue will be referenced as BB followed by issue number, date and year, then page. For example, BB01 August 1963: 4.
3. For full details of titles, channels/stations and dates of recording/broadcast of media appearances, and dates and locations of live shows, see Lewisohn (2000).
4. The phrase "Beatle People" was also sometimes used by the group themselves in interviews. One example can be heard on the group's first Christmas record where the band chimes "Greetings Beatle people" in a gently mocking way, but never cruelly. They would also often refer to themselves as "Beatle John", "Beatle George", etc., for example in the film *Imagine: John Lennon* (Andrew Solt, 1988) where Lennon and Harrison are discussing the whereabouts of "Beatle Ed". This is worth noting especially within the context of Lennon's quote used at the opening of this piece, claiming "we're just us".

References

Badman, Keith. (2000) *The Beatles Off the Record*. London: Omnibus Press.
Barrow, Tony. (2005) *John, Paul, George, Ringo & Me: The Real Beatles Story*. London: Andre Deutsch.
Beatles Book, The. August 1963–December 1969. London: Beat Publications.
Cohen, Stanley. (2011) *Folk Devils and Moral Panics*. Abingdon: Routledge.
Creasy, Martin. (2010) *Beatlemania! The Real Story of The Beatles UK Tours 1963–1965*. London: Omnibus Press.
Davies, Hunter, ed. (2012) *The John Lennon Letters*. London: Weidenfeld and Nicholson.
Doggett, Peter. (2009) *You Never Give Me Your Money: The Battle for the Soul of The Beatles*. London: Bodley Head.

Evans, Mike, ed. (2009) *The Beatles: Paperback Writer. 40 Years of Classic Writing*. London: Plexus.
Frontani, Michael R. (2007) *The Beatles: Image and the Media*. Jackson: University of Mississippi Press.
Gray, Jonathan, Cornel Sandvoss and C. Lee Harrington, eds. (2007) *Fandom: Identities and Communities in a Mediated World*. New York: New York University Press.
Harry, Bill. (1992) *The Ultimate Beatles Encyclopaedia*. London: Virgin.
Heylin, Clinton. (2007) *The Act You've Known for All These Years: The Life, and Afterlife, of Sgt Pepper*. Edinburgh: Canongate.
Inglis, Ian. (2000) *The Beatles, Popular Music and Society: A Thousand Voices*. Basingstoke: Palgrave Media.
Jenkins, Henry. (2013) *Textual Poachers: Television Fans and Participatory Culture*. 20th anniversary edn. London: Routledge.
Lewisohn, Mark. (2000) *The Complete Beatles Chronicle*. London: Hamlyn.
O'Mahony, Sean (2014) Email interview with author, 23 June.
Shirkey, Clay. (1999) "RIP the Consumer, 1900–1999". *Shirkey.com* [online]. http://www.shirkey.com/writings/consumer.html (accessed 30 July 2014).
Southall, Brian. (2007) *Northern Songs: The True Story of The Beatles Song Publishing Empire*. London: Omnibus Press.

Discography

Beatles, The. (1963) *The Beatles' Christmas Record*. London: Lyntone.
—*Please Please Me* (1963) Parlophone.
—'She Loves You' (1963) Parlophone.
—*With The Beatles* (1963) Parlophone.
—*A Hard Day's Night* (1964) Parlophone.
—*Help!* (1965) Parlophone.
—*Revolver* (1966) Parlophone.
—'Yellow Submarine' (*Revolver*, 1966) Parlophone.
—'Love You To' (*Revolver*, 1966) Parlophone.
—*Sgt Pepper's Lonely Hearts Club Band* (1967) Parlophone.
—'When I'm 64' (*Sgt Pepper's Lonely Hearts Club Band*, 1967) Parlophone.
—'Within You, Without You' (*Sgt Pepper's Lonely Hearts Club Band*, 1967) Parlophone.
—*The Beatles* (1968) Apple.
—'Revolution 9' (*The Beatles*, 1968) Apple.
—*Unfinished Music No. 1: Two Virgins* (1968) Apple.
—*Wonderwall Music* (1968) Apple.
—'Get Back' (1969) Apple.
—*Unfinished Music No. 2: Life with the Lions* (1969) Zapple.
—*Electronic Sound* (1969) Zapple.
—*Abbey Road* (1969) Apple.

Author biography

Mike Kirkup is an Associate Lecturer at Newcastle University (UK), based in the School of Arts and Cultures, teaching media studies and popular culture. He was Senior Lecturer and Media Studies Programme Leader at Teesside University from 2005 to 2019, and was Education & Programme manager at Tyneside Cinema from 1989 to 2003. His publications include "'Some Kind of Innocence': The Beatles Monthly and the Fan Community", *Popular Music History* 9.1 (2014), and "Cry Baby Cry" in *The Beatles, or the 'White Album'* (ed. Mark Goodhall; London: Headpress, 2018). He has an MA in Film Studies from Newcastle University and is a Fellow of the Higher Education Council. His greatest musical moment was sitting in as an emergency piano player for The Quarry Men at the 50th anniversary of John meeting Paul event, at St Peter's Church Hall, Woolton, in July 2007.

10 "Misunderstanding all you see": Charles Manson Reading The Beatles at the End of the World

Gerry Carlin and Mark Jones

As their work progressed, The Beatles' music offered to its audiences portals to alternative forms of knowledge; but these were only fully accessible to those immersed in psychedelic culture. This chapter considers how a range of listeners – but most notoriously, Charles Manson – interpreted the band as the principal shapers of cultural consciousness in the sixties, and how this burden of significance mutated to configure The Beatles as functionaries of disillusion at the decade's catastrophic close. Focusing on The Beatles' 1968 "White Album" as a foundational text, the chapter analyses closely the songs 'Glass Onion' and 'Helter Skelter' before surveying and comparing Manson's statements on The Beatles with Lennon and McCartney's differing responses to radical interpretations.

In his insider account of life with The Beatles, Peter Brown, Brian Epstein's personal assistant, recorded an auspicious day in late August 1964 when, in a New York hotel, Bob Dylan turned The Beatles on to marijuana in an act that would, as Brown extravagantly claimed, "affect the consciousness of the world" (Brown and Gaines 1984: 134). Famously mishearing the Lennon and McCartney lyric "I can't hide" as "I get high", and discovering that the band had never experienced the drug before, Dylan was eager to introduce them to new levels of consciousness. The Beatles spent most of the next few hours laughing and giggling; but something else happened too:

> Paul was overwhelmed with the momentousness of the occasion. "I'm thinking for the first time," he said, "really *thinking*". So certain was he of uttering gems of wisdom, he demanded that everything he said that evening be recorded for posterity. He had Mal Evans follow him around the hotel suite, writing down everything he said.
> (Brown and Gaines 1984: 136)

The slow fuse of a psychedelic pop culture was apparently lit in this room in the summer of 1964, and McCartney's response to getting stoned conveys some prophetic, if slightly ludicrous, intimations and insights. Firstly, McCartney confirms what psychedelic voyagers from William James through Aldous Huxley to Timothy Leary had stressed: that the drug experience often seems heavy with intellectual and mystical significance and meaning. Secondly, he immediately adopts the pose of pop-musician-as-guru-and-oracle, a role only recently established by the cultish Dylan, but soon to be refashioned and mass-mediatized by The Beatles. And thirdly, cultural critics and musical historians still pore over such foundational moments like archaeologists in order to reimagine or recover the point at which The Beatles began to "affect the consciousness of the world" and to usher in an era when popular culture was suffused with vision, mystery and promise – when the band were, as Ian MacDonald later claimed, "arbiters of a positive new age" (MacDonald 2008: 221). Here we will consider how such commentators have presented the band as the principal shapers of cultural consciousness in the sixties, and how this burden of significance mutated to configure The Beatles as functionaries of disillusion at the decade's catastrophic close.

Even by the time of their first psychedelic experience, The Beatles were already part of an unwieldy and unprecedented social phenomenon. "Beatlemania" was such a spectacular event that it demanded a response from cultural commentators and arbiters who had not previously been concerned with the apparent transience and commercial vulgarity of popular music. Brian Epstein noted the explosion of analysis prompted by this manifestation of mass fanaticism: "Tens of thousands of words were written in serious newspapers and magazines, and searching attempts were made by star writers to probe the immediacy of the Beatles' success" (Epstein 1964: 17). He went on to cite a feature article by prominent social critic Vance Packard which attributed The Beatles' appeal to the opportunity for inhibited teenage girls to achieve hormonal release. Seen as liberatory by some (Ehrenreich et al. 1992), the same features were perceived as pathological by critics of mass and commercial culture, most notoriously in Paul Johnson's baleful article in the *New Statesman*, "The Menace of Beatlism", which derisively described teenage fans as "a bottomless chasm of vacuity..., bloated with cheap confectionary and smeared with chain-store makeup" (Johnson 1995: 197). While the magnitude of Beatlemania was undeniable, its manifestations were perplexing and its significance was contestable and polarizing. Johnson's assault on The Beatles as vehicles of cultural degeneracy was prompted by a speech to Young Conservatives by government minister William Deedes who saw The

Beatles as an invigoratory force in a moribund society. "They herald a cultural movement among the young which may become part of the history of our time... For those with eyes to see it, something important and heartening is happening here" (cited in Johnson 1995: 195). Deedes's prescient enthusiasm, mocked by Paul Johnson, would actually go on to establish a key interpretive pattern in Beatles analysis, as the band became one of the principal carriers of the 1960s utopian promise.

Only four years after Deedes's effusive endorsement of generational transformation, and The Beatles' first experience of psychoactive drugs, the psychedelic counter-culture was in full flower. Constituted in various proportions by oppositional politics, revolutions in lifestyle, and an independent bohemian intellectualism, its most potent and public ingredient was rock music (Frith and Horne 1987). The Beatles, in their mid-decade move from the Fab Four to the self-conscious artists of *Sgt Pepper's Lonely Hearts Club Band*, were a causative element in the formation of this diffuse movement. The centrality of the band to the spirit of the age was trumpeted most loudly by doctor of psychology and LSD guru Timothy Leary:

> My thesis is a simple one. I declare that John Lennon, George Harrison, Paul McCartney, and Ringo Starr are mutants. Prototypes of a new young race of laughing freemen. Evolutionary agents sent by God, endowed with mysterious power to create a new human species. (Leary 1968: 44)

Leary's messianic statement, tinged with futuristic acid euphoria, is actually a sincere attempt to determine the near-mythic power of The Beatles at this heady time. Their dominant cultural position – massively popular, critically respected, and potentially transcendent – bestowed upon The Beatles a potent if inchoate moral authority and established their works as hieratic documents.

During this period rock music was becoming saturated with allusive and arcane gestures. Whilst these operated partially as exclusionary mechanisms, mystifying the uninformed and "straight", within networks of young people they prompted a counter-cultural autodidacticism, providing references to pursue, authors to read, experiences to chase. To its audiences, music offered portals to alternative forms of knowledge; but these were only fully accessible to those immersed in psychedelic culture. As Todd Gitlin wrote of Dylan's 'Mr Tambourine Man',

> word got around that in order to "get" the song, and others like it, you had to smoke this apparently angelic drug. It wasn't just peer pressure; more and more, to get access to youth culture, you had to

> get high. Lyrics became more elaborate, compressed, and obscure, images more gnarled, the total effect nonlinear, translinear. Without grass, you were an outsider looking in. (Gitlin 1993: 201)

Artists and audiences became involved in feedback loops, mediated by artefacts and fuelled by drugs. These loops operated through mutual relationships cemented by a counter-cultural community, and they made a significant contribution towards the new and populist (anti)politics of the period. This community, loosely but palpably united by popular music, was arguably the first supra-national movement to be created and maintained by a mass medium. Its shared culture was rock music; its networks of affiliation and influence materialized alongside the medium through new mechanisms of production, distribution and consumption. These were enacted locally and continually through such venues as "alternative" shops selling records, books and clothes, and more sporadically and spectacularly in gatherings and events which fed into a nascent festival scene. A key development was the mutation of the musical variety show and publicity tour into rock gigs, where a shared if loose counter-cultural philosophy was as significant as the music. All of these were underpinned by the evolving music press and developing underground media, which carried information but also provided the forums in which the signs, values and significance of this emergent culture could be debated and created.

This concatenation of allusive and complex texts, real and imagined communities, and their associated discursive fields, led to the generation of "interpretive communities". From fans around a record player to professional critics, all were concerned with and influential in the delineation and validation of the new psychedelic community. As noted earlier, a defining feature of this culture was its obsession with meaning and meaningfulness. In a 1968 interview John Lennon acknowledged the ways in which interpretative meaning was being handed over to increasingly receptive and creative listeners, whose readings could reveal aspects hidden even from the artist.

> They can take anything apart.... We write lyrics, and I write lyrics that you don't realize what they mean till after. Especially some of the better songs or some of the more flowing ones, like 'Walrus'. The whole first verse was written without any knowledge. And 'Tomorrow Never Knows' – I didn't know what I was saying, and you just find out later. I know that when there are some lyrics I dig I know that somewhere people will be looking at them. (Cott 1971: 192)

Lennon perceptively acknowledges the democratization of interpretation and appropriation which has become central to the experience and theorization of postmodern popular culture. A foundational text in this interactive interpretation, "which takes the locus of meaning away from the text itself and makes the production of meaning the responsibility of its readers" (Whitley 2000: 123), is The Beatles' 1968 double "White Album". A notoriously ambiguous artefact, the "White Album" encourages acts of decoding in its consumption. A review in British underground newspaper *IT* took such hermeneutic obsessions amongst Beatles fans for granted:

> Naturally those who think they are the fool on the hill, who deciphered a secret message from 'A Day In The Life' by playing it at 16 revs backwards, who discovered that 'Hey Jude' was a message to Dylan asking him to do more live performances, and who found that almost every track on the last 3 albums have been about drugs, will have a field day here: 'Beatles' is loaded with open-ended lines just waiting for someone to decipher! (Miles 1968: 10)

Not just the music and lyrics, but also the mediated presence of The Beatles seemed to demand that the audience engage in decoding activities in order to fully appreciate the significance of the work. Whilst Lennon welcomed this audience participation in 1968, by 1980 – just weeks before his murder – he was more sceptical.

> PLAYBOY: So how did you react to all the misinterpretations of your songs?
> LENNON: For instance?
> PLAYBOY: The most obvious is the "Paul is dead" fiasco. What about the line in 'I Am the Walrus' [*sic*]: "I buried Paul"?
> LENNON: I said, "Cranberry sauce".... That's all I said.
> PLAYBOY: There was no intent in any of the "Paul is dead" thing?
> LENNON: How can there be intent in cranberry sauce? (Lennon and Ono 1981: 74)

The "Paul is dead" rumour, spread by both word of mouth and the mass media in October 1969, was generated by obsessive Beatles fans who loaded random signs drawn from music and iconography with fatal meanings. These fragmentary, inconclusive, and often contradictory rumours dragged The Beatles into the realm of folklore (Bird et al. 1976). The plethora of apparent clues, identified as such only by their generation through a self-fulfilling hermeneutic circularity, created a conspiratorial alternate reality where Paul *was* dead – an ontologically consistent, and therefore irrefutable falsehood.

The "Paul is dead" fiasco, occurring just before the band's demise, was driven by an introspective over-interpretation of Beatles' artefacts; though conspiratorial in form and tone, it was symptomatic of a growing anxiety about the band's fate. Earlier conspiracy theories involving The Beatles, however, were more concerned with the destiny of the West than with the longevity of a pop group. In March 1966, at the height of Beatlemania, in a newspaper interview John Lennon tried to quantify the band's extraordinary success: "We're more popular than Jesus now", said Lennon. "I don't know which will go first – rock 'n' roll or Christianity" (Cleave 1995: 255). When the interview was reprinted in an American magazine some months later, Lennon's casual comparison provoked a furore, chiefly in the Bible belt Southern States, involving communal destruction of records and memorabilia and, most notoriously, the Ku Klux Klan burning a Beatles record on a cross (Sullivan 1987: 313). This was merely the most spectacular aspect of an already extant right-wing and Christian fundamentalist opposition to the group and the cultural degeneracy they were deemed to embody. Most prominent in this movement was David Noebel, an evangelical preacher whose 1965 pamphlet *Communism, Hypnotism and the Beatles* demonstrated the syncretic mix of Christian fundamentalism, anti-communism and the fear of brainwashing which was typical of the paranoid ideologies that the rise of a globalized youth culture evoked.

> In fact Noebel's principal target in 1965 was not the Beatles but rock'n'roll as a whole. Again and again, Noebel addresses himself to "the Beatles, in particular, and rock and roll, in general". The booklet has no references to individual Beatles, no comments on particular songs. The only remarks specific to the band are observations about fan behaviour presented as symptomatic of rock'n'roll as a whole. The Beatles are merely one manifestation of the disease. (Sullivan 1987: 316)

Unconcerned with intent, let alone content, the critiques produced by Noebel and his fellow travellers situate The Beatles as chief representatives of a spiritual and cultural devolution which threatened to destroy Western values – this was the same transformation that Timothy Leary would later welcome as an evolutionary leap. As principal agents in this profound and polarized seismic shift in cultural values, The Beatles consistently provoked responses which were expressed through theological and apocalyptic symbolism. Leary's "agents sent by God" were Noebel's "anti-Christ beatniks" (cited in Sullivan 1987: 315). Extreme as these claims may seem, religiose elements were in fact perceived in Beatlemania from the very beginning. Some fans seemed to believe that The Beatles had the power of healing (Miles 1998: 224). In 1964 Brian Epstein reflected on the previous year, observing that "The Beatles had ceased to be purely a pop group and were becoming a cult" (Epstein 1964:

82). For Paul Johnson, the audience were participating "in a ritual, a collective grovelling to gods who are themselves blind and empty" (Johnson 1995: 198). American child psychologist Bernard Saibel, after attending a Beatles concert in August 1964, reported that "[n]ormally recognizable girls behaved as if possessed by some demonic urge" (cited in Miles 1998: 111). Anti-Beatles protesters could also be demented; McCartney said of Christian demonstrators at a gig in Memphis that "They were zealots. It was horrible to see the hatred on their faces" (cited in Miles 1998: 224). The ecstasies of Beatlemania and the sacrificial ritual of record burning might seem antithetical, but are in essence structurally related.

Obsessive interpretation and sacerdotal readings of The Beatles would climax with Charles Manson's interpretation of the "White Album". The Beatles' 1968 record was a crucial element in the Manson Family's syncretic theology, which was constructed from exegeses of the Bible, The Beatles and native American folklore, together with concepts and methods drawn from psychedelic mysticism, Scientology and counter-cultural communalism. The Family's central doctrine was Helter Skelter – named after the song on the "White Album" – which prophesized an imminent apocalyptic race war, in the wake of which Manson and his followers would inherit the Earth. The notoriously brutal murders of actress Sharon Tate and six others in August 1969 were adduced by the prosecution in the Family's trial as acts intended to catalyse this event.

In the Manson Family murder trial the prosecution's case hung on the jury accepting that Manson's apocalyptic theology was revealed not solely through scrutinizing the Book of Revelation – the traditional source for messianic millenarianism – but also from listening to The Beatles, whom he believed "were speaking to him across the ocean through the lyrics of their songs" (Bugliosi 1994: 414). Though Manson would subsequently deny the primacy of Helter Skelter as motive for the murders (Emmons 1986: 194), the details of the myth were consistently testified to by Family members and their associates. Paul Watkins, ex-acolyte turned prosecution witness, reported one of Manson's many "raps" on the imminent race war:

> They've been taping [sic] into the vibes for a long time. Look at their songs: songs sung all over the world by the young love; it ain't nothin' new. It's all been written down. It's written in the good book, in Revelation, all about the four angels programming the holocaust… the four angels looking for the fifth angel to lead the people into the pit of fire. (Watkins 1979: 147; ellipses in original)

While Noebel feared The Beatles as a force which might "ultimately destroy our nation" (cited in Sullivan 1987: 315) and Leary hailed them as Aquarian harbingers, Manson's esoteric elucidation situates them as prophets of the apocalypse. For all three the phenomenon of The Beatles must signify a kairotic moment – a crisis in history, or, indeed, the end of times.

It is only the extraordinary cultural impact of The Beatles that prevents us viewing the Manson phenomenon and the subsequent trial as utterly fantastical; what legitimizes the prosecution's identification of Helter Skelter as a revolutionary template and motive for murder, as well as a song on a pop album, is the cultural gravitas that The Beatles and their works generated. During their deliberations the jury requested a record player "so they could play the Beatles' White Album, which, though introduced in evidence and much discussed, had never been played in court" (Bugliosi 1994: 535). The defence's plans to summon John Lennon to testify to the meanings of his lyrics "ran aground when Manson's lawyers couldn't find a way to physically administer summonses to each Beatle" (Browne 2011: 220). Whether this would have made any difference to the verdict or not is unknowable – as Lennon stated, "I didn't know what I was saying". It is, though, testimony to the fact that the interpretation of Beatles' artefacts had become as important to the Californian legal system as it had been to the Family. While awaiting trial Manson appeared as cover star and lead feature in *Rolling Stone* magazine. Interviewer David Dalton was initially sceptical about Manson's guilt (Dalton 1999: 70), but was fascinated by his charismatic presence and was as eager as the court might have been to hear the guru's explication of Beatles' lyrics.

> At the end of each song there is a little tag piece on it, a couple of notes. Or like in 'Piggies' there's 'oink, oink, oink'. Just these couple of sounds. And all these sounds are repeated in 'Revolution 9'. Like in 'Revolution 9' all these pieces are fitted together and they predict the violent overthrow of the white man. Like you'll hear 'oink, oink,' and then right after that, machine gun fire. [*He sprays the room with imaginary slugs.*] AK-AK-AK-AK-AK-AK!
> *Do you really think the Beatles intended to mean that?*
> I think it's a subconscious thing. I don't know whether they did or not. But it's there. ... The Beatles know in the sense that the subconscious knows. (Felton and Dalton 1970a: 29)

Manson's "subconscious thing" is an echo of Lennon's lyrics "written without any knowledge". In his espousal of unconscious "automatic" writing – a surrealist technique – Lennon anticipates Manson's insistence on the primacy of interpretation over intention. Unlike his fellow millenarians, but in accord with the paranoiac readers who reasoned that Paul was dead, Manson was fascinated by the textual minutiae of Beatles artefacts, which he continually cited as proof of his theology. For Manson the "White Album" was a cipher whose meanings interlocked and confirmed messages from other, more obviously esoteric and divine sources. Not just a collection of hidden meanings – or, as it is for many critics, a failed album of "fragments" and "bits and pieces" (cited in Whitley 2000: 105) – the "White Album" is revealed as a self-consistent and surprisingly coherent set of instructions for revolution. Like the Book of Revelation, it became a prophetic text: The Beatles were endowed with the same oracular status as the Bible. Manson's interpretations of the "White Album", though ostensibly sourced in textual analysis, are in fact divinely inspired rather than intellectually derived. While many of Manson's readings resemble the usual stoned understandings of "elaborate, compressed and obscure" songs, the point where they metamorphose into psychedelic psychosis is when they tip over into prophecy and personal instructions. The madness in Manson's method enters with the teleological trajectory where all things lead to his own syncretic armageddon. David Dalton asking Manson to explain the "White Album" for the benefit of *Rolling Stone* readers can now be seen as prophetic: Manson has become the gravitational lens through which all interpretations of the "White Album", and, ultimately, the end of the 1960s and its utopian dreams, must pass.

While the earlier Beatles are synonymous with sixties' pop optimism, their later work is intricately bound up with the dark end of the decade. The proximity of the collapse of the band, the end of the sixties, and the Manson Family slayings have led many to discern associative resonances between these events. Repeatedly, commentary on the "White Album" sees it through Manson's eyes, imaging it as a harbinger of cataclysm. Kevin Courrier's *Artificial Paradise* typifies this approach:

> Perhaps the conscious intent behind a song like 'Helter Skelter' has nothing to do with knifing somebody, but when Manson heard *The Beatles* album as a call to murder and a race war, it wasn't just another symptom of his particular psychopathy. There is a hidden violence on this record despite being conceived while the Beatles were learning peaceful mantras in India. The divisiveness inherent in the creation of the album had unquestionably sparked a different reaction in the counterculture than the earlier euphoria of Beatlemania. (Courrier 2009: 228)

Such critical certainty of the album's incontrovertible nihilism is, in fact, questionable. The *Observer*'s contemporary review – untainted by later refractions through mass murder and race war – hailed it as a "deluge of joyful music making" (Palmer 1968: 24), just as Barry Miles welcomed its "very beautiful music", along with its "open-ended lines" and decipherable meanings (Miles 1968: 10). This interpretative openness is still acknowledged in more recent analyses; however, many are now, to a greater or lesser extent, haunted by the spectre of Manson, which channels the readings into historiographies of violence. Nick Bromell's *Tomorrow Never Knows*, while recognizing alternatives, ultimately valorizes Manson's understanding of 'Helter Skelter':

> Intensely aware of its audience's hunger for interpretation, [the "White Album"] teases them with a *glass onion*... And was Charlie Manson completely wrong? What are the final thirty-seven bars of 'Helter Skelter' "about" if not violence, history (returning), drugs, and death? (Bromell 2000: 142)

Manson was a close and careful reader of the "White Album", sensitive to its aural properties, and – like all good cultural commentators – determined to map it onto the chaotic cross-currents of the period. However well argued, though, Manson's eschatological interpretation is only one amongst many potential realizations; it is the extra-textual fact of mass murder that has made it for some the only reading:

> Despite what he [McCartney] says, 'Helter Skelter' – the scariest, the most monstrous of hard rock songs – is not about a playground slide, any more than 'Revolution' was about its being alright. Even words as straightforward as these assume a vastly different meaning when performed over an echoing mass of chainsaw guitars and delivered in such a voice of reverberant cries and noble hysterics as McCartney summons. Here as ever in Beatle music, performance determines meaning; and as the adrenalized guitars run riot, the meaning is simple, dreadful, inarticulate, and instantly understood: *She's coming down fast.* (McKinney 2003: 231)

McKinney's instant (mis)understanding – ostensibly sourced in the text's objective meaning – is an unacknowledged acceptance of Manson's understanding of what was actually "coming down fast". He places Manson's reading of 'Helter Skelter' in explicit opposition to the author's stated intent. This is not Lennon's recognition of audience involvement in the construction of meaning, which pluralizes and democratizes interpretation; rather, it is the legitimization of the "affective fallacy", in which a text's primary meaning is determined by the emotional affect upon the consumer – in this case, Charles Manson. As a commentator in *Rolling Stone* stated,

> *Sgt. Pepper* was such a happy album, such a happy, acid trip, and it made Charlie very happy. And then the white double album was such a down album. I know it affected Charlie deeply.
> And then *Abbey Road* was another happy one.
> And I just can't help thinking: If *Abbey Road* had come out sooner, maybe Sharon Tate would be alive today. (Felton and Dalton 1970b: 33)

Manson's affective reading of the "White Album", which transforms it for subsequent listeners from an intricate assembly of pastiches and experiments into a grim and violent parable, became and has remained the dominant cultural interpretation.

Despite only being mentioned a handful of times, Manson's monopoly on meaning is pervasive in *Revolution in the Head* by Ian MacDonald, one of the most incisive and influential of Beatles scholars. In his discussion of the arch intertextuality of 'Glass Onion' MacDonald suggests that during their psychedelic period the band's obsession with the kind of lyrical obscurity that produced the word and "mind games" that so fascinated their fans actually courted and manufactured disaster:

> Under the influence of LSD and avant-garde art, they came to accept accidental occurrences – and by extension the first things that entered their minds – as intrinsically valid... Listeners were left to generate their own connections and make their own sense of what they were hearing, thereby increasing the chances of dangerous misinterpretation. (MacDonald 2008: 313)

Even the most pessimistic of critics cited previously, for whom the "White Album" reflects or even unintentionally contributes to the Manson Family slayings, do not make the move that MacDonald does here, which is essentially to blame The Beatles for abandoning a generation to an epochal psychosis. The songs that would cause this derangement are left unspecified, but the most likely candidates from the psychedelic period would probably include 'I Am the Walrus', 'Strawberry Fields Forever', 'Lucy in the Sky with Diamonds' and 'A Day in the Life'. Whilst all of these songs exhibit some of the characteristics of surrealism, and foreground ambiguities, they are far from undecipherable; variously they display themes of childhood and nostalgia, evince melancholic affects, or function as social critiques. 'Glass Onion' itself is an irony-laden self-referential melange of Beatles' song references and allusions to writers such as Lewis Carroll and Edward Lear, with a few surreal but hardly unsettling metaphors thrown in; indeed, the song could be seen as a celebration of one of the band's most creative periods and a sardonic acknowledgement of the pleasures of song writing, fandom and interpretation.

It becomes apparent that MacDonald's critique of psychedelic randomness in the band's work is focused on the "White Album", and he follows Manson in making 'Revolution 9' the prime conduit of arcane meanings in The Beatles' catalogue. In his interview in *Rolling Stone*, Manson was asked for his exegesis of the biblical passage Revelations, chapter nine. His response was curt, and his interpretation entirely traditional – "What do you think it means? It's the battle of Armageddon. It's the end of the world". His next comment, though, is less orthodox – "It was the Beatles' 'Revolution 9' that turned me on to it". From this point on it becomes difficult to distinguish between readings of the two texts, as Manson makes their messages analogous. The conflation of the two texts is completed by the interviewer when he asks "Why do you think that this revolution predicted in 'Revolution 9' will be violent?" (Felton and Dalton 1970a: 29). MacDonald's 'Revolution 9' is similarly an evocation of "the revolutionary disruptions of the Sixties", whilst "the actual experience of listening to the track... inclines to the sinister" (MacDonald 2008: 288, 289). MacDonald is clearly right in adjudging it as a soundtrack to a revolution; however, his inability to acclaim it as a creative collage, a cautionary critique, or "[o]ne of the most exciting recordings ever made" (Quantick 2002: 151) is testimony to the limits Charles Manson has imposed on most readings of the "White Album". Even MacDonald's most laudatory statement about 'Revolution 9', that it "must be counted, if only socio-culturally, as one of the most significant acts The Beatles ever perpetrated" (MacDonald 2008: 288), seems an indictment.

Revolution in the Head, although essentially a relatively sober treatment of The Beatles' career structured through a chronological song-by-song analysis, has an ominous undertone. MacDonald writes, "The Sixties seem like a golden age to us because, relative to now, they were" (2008: 37), contrasting the utopian strivings that characterized the period to the materialistic and disunited "waning civilisation" that is the present (2008: 36). Whilst in MacDonald's analysis The Beatles are carriers of this utopian promise, they are simultaneously responsible for its failure. Their experimentalism resulted in a moral relativism "that [could] only escalate towards chaos – and chaos draws psychopaths" (2008: 313). One of these was, of course, Charles Manson; another was Mark Chapman, who killed John Lennon. MacDonald, however, sees the current lack of "demented individuals" stalking popular musicians as "a perverse index of the vacuity of contemporary pop" (2008: 313). He desires profundity in popular music, but simultaneously sees it as a seedbed for assassins. In MacDonald's paradoxical elegy for the sixties' dream, Manson becomes a symptom of The Beatles' influence on history, and ultimately confirms their unique significance.

Whilst Manson and the Family would often wax lyrical about The Beatles' prophetic role, the band were understandably less forthcoming about their place in the Mansonian mythos. John Lennon stated "He's balmy [*sic*], like any other Beatle-kind of fan who reads mysticism into it" (Wenner 1971: 32). Paul McCartney, the writer of 'Helter Skelter', has effectively evaded the topic. He did, though, recognize the potential deleterious effects of irresponsible musical ideologies, in a *Rolling Stone* interview in 1986:

> Let's say a really great group emerged... and say they were advocating, I don't know, killing, Satanism. And they came out with a really great album and turned a lot of people onto Satanism. There's got to be a point where you're gonna say, "Look, guys, we're all for artistic freedom, but maybe we just don't want *de debbil* trampling across America at the moment". (Sullivan 1987: 323)

What is implicit in McCartney's condemnation of evil music is the disavowal of advocacy in his own contribution to musical mayhem. He has consolidated this by his recent reclamation of 'Helter Skelter' as a rock standard in his stadium tours, though it cannot avoid being haunted by its associations (Carlin and Jones 2014: 107). Similarly avoiding any mention of Manson, McCartney has, however, partially confirmed the Family's reading of 'Blackbird' as concerning racial struggle in 1960s America (Miles 1997: 485–86). Despite Ian MacDonald's claim that "Charles Manson made precisely this interpretation" (MacDonald 2008: 292), while Manson's 'Blackbird' is a call for insurrection, leading inexorably to racial armageddon (Bugliosi 1994: 324), McCartney describes his song as a lyrical address to an individual black woman, symbolically represented as a bird; MacDonald's misrepresentation of McCartney's intentions with the song are symptomatic of his over-determination to read "White Album" tracks through Manson.

Unlike McCartney, Lennon did make occasional observations on the Manson Family, demonstrating a knowledge of the trial proceedings and, in particular, Manson's self-representation in his testimony. Lennon's comment that, "A lot of the things [Manson] says are true: he is a child of the state, made by us, and he took their children in when nobody else would" (Wenner 1971: 32), closely mirrors statements by Manson, who proclaimed "I am whoever you make me", and,

> These children that come at you with knives, they are your children. You taught them. I didn't teach them. I just tried to help them stand

> up. Most of the people at the ranch that you call The Family were just people that you did not want, people that were alongside the road, that their parents had kicked them out or they did not want to go to Juvenile Hall, so I did the best I could and I took them up on my garbage dump and I told them this: that in love there is no wrong. (Manson 1995: 216, 215)

Lennon's apparent acceptance of Manson's self-presentation signals a counter-cultural sympathy with the Family's communitarian ideology. He obviously did not endorse their methods, or, crucially, their interpretation of The Beatles, saying "I don't know what 'Helter Skelter' has to do with knifing somebody". Lennon's next comment, though, where he claimed "I've never listened to the words, properly, it was just a noise" (Wenner 1971: 32), is symptomatic of his then recent disengagement from The Beatles and all they seemed to stand for: as he stated lyrically on *John Lennon/Plastic Ono Band*, "I don't believe in Beatles.... The dream is over" (Lennon 1970). This denial of The Beatles' significance and disillusion with the period's utopianism would eventually be confirmed by McCartney, who told Jonathan Green: "In actual fact I don't really think that we thought that we were going to change the world as much as you thought we were going to change the world" (cited in Green 1988: 191).

McCartney's blasé dismissal of The Beatles' cultural importance and Lennon's disbelief in the band and the "dream" they embodied negate the swathes of contemporaneous critics and fans who heralded or feared The Beatles as agents of seismic social change. This usefully includes the more outlandish interpreters, including, of course, Charles Manson. In his trial testimony Manson insisted on the potent social significance of popular music:

> It is not my conspiracy. It is not my music. I hear what it relates. It says: "Rise!" It says: "Kill!" Why blame it on me? I didn't write the music. I am not the person who projected it into your social consciousness, that sanity that you projected into your social consciousness, today. (Manson 1995: 219)

Manson's tragic misunderstanding was to translate interpretation into instruction, and art into action. He was right, though, insofar as an apocalyptic change was in progress; the familiar world of Western society was undergoing irreversible transformations, and The Beatles, if only because of their enormous popularity, were instrumental in that change. This cultural revolution would, of course, ultimately be compromised, and its utopian energies dispersed. In popular historiography, though, the end of the sixties project is a catastrophic betrayal coincident with the end of the decade, the break up of The Beatles, and the Manson Family murders. The popular culture of the seventies, in which communitarian optimism was replaced by the solipsism of the singer-songwriter, the empty bombast of prog and glam, and the eventual nihilism of punk, enacts this disillusion. The Beatles themselves anticipated the emptying of the sixties' dream as the seventies loomed: *Let It Be* (1970) forsook avant-garde impulses for a stripped back-to-basics rock 'n' roll, and Lennon's and McCartney's 1970 solo albums (*John Lennon/Plastic Ono Band* and *McCartney*) evinced primal rawness and an uncluttered amateurism respectively. Popular culture's moment of optimism was over. The over-determined, back-projected readings of The Beatles that we have examined here, in which the "White Album" functions as both index and cause of the period's crises, are expressive of the traumatic loss that the sixties' failure represents – not just the collapse of one potential utopia, but the end of utopianism in popular culture.

References

Bird, Donald Allport, Stephen C. Holder and Diane Sears. (1976) "Walrus is Greek for Corpse: Rumor and the Death of Paul McCartney". *Journal of Popular Culture* 10/1: 110–21.

Bromell, Nick. (2000) *Tomorrow Never Knows: Rock and Psychedelics in the 1960s*. Chicago and London: University of Chicago Press.

Brown, Peter and Steven Gaines. (1984) *The Love You Make: An Insider's Story of the Beatles*. London: Pan Books.

Browne, David. (2011) *Fire and Rain: The Beatles, Simon and Garfunkel, James Taylor, CSNY, and the Lost Story of 1970*. Cambridge, MA: Da Capo Press.

Bugliosi, Vincent with Curt Gentry. (1994) *Helter Skelter: The True Story of the Manson Murders*. New York: W. W. Norton & Co. [orig. 1974].

Carlin, Gerald and Mark Jones. (2014) "'Helter Skelter' and Sixties Revisionism". In *Countercultures and Popular Music*, ed. Sheila Whiteley and Jedediah Sklower, 95–107. Farnham: Ashgate.

Cleave, Maureen. (1995) "How Does a Beatle Live?" In *The Faber Book of Pop*, ed. Hanif Kureishi and Jon Savage, 254–58. London: Faber and Faber. [orig. *Evening Standard*, 4 March 1966].

Cott, Jonathan. (1971) Interview with John Lennon. In The Editors of *Rolling Stone*, *The Rolling Stone Interviews Volume 1*. New York: Warner Communications: 189–205 [orig. 23 November 1968].

Courrier, Kevin. (2009) *Artificial Paradise: The Dark Side of the Beatles' Utopian Dream*. Westport, CT: Praeger.

Dalton, David. (1999) "Rock's Dark Side". *Mojo* 70 (September): 70–76.

Ehrenreich, Barbara, Elizabeth Hess and Gloria Jacobs. (1992) "Beatlemania: Girls Just Want to Have Fun". In *The Adoring Audience*, ed. Lisa A. Lewis, 84–105. London: Routledge.

Emmons, Nuell. (1986) *Manson in His Own Words*. New York: Grove Press.

Epstein, Brian. (1964) *A Cellarful of Noise*. London: Souvenir Press.
Felton, David and David Dalton. (1970a) "The Most Dangerous Man in the World". *Rolling Stone* 61 (25 June): 27–29.
Felton, David and David Dalton. (1970b) "The Book of Manson". *Rolling Stone* 61 (25 June): 31–33.
Frith, Simon and Howard Horne. (1987) "The Rock Bohemians". In *Art into Pop*, 71–122. London: Methuen.
Gitlin, Todd. (1993) *The Sixties: Years of Hope, Days of Rage*. Rev. edn. New York: Bantam Books.
Green, Jonathon. (1988) *Days in the Life: Voices from the English Underground, 1961–1971*. London: Heinemann.
Johnson, Paul. (1995) "The Menace of Beatlism". In *The Faber Book of Pop*, ed. Hanif Kureishi and Jon Savage, 195–98. London: Faber and Faber. [orig. *New Statesman*, 28 February 1964].
Leary, Timothy. (1968) "Thank God for the Beatles". In *The Beatles Book*, ed. Edward E. Davis, 44–55. New York: Cowles Education Corporation.
Lennon, John. (1970) 'God'. *John Lennon/Plastic Ono Band*. Apple Records.
Lennon, John and Yoko Ono. (1981) *The Playboy Interviews with John Lennon and Yoko Ono*. Conducted by David Sheff. Edited by G. Barry Golson. Sevenoaks: New English Library.
MacDonald, Ian. (2008) *Revolution in the Head: The Beatles' Records and the Sixties*. 3rd edn. London: Vintage.
Manson, Charles. (1995) "I Am the Beast: The Trial Testimony of Charles Manson, November 19th 1970. A Transcript". In *Rapid Eye 1*, ed. Simon Dwyer, 3rd edn, 214–23. London: Creation Books.
McKinney, Devin. (2003) *Magic Circles: The Beatles in Dream and History*. Cambridge, MA: Harvard University Press.
Miles. (1968) "Multi-Purpose Beatle Music". *IT* 45 (29 November–12 December): 10.
Miles, Barry. (1997) *Paul McCartney: Many Years from Now*. London: Secker & Warburg.
Miles, Barry. (1998) *The Beatles: A Diary. An Intimate Day by Day History*. London: Omnibus Press.
Palmer, Tony. (1968) "The Beatles Bulls-eye". *Observer*, 17 November: 24.
Quantick, David. (2002) *Revolution: The Making of the Beatles' White Album*. London: Unanimous.
Sullivan, Mark. (1987) "'More Popular than Jesus': The Beatles and the Religious Far Right". *Popular Music* 6/3: 312–26.
Watkins, Paul with Guillermo Soledad. (1979) *My Life with Charles Manson*. New York: Bantam Books.
Wenner, Jann. (1971) "The *Rolling Stone* Interview: John Lennon. Part 1: The Working Class Hero". *Rolling Stone* 74 (21 January): 24–34.
Whitley, Ed. (2000) "The Postmodern White Album". In *The Beatles, Popular Music and Society: A Thousand Voices*, ed. Ian Inglis, 105–125. Basingstoke: Macmillan.

Author biographies

Gerry Carlin retired as a Senior Lecturer from the University of Wolverhampton (UK) in 2020. His publications include writings on modernism, critical theory, and the culture of the 1960s.

Mark Jones is a Senior Lecturer in English at the University of Wolverhampton, UK. He has published on science fiction, horror and crime in various media, and on popular music and pornography.

11 Interlude 2: The Beatles, Interpretation and Influence

Russell Reising, Peter Mills and James McGrath

This second of the three interludes reflects upon the role of the listener and viewer in perceiving and frequently creating frameworks of interpretation and meaning. Special attention is given to the idea of the avant-garde within the structures of the popular musical form.

PM: So, there are the obviously and overtly avant-garde tracks like 'Tomorrow Never Knows' or 'Revolution 9' and George's Indian stuff which would definitely have had that sort of shock of the exotic, but I also think a lot of their more apparently straight-ahead pop writing is avant-garde in the way that it uses and plays around with the conventions of 'straight-ahead pop writing' and does something else with them. The jazz chord McCartney mentions to Rick Rubin as being "hidden" in 'Michelle', for example.

JM: I always found 'Eleanor Rigby' quite striking in that way because although I suppose Ray Davies was starting to write in a similar direction, it's almost the absolute opposite of the 'From Me To You' technique – you know how those early songs had "you" or "me" or "us" in the title – but 'Eleanor Rigby' dispenses with all of that: "look at all the lonely people". It's a really different approach to song writing isn't it.

RR: It is. You know I think one way of tracing The Beatles' evolution is who they mean by "you". Once they get to 'All You Need Is Love' (1967) I think they're talking to everybody whereas the "you" earlier on is an object of desire but there it becomes like The Beatles embarking on their ministerial preaching!

PM: Yes, *you* say *you* want a revolution...

RR: Yeah I mean that "you" becomes transcendent: maybe after all the lonely people, when they get beyond boy loves girl, boy wants girl, look out girl, run for your life if you can little girl. Once they get beyond that and of course from my point of view that was all the LSD, you know their transformation and I think even in this concept of who the you's are in the songs has a lot to do with their really significantly expended visions. John Coltrane said the morning after his first LSD experience, he said "I experienced interrelatedness of all life forms" and I think that's what The Beatles and a lot of the more reflective introspective psychedelic lyricism was all about. You know before LSD nobody was writing stuff like just take a pebble and cast it to the sea then watch the ripples that unfold into me, they were saying "let's get in the back seat and do it"!

It was a real big change, and, just to introduce that race element, I think after *Revolver* The Beatles become really "white". I mean they covered songs by – I did a count – over forty different R'n'B acts over the course of their early career, a couple of hundred songs they covered in performance as The Quarrymen and as The Beatles. In the later phase, Billy Preston starts adding that soul sound but aside from that they go from being a group strongly influenced by blues and R'n'B to a group really flying free of lots of influences from their musical roots.

JM: How about the "White Album" though? Because I detect Chuck Berry's influence in 'Revolution' and 'Back in the U.S.S.R.', and B.B. King on 'Yer Blues' and so on.

RR: Yeah that's true, but I've never been sure whether that it wasn't parodic. It might be and if it *is* parodic it doesn't mean it's not "influence". We can also think of how that seemed even at the time – interestingly nostalgic somehow even in '68? – and with Eastern Europe, the former Soviet Empire, wide open, that song *really* seems nostalgic now. So, it's as if they almost anticipated what would be a double layer of nostalgia in that. When I was in college, I was taught by a professor who had a big influence on me, he used to hate The Beatles because he said all they were doing was stealing black music and not giving the original musicians and writers credit for it. Now that wasn't true. The Stones gave greater credit, I suppose, but they were more deeply indebted. I mean The Beatles liked to hang out with the Ronettes but I don't think that was necessarily...

PM: [Laughs] discussing chord shapes.

RR: [Laughs] exactly!

JM: To move on a little, what do you think about 'Blackbird'?

RR: McCartney's stories about how, why and where he composed it are really conflicting; one says he wrote it in Rishikesh after hearing a blackbird singing in the early morning. Later on, he said it was really a response to the racial tensions and problems in the United States around the time of the "White Album", and people have reported that it is really addressed to a black woman. Take your pick!

JM: It's interesting isn't it, because McCartney there is doing something that's more aligned to literary criticism and it's the kind of thing that we do I suppose isn't it, the retrospective interpretation. Lennon was similar because although 'I Am the Walrus' was famously a send up of, well, possibly people like me, he did go into a lot of detail about where he got the inspiration from for the lyric: he did encourage that kind of interpretation when it suited him.

PM: It's interesting though isn't it; the act of interpretation, whether it is retrospective by the composer or whether it's our job – it can be both 'serious' and also kind of game playing a la 'I Am the Walrus'. That's what popular music can do. Bundle up these very concentrated messages in concise bundles. I'm also interested in the issue of sleeve design: the album covers, in this case the famous (infamous) "White Album" sleeve design.

There's the blankness, the whiteness: do you know that scene in *This Is Spinal Tap*? "Look at The White Album, what's on that cover, nothing!" I've always understood it as a sort of sidestep from the habit of 'reading' covers: think of the luxuriance of design on *Revolver* and its brilliant full cover equivalent on *Sgt Pepper*: insanely loaded with detail. The former all self-referential, the latter only partly so – in fact it's almost elegiac. The flowerbed, the waxworks, the former selves.

RR: Well, all that detail certainly influenced how we thought about what we were going to hear.

PM: It makes you listen a way, a certain way. There's a totality of meaning between visuals and music.

RR: I mean when you see *Revolver* that sets you into a certain mindset and then you hear 'Taxman' and of course whatever direction you're heading in is confirmed almost automatically and of course with *Sgt Pepper* as well. I won my first copy of *Sgt Pepper* at a Fourth of July post fireworks dance because I'm where the outsiders are from and, you know, in addition to being the first album that ever printed the lyrics that was an album that you could spend as much time with the cover as you could with the music. When 'Yesterday' came out that was a really dark day because that was the day our parents started liking The Beatles. I mean that was really interesting because they went from being something that my friends and I could rally around and identify with to something that our parents wanted us to put on again to hear that beautiful song: not that beautiful songs are a problem but that transgenerational appeal you were talking about, you know 'Yellow Submarine' and the cartoon and things like that they also opened it up to people my parents' age and to the younger ones.

JM: I suppose things like 'When I'm Sixty Four' probably continued that process, as did a song like 'Honey Pie' on the "White Album".

RR: I don't think they were pandering, I just think it's that their music – their *vision* – was so capacious that there was no way to keep them in any sort of corral.

PM: When we're talking about moving from one audience to another, all those kind of transitional things that is a kind of a remnant of the era where pop was understood as a kids' thing or a rite of passage thing, strongly identified with your peer group as you noted before. So, even if it was as phenomenally successful as they were, there was still something about it that belonged to you, or this particular group over here, rather than your parents. Having said that, it's obvious that a song like 'Yesterday' is going to be more interesting to somebody who was fifty-five in 1965 than 'I Don't Want to Spoil the Party'.

RR: Or 'Paperback Writer'.

PM: Both of which are fantastic songs but the older listener would almost certainly say well, that's *your* music, but what we were talking about right at the beginning, the pan-generational thing, we can now probably project generations into the future and say well they will probably know this music. There are two things going on there: one is that post-1945 pop now has a history just a little longer than the lifespan of its first audience, so it begins to be thought of differently as a cultural form. Secondly, the advent of recording means that all this stuff is accessible. Who were the great singers of the early 19th century? We can find their names in books but we'll never hear them. And that's a massive difference. The Beatles, however, will continue to be heard in the immediate future, certainly by my grandchildren, if my kids have kids they will hear them and so it will go on. So, is that because people no longer think that way about sort of generational branding or sort of the tribal aspect of it or is it that somehow that certain music reaches a point of where it truly does belong to everybody?

RR: Well that's an interesting question, you know I think of movies like *Rock Around The Clock* (1954) that was clearly a generational struggle, you know the struggle for that music: in those movies it's always the kids [laughs] "rockin'" and their parents working but there's always some super cool older person who sees the potential of this and wants the kids to have their fun. As for my personal experience, I don't think my parents ever really warmed up to my music although my parents were really lower-middle/working-class types with no sophistication although I was raised on Hank Williams and The Drifters. My mother loved Hank Williams and she loved The Drifters so I had some, you know, some pretty solid stuff to be hearing.

PM: That's not bad.

RR: No that wasn't bad at all, but regarding that transgenerational thing, I think even an older person – say a hypothetical Martian with the sensibility of a seventy-year-old! – could come and find stuff in The Beatles to like. It's not just variety. When they do this other stuff they do it really well. Even 'When I'm Sixty-Four', a song that I don't like at all – I wish it would have been left off *Sgt Pepper* in favour of 'Strawberry Fields'! – but even that song is done so damn well it doesn't just *refer*, it *evokes*.

JM: On that topic of *Sgt Pepper*, I probably listen to it less than almost any Beatles album other than the first two and I think it's because it's as if it has a 'novelty' element for me. I mean, I love 'A Day in the Life', 'She's Leaving Home' and 'Getting Better'. The other tracks… I'm just not as attached to them as I am to most other Beatles material for some reason.

RR: Interestingly, within that era, John Lennon said he wanted 'Tomorrow Never Knows' to sound like a thousand monks chanting from a mountain in Tibet. What did he say about 'Being for the Benefit of Mr Kite!', which is my favourite song on *Sgt Pepper* by the way? He wanted you to be able to smell the sawdust of the circus. You know, that's a commitment to an aural sophistication that I'm not sure anybody else had. It sounds now as like an example of what they were hoping to get from George Martin but it's also a sense of the absolute depth of their commitment to creating something more than a soundscape. I think they do that. 'When I'm Sixty-Four', even 'Lovely Rita' as well as 'Being for the Benefit of Mr Kite!': those songs are all a part of it in that they really do evoke more than a sonic sense. They're evoking something from the past with a sonic signature of where they were at the time, so it wasn't just that they were going to the past to steal styles and gestures, they were also digging into it, almost like a creative archaeology. An emotional archaeology of the eras they write about.

PM: That's so interesting and this is what I was trying to articulate earlier about the avant-garde element – you've got the tracks that will sound 'avant-garde', you can play them to anybody and say yeah that's one of the avant-garde ones, but within these tracks, such as 'Being for the Benefit of Mr Kite!' there's something happening all the time and it's playing out and going round your head. Even though the sound of it isn't immediately or obviously 'avant-garde' the way it's put together, the ambition of it seems avant-garde to me even though when you listen to it you think "oh that sounds a little bit like that music I heard at the circus" or "that's a piano, it's behaving like pianos behave in music". Making the everyday feel just off balance enough.

JM: That's like that thing of throwing the tapes into the air or something and then sticking them back together after they've been cut up.

RR: Yeah, they cut tapes of actual circus rides and looped them back together. When we had a conference on the fiftieth anniversary of the "White Album" everybody was saying okay, if you could only have it be one LP what would it be and I became quite unpopular by insisting that you can't have a "White Album" without 'Revolution 9'.

JM: I completely agree; I find it absolutely fascinating you know and strangely uplifting actually, because there aren't many musical experiences that so capture the feeling of confusion in life.

RR: I mean people say, well that's one third of one side you know, well I don't care! I mean, if other stuff has to go we can leave 'Ob-la-di, Ob-la-da', leave 'Why Don't We Do It in the Road', we can leave 'Wild Honey Pie'. I mean I'd rather leave out some really important songs than leave out what I think is the signature song of the album. It demonstrates the commitment to the avant-garde and this is where I think Yoko really helped consolidate those final years of The Beatles with her own commitment, and she just sort of like pushed John farther and farther in that direction. Although I was in Chicago two weekends ago and I saw a car had a bumper sticker that said "I still blame Yoko".

JM: Just at the point where John met Yoko, Paul was starting to go, it was as if, you know with his experiments on *Revolver* then *Sgt Pepper* but after the failure of *Magical Mystery Tour* he sort of turned back didn't he, like 'Lady Madonna' is much more conventional in some ways than anything he'd been doing for several years and at the time that he's going further into 'When I'm Sixty Four'. Actually, within about three years of that song coming out, McCartney was living just that lifestyle.

RR: He sure was.

JM: Cottage gardening, you know, it was part of his image by the time he was twenty-seven.

RR: Yeah, well then of course eventually John Lennon becomes the breadbaking househusband I guess so they all moved in that direction. The other thing I want to get back to in 'She's Leaving Home' is that line "Daddy our baby's gone". That's a fascinating line for how old they were when they wrote that. To be able to internalise that – "Daddy, our baby's gone" – that's part of what I was getting at with that idea of emotional archaeology that ended up being really integral to their song writing. You know, lots of other groups there's the whole Pure Prairie League and The Grateful Dead writing about, you know, the Old West or outlaws or something like that but something like 'Friend of The Devil' doesn't have any depth to it. It's a great song and all that but I don't know of anybody else who committed themselves. Of course The Beatles knew nothing about the black hills of Dakota [location for 'Rocky Raccoon'] you know, but they managed somehow to evoke that atmosphere: whether it was some sort of strange remote viewing or something like that I couldn't say, but they managed to make the songs not just refer to but to resonate with either the past or the future and I think that might be the key to their endurance.

PM: It just floats free. 'She's Leaving Home' to me was a little like 'Eleanor Rigby' actually, in that when I was little and I used to hear those songs they used to frighten me; think how the strings lunge in after he sings "Daddy our baby's gone", that stab of realisation, it's like Bernard Herrmann you know? It's just sticking it right in there.

RR: Absolutely, they were kind of scary. The first time my son heard 'Eleanor Rigby' I was watching a high-def version of the movie *Yellow Submarine* and he was walking through the room and he literally stopped in his tracks, it was like he was electrified and he said "what is that". He didn't think it was beautiful, he said "that is so weird". I'm not sure that I had even seen *Psycho* when I first heard 'Eleanor Rigby'. Imagine it's two string quartets in 'Eleanor Rigby', imagine them sounding frightening in 'She's Leaving Home', you know, imagine high culture being brought into a pop song in a way that is unnerving rather than soothing.

PM: Rather than sweetening or ornamentation which is often what strings are used for in pop.

RR: Sure or harpsichord or things like that, but of course then you have something like 'Good Night' and in some ways that is pure schmaltz. I always thought it was heading for the end of things when rock groups started incorporating symphonic sounds or string quartets or things like that, but it never struck me as a problem with The Beatles. Except, as I said, it meant that my parents started liking them which was anathema at the time. Of course, my mother loved The Beatles doing cover versions by The Marvelettes or The Miracles and things like that but that's because, oddly enough, these white guys from England seemed less threatening if they evoked African American music which was in itself threatening to white Americans once it got beyond, you know, radio stations that only played race records. I think the idea that these four white kids, these four Brits, would be able to neutralise the threat previously posed by somebody like Little Richard. Their ability to translate stuff seemed endless.

PM: They introduced Motown to the UK in a way: well, the Tamla Motown stuff had come out in this country and there'd probably even been a package tour or two, but it was the effective endorsement of having Motown songs on the early albums that really opened the door because people would think "well, what is this stuff? We'll have to find out who W. Robinson is" and then go and find the music.

RR: I grew up near Detroit and so we had one of the really significant AM radio stations that premiered all of the Motown stuff. The station was in Windsor, Ontario just across the river from Detroit and so when I was first hearing all this stuff it was an absolute jumble. We would hear Johnny Cash followed by Smokey Robinson followed by The Animals followed by Herman's Hermits followed by The Monkees, you know? It's really hard for people to understand how we heard the music at that time, you know, because whatever new Beatles cut was new you'd hear it twenty times a day but you'd hear it in the environment provided by music as different from the Beatles as it possibly could be. It was really fascinating just hearing, you know, 'Rainy Day Women' followed by 'A Day in the Life' followed by 'Micky's Monkey' followed by Linda Ronstadt and the Stone Poneys. That's something that you'd be pushed to find even in the most avant-garde college radio these days: nobody is that anarchic in terms of genre hopping.

PM: Absolutely, that feels like an extraordinary level of eclecticism. I can't think of a radio station here that would have a playlist like that. Themed or genre radio has snuffed that out, even in the UK. BBC 6Music maybe, on a good day, might get close.

RR: Yeah, there was nothing else in this country and it was because of Motown and CKLW there was a direct connection between the secretary at Motown and the secretary at the radio station so everybody else probably got all the other stuff but the Motown infusion into that. And to a certain extent it made The Beatles seem even better because, you know, they stood out not just compared to Gerry and the Pacemakers or The Dave Clark Five but next to The Marvelettes or Martha Reeves and the Vandellas; there was a notion that they were all in a community, with The Beatles, who were number one among equals as well as the chart, as standard bearers.

Author biographies

Russell Reising is Professor emeritus at the University of Toledo, Ohio, USA. Professor Reising has taught, spoken, and published widely on topics in American literature and culture, Japanese literature and culture, popular culture and popular music. He has lived, studied, and taught all over the world, including Taiwan, Japan, Finland, England, and the United States. Russ's academic work has also resulted in his being commissioned to present workshops and lectures in England, Italy, Spain, Finland, Estonia, Bulgaria, Poland, the Czech Republic, Austria, Australia, and Japan. He was also an original member of the Educational Advisory Board at the Rock and Roll Hall of Fame and Museum. In 2008, Russ was one of only thirty Americans invited to participate in the People's Republic of China's first international literary conference.

Dr Peter Mills is Senior Lecturer in Media and Popular Culture in the School of Humanities and Social Sciences at Leeds Beckett University, UK. He has previously published on Samuel Beckett, Van Morrison and The Monkees. Peter is currently working on a series of short books on individual songs, a book chapter on the history of live music in Roundhay Park in Leeds, and an ambitious project looking to catalogue the history of live concerts at Leeds Beckett University since 1970.

Dr James McGrath is Senior Lecturer in English Literature and Creative Writing in the School of Humanities and Social Sciences at Leeds Beckett University, UK. He completed his doctoral thesis on the work of John Lennon and Paul McCartney, and his first book *Naming Adult Autism: Culture, Science, Identity* was published by Rowman & Littlefield International in 2017. His poems have been published in various literary periodicals.

Part Three

Savoy Truffles:
Further Perspectives

12 Paul in the Picture: Anatomy of a Snapshot

Martin Malone

In an age when the act of creation so often feels subsumed to that of curation, there is no ghost economy more lucrative than that dealing in Beatles ephemera. As their stock rises with each passing year, it feels ever more unlikely that one should encounter anything Beatle under an un-turned stone. The author's chance encounter, then, with a pristine Box Brownie snap of a pre-fame Paul McCartney – Höfner in hand, Beatles' bob, sporting a proto-Fab suit – in a small Scottish venue is what initiated the work of this chapter. What follows is a picaresque stroll around north-east Scotland during the short Beatles tour of January 1963. Ostensibly, a search for the provenance of a snapshot, the chapter becomes an impressionistic meditation upon the randomness of fame and the prosaic truths that so often prop up our sense of legend. By February of the following year, The Beatles had been on the Ed Sullivan Show *and the rest was history.*

Figure 1: Paul McCartney (photographer unknown, courtesy of Martin Malone).

"Tell you what, just pick out something small you'd like and you can have it."

"What, really? You sure?"

"Yeah, why not? You've been a good customer here, go for it."

The lady had a knack for sourcing great stuff, so I knew this might be good. But I had absolutely no idea it might turn up what I was about to find. Let's start here, then, with my scanning the room…

In the summer of 2017, my four year-old, his mother and myself moved from our university flat in Aberdeen to a quirky old house on the seafront at Gardenstown, a village, snug to the cliffs of the Banffshire coast that sometimes feels like the living incarnation of *Llareggub*, the fictional town conjured up by Dylan Thomas for 'Under Milk Wood'. The house, itself, needed a lot of work – still does – but we figured that it was no worse than anything either of us had encountered as students in the 1980s; indeed, it would situate at the more luxurious end of that particular scale. Besides, our wee boy was turning four, about to start school and, well, what better childhood could he have than growing up on a beach? I so often find that when you take a chance like this, the universe tends to provide. Sure enough, the moment we discovered our much-loved couch was too big to get into the house, we also found a great antique shop, just five miles away, in an old garage building at the side of the A98 running between Fochabers and Fraserburgh. *Templars Antiques & Fine Furniture*, by its own lights, specialized in: "Antiques, up-cycling, curios, gifts, vintage, and reclamation. We stock an eclectic mix of goodies." And, true to her word, Gabby had a talent for finding great stock then selling it on at prices we could afford without much lost sleep. I'd already bought a replacement couch, leather jacket, some trench art and ("say nothing of this to Jenn") a box of classic jazz LPs reissued on high quality 180-gram vinyl. So, I liked Gabby and she appeared to like us in turn, particularly wee Fíonn, who was never slow to make himself comfortable among the vintage toys and teddy bears. She, herself, had a young daughter and was looking after a Polish husband still recovering from injuries sustained, three years earlier, in a vicious racially aggravated attack. We'd drop by on Saturday mornings for a coffee and a chat *en route* to the weekend shop: newcomers to the area, exchanging small talk and thrilling over her latest finds. Business was ticking over but Gabby was hampered by a pig of a landlord who complained about everything and wanted to double the rent. Suddenly faced with an unprofitable set-up, she was moving out at the end of the month to go online, hence the kind offer of this freebie by way of a leaving present.

A familiar indecision rose up in me, as it used to do in sweet shops when I was a kid or, later, whenever I walked into a record store. With so much to tempt me, I simply froze in the headlights of choice. But, on this occasion, I almost immediately clapped eyes on a black-and-white photograph – about three-by-three inches – clip-mounted behind a plain glass frame; of the sort I'd used to showcase significant gig tickets when I was a teenager, in the hope of impressing anyone subject to the dubious pleasures of my bedroom. Perhaps it was this instinctive connection which drew me to the small picture, placed innocuously on a table of bric-a-brac among the lace doilies, cake stands, cap badges and china. Or, perhaps, we have hard-wired into our early twentieth-first century brains a cadre of *leitmotifs* so unmistakable that we'd have to be visiting from another planet for them not to resonate: Ghandi, Nagasaki, the moon landing, Kennedy assassination, Bloody Sunday, 9/11 and so on. Because this was Paul McCartney, surely. Not only that, but prime-era early Fabs Macca, in proto-Beatles suit, mop-topped and plucking on the 1961 Höfner 500/1 bass recognizable to, well, *everyone*.

"Have you seen this?", I asked Gabby.

"Yeah, cute isn't it?"

"*Cute?* It's amazing. What's it doing here, I wonder."

"Well, they toured up here in the early 60s, you know."

Did I know? I'm not sure I did. My Dad was a Scouser, Aunt Pat allegedly went on a date with Paul back in the day, my football team is reputedly his also, and I'd lived in Liverpool for twenty-four years; that's seven longer than anywhere else. For several of those, I'd been the near neighbour of Allan Williams – aka "the man who sold The Beatles" – in Pelham Grove, Aigburth. At the same time, I was dating a girl from Menlove Avenue, whose house overlooked Mendips and the yet-with-us Aunt Mimi. All in all, then, I've some degree of personal exposure to The Beatles' origin story. A child of punk and post-punk, however, I held them off for many years in blind-purist obedience to The Clash's year-zero declaration from 1977: "No Elvis, Beatles, or The Rolling Stones". With maturity, this changed significantly of course, though I remain far from the sort of Fabs nerd I'd often encounter on my doorstep in Percy Street or on Penny Lane. But, even in an Aladdin's Cave of interesting bric-a-brac, there was absolutely no competing with this 3×3 snapshot of a young James Paul McCartney at play: I scarfed it with gusto and so began this search.

What I'm now looking at is clearly a view of Paul taken from the stage-front of one of those halls familiar to anyone who attended dances or school assemblies during the first two or three decades after the Second World War: lots of dark-wood and hard surfaces, framing a stage raised about four or five feet above the audience. He's singing into a classic ribbon mic, typical of the times (possibly a Reslo RBT/L), at an angle of about 60° elevation above the photographer who is stood below him to his left. Picking at his bass with that beat-era index and middle finger style you'll see a lot on re-runs of *Ready Steady Go*, McCartney is singing in a manner relaxed enough to suggest a slower number, rather than him rolling over any Beethovens. There's a skinny black tie and the sort of mod-cut suit they were soon to exploit on a global scale, ditto the hair which is shaping towards the famous mop-top and – nice touch, this – what appears to be a cufflink poking out from underneath the single-button jacket sleeve. Crucial to it all is that 1961 Höfner violin bass, a model with which I'm quite familiar, having liberated and restored a neglected one from a flat on Windermere Terrace, Toxteth, in the early 1990s. To say this instrument is "iconic" would stretch definitions of understatement, I feel, so burned is it into the modern world's visual consciousness. Taken as a whole, the snapshot's composition is like one of its subject's better melodies: so instinctively familiar that you feel it's always been there, known long before its penning, or, in this case, before I clapped eyes on it. The photograph has that same wonderful in-the-room and in-the-moment quality one may glean in pictures from the black-and-white era of, say, your own parents' wedding. The print quality dates the snapshot unmistakeably and, I have to say, that it has aged rather well, given that it was taken three months before my own birth. Having scoured the photographic archives, I've come up with nothing quite like it, so it's certainly a one-off fan original and clearly begs the questions: who took it? where? and when?

Triangulating evidence of this kind is so much easier than in pre-internet days but, even now, given the level of fame subsequently enjoyed by the picture's subject, it is far trickier than it may seem. Firstly, I wanted to learn more about those tours of northern Scottish dance halls; to such unlikely places as Keith, Forres, Nairn, Fraserburgh, Peterhead, Bridge of Allan and Elgin. Here, I shall be ever-grateful to the trove of relevant material found on the *Scotbeat* website, which bills itself as providing: "1960's beat era Scotland features, exclusive music-related materials from the Albert Bonici archives. The Beatles, The Copycats, and many other musicians and vocalists booked by Albert Bonici of Elgin." It more than holds good on this promise with an absolute wealth of information, articles, weblinks, show-bills and press cuttings from the era: the perfect place to start, then. Bonici was something of a major-domo of the Scottish dance-band and beat scene. He ran the LCB Agency which booked acts to tour the north of Scotland as well as representing local talent. This operation centred around the Two Red Shoes Ballroom in Elgin which opened in 1960 and fronted an unprecedented flourishing of the local music scene. From direct experience, I know for sure there are gentlemen of a certain age, in small towns like Buckie, still dining out on the fact that they "supported The Beatles" back in the day, and why not? I heard a lot similar in the bars of Liverpool. And, while I have come across a couple of offerings in the vein of photo-journalism, there remains a great book to be written about both the beat scene up here and Bonici himself, who's mentioned in most Fab Four biographies of that time. This includes the near-Proustian epic that is *The Beatles All These Years – Volume 1: Tune In*, by Mark Lewisohn, which I also turned to for my research into the possible provenance of the snapshot. Tantalizingly, that first tome ends on 31 December 1962, just two days before the Beatles' short, five-day tour of northern Scotland in January 1963, a fact that may assume significance here, given that Lewisohn's *Volume 2* will not be available until 2023 at the earliest, according to the author's own website.

What is clear is the significant link to northern Scotland which The Beatles had in their formative years. As early as 1960 – with Paul about to do his A-Levels, George an apprentice electrician and John grifting his way towards dropping out of art school – they were engaged as backing band to Johnny Gentle for his "Beat Ballad Show", which toured north-east Scotland between 20 and 28 May of that year. The tour, taking in such rock 'n' roll hotspots as Fraserburgh, Forres and Keith, was the oblique result of their failed audition to become Billy Fury's touring band and, by their own admission, the trip found them under-prepared in terms of gear and musical chops: in *The Beatles Anthology*, George described the band as "crummy. The band was horrible, an embarrassment" (Beatles 2000: 83). It did, however, amount to a baptism of fire that proved essential in terms of bonding, growing up in public and learning how to cope with touring and each other. Years later, in an interview recalling the tour, Paul McCartney told *The Times* newspaper: "Not a lot of people knew about us before then, so this is kind of pre-history. But we loved it and it was invaluable experience for us because, after that, we knew it was no breeze, you had to work hard and you had to sort out where the money was coming from. It taught us a lot of lessons." There is, indeed, an intriguing body of stories and recollections of this tour from The Beatles themselves and the people they encountered in north-east Scotland. Most of these can be found in the Lewisohn book or, indeed, Ken McNab's invaluable 2008 book *The Beatles in Scotland* and in the "Tartan Beatles" chapter of Richard Houghton's collated fan memoir of Beatles gigs, *I Was There*, each of which proved invaluable to this investigation.

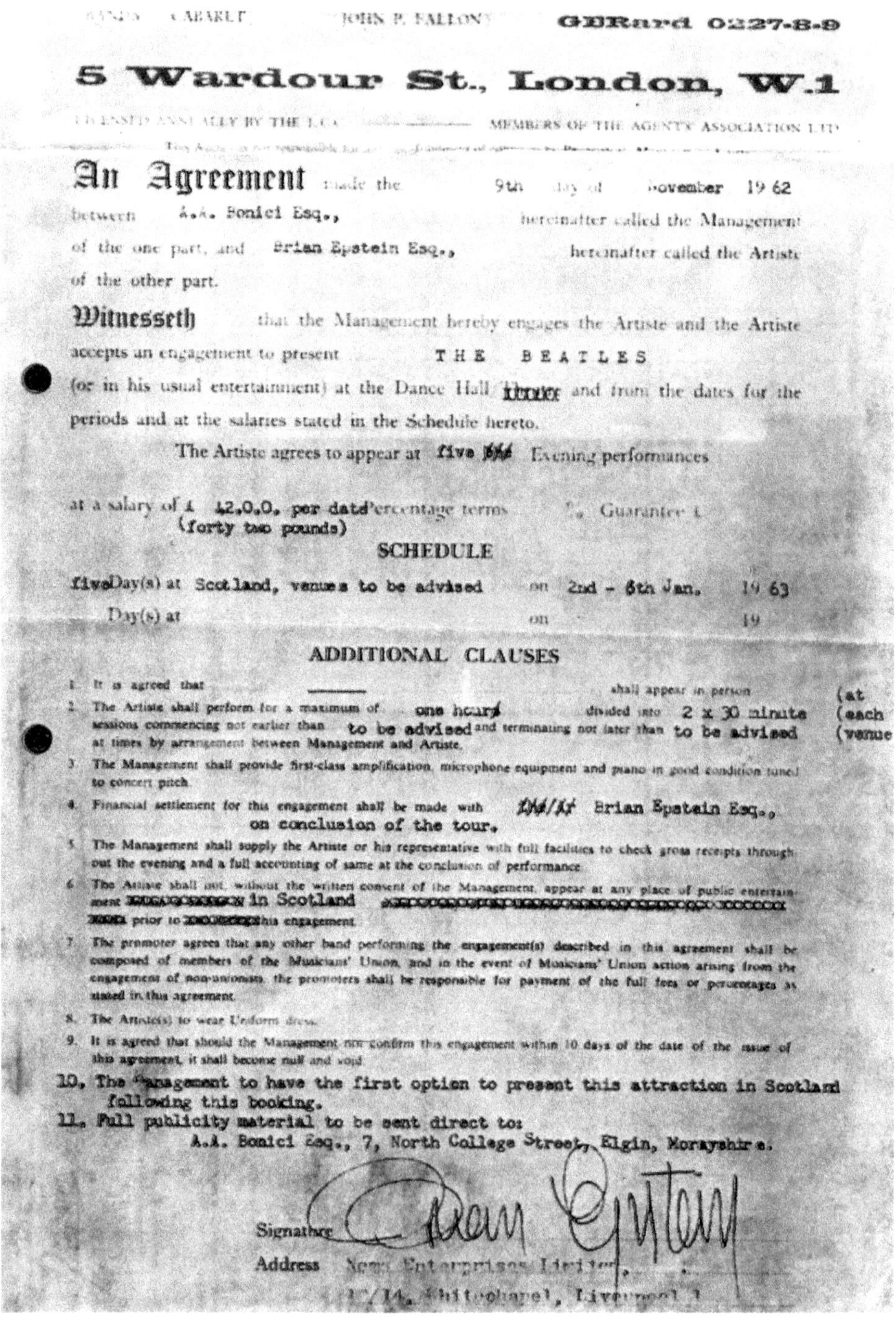

JOHN P. FALLON GERrard 0227-8-9

5 Wardour St., London, W.1

MEMBERS OF THE AGENTS' ASSOCIATION LTD

An Agreement made the 9th day of November 1962 between A.A. Bonici Esq., hereinafter called the Management of the one part, and Brian Epstein Esq., hereinafter called the Artiste of the other part.

Witnesseth that the Management hereby engages the Artiste and the Artiste accepts an engagement to present THE BEATLES (or in his usual entertainment) at the Dance Hall and from the dates for the periods and at the salaries stated in the Schedule hereto.

The Artiste agrees to appear at five Evening performances at a salary of £ 42.0.0. per date Percentage terms % Guarantee £ (forty two pounds)

SCHEDULE

fiveDay(s) at Scotland, venues to be advised on 2nd - 6th Jan. 19 63

Day(s) at on 19

ADDITIONAL CLAUSES

1. It is agreed that shall appear in person
2. The Artiste shall perform for a maximum of one hour divided into 2 x 30 minute sessions commencing not earlier than to be advised and terminating not later than to be advised (at each venue) at times by arrangement between Management and Artiste.
3. The Management shall provide first-class amplification, microphone equipment and piano in good condition tuned to concert pitch.
4. Financial settlement for this engagement shall be made with Brian Epstein Esq., on conclusion of the tour.
5. The Management shall supply the Artiste or his representative with full facilities to check gross receipts throughout the evening and a full accounting of same at the conclusion of performance.
6. The Artiste shall not, without the written consent of the Management, appear at any place of public entertainment in Scotland prior to this engagement.
7. The promoter agrees that any other band performing the engagement(s) described in this agreement shall be composed of members of the Musicians' Union, and in the event of Musicians' Union action arising from the engagement of non-unionists the promoters shall be responsible for payment of the full fees or percentages as stated in this agreement.
8. The Artiste(s) to wear Uniform dress.
9. It is agreed that should the Management not confirm this engagement within 10 days of the date of the issue of this agreement, it shall become null and void.
10. The Management to have the first option to present this attraction in Scotland following this booking.
11. Full publicity material to be sent direct to: A.A. Bonici Esq., 7, North College Street, Elgin, Morayshire.

Signature Brian Epstein

Address Nems Enterprises Limited, 12/14, Whitechapel, Liverpool 1

Figure 2: Contract between Brian Epstein and Albert Bonici setting out the terms for The Beatles' tour of northern Scotland, January 1963 (courtesy of the Albert Bonici archive).

What could reasonably be described as the pre-fame Fabs toured northern Scotland on two occasions.[1] As I have already mentioned, the first of these took place during May 1960, with the boys trading under their earlier name of The Silver Beetles. Here, they provided backing for Johnny Gentle, using the pseudonyms Paul Ramon (McCartney), Long John (Lennon), Carl Harrison (George) and Stuart de Stael (after Stu Sutcliffe's favourite painter, Nicholas de Stael). Local accounts of this tour abound, in both the McNab and Houghton books and elsewhere, in less well-known publications such as the article written by Stan Williams, "The Silver Beetles in Fraserburgh" (Williams 2014), which can be found, among others, on the *Scotbeat* website. In terms of my research, however, it is pretty clear that photographic images extant from this era rule out identification with my picture of Paul: the boys look appreciably younger and cut something of a rockabilly look in comparison with the recognizably Fab-look modelled here. So, in terms of narrowing things down to the most likely provenance for Paul in the picture, we can, with some degree of confidence, date the snap to The Beatles' January 1963 mini-tour. By this time Ringo had joined the group and their first single 'Love Me Do' had grazed the lower reaches of the Top Thirty, prompting them to be billed in some posters as "The Love Me Do Boys" for their show at the Two Red Shoes Ballroom in Elgin on 3 January. In a very real sense, then, this was a significant early moment in the worldwide cultural phenomenon they were soon to become, all-the-more fascinating for its relative anonymity and the small venues played. The tour was, as previously suggested, put together by local entrepreneur and promoter, Albert Bonici, who visited Brian Epstein's Wardour Street office to sign a contract which makes for interesting reading:

Here, we see that The Beatles were scheduled to play five "Evening performances" "at a salary of £42 per date" between 2–6 January 1963 at venues "to be advised". The group was contracted to play for a maximum of one hour to be split over "2 × 30 minutes" sets at each venue. The contract is dated on "the 9th day of November 1962" and the shrewd Bonici was soon to secure the exclusive rights to promoting all future Beatles concerts in Scotland. As it turned out, the scheduled five-date tour fell foul of the arctic conditions which beset the UK during that notoriously cold winter of 1962–63, resulting in the first of the proposed dates, at the Longmore Hall in Keith, being cancelled. The band's flight, having been diverted from Edinburgh, landed them at the nearer Aberdeen airport but they were still unable to reach the venue due to the snowbound roads. The Beatles' roadie, Neil Aspinall, had yet to complete the treacherous journey by road in a van with the band's gear, so this show appears to have been doomed from the start. Ken McNab notes that:

> Rather than hang around for a day, John Lennon used the unexpected break to fly back down to Liverpool to see his by-now-pregnant girlfriend Cynthia. Lennon promised to be back in time for the band's first gig at the Two Red Shoes the next night. Typically, though, he was racing against the clock and only made it to the venue with a little over an hour to spare, much to the relief of his three bandmates who would have been faced with the awkward situation of having to cancel a second successive show, a move that would have undoubtedly infuriated Epstein and Bonici. (McNab 2008: 69)

These details narrow down my own search, therefore, to the four dates that *did* take place, which were:

   3 January: Two Red Shoes, Elgin.
   4 January: Dingwall Town Hall, Dingwall.
   5 January: Bridge of Allan Museum Hall, Bridge of Allan.
   6 January: Beach Ballroom, Aberdeen.

I am utterly convinced that my photograph comes from one of these shows but pinning down its precise location and date has proved far more difficult than I had initially anticipated: there are factors which first advocate and then appear to eliminate each venue. Ultimately, I would go so far as to suggest that my task is possibly made harder by the uncertain provenance of earlier more known pictures, which may not actually be what they have hitherto been understood to be. "Possibly", "may not", "suggest": clearly, this inquiry will be one that rests on a balance of probability, though my reasoning and research are sound enough... or so it seems to me.

There *are* tells in the photograph which ought to help date and locate it in time and space: the Höfner bass, McCartney's suit and haircut, the angle, depth and focus of shot, the apparent size, scale and decor of the venue, the microphone and stand. That microphone will cause me a big headache late in the day. There is also an appreciable abundance of extant photographic stock, from private sources and local press coverage which should confirm, or at least, strongly suggest which of the gigs we're witnessing. However, what we must remember is the fact that this *is* a moment – perhaps one of the very last – when The Beatles were just one of any number of hard-working beat combos seeking to cash in on their fifteen minutes of fame, while they had a record in the lower reaches of the charts and enjoyed some airplay on Radio Luxembourg. As a result, none of the pictures taken during the '63 Scottish tour were taken in the memorializing spirit of a set-piece image designed to fix greatness in a clearly recognizable context. Fan photos and pop music itself are intrinsically ephemeral; indeed, this remains its key aesthetic, even now, in an age when popular culture has started to assume the appearance of significant history. So, my shot, like all the rest, is and shall always be vague in nature and flighty in the face of historical specificity. Such is rock and roll. Personally, I wouldn't change that for the world and certainly not for any nerd-spotting kudos to be had from a definitive identification. This way it is poetry. Though let us, anyway, enjoy the hunt and the journey.

The Two Red Shoes date on 3 January is the first candidate which comes to mind but the easiest to discount. Despite it being geographically closest to the location of my find, one look at a picture of the ballroom in its heyday will tell you that this is not the stage occupied by McCartney in this shot: it is too low, set up in a corner of a room more brightly painted than the one we're looking for, and altogether too cramped to match the insouciant ease of the man playing bass in my snapshot.

Figure 3: The Two Red Shoes Ballroom, Elgin, circa 1963 (courtesy of the Albert Bonici archive).

Figure 4: Beach Ballroom, Aberdeen, 6 January 1963 (courtesy of the Albert Bonici archive).

Nonetheless, I did send the picture to the *Scotbeat* editor and keeper of the Bonici archive, David Dills, who agreed with me but posted it on the site blog with an invitation to anyone who may have seen the tour to help in sourcing the photograph. As I write, we have not exactly been overwhelmed by the response, though some did help to confirm the hunch that my picture was also *not* taken at the Beach Ballroom in Aberdeen, which continues as a venue for touring rock bands to this day and is altogether too large of scale to correspond with the apparent size of the room we see in my photograph. For a moment, the vertical wooden beams above the stage back-cloth behind McCartney's head did tease me with their suggestion of something similar at the Beach Ballroom but, in the end, there is a clear mismatch of scale and depth-of-field in either space for them to be one and the same. Such factors danced in and out of my reasoning throughout this research, always offering an argument for one venue over another but ultimately crumbling under closer scrutiny. Those mics, however. They'll be back.

We are left with two venues from which to decide the most likely location of my snap, then: The Bridge of Allan Museum Hall and Dingwall Town Hall, both of which made for evenings notable in very different ways; and, in each case, for reasoning somewhat thwarted on my part. The Bridge of Allan gig was, according to audience member accounts, notable for its raucous crowd and a reception of The Beatles that was somewhere between hostility and indifference. According to audience member Neil Cunningham:

> Upstairs there were just a few couples, I remember about 20 or so young people scattered around the seating, huddled in pairs. The main hall lights were lit and the coloured footlights illuminated the stage curtain.
>
> Downstairs a crowd eventually gathered, about a hundred or so I suppose. The curtains parted as this new group began to play. There were four of them – the most striking thing about them was their hairstyle.
>
> … About 10 minutes or so into the session, the crowd downstairs became restless. From the remarks that floated up from the floor of the hall I gathered that the punters were not too charmed with the act, and someone began calling out that everyone should leave and go to the Stardust Club in Dunblane. The crowd disappeared within the next 20 minutes or so, and eventually all that was left was the upstairs few, probably too lazy to leave… (McNab 2008: 120–21)

Ah, how many reputedly "legendary" gigs have I been to, myself, where the reality was altogether more prosaic like this one! For present purposes, however, this account throws up some visually significant details: the old-fashioned proscenium arch borough hall stage, the stage curtain, mention of the group's distinctive hairstyle, are each factors that accord with those of my photograph. Another account of the gig is to be found in Richard Houghton's *I Was There* book. This one, from the ground floor, certainly feeds my fascination with the harsher realities of "legendary" gigs but is, perhaps, more significant for coming from Albert Bonici's co-promoter of Beatles gigs in Scotland, Andi Lothian:

> … I ran the last night, which was a Saturday night in a place called Bridge of Allan near Stirling. There were a hundred people there

> – 96 drunk young farmers and 4 women. So the place was just a rammie. I had only one doorman with me so I was doing a lot of the bouncing as well.
>
> The Beatles went on, did their stint and a penny hit Paul's guitar and chipped it. I was quite despondent about it because we had lost money on the event. (Houghton 2016: 61–62)

Now, if I could only make out a chip on McCartney's bass in my photograph then we'd have our gig. Alas, I can see no such thing and the Bridge of Allan concert seems destined to remain a moment of negative capability – the trump card of perpetual possibility – since, despite my best efforts, I have drawn an absolute blank on images of the gig itself. Almost certainly, some exist but if they do, they aren't available in any of the obvious places one might look for such pictures. But, while this outside chance abides, there remain a few factors that incline me to rule out the Bridge of Allan concert as the location for my snapshot: firstly, despite its current proximity to a shop called "Funky Village", the Museum Hall is in a central belt town quite distant from the Banffshire coast where I found the picture. This surely reduces its likelihood as the venue, human behaviour being what it is. Though it is not *impossible*, I admit. Secondly, given Andi Lothian's testimony, the Paul in *my* picture doesn't exude the air of a man being heckled by 96 drunk young farmers nor of one facing the old-penny firing-squad.

... Which leaves us with the previous night at the Town Hall in Dingwall, a gig remarkable for quite different reasons: chiefly its dearth of punters. Estimates vary but not much, given that they range between 19 and 20 audience members for a gig described by attendee Margaret Patterson as "the night the Beatles died onstage before the showbiz equivalent of two men and a dog" (McNab 2008: 118). Given that, as McNab points out, this was a group only weeks away from becoming a household name, it is worth dwelling on the wall of indifference which faced the not-so-Fab Four that night in Dingwall. To anyone who has been in a band – and I've been in quite a few – these accounts will be familiar and make for a healthy dose of *Schadenfreude*. A 17-year-old Billy Shanks was, in the end, *not* one of the audience, unless he was the floating 20th member. He remembers it like this:

> And the funny thing is that when I went in the door to go in and go upstairs the doorman said: "Before you pay, go up and have a listen". They actually played that song 'Love Me Do' when I looked in the door and I thought, "No, no this is not my type of music".
>
> I walked out and went to the local village hall five miles away to hear the Melotones. (Houghton 2016: 59)

That Melotones gig at the Strathpeffer Pavilion on the same evening drew a crowd of 1,000, including a chastened post-gig Beatles. The 17-year-old Margaret Patterson, who stayed for the whole Beatles set, was actually stood up by her future husband Tommy in favour of the other gig. She has since organized reunions of the 19-person Town Hall audience and, with the benefit of hindsight, reflects:

> In just five days, their second single would be released by their record company, EMI. Five days. Yet tonight, the Beatles couldn't even compete with the local foot-stompers at the Strath. And there would be precious little sympathy for the motley crew that made up this husk of an audience at the town hall. (McNab 2008: 118)

Remarkable, then, that there are images of this night at Dingwall Town Hall: images that demand consideration in the light of my search. There is also another comment made by Margaret Patterson which may be of assistance here:

> I sat on the stage all night chatting to The Beatles, and Paul in particular, who told me not to be upset as there were far more fish in the sea than ever came out of it. He was lovely! They said "Where is everybody? This town is dead!" And I replied, "Oh, no offence boys, but there is a great band on at the Strath and everybody is there and I'm going there soon. Why don't you come?" (Houghton 2016: 60)

Now, doesn't *this* mellow tone accord with my own picture of a somewhat unhurried Paul on bass, taken from an angle and situation that surely suggests a somewhat low-key affair? I confess, I so want my snapshot to be of this particular concert. There, I've said it. Notwithstanding the fact that Dingwall, though nearer here as the crow flies, is probably a longer trip to make than the better transport-connected Bridge of Allan, near Stirling. There is something inescapably romantic about the notion that we are witnessing a final moment of lesser mortality on the part of the Fabs, before they were catapulted into the stratosphere, as *the* biggest stars popular culture is ever likely to create. But the few photographs of that night bring as many caveats as positive leads.

Figure 5: The Beatles onstage at Dingwall Town Hall, 4 January 1963 (courtesy of the Albert Bonici archive).

If we were to be steered by concert ambience alone, this is surely the one: the intimacy and relaxed atmosphere of a small venue, a sparsely attended gig, the stage raised to about the same height suggested by my picture of Paul, the clear match of stage clobber, that 1961 Höfner violin bass, the back cloth... I swear I can even locate the possible shooter in the fair-haired chap to the far right, whose attitude *may* suggest he is in possession of a 35mm Kodak Retinette or Canon Demi. It could even be that my picture was taken by Margaret Patterson as she sat on the stage. The angle and depth of field would be about right if it were, except that she would have had to be prone at John Lennon's feet if we are judging by my foraged photograph. But then things start to break down: that back-cloth has stars on it, mine does not, that back-cloth is surmounted by the sort of white curtain swags you'd find at your Auntie Eileen's, mine is not. I think, too, that we'd get a hint of George's Vox AC30 amp visible in the Dingwall picture but not in my own. And then there are the microphones. Oh, those mics. They are clearly different, as are the mic stands. Paul is singing into different microphones for each picture and it is highly unlikely these were ever changed mid-set. So, alas, the Paul in *my* picture is not in Dingwall Town Hall. Darn it.

In the final analysis, this was never intended to be an archival act. The precise location of my McCartney picture would gain us, what? Mere factual confirmation. When, to my mind, the new snapshot represents something altogether more ephemeral and poetic. As a poet, surely, I'll stick with that. For the record – and if it helps those wired for facts – I'm now inclined towards identifying the venue as the Beach Ballroom on Aberdeen's seafront, where they played the last date of the tour on 6 January. Let's go back to a section of that Aberdeen picture and see that certain details do, after all, correspond to what we see in my photograph: the height of the stage, the plain black stage background, the straight mic-stand and, crucially, those microphones, which look exactly like the Reslo-style ribbon mic we see in my McCartney pic.

Figure 6: Detail – Beach Ballroom, Aberdeen, 6 January 1963 (courtesy of the Albert Bonici archive).

With some zooming-in, he can just be made out, beyond John, stood stage right in his proto-Beatles suit. That mic stand is positioned close to the front of the Ballroom's stage, allowing for precisely the correct angle of shot from one of those likely lads pressing forward. There remains the issue of field-depth – my shot suggests a stage back cloth far closer to Macca than looks possible in the vaulted space we see here on the Aberdeen stage, but maybe this could be accounted for by an optical illusion created by the angle. Again, "maybe", "perhaps" and "possibly". But, if I may flirt with the notion of psychogeography for a moment, there is psychological plausibility in the likelihood of my snapshot having been taken by a Banffshire resident at the Aberdeen gig; since, to this day, the city exerts the requisite cultural pull for a big night out for folks up here. Perhaps, too, the fan taking this picture was a *big* fan, who'd seen them in Elgin earlier on the tour and been impressed enough to come see his or her heroes again. Which music lover *hasn't* done that in their time? On the balance of considered probability, then, I name Aberdeen Beach Ballroom as the location: on Sunday 6 January 1963, when The Beatles played their last Scottish date before Beatlemania set in and there was no going back. So what? For me the thrill lies in an interplay between possibility and the one certain fact that my snapshot was from this particular tour and, quantifiably, at this moment of pre-fame status. Ultimately, the photograph's main value is altogether less historical than esoteric in its proof that tomorrow, indeed, never knows what today will become. So, enjoy my picture, turn off your mind, relax and float downstream.

Notes

1. I am defining "fame" here as a condition that irreversibly set in with Beatlemania which grew over the course of 1963, in the months immediately following their January tour of northern Scotland.

References

Beatles, The. (2000) *The Beatles Anthology*. London: Chronicle Books.
Houghton, Richard, ed. (2016) *I Was There (1957–1966)*. Falmouth: Red Planet Books.
Lewisohn, Mark (2013) *The Beatles All These Years – Volume 1: Tune In*. London: Little Brown.
McNab, Ken (2008) *The Beatles in Scotland*. Croyden: Polygon.
Williams, Stan. (2014) "The Silver Beetles in Fraserburgh". *ScotBeat*. https://scotbeat.wordpress.com/2014/05/26/the-silver-beetles-in-fraserburgh/

Author biography

Martin Malone lives in north-east Scotland. He has published three poetry collections: *The Waiting Hillside* (Templar, 2011), *Cur* (Shoestring, 2015) and *The Unreturning* (Shoestring, 2019). *Larksong Static: Selected Poems 2005–2020* was published by Hedgehog Poetry in December 2020. An editor at *Poetry Salzburg* and Honorary Research Fellow in Creative Writing at Aberdeen University, he has a PhD in poetry from Sheffield University. Currently, Martin is a Poetry Ambassador for the Scottish Poetry Library and a board member at An Tobar & Mull Theatre.

13 The American Beetles: How a Fake Beatles Band Defined a Movement, Changed a Culture, and Beat The Beatles at Their Own Game

Ed Prideaux

In this chapter the author explores the remarkable story of "The American Beetles", arguably the first ever Beatles tribute act, equally possibly a huge confidence trick played on audiences, promoters and broadcasters in mid-1960s South America – but also one which speaks of the way the music business worked in the mid-1960s and how to some extent it still does. An American entrepreneur put together an act that was purported to be The Beatles without ever actually promising that they were the real thing. Issues of identity, authenticity and audience are all brought to the table in this extraordinary tale which starts with glimpses of unimagined success for the musicians involved and ends with disappointment for band, promoters and audience. The fevered politics of South America in the period also add much to the mix, while a blend of personal reminiscence, contemporary comment and historical perspective allows the details of this little-known story to shine through for perhaps the first time.

It is late June, 1964. On Dick Clark's *American Bandstand*, a flagship nightly entertainment show, an unusual act is due to appear.[1] They will follow Wayne Newton, a greasy-haired lounge singer known to his fans as "Mr Las Vegas". "It's guest time, ladies and gentlemen", Clark announces from behind the desk. They take the stage.

The group is four in number. Draped in dapper grey suits and thick heels, their heads are curtained by mops of silky brown hair. Opening with an earnest four-beat hand clap and a crunchy Chuck Berry-ism, the group segues to a familiar lunge of toe-tapping rhythm-and-blues. The tall one – a guitar player and the main singer – leads the pack, with their lyrics checking common themes of going to school and liking rock and roll.

Their faces project an almost-permanent beam. The rhythm player grins, the drummer jollies, and the bassist – initially the least mobile of the lot – soon begins a reluctant-looking leg dance. And after only two minutes and ten seconds, the band will bow their heads. "Hi Ringo, if you'll come down from up top there!", Clark booms to the drummer. "I should first of all find out the primary question: is this your own, all your regular-type hair?" "Yes sir, we're growing it", the drummer responds. "It isn't a wig, is it?", Clark jabs. The bassist can't stop smiling. "May I have your first names please?" "Dave". "Tom". "Vic". "Bill".

For the Beatle experts among us, there would have been something amiss well before the names. For starters, The Beatles never performed on Dick Clark's show;[2] George Harrison, Paul McCartney and John Lennon were all the same height, so no single Beatle was the "tall one", either; and with the exception of 'Bad Boy' and 'Getting Better', recorded respectively one and three years after this performance, The Beatles would never release a song about school.

But for those who'd watched *American Bandstand* that night, the differences would have been far more apparent. Simply put, the band isn't The Beatles at all. They are "The American Beetles": a Beatles parody cash-in band formed just a few months before. It even says as much on "Ringo's" drum skin. And in place of four lads from Liverpool, The American Beetles comprise a quartet from Palm Beach, Florida: Vic Gray, Dave Hieronymous, Bill Ande, and Tom Condra, each of whom would later self-describe as a medical student, a passionate water skier, an aspiring horror actor, and an "amateur composer".[3]

> "You are doing what I guess a lot of people would like to do: let their hair grow long, play the Beatles stuff and so forth. How does this strike you? Did you ever meet these fellas [The Beatles]?", Clark asks.
> "We met 'em in Miami".
> "What happened? Did you have an all-out war? Did they receive you well? Were you going to see them or vice versa?"
> "No, they came to see us. We were playing a club in Miami and they came in".

It is a night that Bill Ande, the band's lead guitar player and the "tall one", and Bob Yorey, their manager, still remember fondly. Even Ringo would recall that evening in *The Beatles Anthology*, although more for The Coasters than the Fab Four's American counterparts.[4] "We did the little 'Beetle routine'. A couple of them were in the audience. I think it was maybe John and Ringo", Ande says. "We were backing up The Coasters. We backed up The Coasters, and The Drifters, and every act you can think of. We had a real good rhythm section".[5]

Their manager remembers differently. "Paul McCartney came in with his girlfriend at the time, Jane Asher, and then Ringo came in. I thought that when the cops came, we had a problem... because I was advertising The American Beetles! I got so much publicity from that".[6]

The band weren't always Beatles parodists. They had started out as a doo-wop-influenced R'n'B act named The Ardells (sometimes spelt The R-Dells). "We had a little vocal group... Like four or five of us would sit around at the drive-in at a restaurant and sit in a car and harmonise", Ande, the lead guitarist, remembers.

The band found some early success. They cut a halfway hit – "kind of like a country song", Yorey recalls – for Columbia Records, and were making the rounds gradually in the Palm Beach club scene. But when Beatlemania struck in early 1964, Bob Yorey, a grifting nightclub owner and boxing entrepreneur, was quick to spot the opportunity. "I said, 'You know what? They're the English Beatles. I'm gonna make up a group. I got these four guys and I said, 'Listen. Grow your hair and we're gonna call you 'The American Beetles'".[7]

"When The Beatles came out, one night we just combed our hair down... and we did our normal rock 'n' roll show. And we announced ourselves as 'The American Beetles'", Ande says. "We wore our hair the same, we dressed the same, we wore suits. It was pretty good".[8]

They may have looked the part, but The American Beetles would never actually play any Beatles originals. Not that this mattered much for their Beatle-hungry audience, Ande noted: "We did some original songs, and we did a lot of rock 'n' roll. We did everything from Jerry Lee Lewis... We did everything from Ray Charles, 'Summertime Blues'. We were just a rock band, you know. And it kind of just blew up".

Amid the PR wave generated by their chance meeting with the real band, The American Beetles began forging valuable links in the music industry. They made their way to California, performed on the Sunset Strip, and made contact with Johnny Rivers, a producer who had found fame with 1966's no. 3 chart hit, 'Secret Agent Man'.

It was a routine performance at Palm Beach's Mau-Mau Lounge, however, that would change the band forever. An Argentine businessman named Rudolfo "Rudy" Duclós was in the audience. Duclós liked their sound. He liked The Beetles' look, too. But more than anything else, he liked their name. "After a while, a guy from South America came in and saw it and wanted to book us on a tour... So, we said, 'Well, what the heck!'", Ande remembers.

As with everywhere else in the world at the time, Beatlemania was going viral in Argentina. An EMI shipment, comprising bumper packages of the band's single, 'From Me To You/Thank You Girl', and *The Beatles' Hits* compilation LP, had landed in June the previous year and gone straight to the top of the respective charts. And following a brief experiment by EMI's Argentine subsidiary – in which the band's name was temporarily translated to the literally Spanish '*Los Grillos*' – demand skyrocketed with The Beatles' visit to the USA in February 1964. EMI was more than willing to accommodate, and two fresh singles were cut by April.

Notwithstanding the country's enormous demand, The Beatles had no plans to tour in Argentina or indeed anywhere in South America at all. And as with any market that needs clearing, Duclós spotted a gap. After signing the relevant papers, The American Beetles were headed on a round trip to Argentina, Venezuela, Uruguay, and Peru, with brief starting performances in Spain and Mexico. It seemed like everyone would be a winner. Yet there was something Duclós hadn't quite mentioned to his contacts. It wasn't *The Beatles* that had been booked. He'd sold the Americans as the real thing.

The South American press lapped it up. Peru's *La Prensa* announced their arrival for the following May, with the band (including 'Paul McCarthey' [sic]) "almost, almost done" signing the contract with the Peruvian Channel 4's commander, Mauricio Arbulú.[9]

"The Beatles Are Coming!", declared Argentina's *La Crónica*,[10] and Duclós swung them a spot on Argentine Channel 9's *The Laughter Festival*. "I was working at the video room, and we couldn't believe it ourselves that The Beatles would be coming here", said Roberto Monfort, who worked at Channel 9 in 1964.[11] "Alejandro Romay [Channel 9's owner]... claimed to have secured a fabulous deal. He generated a tremendous expectation... [He had] a huge advertising campaign on the TV channel. The Beatles' case, it broke with everything known so far. I mean, it was an impressive moment".

Boarding the media wave, the "Disc Jockey" label cut a double disc[12] of The American Beetles in June, comprising 'You Did It', 'Don't Be Unkind',[13] 'Great Day' and 'Walking With My Baby': tracks in which many, including Argentine rock superstar Felix "Litto" Nebbia, still find musical merit.[14] The scam was working. Not that The American Beetles knew anything about it, though. Ande insists,

> We didn't know any of that [false promotion] was happening, because, and number one, we didn't spell our name the same. We always said 'The American Beetles': B-E-E-T-L-E-S. And that's what surprised me, because we never, ever pretended to be them... We

were *us*. And we thought it'd be funny to be America's version, so to speak.

What is more, even months before their arrival, there are some retrospective signs that the "American" identity of the group was emerging. The major Argentine daily paper *Clarín*, for example, wrote of "the authentic, that is to say, the Made in England" quality of the real Beatles as early as that May,[15] and on the week of The Americans' arrival – a time when any press embargoes would presumably be under careful watch – the paper lambasted the band's "imitated bangs... of the famous modern English ensemble".[16]

But if the scam's target audience was children, perhaps it was unlikely that any minor press disclosure would compromise their spoils. Carlos Santino recalled the news fondly. "I remember the moment when they announced that The Beatles [would] come to Argentina because of my cousin. She was going nuts. And I'm not even talking about going to the theatre to get to see them. The mere fact of watching them on TV represented a significant experience already".[17]

The American Beetles' appearance on Dick Clark's *American Bandstand* took place only weeks before the scheduled flight. The American Beetles would arrive in Buenos Aires at the height of Argentine winter. And to witness their descent, large crowds of excited teenagers had amassed in the ranks. Suited up and filing down the escalator, one can only imagine the excitement that Tom, Vic, Bill and Dave were feeling. But it didn't take long for the dream to come crashing down.

Again, behind the band's backs, Duclós had sold The American Beetles to both Channel 13 and Channel 9 for the same night.[18] What may have been a canny commercial play in the first instance had since become a difficult legal wrangling, and a hasty court mediation was arranged on their immediate arrival in the continent.

Joined by lawyers and executives from both sides, the band entourage was dragged to a backroom at Buenos Aires airport to settle the score. While Romay and the bosses at Channel 9 had signed a contract, Channel 13 held some useful *sub rosa* links with the capital's authorities. These connections would prove decisive.

Channel 9's Alejandro Romay wasn't called the "Czar of television" for nothing, however. He didn't like to lose. He had an "unorthodox" solution planned. Romay called up Karadajian, the star of a wrestling programme called *Titans in the Ring*, and asked the giant to bring "all [his] heavyweights at my hand".[19]

Romay explained more than thirty years later, "The bouncers went right over to the five boys, and they practically hung them over their shoulders.

Everybody was chasing them: the police, the people from Channel 13, the judge". The band's manager recalls, "The police and the bodyguards said 'Listen, you get inside there' – they made a 'V' – 'and the minute we start running, don't stop, just continue'". "There were a lot of people at the airport, and they didn't want no problems. It was kind of scary".[20]

"Already in Palermo [a neighbourhood in Buenos Aires], I had the trucks and everything set up", Romay said. "We went to a hotel [in] the suburbs in San Telmo that nobody knew about and we locked them up".

The band's lead guitarist adds some fresh detail. Not only did Karadajian and his wrestling minions remain with them throughout the tour – "we'd make them wrestle in hotel lobbies", Ande remembers – but it seems that Channel 13 briefly stole their drummer back. "When we got off the plane, they took us to a TV station. Our drummer was kidnapped by a different station. And they went through a whole thing to get us back and everything".[21] Kidnappings and getaways notwithstanding, the band soon made it to Channel 9 studios in one piece. It was rehearsal time.

The press, meanwhile, was hot on the trail. The legal dispute – followed, of course, by Romay's escape – made for a thoroughly newsworthy denouement, and the slowly-emerging subterfuge of the entire tour only legitimized the blood-baying of Argentina's conservative commentators. "*The Beetles: 2 Channels Enjoy Your Howls*" wrote *La Crónica*.[22] Positioning the case as a politico-legal scandal, the paper co-opted police slang in a small paragraph on each "suspect" in the case. The paper would supply a more fascinating example the following day.[23] In the confused aftermath of Romay's "unorthodox" solution, Argentina's tabloid would scoop an exclusive with the mediation judge himself. And in their brief but characterful exchange, the older Argentine seems to echo the scepticism of an entire generation.

"Moving away from the legal dispute, what do you think of these young people?", the reporter asked.

"What do you want me to say? I remember that, in our time, the Charleston and its movements were also disparaged. But the truth is that I do not understand..."

"Would you let your children go see The Beetles?"

"That is their thing. I wouldn't see them even if I was crazy".

Compared to past coverage (and indeed that still to come), this exclusive was fairly soft on the band. In the last few months, the newly arrived "Beetles" had gained notoriety in Argentina in accordance with the real Beatles' attraction of reactionary press vitriol from some quarters. *La Crónica*, a paper that otherwise centred on "*artistaspopulares*" such as Bing Crosby and Chico

Navarro,[24] found rich ammunition in the "manes" of the Fab Four. They were "howlers-trepidants", their "artistic quality almost nil", and "the scream" – presumably the kind found in 'Twist and Shout' – was ordained "a sharp, piercing howl, stinging and groaning... not related to music", yet "in keeping with... Parkinsonian contortions [and] epileptic rictus".[25]

Quite the commentary. Back at Channel 9's studios, Romay, the station's Caesar-like owner, was growing disgruntled. "They were shameless, dirty, filthy", Romay said of his new booking. "They were the worst! And when it was time to sing, I thought, 'Well, but can they sing?'[26] So, we came to this studio. I was there, so I said, 'Well, let's see: you have to do a rehearsal'. They said, 'Put the record on!' Well, that was the last straw. 'Put the record on? Which record?!'" "'Well, we're going to do lip sync, since we can't sing!'"

To this day, however, Ande and Yorey maintain that their performance was completely live.

> There were articles that were written when we were down there... And some of them were very cruel. And they accused us of, like, lip-syncing our songs, not playing very well, and not singing very well... But I'll tell you something: we had a really good band. And we sang good, we played good, we did everything live.

Hector Zarraga, a Channel 9 employee of the time, sides with Romay. "No, no, it was all lip sync. We put some speakers on the side, they listened, and they pretended. They didn't speak".[27] Whatever the nature of their performance, The American Beetles would grace the stage of *The Laughter Festival* that week.[28]

"Our television programming is based on the best that the current Argentinian youth has [to offer]", the *Festival*'s bow-tied presenter proclaimed. "But our goals are much higher: the conquest of the Latin American markets. The Beetles... represent a reaction against materialism... They represent it in a single word: dignity. Of course, you might ask me, 'Can dignity be displayed in that way? With those clothes, that hair?'"

"I remember so vividly the announcer introducing The Beatles", reflected Carlos Santino, who was then a child glued to the screen.[29] "And there was like a circle made of paper – it was huge. They broke that circle and came on the stage. They headed to their instruments". His cousin was "going nuts".

Then the inevitable happened. When she saw it wasn't Paul McCartney who was coming out from behind the curtain, she started to cry inconsolably. Mabel Schajris, likewise a child in 1964, noticed the oddity early on. "They [hadn't] spelled the name. It spelled with a double E", she said.[30] Studio decks were packed to the brim. As the band tore into 'Twist and Shout' – the only number they seemed to share with the real deal – the audience was apparently captured by a deranged cognitive dissonance.

"BEE-TLES! BEE-TLES!", the crowd chants. As hands clap and feet stamp, the teenage spectators appear in the throes of a tribal ecstasy. "The audience that had access were delirious. They really were delirious... It was like watching a fantasy", said Roberto Monfort, the Channel 9 staffer who had hitherto been caught in the "tremendous expectation" of Romay's media *coup*.[31] "It was hysteria – real hysteria".

Luis Rodriguez-Corti was among the hysterical crowd:[32]

> There was no audio monitoring. The only thing you could hear were the drum and the guitar – they were blaring out.... Everybody was jumping around me and I couldn't hear a thing. Suddenly I found myself shouting like everybody else. But I didn't understand why, because in the end it was all a charade.

It wasn't all euphoria, though. "Between indignation and laughter" is how Monfort described much of the night. "Because there were some people that were having fun, but some others were waiting for the real Beatles. And they felt defrauded". Jacko Zeller felt the occasion "pretty sad... because they were musicians – actually, they were not good musicians", he hedges. "The only thing they had was the wig. They could play, but it was a disappointment".[33]

As it happens, Romay wasn't in the studio that night. Shortly before the performance, the Channel 9 mogul was apparently consumed by a rare moment of compunction. "I want no part in this lie to the people. I'll take a plane and go to Punta del Este [an Argentinian beach resort]", Romay is said to have told his crew. "I don't want to know a thing about what's going on". It seems he checked at some point, though. "No, people went crazy! They bought it!", Romay maintained in 1998. "We had 63 rating points with The Beetles. I think it was the highest peak in the [channel's] history".

While lucrative, the TV performance drew sharp attacks in the national press. *La Crónica* declared the quartet "*antimelodicos*", "howling songwriters" and "*pelucones con sillidos*", a wry comparison to the fusty wig-helmed aristocrats of 19th-century Chile.[34] A headline later in the week declared that "*They Have Hair in Their Vocal Chords! They Sing Bad, But They Act Worse!*"[35]

> At 21.17, the expected, the dilated, the 'irreplaceable' American Beetles... were announced more or less as you already knew. Long, straight hair, hairstyles, with spry, tight pants; four faces in which it could be doubtless said that every sign of intelligence was conspicuous by its absence.

The band's concert performances would only attract more (and sometimes more dangerous) attention. "Most everybody really liked our music and what we were doing", Bill Ande says. But "a certain element" – "jealous guys, you know", he speculates – would "throw coins, maybe rocks. We'd do a concert and have to get the hell out!"[36]

The press covered these incidents with glee.[37] "A lot of people, after they saw them, went, you know, 'This is not Ringo, this is not Paul McCartney!'– you always had a few people in the crowd that made noise and so forth", remembers Bob Yorey, The American Beetles' manager. "But it was okay. It was a great gig for the guys. I thought they were received very well".

As the tour progressed, the news coverage showed no sign of slowing down. Story by story, column inch by column inch, The American Beetles were fast becoming the media sensation of the South American winter. The saga was moved by *La Crónica* and *La Nación* from their cultural pages to those of "*informacion general*", and in those newspapers that neglected the change The American Beetles still boasted a nigh-on monopoly.[38] Even when *A Hard Day's Night*, The Beatles' record-breaking film, was released in the week after The Americans' Channel 9 performance, the news was comparatively overlooked.

For two months, The American Beetles (even once, and in large part because, Duclós's ruse was up) displaced The Beatles proper from the Argentinian media. Taking January to December 1964 as a whole – a period that long precedes and outdates The Americans, and includes further Beatles releases, a smash film and the Beatlemania phenomenon altogether – The Beatles had only a slight edge on their American counterparts in news mentions and press imagery.[39] It was a PR *coup* to say the least.

So intense was the media circus, in fact, that *Primera Plana* magazine ran an editorial condemning the fickleness of the Argentinian press.[40] In the article, the author despaired that newspapers "seemed to be more concerned about the appearance of four American students" than the earthquake or presidential election in Mexico, or the fast-erupting war in South Vietnam.

Don't mistake this for an endorsement of the band, though. "No one who heard the quartet can believe that the permission granted to hoot freely has made one a better human being", the author warned – and "concealed behind their brand-new manes [lies] an inability to sing which no specialist had doubted, even before hearing them".

The Beatles machine would have to respond eventually.[41] EMI Odeon soon published a press release clarifying the identity of the group, explaining that The Beatles had never been to Argentina. It is estimated that EMI increased the authenticity checks on future releases by as much as three-fold. *A Hard Day's Night*, the soundtrack released a month after the film, was rechristened, "*Yeah,*

Yeah, Yeah: Paul, John, George and Ringo!", and the accompanying singles were published as 'The Real Beatles' at the company's insistence.

In another bizarre turn, The American Beetles themselves inspired the creation of new Beatle-imitating bands. *Los Búhos*, translated as "The Owls", scored articles in *La Crónica* and *Antena* magazine that month,[42] with the group's members – "Juan", "Yusti", "Jorge" and "Rango" – declaring their sound "more Beatles than The Beetles". *Los Búhos* were joined the following month by *Las Beatlas*, "a musical ensemble of hairy young girls"[43] that appeared on Argentinian TV. And when a suspicious bootleg began circulating in the underground market, The American Beetles were forced to issue their *own* clarifying press comment on the imitative record's inauthenticity.

But as the press amassed in quantity, a race to the bottom was afoot on quality. "Some of the reporters gave us negative press. And because we had long hair, they considered us gay people, *maricóns*", Bill Ande says. "I remember making a remark, 'Bring us your wife and daughter, and let me spend the night with them', and he didn't like that, you know. It would piss you off... They did things to insult us."

Under the taxing headline of "*The Beetles and the amazement of a chronicler in the face of an idolatry hard-to-justify*", *Clarín* ran an opinion piece filled with homophobic dog whistles.[44] The author relates their TV appearance to the "decline of the human condition" and the arising of the "intersex state". The band are positioned as "examples of notorious ambivalence", with their "hair in the way of disheveled girls, their tight pants and the way they swing to the rhythm of their songs". Vic, the band's bassist, is pictured "undergoing makeup" before the TV performance: a sexual signal that further "accentuates the characteristics of his ambiguous personality".

The article even questioned the Americans' very identity as humans.[45] Referencing the work of American anthropologist Ralph Linton, the piece compares the band to "a rat or a fossil", insofar as – like other sub-human entities – people can study them with an "impassiveness" and objectivity not afforded for real human subjects. Argentina, even in advance of the military coup of 1966, was not quite ready for the wilful ambiguities of Anglo-American pop.

La Crónica added to the storm.[46] The band were "*cascarudos*", or Torito bugs, whose resemblance to men is "pure coincidence". In a racialized jab at the band's booking agent, *Atlántida* magazine's special feature, "*The Sham of The Bangs*",[47] deemed Duclós a denizen of corruption and "creole liveliness": the creoles being a long-victimized race of West Africans and ancestral colonial Spaniards common to South America.

Other criticism was more condescending. *Clarín* described The Beetles as "'artists'"[48] and "'treasure'",[49] while *La Crónica* – in a scattergun of upturned noses and quotation marks – took aim at "the 'singers' (as somehow you have to call them)" and "interpreters", and even ironicized the concepts of "stars", "fans" and "gossip".[50]

As much as the band itself, the media's incensed reaction was a result of broader changes capturing the world at the time. That the band could attract such venom – as did anything remotely colloquial, too, it seems – is a sure-fire sign of a widening Generation Gap, or *Brecha Generacional*,[51] that was colouring basic elements of language and culture. Where The Beatles proper were manna from heaven for the kids, their sound was "Parkinsonian" to the parents. Young and old were in parallel universes.

Duclós's scam was drawn arguably from the same thread. While their only commonalities were half a name, four moptops and some suits, to assume that The American Beetles were indistinguishable from the real deal betrays the very elitism that The Beatles proper would later vanquish.

Litto Nebbia, who witnessed and enjoyed the American Beetles phenomenon, found fame in the *rock nacional* movement of the late 1960s. "'Let's say they are The Beatles – who would ever notice it?!' Well, but that's absurd. I don't know how somebody can come up with that idea – and say that Chaplin is coming tomorrow but Carlos Balá [Argentine comic actor] comes instead".[52]

Approaches along these lines had been deployed before, according to Sergio Pujol, a music historian and cultural critic. "Those were the times when they were mass-producing local idols in the image and likeness they were producing in Motown… and England".[53] And looking at contemporary exploitation films like *El Club Del Clan*, it is hard to contest Pujol's assessment. "It looked like some idea of rebellion, but yet a little washed out".

Perhaps The American Beetles themselves have questions to answer, too. They may have sidestepped the active deception of their booking agent, but the band's occupation of The Beatles through a mere change in appearance hints at a different kind of reductionist cynicism. We can sit and chuckle as Dick Clark, the *American Bandstand* host, obsessed over their hair – and neglected to ask even one question of their music – but the group's rebranding shows an act more than willing to play the part.

An advertisement in *Clarín* would take this reductionism to its logical end. Promoting The Beetles' forthcoming performance on Radio Splendid, the band is shown with no visual identifier other than – quite literally – four faceless moptops.[54] It is interesting to note, however, that their performance on Radio Splendid would never actually go ahead. As well as more longer-term demographic changes, The American Beetles' culture war was shaped by active political resistance, too. Both Radio Splendid and Radio Liberty cancelled their showings under pressure from the Administrative Commission, a government agency that monitored the press.[55]

Professor Nélida Baigorria, the Commission spokesperson, described The American Beetles as "absolutely free of artistic value" and as displaying "sexual ambiguity". "We knew perfectly well what their artistic qualities were – if what they do can be called art – and that is why we adopted this measure... Bear in mind that the State has the obligation to take care of the physical and moral health of the people".

For Baigorria, the lack of any "legal instrument that enables us to intervene in cases like this" wasn't necessarily a problem. She pledged that "work is underway" on a new regulatory framework, and "the means will be given to defend listeners and viewers from this type of pseudo-artistic manifestation" in the future. Such a move was not unheard of. In 1964, Argentina and South America altogether were cycling between explicit and implicit forms of fascism. "The country remains a contradiction", the *New York Times* reported at the year's outset, with its "shanty-built structure" said to be "in considerable disarray" amid "the political tornadoes of the last two years".[56] The country's President was overthrown in a military *coup d'état* just two years later, and even while purging the country's political surface of Peronism (the hyper-conservative populist system of Peron, the ex-dictator of Argentina), the ideology remained stubbornly present in Argentine culture.

The American Beetles scandal was peppered with such ideology. Putting aside its machismo-chauvinism, one need only consider the media's recurrent anti-Americanism, with the band dismissed by *La Crónica* as "American howlers". "Let's not forget, they are Yankees", the paper said the next day,[57] offering a barbed apology for the band's "measured howls" and bad singing ("luckily they sing little").

Political turmoil would follow the band throughout their tour. "When we went to Caracas, Venezuela [a country riven by anti-American sentiment],[58] and we went to the TV studio when we arrived, there were soldiers on the roof with machine guns. There was a whole uprising we didn't know about", remembers Bill.

During a pit stop in Franco's Spain, The American Beetles were even caught in a likely eruption of fake government news. The band performed in the Plaza de Toros de Las Ventas, Spain's largest bullfighting ring and a venue capable of housing more than 25,000 spectators, in an evening billed as a "fast-paced show with modern rhythm". According to *ABC* and *Pueblo*, the music so excited the impressionable audience that "outrageous troublemakers" stormed the stage, and a "ridiculous collective madness" spread to riots and vandalism in

Madrid's subway system. "Bola", a local teenager, is singled out for his role in the apparent carnage, but friends were keen to recast him as a "calm, very modern boy incapable of killing a mosquito".

For all the "deafening pandemonium", perhaps it is surprising that Bill Ande remembers none of the above ever having happened. *Fonorama* magazine, a pop periodical, debunked the claims and issued a potent and courageous response. "For our part, we just want to add that when bad faith takes over a person and this person is also a journalist, the truth of the facts can be distorted in many ways".

In Brazil, a serious military *coup* had overthrown the government just months before the band's arrival. A similar coup would occur in Bolivia that November in 1964. By that time, Brazil's culture war over The Beatles and electric music would soon reach fever pitch.[59] Dismissed by left and right as a virus of "cultural imperialism" and a threat to Brazilian sovereignty, the height of Brazil's anti-Beatlemania in 1967–68 would see traditional folk singers releasing songs about the band's toxic influence (embodied especially in Brazil's so-called "Yeah, Yeah, Yeah" sound) almost semi-regularly, and even a "March Against The Electric Guitar" on the streets of São Paulo.

But just as The Beatles had their countercultural supporters,[60] The American Beetles had a share, too. The band would provide the direct and proximate inspiration for Hugh Fattoruso to found *Los Shakers*, a band that remains one of South America's most enduring and significant musical exports.

Seeing The American Beetles on TV in Uruguay, Fattoruso remarked that the group was "the first time we saw guys with long hair making music". "A week after seeing these guys, news arrives in Montevideo that there is a group like this in England, and that women go crazy and the cities stop when they talk about them on the radio. It was The Beatles, and I went to a short film about them."[61] And judging by *Los Shakers*' aesthetic, it is hard not to distinguish The Be(e/a)tles' influence.

Towards the end of the year, *Leoplán* magazine would consider the American Beetles episode "the coolest" of 1964.[62] Where the band lacked originality, the judges found the band's "coolness" "in its most illicit sense" – "that is, in other words, what corresponds to 'self-confidence', 'self-impunity' and considerable audacity".

Yet, even when The American Beetles were trashed and lambasted, the band provided influence in a paradoxically more positive way. For the more they were criticized, the more The Beatles proper would rise in comparative stature and currency – albeit reservedly – in the mainstream press.

At the start of The American Beetles' tour in July 1964, the best the press had to say of The (real) Beatles could perhaps be found in *Primera Plana* magazine, which praised the band's "incredible aptitude for human communication" while acknowledging their "musical precariousness".[63] By the time the Americans left in mid-August, though, *Atlántida* decried "the artistic inferiority of American substitutes" and celebrated their "bombard[ment]... with nuts and other iron 'flowers'".[64]

Clarín's eyes, meanwhile, were opening to the historical moment at hand.[65] Only a handful of new Beatles songs were released in the American Beetles interim – with the musical style largely maintained – but the "Beatles denomination" was now recognized as "having produced a deep rift in show business, to the point that some already use the name as a landmark in the history of the sector".

A journalist interviewed in *Leoplán* – the magazine that elected The American Beetles the "coolest" of 1964 – offered his support for the nascent youth movement the following month.[66] "[The Beatles] represent a healthy youth. There is nothing morbid, no aberration, nor equivocal cases". He contrasts organic Argentinian stars such as "Palito Ortega, Leo Dan, Juan Ramón" with the falsity of The American Beetles, whom he considers unsuited candidates to lead the "New Movement". "In Argentina, the youth prefer to be represented by a normal being and not by someone bizarre."

It may seem a small step, but for a media climate that had only recently dismissed such terms as "gossip" and "fan", the change marks a rapid evolutionary leap. "There is no doubt that the members of this musical quartet have achieved a popularity that recognizes world dimensions", *Clarín* would write that September. "And although their clothing style... and long hair have been erected as symbols of the attitude of rebellion and anti-conformity of a certain sector of modern youth, it is equally true that their musical gifts are relevant and come, to a large extent, from a disciplined professional conduct".[67] Likewise, *La Crónica* deigned to recognize the group as "interpreters of acceptable musical conditions" and their hair as "peculiar" and "unique".[68]

And in a final *coup* for the youth movement, *Clarín* could comfortably call The Beatles "decidedly unique and talented" the next month,[69] and *La Nación* – a *cognoscenti* broadsheet that described itself as a "journalism of ideas" – acknowledged the band's songs as "catchy".[70]

To this day, The Beatles remain an enormous cultural agent across Latin America. Digital populations in Mexico and Argentina rank respectively as the second and fifth most engaged audiences for The Beatles music on YouTube.[71] Uruguay, positioned at number eight in the rankings, is nearly ten per cent more engaged than the UK, which sits at number ten. Mexico's top classic rock radio station is said to play The Beatles for a summative two hours every day,[72] and Argentina's Beatles museum – the personal stock of Rodolfo Vásquez, the most prolific Beatle collector on earth[73] – is bigger than any other.

Once their planes left the tarmac that winter, though, The American Beetles' fifteen minutes of fame were well and truly up. "We did The American Beetles thing, and then after we couldn't get any DJs in the United States to play any of our songs", Bill Ande said. "You know, our originals. So, we just stopped that. And after we got back from South America, we changed our name to The Razor's Edge and had a couple of decent records here. That's basically the whole thing."

The Razor's Edge didn't catch on. "One person had left, they brought in a new bass player, and then it kind of fell apart. The guys were tired of travelling and so forth", says Bob Yorey, who remained their manager.

For all their unlikely influence on South American culture, perhaps it is a shame that The American Beetles should remain so obscure in the continent today. But an arguably greater shame consists in their having been necessary at all. Indeed, if The Beatles proper had cleared their schedule, venues filled their pockets, and appeared in the Americans' place on Channel 9 that night, one simply cannot overstate the impact they may have had on Argentinian culture. It is no coincidence that The Beatles were the ones inspiring rafts of parody bands and opportunists.

Unlike any musical phenomenon before or since, The Beatles were so popular, and inspired such devotion, that their reception bordered on the genuinely religious.[74] And in telling the story of that extraordinary band – and their absurd Floridian mix of R'n'B, politics, press, and commercial fraud – The American Beetles should never be overlooked. Some things really aren't too good to be true.

Notes

1. Dick Clark's *American Bandstand*, Season 7 Episode 39. Relevant clip: https://www.youtube.com/watch?v=UJdNN3dMcgc
2. In 1967, Clark was forced to use a pre-recorded PR "interview" with The Beatles in one of his shows. Clark claimed to have "conducted" it three years earlier. https://www.youtube.com/watch?v=_vArN-3wUGE
3. *Primera Plana*, 14 July 1964.
4. "I had another disastrous evening in Miami. We went out to see The Coasters, who were heroes with 'Yakety Yak'. People were *dancing* to them in the club, and I just couldn't understand it. These were rock 'n' roll gods to me, and people were dancing! I was just so disgusted. But The Coasters were great, and it was a thrill to see American artists. We'd never seen them before like this, *in America*." https://www.beatlesbible.com/1964/02/13/travel-new-york-miami/ Funnily enough, The American Beetles' bassist, Vic Gray, recalled to Dick Clark that both Ringo and Paul had danced to their music – quite a double standard, Ringo!

5. Author interview with Bill Ande – all later quotations from Ande are drawn from this interview unless otherwise specified.
6. Author interview with Bob Yorey – all later quotations from Yorey are drawn from this interview unless otherwise specified.
7. Interview with F. Pérez in "When Beatles Came to Argentina" (2017) – https://www.youtube.com/watch?v=PaRWOSWg_oU.
8. Author interview with Bill Ande. First published in BBC Culture, "How the Fake Beatles Conned South America", http://www.bbc.com/culture/story/20200423-how-the-fake-beatles-conned-south-america
9. See original cuttings here: http://www.arkivperu.com/los-beatles-en-peru-1964-65/.
10. 26 June 1964. As with all other Argentinian press unless specified otherwise, this clipping was originally drawn from R. Bujan, "The Fab Four?: Strategies to Build The Beatles in the Graphic Press in Argentina during 1964" (Faculty of Social Sciences, University of Buenos Aires, 2006), accessed at http://rodbujan.com/wp-content/uploads/2019/05/tesina-comunicacion-beatles-rodrigo-bujan.pdf.
11. Pérez, "When Beatles Came to Argentina".
12. Releases accessed at: https://gripsweat.com/item/301385527840/the-american-beetles-americanos-lo-hiciste-3-fake-beatles-argentina-ps-7-ep
13. The thoroughly Beatle-styled recording can be found here: https://www.youtube.com/watch?v=2LFbXJ6Nk-c.
14. Pérez, "When Beatles Came to Argentina".
15. 12 May 1964.
16. 1 July 1964.
17. Pérez, "When Beatles Came to Argentina".
18. The American Beetles would later "distance themselves from Duclós when he left an unpaid account in the United States in the group's name". Bujan, "The Fab Four?", 34.
19. Interview with *Zoo TV* (1998) – https://www.youtube.com/watch?v=qVFBw_5W7jk.
20. Author interview with Bob Yorey. First published in BBC Culture, "How the Fake Beatles Conned South America", http://www.bbc.com/culture/story/20200423-how-the-fake-beatles-conned-south-america.
21. Author interview with Bill Ande. First published in BBC Culture, "How the Fake Beatles Conned South America", http://www.bbc.com/culture/story/20200423-how-the-fake-beatles-conned-south-america. More than half a century later, though, extracting any further detail proves a challenge.
22. 7 July 1964.
23. 8 July 1964.
24. One such story covered the momentous event of "Palito Ortega moves to Palermo" (25 November 1964).
25. 10 March 1964.
26. Ahead of the performance, *Clarín* asked the same question: "What will happen when they open their mouths and pretend to sing?"

27. Pérez, "When Beatles Came to Argentina".
28. See a clip from their appearance here, with the band performing 'Mean Woman Blues': https://www.youtube.com/watch?v=sCb-zVUwQhk
29. Pérez, "When Beatles Came to Argentina".
30. Pérez, "When Beatles Came to Argentina".
31. Pérez, "When Beatles Came to Argentina".
32. Pérez, "When Beatles Came to Argentina".
33. Pérez, "When Beatles Came to Argentina".
34. 7 July 1964.
35. 9 July 1964.
36. Author interview with Bill Ande. First published in BBC Culture, "How the Fake Beatles Conned South America", http://www.bbc.com/culture/story/20200423-how-the-fake-beatles-conned-south-america.
37. *La Crónica*, 26 July 1964: "They filled them with tomatoes and eggs, in addition to trying to teach them to sing with their own hands."
38. Bujan, "The Fab Four?", 66.
39. Bujan, "The Fab Four?", 66.
40. 14 July 1964.
41. Bujan, "The Fab Four?", 35.
42. 29 July 1964 and July edition, respectively.
43. *La Crónica*, 29 August 1964.
44. 10 July 1964.
45. The Beatles proper would later receive similar treatment (30 August 1964). The band were zoomorphised by *Clarín* as dogs – named "The Beagles" – and Ringo a long-nosed bird.
46. 7 July 1964.
47. August 1964.
48. 10 July 1964.
49. 7 July 1964.
50. 7 July 1964.
51. M. F. Osuna, "Policies Implemented by the Last Argentine Dictatorship to Bridge the 'Generation Gap'", *Latin American Journal of Social Sciences, Children and Youth*, Universidad de Manizales, 2017 – accessed at https://ri.conicet.gov.ar/handle/11336/76225.
52. Pérez, "When Beatles Came to Argentina".
53. Pérez, "When Beatles Came to Argentina".
54. 14 July 1964.
55. "Foreign Acts Visit Brazil 1957 to 1968" blog – http://cartazes-internacionais-no-brasil.blogspot.com/2012/06/american-beetles-1964.html.
56. https://www.nytimes.com/1964/01/17/archives/argentina-faces-growing-deficits-decline-in-political-unrest-gives.html.
57. 7 September 1964.
58. A. McPherson, "Anti-Americanism in Latin America and the Caribbean", in *The Anti-American Century*, ed. A. McPherson and I. Krestev (New York: Berghahn Books, 2006), accessed at https://books.openedition.org/ceup/974?lang=en.

59. G. Alonso, "'Tomorrow Never Knows': The Influence of the Beatles' Music in Brazil", *Journal of World Popular Music* 4:2 (2017), accessed at https://www.researchgate.net/publication/321653872_Tomorrow_never_knows_The_Influence_of_the_Beatles"_Music_in_Brazil.
60. In **Argentina**: T. Wilson and M. Favoretto, "*Rock Nacional* in Argentina during the Dictatorship" (2016), accessed at https://oxfordre.com/latinamericanhistory/view/10.1093/acrefore/9780199366439.001.0001/acrefore-9780199366439-e-368.

    In **Brazil**: "From 63 to 70 I drank, ate, smoked and breathed Beatles", Rita Lee, the famous Brazilian Tropicalista, said to *Rolling Stone Brazil* (2007).

    Caetano Veloso, quoted in *Pitchfork*'s (2016), "God Is On The Loose!": "The idea of cultural cannibalism fit Tropicalistas like a glove; we were 'eating' the Beatles and Jimi Hendrix. We wanted to participate in the worldwide language both to strengthen ourselves as a people and to affirm our originality".

    In **Peru**: see https://andina.pe/agencia/noticia-influencia-mccartney-y-the-beatles-revoluciono-a-juventud-peruana-los-anos-60-357303.aspx.
61. *Página 30* magazine, April 1993.
62. 16 December 1964.
63. 14 July 1964.
64. August edition.
65. 19 August 1964.
66. 16 September 1964.
67. 14 September 1964.
68. 15 September 1964.
69. 3 October 1964.
70. 2 October 1964.
71. https://chartmasters.org/2019/07/beatles-global-heatmap/
72. https://www.nytimes.com/2016/12/02/world/what-in-the-world/for-mexicos-beatlemaniacos-all-you-need-is-nostalgia.html
73. https://www.guinnessworldrecords.com/world-records/largest-collection-of-beatles-memorabilia
74. J. Lennon, P. McCartney, G. Harrison, and R. Starr, *The Beatles Anthology* (San Francisco: Chronicle Books, 2002), 142–43.

Author biography

Ed Prideaux is a freelance journalist and researcher who specializes in coverage of psychedelic culture. Ed has written for the BBC, *The Guardian*, the *Financial Times*, *The Spectator*, *Unherd* and others. He recently completed a Master's degree in Psychology, during which he pursued research on the adverse effects of psychedelic drugs.

14 Interlude 3: Listening and Remembering

Russell Reising, Peter Mills and James McGrath

The final interlude considers the duality of listening and remembering via reflections on misheard lyrics, individual responses and the importance of sound, especially in relation to recordings. We 'remember' the first time we heard a song, or a band, and other reflections on our lives accrete around those sounds. The recording does not change, but the listener does.

PM: This idea of reimporting American music via Liverpool, what kind of influence would you say that had on the American music that was kind of prompted by the British invasion?

RR: Well again I can speak almost for a generation, and we loved it! I mean we thought if it was British it had to be cool and I had friends who affected English accents! It wasn't really selling it back to us as much as it was introducing us because a lot of the stuff that The Beatles had covered was brand new to a massive part of their audience. As for me and my music-mad friends, a lot of the stuff they covered we were listening to every day anyway – Sam Cooke or The Drifters or The Shirelles or Fats Waller or Chuck Berry, you know, they were never off the scene – but what they *did* do was break the barrier between what had been race music and the mainstream.

PM: Right.

RR: And I'm not sure I knew, I don't think I knew anybody who thought of it as The Beatles getting us back to our music because it was music that hardly anyone else had access to. It was like introducing it by opening the doors. I had a dear friend Sam Andrew who was with Big Brother and the Holding Company the last time I saw him and we were talking and he was telling me about a time that he and Janis Joplin went to see Big Mama Thornton. Janis Joplin worshipped Big Mama Thornton and Big Mama Thornton gets up on stage and sees Janis Joplin and just annihilated her saying "what I see there is a white girl in the audience tonight who's making lots of money off of my songs and I can hardly make a dime" and she was just like reading the riot act to Janis Joplin. Sam said Janis literally slid under the table and was sobbing, you know, she was there to pay homage to Big Mama Thornton, but Big Mama Thornton clearly saw her as little other than a parasitic Texas waif that The 13th Floor Elevators had rejected as their lead singer.

PM: Oh God, poor Janis, I always think that – poor Janis!

RR: Yeah, I mean evidentially it wasn't near the end of her life, it wasn't like it precipitated the end but it was an absolute knock in the head, it was like Maxwell's Silver Hammer. By the way I wasn't able to go to that Abbey Road conference but, I guess, good friends of mine were there and I guess they discussed Maxwell's Silver Hammer quite a bit. It was one of the songs that dominated the discussions and I can't wait to find out why.

PM: You don't like that song, do you James? We've known each other for nearly twenty years and it's one of the very few Beatle tunes I've heard you express a dislike for. Why don't you like it?

JM: I liked it the first few times I heard it when I was about six but then I became more interested in 'Come Together'. The thing about 'Come Together' was that strange sound Lennon makes, some people say he's singing "shoot me".

PM: I think it's just a bit of mouth percussion, isn't it? A bit of shoo-be-doo-wah. That's what I think anyway – the "shoot me" thing seems something of an irresponsible reading, really.

JM: But it almost felt like "is that record scratched" or something, I remember that was one of my first thoughts, you know like a strange something that you couldn't put your finger on it, it almost sounded like a fault on the record.

RR: And of course we got lots of faulty records back then that you know you had to take back because the pressing was so poor and so we didn't even really know what was meant to be on there. By the way one thing that was brought up at this Abbey Road conference, and I think this is new, you know that beautiful moment in 'Here Comes the Sun' when there's that synthesizer line that goes "doooo" [0:12-15].

JM: Yeah?

RR: That was a broken synthesizer. That key was broken and they figured out a way to take a defective instrument and turn it into one of, I think, the beautiful moments on the whole album. I mean you can't believe that it's not meant to be like that. Of course it *is* meant to be like that but it was discovered as a result of having a faulty electrical circuit on the synthesizer.

JM: That's amazing!

RR: So, what else is in this book?

JM: There's a chapter on local Black influences on The Beatles in the very early days, so pre-1962 particularly, Lord Woodbine I don't know if you've come across that name much? On the famous photo of The Beatles on the way to Hamburg he is there with them and he kind of, he drove the van and things; he was a friend of Alan Billings but what's not so well known is that he was a, quite a highly regarded calypso musician and songwriter. He was born in Trinidad in 1929, came to England on the *Windrush* in 1948 and by the late fifties was living in Liverpool. He ran a number of steel bands but the interesting thing is he was the first singer/songwriter that John and Paul ever met. They didn't often talk about him in interviews but in Liverpool this is quite a well-known story. I mean he never became a recording artist but he was close friends with Lord Kitchener who was also on the *Windrush*.

I noticed in Mark Lewisohn's book [*All These Years: Tune In*, 2013], it is stated that Lennon's first composition was called 'Calypso Rock'; Lennon himself named it in a 1971 interview and I think it might have been an instrumental. It's just intriguing that in the late fifties one of two LPs that Lennon owned as an art student, one was a Buddy Holly compilation and the other was Lord Kitchener's *Calypsos, Too Hot to Handle*, so my chat with Mark Christian is focusing on this hidden black Beatles history.

RR: I'll be darned, the guy's name was Desmond Jones huh? Yeah coz they do that whole "Ob-la-di, Ob-la-da" thing and it has that Caribbean flavour at least. I got stoned once with Tony Sheridan in Japan.

PM: [laughs] Now that's a hell of an opening line, Russ.

RR: [laughs] Yeah, it was at an international conference and they brought him over to talk about The Beatles in the Hamburg days and then he jammed with the Japanese house band all night and during the break, I mean this guy carried marijuana into Japan, I thought this guy's totally insane and we were in this little back alley getting stoned and nobody talked with Tony Sheridan, he just did Monty Python rips the whole time, but it felt pretty cool to be hanging around with him like when once in Liverpool I ran into Allan Williams.

JM: Yes, yeah that's always an unforgettable experience.

RR: Oh it really is, he drinks red wine on the rocks. I was telling a story about Tom Waits, I'd just seen Tom Waits on TV the night before and he was telling a story about how he's never recognised when he goes anywhere, you know he goes to a music store and he leans on the piano and nobody sees him, he picks up a guitar and nobody sees him and he says then I took my kids on a field trip to the dump and as soon as I got to the dump everybody there recognised him. And Allan Williams is walking by and he says "oh and who are you sir that you should be recognised" and I said oh no no I'm just telling a story about someone else, and he says "well nobody recognises me either" and I had just finished reading *The Man Who Gave Away The Beatles*. I didn't know it was him but he sat down and regaled us with stories as long as we kept buying him cheap red wine on the rocks.

JM: I had a similar experience meeting up with Allan Williams in the Jacaranda pub in 2010. Together with Lord Woodbine though, Allan was a major figure in The Beatles' early history. He was one of the great raconteurs of the era.

RR: Have either of you, I forget which book it is but Timothy Leary in, I think, well it was in one of his many autobiographies, he has a chapter in which he rips on *Sgt Pepper* when it first came out and he writes a long discussion of something and in the margins he has the lines from 'Sgt Pepper's Lonely Hearts Club Band' that he's thinking about as he's saying these things.

JM: Could it be *The Politics of Ecstasy*?

RR: *The Politics of Ecstasy*! Yes, that's it. It's really fascinating: you know our students might say sort of weird things about *Sgt Pepper* and we'd give them a D but when Leary's saying it he weaves in between images and references and lines from the songs into his own dialogue about what's going on in his life at the time.

PM: We're keen to bring in a few more creative responses to the music, via fiction, non-fiction or poetry as well as academic essays.

RR: Well it was The Beatles that turned me into a reader because when I went to school it was really low grade; all the teachers were teachers because they had to justify their salaries as football and baseball coaches so there was zero stimulation there. However when *Sgt Pepper* came out all of a sudden there were the lyrics and the "White Album" came out and there were the lyrics and all of a sudden – ah! – I became interested in poetry.

JM: It was a very similar experience for me.

RR: I bet that's true of a lot of people. Before that we had struggled to understand but all of a sudden these were poems, you know? You could see them, they had lines, you could scan them, you could actually know the words, adding to the visualisation of the songs. The words contributed so much you could see things that you wouldn't necessarily hear.

JM: Definitely yeah. I would often struggle to make out the words sometimes especially when you're talking very basic 1960s record players.

PM: I used to just transcribe them, you know, lyrics of songs that I liked. They were often wrong – not always but often! – and occasionally I would prefer the one I'd heard to the actual lyric so, as you say, you "see" through the sound to what might not even be "there" in the conventional sense. So, we find different responses to what is heard, according to who is listening; the listener brings the weight of their own experience to bear upon the interpretation even in the sound or weight of a phrase rather than its actual meaning.

RR: Absolutely – talking of such things, what's this book going to be called?

JM: *Carnival of Light* is the title.

PM: It came to me on a flight to Japan. It's the great "lost" Beatle recording, of course.

RR: Yeah, I really like that title.

Author biographies

Russell Reising is Professor emeritus at the University of Toledo, Ohio, USA. Professor Reising has taught, spoken, and published widely on topics in American literature and culture, Japanese literature and culture, popular culture and popular music. He has lived, studied, and taught all over the world, including Taiwan, Japan, Finland, England, and the United States. Russ's academic work has also resulted in his being commissioned to present workshops and lectures in England, Italy, Spain, Finland, Estonia, Bulgaria, Poland, the Czech Republic, Austria, Australia, and Japan. He was also an original member of the Educational Advisory Board at the Rock and Roll Hall of Fame and Museum. In 2008, Russ was one of only thirty Americans invited to participate in the People's Republic of China's first international literary conference.

Dr Peter Mills is Senior Lecturer in Media and Popular Culture in the School of Humanities and Social Sciences at Leeds Beckett University, UK. He has previously published on Samuel Beckett, Van Morrison and The Monkees. Peter is currently working on a series of short books on individual songs, a book chapter on the history of live music in Roundhay Park in Leeds, and an ambitious project looking to catalogue the history of live concerts at Leeds Beckett University since 1970.

Dr James McGrath is Senior Lecturer in English Literature and Creative Writing in the School of Humanities and Social Sciences at Leeds Beckett University, UK. He completed his doctoral thesis on the work of John Lennon and Paul McCartney, and his first book *Naming Adult Autism: Culture, Science, Identity* was published by Rowman & Littlefield International in 2017. His poems have been published in various literary periodicals.

Index

NB: Page numbers in *italics* indicate illustrations.

Abbey Road 39, 41, 109–10, 130, 140, 195
Abercrombie, Nicholas 118
Aberdeen 216, 221, 224–5, *224*, 229–30, *229*
Abram, Michael 146–7
Across the Universe: Fan Fiction Archive 149
'Across the Universe' (song) 50
Afghanistan 48
African American musicians 37–8, 40, 209
'Ahab the Arab' (Stevens) 46
Alexander, Arthur 38, 40
'All You Need is Love' 81, 202
Alpert, Richard 47–8
American Bandstand 231–2, 235, 241
American Beetles, The
    mop-top image 231–2, 237–8, 240–1, 244
    in South America 233–45
American musical influences
    African American musicians 37–8, 40, 209
    reimported to USA 249
    rhythm and blues (R&B) music 18, 25, 37–8, 209, 233
    rock 'n' roll 67, 90–1
amphetamines 76, 90, 92
Ande, Bill 232–37, 239–40, 242–3, 245
Andrew, Sam 249–50
Antena 240
Anthology albums 2, 8
Apple Corps
    alternative type of organisation 81, 100–1
    disputes/difficulties 74, 161, 180
    International Business Festival 127
    legacy management 4, 128, 132, 143, 154–5, 160
    rooftop concert 120, 129
Argentina 233–42, 244–5
Aronowitz, Al 97–8
art students/artistic identity 88–90, 93–8, 101–2
Asher, Jane 21, 99, 170
Asher, Peter 99–100
Asian musical forms 44–6, 49–50, 173, 202
'Ask Me Why' 37
Aspinall, Neil 138, 165, 221

Atlántida 240, 244
audiences *see* performer–audience relationship
Austria 73
autobiographical lyrics 19–21, 30
avant-garde
    The Beatles 98–9, 176, 195, 202, 207, 210
    Lennon 28
    McCartney 20–21, 99–100
    Ono 55, 100, 207
    Roxy Music 111

'Back in the U.S.S.R.' 71, 81, 203
Baez, Joan 21
Bahamas 73
Baigorria, Nélida 242
Barrow, Tony (Frederick James) 164–6, 172
Batchelor, Stephen 48
BBC 27, 94, 163, 210
Beach Ballroom, Aberdeen 224–5, *224*, 229–30, *229*
Beat movement 86–90, 92, 94–5, 97–100
Beat poetry 87, 89–90, 95, 97, 100
"Beatle People" 161, 166–7, 169, 171–2, 175
Beatlemania
    The American Beetles 233–4
    Beatles Monthly 139–41, 170–71
    beginning of 60, 63
    discussion of 66, 117, 120, 173, 180, 186, 190–91
    A Hard Day's Night 63, 70, 156
Beatlemania museum, Hamburg 122–5
The Beatles, naming of 72, 90, 159
The Beatles ("White album")
    critiques 25, 175–6
    Manson's use of 191–7
    race 191, 203–4
    recording process 44, 79
    songs 28, 39, 189, 207, 253
Beatles and Beyond 126
The Beatles Anthology 219, 232
The Beatles Book see Beatles Monthly
Beatles Britain app 132
The Beatles fan club 138
Beatles for Sale 81
The Beatles: Live at the Internet 116, 132

Beatles Monthly
 beginning of 138, 164
 fans, empowerment of 139–41, 160–63
 final issue 180–1
 layout and content 166–8
 letters page 139, 166–7, 169–76, 179
 photographs 160–1, 165–6, 168–9, 178–9, 182
'Beatles Movie Medley' 2
Beatles scholarship 1, 4, 108, 137, 139, 154
Beatles! Slash: All You Need is Love 150
beatniks 87–90, 94, 97–9
'Being for the Benefit of Mr Kite!' 206–7
Bell, Charles 52
Bell, Rachel 15–16
Benzedrine 90
Berry, Chuck 18, 203
Best, Mona 35
Best, Pete
 in The Beatles 35–6, 91, 122
 at Beatles conventions 141–3
 education 102
 replaced by Ringo 64
Bible 191, 193, 196
Big Mama Thornton 249–50
Black Dwarf 24
Black musical influences 25, 203, 249
 African American musicians 37–8, 40, 209
 calypso/Caribbean 19, 26, 251
 in Liverpool 18–19, 27, 29, 38–40, 251
'Blackbird' 197, 203–4
Blavatsky, Helena 51, 56, 99
Bloustien, Gerry 123
bohemianism, definition 5–6, 85–6, 92
Bonici, Albert 218–19, *220*, 221, 225
Bonvalot, Gabriel 51
'Borrowed Time' (Lennon) 29
Bramwell, Tony 165
Brando, Marlon 91–2
Braun, Michael 60, 163
Brazil 243
"breathless345" 4
Bridge of Allan Museum Hall 225–6
British Beatles Fan Club 126
Bromell, Nick 62, 76–8, 81, 194
Brown, Peter 185
Brubeck, Dave 45–6
Bryce, Leslie 138, 165
Buddhism 48, 109, 144; *see also* Tibetan Buddhism
Burgess, Jean 148–9, 154

Caen, Herb 87

Cage, John 28, 99–100
California 81, 86, 133, 192, 233
Callaghan, James 25, 27
calypso/Caribbean music 19, 26, 251
cannabis *see* marijuana
'Can't Buy Me Love' 63
'Carnival of Light' 7–8
Carson, Christie 121–2
Caulfield, Ian 17
Cavern Club 4, 18, 36, 95, 101, 120
celebrity, definition 117–18, 122
Chapman, Mark 138, 145–7, 162, 196
China 51–4
Christianity 47, 190–91
The Christians 36
Churchill, Winston 45
Clarín 235, 240–1, 244
Clark, Annie (St. Vincent) 133
Clark, Dick 231–2, 235, 241
class *see* middle class; working class
classical/orchestral music 14, 22, 24, 28, 39, 174, 208–9
Cleave, Maureen 20–21
The Coasters 232–3
Cohen, Stanley 171
Cohn, Nik 79
Collingham, Anne *see* Sumpter, Valerie (Anne Collingham)
Collins, Marcus 15, 29
colonialism 25–6, 46, 48, 51, 53, 56, 67, 75
Coltrane, John 203
'Come Together' 81, 130, 250
commercialism 60, 64, 71, 81, 95–9, 127, 186
confessional songs 19, 30
Connell, John 125
Connolly, Ray 87, 89
consciousness, modes of 46–7, 53, 65, 145; *see also* drug use; meditation; subconscious
consumption
 changing structures of 131, 153–4, 181
 consumers as co-owners 116–17, 127–8
 see also fans/fandom; user-generated content
cosplay (fans) 119, 131, 141
counter-culture, definition 48, 85, 100–101, 144–5
Courrier, Kevin 193
cover art/sleeve design 63, 124, 156, 204
cover versions 5, 37–8, 152, 209
The Crack 87
crowdfunding platforms 126–7
Cunningham, Neil 225
Curtis, Jim 76

Index 257

The Daily Mail 16, 19
The Daily Mirror 27, 60
Dalai Lama 54
Dalton, David 192, 195–6
David-Neel, Alexandra 52
Davies, Hunter 90–91, 93–4, 143–5
Davies, Ray 46, 202
'A Day in the Life'
    lyrics and music 19, 22–4, 41, 72, 174, 189
    studio 45, 110, 179
'Day Tripper' 63, 69
de Certeau, Michel 76
Dean, James 71, 91–2, 166
Dean, Johnny *see* O'Mahony, Sean (Johnny Dean)
Deedes, William 186–7
digital media 116–19, 121, 125–33, 181; *see also* YouTube
Dills, David 224
Dingwall Town Hall 226–8, *228*
Douglas, Eva 48
dreams 47, 68, 70, 74–6, 81
The Drifters 206, 233
'Drive My Car' 69, 72
drug use 46–8, 50, 94, 175, 180; *see also* amphetamines; LSD; marijuana
Duchamp, Marcel 28
Duclós, Rudolfo "Rudy" 233–5, 239–41
Duffett, Mark 146–7
Dunbar, John 99–100
Dylan, Bob 1–2, 97–8, 109, 185–8

Eagleton, Terry 17
The Ed Sullivan Show 36, 69, 79, 129, 132
Edwardian aesthetics 67, 75, 90
Ehrenreich, Barbara 66, 79, 139–40, 186
'Eleanor Rigby' 22, 26, 63, 202, 208–9
Elgin 219, 221–3, *223*
Elizabeth II, Queen 64
Elliott, Anthony 14, 22
Ellis, Royston 18, 89–90
EMI 8, 120, 227, 234, 239
Empress Pub 127
Epstein, Brian 96, 164, 186, 190
    The Beatles' image 64, 79, 95, 120, 140, 161
    Beatles Monthly 138, 140, 164–5
    contract with Bonici *220*, 221
    death 98, 170
establishment 60, 65–8, 70, 73–5, 77, 81
Evans, Mal 138, 165, 185
Evans, Mike 102
Evans-Wentz, Walter Y. 52

Evening Standard 20
Exis/Existentialists 86, 93–5

facial hair 177–80
Fainlight, Harry 100
fan conventions 141–3
fan fiction 138, 149–50
fanaticism 145–7, 162–3
fans/fandom
    definitions 118–19, 156, 162–3
    identity through 116–19, 122–5, 128–31, 133, 140
    see also "Beatle People"; Beatlemania; *Beatles Monthly*; female fans; journalist/fan; tribute bands; user-generated content
fanvids 147–8, 153
fascism 53, 242
Fattoruso, Hugh 243
female fans 66, 139–41, 172, 186, 191
'Ferry Across the Mersey' 36
Ferry, Bryan 111
Florida 232–3
Fonorama 243
'For You Blue' 3
Forthlin Road, Liverpool 16
Frith, Simon
    The Beatles and psychedelia 187
    The Beatles' art college bohemianism 88–9, 101
    live performances 120, 123, 131
    pop music consumption 116–18
'From Me to You' 202, 234
Fury, Billy 102–3, 166, 219

Gambier Terrace, Liverpool 88, 90
Gentle, Johnny 103, 166, 219, 221
Get Back (film) 2–4
'Get Back' (song) 27, 74, 80
Gibson, Bob 138, 167, 169, 179
Gibson, Chris 125
Gillett, Charlie 69
Ginsberg, Allen 86, 97, 100
Gitlin, Todd 187–8
'Give Peace a Chance' (Plastic Ono Band) 28, 30
'Glass Onion' 145, 194–5
Goldsher, Alan, *Paul is Undead* 149
'Good Night' 76, 209
Goons 67–8
Gotlop, Philip 165
Govinda, Lama Anagarika 53
Graceland 69, 71, 125

Green, Jonathan 46, 48, 198
Green, Joshua 148–9, 154
Gregory, Georgina 151–2
Grenard, Fernand 51
Grossberg, Lawrence 78, 118–19, 127
group identity 4, 13, 62–7, 75, 78–80; *see also* mop-top image
The Guardian 146
Guitar Hero 128–9, 131
guitars *see* Höfner violin bass guitar
Gunn, Simon 15–16

hair *see* facial hair; mop-top image
Hamburg
    art college 93, 101
    Beatlemania museum 122–5
    career milestone 35, 70, 91, 96, 120
    Exis 93–5
    Lord Woodbine 18, 38, 251
    Raving Texans 71
    Reeperbahn 93, 123, 125, 164
    'The Sheikh of Araby' 46
    'Ticket to Ride' 69
'Happy Xmas (War Is Over)' (Lennon) 29
A Hard Day's Night (film)
    The Beatles' image 62–5, 75, 79–80
    drug use 76
    establishment 65–7, 73
    fans, importance of 77–8, 145, 155–6
    fee 96
    humour 60, 64, 67–9, 78
    journeys 70–71, 73–4
    South American response 239
    title 61
'A Hard Day's Night' (song) 20, 23
Harmonix 128–9
Harrer, Heinrich, *Seven Years in Tibet* 53
Harrison, Dhani 128, 146
Harrison, George
    attempted murder of 146
    education 102–3
    pseudonym (Carl Harrison) 221
    quotes 61, 64, 70–71, 75, 80, 98–9, 120, 178–9, 219
    religion 144
Harry, Bill 40, 87, 95, 164–5
Hedin, Sven 51
Heilbronner, Oded 15, 22, 25, 27
Help!
    content of 49, 60, 64–5, 68, 79–80
    drug use 76
    locations 73, 78
'Helter Skelter' 69, 191–4, 197–8

Hendrix, Jimi 110
Henry, Tony 18–19
Herbert, Ian 151
'Here Comes the Sun' 250
heroin 55
Hess, Elizabeth 139
'Hey Jude' 137, 155–6, 189
Heylin, Clinton 172
Hills, Matt 118–19, 140–1, 147
Hillsborough tragedy 36
Hilton, James 54, 56
Himmler, Heinrich 53
Hinduism 49–50, 54, 144
hip hop music 37, 153
hippy culture 54–5, 85, 144, 175
hipster-rockers 91–3
Hoffmann, Dezo 63, 67
Höfner violin bass guitar 128, *215*, 217–18, 222, 226, 228
Hoggart, Richard 22–3
Holly, Buddy 251
'Honey Pie' 67, 71, 205
Horne, Howard 88–9, 101, 187
Houghton, Richard 219, 221, 225–7
Huxley, Aldous 46–8
Huyssen, Andreas 28

'I Am the Walrus' 188–9, 204
'I Don't Wanna Be a Soldier' 29
'I Feel Fine' 110
'I Want to Hold Your Hand' 20, 63, 68
'I Want to Tell' 76
'I Want You' 110
'Imagine' (Lennon) 30
immigration 18, 25–7, 29, 46
In His Own Write (Lennon) 97
India
    links to Tibet 53–4
    musical forms 46, 49–50, 173, 202
    Rishikesh 25, 49, 72, 153, 204
    tourism 48–9
'India' (song) 153
Indica bookshop 50, 100
Inglis, Ian 91, 93–5, 160
'The Inner Light' 49–50
interactivity 116–17, 122–5, 130–33, 154, 162, 188–90
International Business Festival 127, 159
International Times 100
interpretation vs. intention 188–90, 192–6, 198, 204, 253
Isley Brothers 38
ITN 177

ITV 2, 163, 174, 177

The Jacaranda 18, 87, 90, 252
Jackson, Peter 2–3
Jacobs, Gloria 139
Jamaica 26
James, Frederick *see* Barrow, Tony (Frederick James)
Japan 29, 55, 151, 160, 251
jazz 29, 46, 90, 92, 202
Jenkins, Henry
　commodity culture 122
　digital media 116, 118, 133, 150, 162–3
　participatory culture 116, 118, 125, 128, 133, 155
　Textual Poachers 140, 147, 155, 162–3
Johnson, Paul 186–7, 191
Johnston, Shelagh 89
Jones, Peter (Billy Shepherd) 166–7
Joplin, Janis 249–50
journalist/fan 143–5
'Julia' 55

Kaiserkeller Club 93, 123
Karadajian 235–6
Kay, Rob 131
The Kazakhstan Beatles 151
Kerouac, Jack 86
Kerr, Aphra 117
King, B. B. 203
King Curtis 29
The Kinks 46
Kirchherr, Astrid 79, 91, 93–4
Ku Klux Klan 190

La Crónica 234, 236–42, 244
La Nación 239, 244
'Lady Madonna' 27–8, 208
Laing, Dave 15, 87, 103
Landau, Jon 25
Lapidos, Mark and Carol 141
Las Beatlas 240
Las Vegas 141–2
Leary, Timothy
　The Beatles as "agents sent by God" 187, 190, 192
　political campaign 81
　The Politics of Ecstasy 85, 252
　The Psychedelic Experience 47–8, 50, 52, 54–6
Lefebvre, Henri 81
Lennon, Cynthia 20, 164, 222
Lennon, Freddie 17

Lennon, John
　childhood 16–17, 70
　class 14–18, 23–4, 28–31
　education 17, 36, 87–90, 94, 102–3
　"granny glasses" 177–9
　murder of 144–7, 196
　musicianship 18, 39
　pseudonym (Long John) 221
　quotes 3, 21, 26, 29, 60–62, 69–72, 74, 77, 80, 91, 94, 96–101, 141, 159, 174, 188, 190, 192, 197–8, 206
Lennon, Julia 17, 55
Leoplán 243–4
Lester, Richard (Dick)
　A Hard Day's Night 60, 63, 67–8, 74, 76, 78, 80, 156
　Help! 73, 76
Let It Be (album) 3, 39, 199
Let It Be (film) 3, 66, 74, 78, 80, 120
Lévy, Pierre 118
Lewisohn, Mark 1, 8, 14, 16–19, 177, 219, 251
Lhasa 51, 53
Life 64, 77, 174
Lindsay-Hogg, Michael 3, 66, 120
Little Richard 27, 37–8, 209
live performances
　The Beatles' ceasing of 72, 75, 98, 120–21
　digital alternatives 129–33
　performer–audience relationship 120–21, 124
Liverpool
　accents/slang 70, 77–8, 151
　anti-immigration 26
　Black music scene 18–19, 27, 29, 38–40, 251
　A Hard Day's Night premiere 63–4
　Lennon and McCartney's childhoods 16–17, 23, 36, 69–70
　tourism 4, 40–41
　Toxteth (Liverpool 8) 18, 38–9, 87–9, 126–7
　Yellow Submarine (film) location 74
Liverpool College of Art 87–91, 101
Liverpool Echo 70
Liverpool Football Club 36
London 20–21, 46, 70, 73, 79, 90, 99–100
'Long Long Long' 110
Longhurst, Brian 118
Look 159
Lord Kitchener (Aldwyn Roberts) 19, 251
Lord Woodbine (Harold Phillips) 18, 26, 38–40, 251
Los Búhos 240

Los Shakers 243
Lothian, Andi 225–6
'Love Me Do' 2, 160, 163, 221, 226
'Love You To' 109, 173
LSD 46, 101, 143, 195, 203
　films 75, 77
　Leary, influence of 47–8, 50, 54–6, 187
　McCartney in *Life* magazine 161, 174
'Lucy in the Sky with Diamonds' 65, 76, 174

McCartney, Jim and Mary 16
McCartney, Paul
　avant-garde/bohemianism 20–21, 28, 87–8, 99–100, 103
　'Carnival of Light,' hope for release of 8
　childhood 16–17
　class 14–18, 21–4, 28, 30–31
　drug use 161, 174, 185–6
　education 17, 102–3
　musicianship 18, 39, 45
　"Paul is dead" rumour 140, 189
　photograph, newly discovered 215, 217–18, 221–30
　pseudonym (Paul Ramon) 221
　quotes 19, 20–22, 26, 37, 61–2, 74, 79, 87–8, 91, 94–8, 101, 128, 164, 178, 197–8, 219
　as ultimate Beatles tribute act 152
MacDonald, Ian 15, 19, 82
　The Beatles ("White album") 28, 44, 195–7
　The Beatles and psychedelia 50, 54, 74, 186
　The Beatles' early influences 18, 22, 72
　as journalist/fan 143–5
　'Tomorrow Never Knows' 44, 50, 54–5
McGrath, James 21, 144–5
McKinney, Devin 194
McNab, Ken 219, 221–2, 225–7
Madryn Street, Liverpool 126–7
Magical Mystery Tour
　artistic experimentalism 27, 99, 208
　The Beatles' image 62, 80
　Beatles Monthly 175
　establishment 66, 68
　locations 73–4, 78
　musical hall 67
　psychedelia 65, 75–7
Maharishi Mahesh Yogi 25, 49, 55, 72, 101, 153
Mann, William 14
Manson, Charles 145, 162, 191–8
marijuana 48, 69, 76, 81, 97, 180, 185, 251
Marshall, P. David
　celebrity, definition 117–18, 122
　commercial structures, changes 116, 127
　live performances 120–21, 123–4, 131
　video games 130
Martin, George 77, 91, 178
　art vs. commercialism 71, 98–9
　music production 22, 39, 45, 56, 110, 206
Martin, Giles 129
'Maxwell's Silver Hammer' 109–10, 250
meaning/meaningfulness 188–90, 192–6, 198, 204, 253
meditation 25, 49, 81
Melly, George 61, 64, 78, 80, 90–91
Melody Maker 1
Melotones 226–7
Mendips, Liverpool 16, 23, 217
mental illness 146–7, 193
Merseybeat 70
Metzner, Ralph 47–8
Mexico 48, 234, 244
Michael X (Michael Abdul Malik) 29
'Michelle' 202
middle class
　bohemianism/beatniks 85, 88, 103
　consumption 81
　Lennon and McCartney 15–18, 21, 23, 28–9
　suburbia 69
Miles, Barry
　The Beatles as cult 190–91
　The Beatles' films 62
　The Beatles' music 8, 21–2, 26–7, 189, 194, 197
　Exis 93–5
　McCartney 16, 20–21, 28, 87–8, 99–100, 103
military spaces/uniforms 65, 73–6
Mojo 26
Moltenbrey, Karen 130
Monfort, Roberto 234, 238
The Monkees 2, 173
mop-top image
　acceptability 66, 128, 179
　The American Beetles 231, 237–8, 240–41, 244
　fan cosplay 119, 123, 132
　move away from 56, 177–9
　mythology of 62, 152, 162
　Scotland tour, pre-fame 217–18
Motown label 36–7, 209–10
Mozart, Wolfgang Amadeus 39, 45
'Mr Tambourine Man' (Dylan) 187–8
Mulligan, Brian 164
Munday, Rod 130

Murden, Jon 23
music hall (vaudeville) 67, 69, 75
musical theatre 62–3
musique concrète 28, 45, 56
mysticism 46, 74, 185–6, 191, 197

National Trust 4, 16
Nebbia, Felix "Litto" 234, 241
New Left 15, 25
New Left Review 24
New Statesman 186
New York 36, 86, 141, 146, 185; *see also* Shea Stadium, New York
New York Times 14, 28, 242
Noebel, David 190, 192
Norman, Philip
    The Beatles' humour 64
    The Beatles' influences 18, 49–50, 87, 89
    The Beatles' songwriting 21, 45
    as journalist/fan 143–5
    Lennon's childhood 16, 30
North End Music Stores (NEMS) 164–6
'Norwegian Wood' 21–2, 49

'Ob-la-di, Ob-la-da' 26–7, 251
The Observer 193–4
'Octopus's Garden' 110
O'Grady, Alice 125, 131
O'Mahony, Sean (Johnny Dean) 138, 160–1, 164–70, 175–6, 179–80
Ono, Yoko
    avant-garde 28, 55, 100, 207–8
    Beatles Monthly 161, 170–1, 176
    Lennon's legacy 16, 128
    music, with Lennon 27–8, 30–31
    politics 28–9
orchestral/classical music 14, 22, 24, 28, 39, 174, 208–9
Orientalism 21, 46, 55–6

Packard, Vince 186
Pallis, Marco 52–3
Palm Beach, Florida 232–3
'Paperback Writer' 20, 205
Parlophone 110
participatory culture
    Beatlemania museum 125
    digital media 118, 122, 128, 130, 132–3, 147–50, 154–5, 162
    Save Madryn Street campaign 126
Patterson, Margaret 226–7
"Paul is dead" rumour 140, 189
Payne, Maureen (Bettina Rose) 166–7

Payne, Valerie 170
Penny Lane (place) 4, 40, 217
'Penny Lane' (song) 22–3, 75, 177, 179
The People 87–8
performativity 117, 119, 122, 131
performer–audience relationship
    digital media 118, 121–2, 125, 127–8, 130–33, 147–9, 155
    live performances 120–21, 124
    staged 137, 155–6, 159
Peru 234
Philippines 146
Phillips, Harold *see* Lord Woodbine (Harold Phillips)
'Piggies' 81
Plastic Ono Band 28, 30, 198–9
Playboy 85, 189
Please Please Me 36–37, 41
poetry 103, 252–3; *see also* Beat poetry
police
    in Beatles films 60, 65–6, 73, 81
    in reality 92, 236
politics
    Apple Corps 74
    films 65–7
    music 14–15, 22, 24–31, 81
Pop Go The Beatles 163
popular music scholarship 1, 108, 116–17
postmodernism 25, 111
Powell, Enoch 25–6
'Power to the People' 29
Preludin 94
Presley, Elvis 90, 97, 102, 111, 125, 140
Preston, Billy 3–4, 27, 110, 203
Primera Plana 239, 243–4
prophetic messages 186, 192–3, 197
protest songs 29–30
psychedelia
    art 100
    Leary, influence of 47–8, 50, 52, 54–6, 187–8
    Magical Mystery Tour 65, 75–7
    music 65, 69, 77, 174, 195, 203
    mysticism 186, 191
    psychosis 193
Pujol, Sergio 241
The Punkels 151

The Quarrymen 90, 203

race 203–4, 209; *see also* Black musical influences
race war, USA 191, 193, 197

racism 27, 38, 56
Radio Luxembourg 222
Radio Splendid 241–2
Ram (McCartney) 1
Raving Texans 71
The Razor's Edge 245
Reck, David 22, 46, 49
Record Mirror 89, 166
Reeperbahn, Hamburg 93, 123, 125, 164
Reporting 66 177
Revelation, Book of 191, 193, 196
'Revolution' 15, 24–5, 27, 44, 81
'Revolution 9' 28, 98, 176, 192, 196, 202–3, 207
Revolver
    Beatles Monthly 170, 173
    cover art 204
    experimentalism 41, 77, 203, 208
    'Love You To' 109
    'Tomorrow Never Knows' 45, 50, 56, 111
rhythm and blues (R&B) music 18, 25, 37–8, 68, 203, 209, 233
Rishikesh 25, 49, 153, 204
Roberts, Aldwyn *see* Lord Kitchener (Aldwyn Roberts)
Roberts, George 18
rock 'n' roll music
    African American influence 38, 40
    art/bohemianism 90–3, 99, 101, 103, 199
    Britain 61, 69–70
    Hamburg 123, 164
    merged with music hall 67–8
    opposition to 190
    psychedelic culture 187–8
    teenagers/youth 67–8, 117
Rock Around the Clock 61, 206
Rock Band: The Beatles (video game) 116, 128–31
rockers 91, 93–5, 171
Rodriguez-Corti, Luis 238
Rolling Stone magazine 192–6
Rolling Stones 70, 109, 111, 203
romanticism 86, 88–9, 95, 101
Romay, Alejandro 234–8
rooftop concert 3–4, 66, 74, 120–21, 129
Rooftop Sessions (online forum) 149
Rose, Bettina *see* Payne, Maureen (Bettina Rose)
Roszak, Theodor 25
Roundhouse 7, 162, 170
Roxy Music 111
Rubber Soul 25, 41, 80

Saibel, Bernard 191
Said, Edward 55
St. John's Hall 35–6
St. Vincent (Annie Clark) 133
San Francisco 29, 72, 86, 120, 177
Sandvoss, Cornell 116, 118
Santino, Carlos 235, 237
Save Madryn Street campaign 126–7
Schajris, Mabel 237
Scotbeat website 218, 221, 224
Scotland 163, 216–19, *220*, 221–30, *223*, *224*, *228*, *229*
Sgt. Pepper's Lonely Hearts Club Band
    Beatles Monthly 170–5, 179
    cover art/aesthetics 75, 124, 204
    Leary 187, 252–3
    musical content 22, 39, 41, 140, 195, 206, 208
    performance 67, 80
    recording process 62
sexual objectification 139–41, 150
sexual revolution 66, 140
sexual themes 68–9, 77, 149–50, 242
'Sexy Sadie' 67
Shankar, Ravi 46
Shanks, Billy 226
'She Loves You' 20, 78, 140, 163, 165
Shea Stadium, New York 120, 123–4, 132
'The Sheikh of Araby' 46
Shenson, Walter 62, 78
Shepherd, Billy *see* Jones, Peter (Billy Shepherd)
Sheridan, Tony 251–2
'She's Leaving Home' 22–3, 54, 208
Shipper, Mark, *Paperback Writer* 149–50
Shirkey, Clay 162, 181
The Silver Beetles 90, 221
Sinatra, Frank 39, 140
sitar 46, 49, 173
slash fiction 138, 149–50
sleeve design/cover art 63, 124, 156, 204
Smith, Mary ("Mimi") 16, 102, 217
social media 116, 118–19, 126–7, 131, 162, 167
'Something' 39
South America 233–45
Southon, Mike 159–60
Spain 234, 242–3
Spinetti, Victor 60, 142–3
Spitz, Bob 21, 93
Starline Club 18
Starr, Ringo (Richard Starkey)
    American West, love of 71
    education 105

film lines 67, 69
joins The Beatles 64
quotes 1, 70, 75, 96
see also Madryn Street, Liverpool
Stevens, Ray 46
Stockhausen, Karlheinz 20, 28, 99–100
Strathpeffer 227
Stratton, Jon 26
'Strawberry Fields Forever' 22–4, 75, 177, 179
studio techniques 44–5, 110, 250–51
subconscious 75, 192; *see also* dreams
Sullivan, Henry W. 14, 17
Sullivan, Mark 190, 192, 197
Sumpter, Valerie (Anne Collingham) 166–7, 169, 171
Sunday Night at the London Palladium 69, 96, 132, 164
Sunday Times 178
surrealism
    fan fiction 138
    films 65, 67–8, 73–4, 76
    songs 60, 65, 111, 192, 195
Sutcliffe, Pauline 89, 95
Sutcliffe, Stuart
    art student 87–90, 94, 102
    in The Beatles 72, 91, 124–5
    death 125
    in The Silver Beetles 221

Tarantino, Quentin 61
'Taxman' 25, 204
Taylor, Linda 175
Teddy Boys 90–91, 94–5
teenagers
    Beatles fans 62, 65–6, 140, 163, 173, 186
    cultural phenomenon of 66, 68, 71, 90–91, 117, 140
    Lennon and McCartney as 14, 16–17, 99
Templars Antiques & Fine Furniture 216
'Thank You Girl' 63, 234
Theosophy 51–2
Tibet 50–56, 206
Tibetan Book of the Dead 48, 52
Tibetan Buddhism 47, 50–56
'Ticket to Ride' 69
The Times 14, 219
'Tomorrow Never Knows'
    in context on *Revolver* 45, 50, 56, 111
    MacDonald's reading of 44, 50, 54–5
    orchestral passages 22
    psychedelia/avant-garde 77, 188, 202, 206
    recording process 43–5, 111
Tow, Vinnie (Vinnie Ismail) 18

Toxteth (Liverpool 8) 18, 38–9, 87–9, 126–7
tribute bands 132, 138, 141, 150–51, 240; *see also* American Beetles
Trinidad and Tobago 5, 18, 29, 251
Tuesday Rendezvous 163
Turkey 45–6
'Twist and Shout' (EP) 36, 163
'Twist and Shout' (Isley Brothers) 38
'Twist and Shout' (*The American Beetles*) 237–8
Two Red Shoes Ballroom, Elgin 219, 221–3, 223

United States of America (USA)
    Beat movement 86–7, 90, 92
    influence of 64, 70–71, 90–91, 190
    race war 191, 193, 197, 204
    see also American musical influences
Uruguay 243–4
The US vs John Lennon (Leaf and Scheinfield) 29
user-generated content
    Beatlemania museum 123, 125
    social media 116, 118–19, 131, 162
    YouTube 131–2, 138, 147–9, 153–5
utopianism
    Apple Corps 101
    The Beatles' embodiment of 187, 193, 196, 198–9
    films 62, 65–6, 81

Vásquez, Rodolfo 245
Venezuela 242
video games *see Rock Band: The Beatles* (video game) 116, 128–31
virtual reality 116, 132–3
Vollmer, Jürgen 93–4
Voorman, Klaus 93–4

Waits, Tom 252
Watkins, Paul 191
Wellington, Anthea 171
Wells, H. G. 46–7
Westerbrook, Cath 175
'What You Got' (Lennon) 29
'When I'm Sixty-Four' 23, 205–6, 208
"White album" *see The Beatles* ("White album")
Whiteley, Sheila 15
Wiener, Jon 14, 22, 24–5, 29, 100
Wikstrom, Patrik 147
Williams, Allan 18, 38, 87–8, 217, 252
Williams, Eric 29
Williams, Stan 221
'With a Little Help From My Friends' 23

'Within You, Without You' 49, 55, 155, 173, 175
Womack, Kenneth 96
working class
   entertainments 22–3, 67–8, 73, 77
   establishment acceptance 64
   Lennon and McCartney 14–18, 22–6, 28–31
'Working Class Hero' (Lennon) 16, 30

Yellow Submarine (film)
   aesthetics 75, 78
   appeal to children 65, 109, 209
   The Beatles' image 79
   Beatles Monthly 171
   drug use 65, 76–7
   establishment 64–6
   surrealism 65, 68, 74, 76
'Yellow Submarine' (song) 77, 109, 172, 205
'Yer Blues' 203
'Yesterday' 22, 79, 205
Yorey, Bob 232–3, 237, 239, 245
Younghusband, Sir Francis 51
youth/youthfulness 60–61, 63–7, 187–8, 190, 244; *see also* teenagers
YouTube
   The Beatles' performances 37, 147, 153, 244
   user-generated content 4, 131–2, 138, 147–9, 153–5

Zarraga, Hector 237
Zeller, Jacko 238

www.ingramcontent.com/pod-product-compliance
Lightning Source LLC
Chambersburg PA
CBHW042041240426
43667CB00047B/2941